APOSTLES OF EQUALITY

APOSTLES OF EQUALITY

The Birneys, the Republicans,
and the Civil War

D. Laurence Rogers

Michigan State University Press

East Lansing

∞ The paper used in this publication meets the minimum requirements of ANSI/NISO Z39.48-1992 (R 1997) (Permanence of Paper).

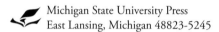 Michigan State University Press
East Lansing, Michigan 48823-5245

Printed and bound in the United States of America.

17 16 15 14 13 12 11   1 2 3 4 5 6 7 8 9 10

LIBRARY OF CONGRESS CATALOGING-IN-PUBLICATION DATA

Rogers, D. Laurence.
    Apostles of equality : the Birneys, the Republicans, and the Civil War / D. Laurence Rogers.
        p. cm.
    Includes bibliographical references and index.
    ISBN 978-1-61186-015-3 (cloth : alk. paper) 1. Birney, James Gillespie, 1792–1857.
2. Abolitionists—United States—Biography. 3. Presidential candidates—United States—Biography. 4. Antislavery movements—United States—History—19th century. 5. United States—Politics and government—1815–1861. 6. Birney family. 7. Republican Party (U.S. : 1854)—History—19th century. 8. United States—History—Civil War, 1861–1865. I. Title.
    E340.B6R64 2011
    973.71'14092—dc22[B]   2011006668

Cover design by David Drummond, Salamander Hill Design, Inc.

Book design by Scribe Inc. (www.scribenet.com)

Cover painting of the World Anti-Slavery Convention, London, 1840 by Benjamin Robert Haydon is used with permission (©National Portrait Gallery, London).

g green press INITIATIVE Michigan State University Press is a member of the Green Press Initiative and is committed to developing and encouraging ecologically responsible publishing practices. For more information about the Green Press Initiative and the use of recycled paper in book publishing, please visit www.greenpressinitiative.org.

Visit Michigan State University Press on the World Wide Web at:
www.msupress.msu.edu

Contents

Preface   vii

Introduction   xi

PART 1. THE BIRNEYS

1. Rising Immigrant Tides   3

2. Birthing Kentucky and a Birney   13

3. Roots of the Conflict over Slavery   31

4. Trapped in the Golden Circle   49

5. Defending the Cherokee, Launching Abolition   65

6. The Colonization Debacle   73

7. Birney's Epiphany   81

8. Saving the South from Destruction   95

9. The Tar and Feathers Agenda   107

PART 2. THE REPUBLICANS

10. Lincoln's Prophet   121

11. Henry Clay's Nemesis   135

12. Uncle Tom Comes Alive   145

13. Michigan's "Wonderful Revolution"   153

14. Flight to Eagleswood   169

15. The Republican Phenomenon   175

PART 3. THE CIVIL WAR

16. The Birneys in Battle   195

17. The U.S. Colored Troops Tip the Balance   211

18. Appomattox Sundays   223

Epilogue   235
Appendix 1. Birney's Writings   253
Appendix 2. First Republican Platform   257
Notes   263
Bibliographic Essay   291
Index   297

Preface

ONE OF THE NATION'S LEADING ANTISLAVERY SCHOLARS AND authors, Professor Dwight Lowell Dumond of the University of Michigan, rescued the papers of James Gillespie Birney in the basement of Birney's grandson, George Birney Jennison, in Bay City, Michigan, in 1936. Without that find, the story of Birney's contribution to the history of the nation would have been incomplete. Those papers, spanning from 1831 until Birney's death in 1857, are preserved in the William L. Clements Library at the University of Michigan. The midwestern location of the library is far from where most of the research on abolition was conducted—in the East. As it was, research and writing on the Birney legacy languished for about a century while authors lauded other abolitionists such as William Lloyd Garrison. Another aspect affecting the historiography of James G. Birney is the work of political detractors such as Theodore Roosevelt, who, in his 1887 biography of Senator Thomas Hart Benton, described Birney's presidential candidacy as "a political crime." He also denied that the work of Birney and the political abolitionists had anything to do with the formation of the Republican Party. However, it is clear that Birney's Liberty Party and successor Free Soil Party laid the foundation for the greatest shift in political opinion in American history, from a nation that supported slavery to one that opposed it. Only lately have historians and legal scholars begun to credit James G. Birney. His advocacy for Native Americans in Alabama and Georgia in the late 1820s actually started the abolition movement, some scholars have written. Birney's 1840 declaration to the New York legislature that there was "a higher law" predating the Constitution that obviated slavery was adopted first by Salmon Chase and then by Abraham Lincoln. And his writings laid the foundation for the Fourteenth Amendment to the Constitution, granting citizenship to former slaves and extending "due process of law" and "equal protection" guarantees in all states to other constitutional provisions. Also, some scholars assert that Birney's writings undergird the *Brown v. Board of Education* ruling of the U.S. Supreme Court in 1954, which led to desegregating schools.

Growth of the Antislavery Vote in the United States

1840	William H. Harrison, Whig	1,275,017
	Martin Van Buren, Democratic	1,128,702
	*James G. Birney, Liberty	*7,453*
1844	James K. Polk, Democratic	1,337,243
	Henry Clay, Whig	1,299,068
	*James G. Birney, Liberty	*62,103*
1848	Zachary Taylor, Whig	1,360,101
	Lewis Cass, Democratic	1,220,544
	*Martin Van Buren, Free Soil	*291,263*
1852	Franklin Pierce, Democratic	1,601,474
	Winfield Scott, Whig	1,386,578
	*John P. Hale, Free Soil	*155,900*
1856	James Buchanan, Democratic	1,927,995
	*John C. Fremont, Republican	*1,391,555*
1860	**Abraham Lincoln, Republican*	*1,866,352*
	Stephen Douglas, Democratic	1,375,157
	John Breckenridge, Southern Democratic	845,763
	John Bell, Constitutional Union	589,581
1864	**Abraham Lincoln, Republican*	*2,216,067*
	George McClellan, Democratic	1,808,725

*designates antislavery candidate

I need to thank Elizabeth Fladeland, a student of Dr. Dumond, whose transcription of Birney's letters led to her doctoral dissertation and a 1955 book, *James Gillespie Birney: Slaveholder to Abolitionist,* published by Cornell University Press. Ms. Fladeland gave me personal advice on the study of Birney by telephone several times from the start of my research in 1997 until her death in 2008. Also, John Dann, former director of the Clements Library, was always helpful in facilitating the use of the Birney materials and providing insights on the location of other information. The library's new director, J. Kevin Graffagnino, an eminent bibliographic authority, who succeeded Mr. Dann in 2008, was also of great assistance. Brian Leigh Dunnigan, curator of the library's map division; Cheney Schopieray, assistant curator of manuscripts; and Clayton Lewis, curator of graphics, were all extremely helpful as well.

The University of South Florida's research section in Tampa was a productive place for Civil War information relating to Birney's sons William and David, both Union major generals. Andy Huse, assistant librarian, special collections, at the university rendered assistance on many research topics related to the book. Nothing could have been accomplished without the advocacy and guidance of MSU Press editor Julie Loehr and the assistance of the staff.

Marvin Kusmierz, who conducts the Bay-Journal.com website on Bay City history, and Alan Flood, retired Great Lakes mariner and volunteer researcher at the Bay County Historical Society, with diligent detective work, found many insights that added to the understanding of the Birney story. Dee Dee Wacksman, an avid Civil War researcher and reenactor, provided considerable inspiration to complete this work. Dr. Paul Connors, of Lansing, Michigan, a Loyola University–trained historian and author, provided invaluable insight and advice in the editing process. Also, constitutional scholar Dr. Roger F. Pajak, of Washington, D.C., longtime government intelligence official and author and adjunct professor at the University of Virginia, took an interest in the work and provided invaluable advice and encouragement.

Birney descendants Frank Birney, an actor, and his wife, Betty Birney, an author, in California, along with Herman Hoffman "Topper" and Sherry Birney in Huntsville, Alabama, provided valuable family information. The late Rt. Rev. David Bell Birney IV, of Danville, Kentucky, and his wife, Virginia, became my friends and were helpful on my visits to Danville, and Virginia Birney came to Bay City to rededicate Pine Ridge Cemetery in 2003. Birney sons Judge James Birney (1817–1888), onetime lieutenant governor of Michigan and U.S. Minister to The Hague, and his brother, George (1832–1856), are buried in Pine Ridge, a historic burial ground established by Judge Birney in 1858.

Help also came from Paul Davis, Gerald Pergande, and James Petrimoulx, all dedicated researchers on local and Civil War history and fellow members of the Seventh Michigan Cavalry Civil War Round Table. Veterinarian Philip Engelhardt, a neighbor, was a frequent visitor to my home bearing Birney research information, and his son, Paul, has written of Birney in his studies at Hamilton College. Support and information also were provided by my bibliophile physician, Gary Dardas, along with journalist Eric Jylha and curator Ron Bloomfield of the Bay County Historical Society along with history enthusiasts Joy Baker, Ray Chapman, J. Donald and Suzanne

David, Tom Hickner, Arthur I. Nixon, and Louis Rupff. And my wife, Mary Dolores Barron-Rogers, has, as always, been a source of advice, inspiration, and help. I thank all who took an interest in this book and apologize to those who may have been forgotten.

Introduction

IT WAS A STRANGE SIGHT IN RURAL TENNESSEE: A LONE WELL-DRESSED man on horseback, jolting along a dusty road. It was December 1831, and the rider had been on a mission—to find a new home away from the South.

He was a thirty-nine-year-old political maverick from Huntsville, Alabama, named James Gillespie Birney. After a Southampton, Virginia, slave insurrection that August resulted in the death of sixty whites and more than one hundred blacks, including instigator Nat Turner, Birney determined to seek a quieter place to rear and educate his children. He would not continue in Alabama nor return to Kentucky, his birthplace. He had visited Ohio, Indiana, and Illinois and finally settled on Jacksonville, Illinois, where Rev. Edward Beecher, a noted eastern scholar, preacher, and educator, was to be president of a new college. The place was in southwestern Illinois not far from Sangamon County, where would-be politician Abraham Lincoln was practicing law.

Although vigorous and intent, Birney had failed as a plantation owner, primarily because of a major flaw: he was too sympathetic to his slaves and failed to demand the labor required to extract enough cotton from the rich, productive soil to make himself wealthy. Unlike many slaveholders, he could not even order an unruly slave to be whipped, his son William had observed. Neighbors gossiped about deeper character issues. The outlander from Kentucky had succumbed to the aristocratic curses of strong drink, gambling, and horse racing that were the passion of his wealthy neighbors. Not only had he neglected his plantation, but he had also found himself deep in debt from losses on failed crops and multiple vices.

Chastened and nearly bankrupt, Birney had subdued his pride and mortgaged his four dozen slaves, including his household favorites, Michael Matthews and his family, whom he had brought from Kentucky. He swore off liquor and gambling and joined the reformist Presbyterian Church. Elected mayor of Huntsville, he battled the saloon keepers who ran the town. Slowly he was rebuilding the law practice and the fine reputation he had earned in his first years in Alabama as state solicitor for five counties, prosecuting murderers and breaking up a lynch ring, and he had bravely defended the Cherokee who were being pushed off their land.

His political career in Alabama had been virtually destroyed when he opposed the Democratic god of the frontier, General Andrew Jackson. The legendary "Old Hickory," now president, was idolized by frontier folk whose land he had wrenched from the Cherokee and other tribes and whose futures he had salvaged from the second British invasion in the War of 1812. It was either a courageous or foolhardy man who would openly oppose President Jackson politically. But such action was Birney's nature.

Birney was an idealist in the land of realists, a dreamer who took refuge in the words of the Declaration of Independence "all men are created equal" to underpin his opposition to injustice against both white and black citizens. Although he had grown up owning slaves in Kentucky, his attitudes had been broadened by antislavery preachers of his youth and among the abolitionists of Princeton University and the Quakers of Philadelphia, where he had studied law. At this point in history slavery had been part of the accepted order of things for more than two centuries, since the first Dutch ship carried African men and women into Virginia in 1619.

As Birney rode slowly south along that lonely stretch of Tennessee road, he suddenly heard wailing human cries from an outbuilding at the rear of a ramshackle inn. Unable to ignore the agonizing screams, the curious and fearless lawyer reined up and strode to the building. Throwing open the door, he was startled to see a Negro woman in her early twenties, stripped to the waist and bleeding from her back, arms, and legs. She was tied like a side of beef to an overhead beam so that only the tips of her toes reached the floor. The young woman slumped in her bonds, her body jerking as blood spurted with each slash of the cruel flat cowhide whip. The stocky, powerful abuser, whom Birney later learned was the wife of the innkeeper, was angrily beating the helpless black woman as the woman shouted defiantly. The cries did little to deter the assault, and the innkeeper's wife barely looked up as the concerned lawyer entered the shed. A small biracial girl, perhaps five years old, cowered in the corner.

Awkwardly injecting himself into the violent scene, Birney's sympathetic small talk distracted the abuser as she panted from her brutal efforts. "The voice of sympathy was to the poor slave as the voice of an angel of God," William Birney later wrote. The elder Birney decided instantly to try to rescue the black woman and her child from the raging matron. A Birney biographer observed, "The child was hers by the innkeeper, and as a consequence the outraged wife took every opportunity to wreak her vengeance on the slave woman."[1]

Thus the man whose conscience told him slavery was wrong, and who had determined to oppose it despite the risks, had done what he had pledged never to do again: buy slaves. Birney made a deal with the innkeeper for the mother and child, put them in the stagecoach at the local livery stable, and took the happy pair along with him to Alabama. William Birney remembered "the wretched plight of the woman and child when they arrived, and that for a year or two afterward the child did not entirely lose the nervous, frightened look of a timid and hunted creature."[2]

From that point on Birney would free slaves, not buy them, and, in a misguided effort to protect black people and perhaps initiate talk of emancipation, would advocate colonization—the back-to-Africa movement. Soon, frustrated by the failure of colonization, he turned to supporting gradual freedom and finally championed immediate emancipation. Birney's philanthropic course, decided upon after encountering injustice along a dusty road in Tennessee, would lead to abolitionist publishing and politics, his two candidacies for president, evolution of the Liberty and Free Soil parties into the Republican Party, and the greatest civil war in world history. Freedom finally flowed from the wellspring of blood.

The story of the courageous life journey of James Gillespie Birney, his family, and those who followed his pioneering abolitionist political crusade is one this book aspires to tell.

PART 1

The Birneys

CHAPTER 1

Rising Immigrant Tides

The Effect of this kind of Civil Society seems only to be, the depressing Multitudes below the Savage State that a few may be rais'd above it.

—BENJAMIN FRANKLIN, ON IRELAND

YOUNG JAMES BIRNEY OF COOTEHILL, COUNTY CAVAN, IRELAND, may have been affected by conditions Benjamin Franklin saw on a visit to Ireland in 1771, when Birney was a four-year-old still in knee pants. The sage of the American colonies wrote his impressions: "I have lately made a Tour thro' Ireland and Scotland. In these Countries a small Part of the Society are Landlords, great Noblemen and Gentlemen, extreamly opulent, living in the highest Affluence and Magnificence: The Bulk of the People Tenants, extreamly poor, living in the most sordid Wretchedness in dirty Hovels of Mud and Straw, and cloathed only in Rags." Franklin wrote about his fears that Britain's continued exploitation of the American colonies might soon leave them in decay and poverty much like Ireland. Perhaps the corruption and injustice that pervaded their country gave motivation to sixteen-year-old Birney and thousands of other Irish to immigrate to America. But America had its own form of corruption and inhumanity— slavery—and Franklin's Philadelphia personified it despite being the vortex of the successful revolution and separation from Britain that proclaimed freedom and justice for all.

As his reeking ship jammed with refugees from Dublin docked in Phila- delphia in 1783 after a tortuous two-month journey, the ruddy-faced Irish immigrant Birney could scarcely avoid seeing the slave ships with African human cargo also arriving at the quay. Cries of the hapless captives were not as loud as they might have been, since the weak and ill had been jettisoned at sea, drowned alive like so many rotting fish. Even the ships from Ireland were known as "coffin ships" because of their cramped and disease-ridden quarters. As Birney debarked in America, free to start his new life, the African coffles were auctioned in Philadelphia and condemned to lives of involuntary servitude, most in the South. That would be the main pattern of the mass crime of slavery that continued over two centuries: the North would import the captives from Africa and profit from their transportation, retaining some slaves, and the South would purchase a labor force to do the arduous hand cultivation required to produce agricultural bounty.[1] The financial elites in both the North and South sections of the country were enriched as a result of such an evil collaboration. The ingrained system became impossible to stop, and no American presidential candidate, except—eventually—the son of the Irish immigrant who landed in Philadelphia in 1783, ultimately had the courage to say, "Halt! These are our fellow humans, and our nation is violating God's law!"

The Irish James Birney, first of a long line of Birneys with the same proper name, was among the waves of immigrants that began washing up on the shores of America at the start of the eighteenth century. It was the dawn of a new nation that promised freedom for all in its Declaration of Independence. Word had flashed around the world that the new land welcomed settlers. After voyages during which they were jammed elbow-to-elbow on pitching seas, in rickety two-masted schooners, braving disease and ocean disaster, the Irish immigrants were as happy to see their adopted land as they were to wiggle out from under the crushing English boot. Birney came to America too late to fight in the revolution that was at its end in 1783, but was on hand for the economic boom that followed.

As Birney Senior began his five years in Philadelphia, he was surrounded by slaves who were forced to work for nothing. The ambitious young immigrant was more intent on making his fortune in the New World than getting too much involved in the politics of the early republic. His innate intelligence and neat handwriting won Birney a job clerking in a wholesale and retail dry goods store. The fact of his employment at such a position perhaps indicated his higher class and some education, since many unskilled Irish were forced to work at low wages if they could get past the "No Irish Need Apply" signs on most establishments. Besides, being a Protestant, he didn't face the inherent prejudice most Irish Catholic immigrants faced in an anti-papist environment.

Philadelphia presented a dramatic dichotomy: while it was a thriving center of the slave trade, it also was the wellspring of freedom and abolition. Some ships arriving carried groaning human cargoes, those who survived the wracking Atlantic voyages often sick and helpless, chained in fetid holds like animals. About 15 percent of slaves died before they reached America.[2] Powerful, warlike African native chiefs sold their own people and captives as well to European, Caribbean, and North American traders with vessels specially designed to hold humans packed together below decks inhumanely. The Atlantic Ocean region linked European and Euro-American interests leading to the development of modern capitalism, according to Aaron Fogelman, of Northern Illinois University.[3] The world was made aware of the horrors of the slave trade as early as 1791 when a young African, Olaudah Equiano, told of being kidnapped at age eleven from his village in present-day Nigeria. Equiano documented the horrors of the "Middle Passage" in an autobiography published in New York, telling of fellow captives preferring death to slavery and jumping, chained, into the sea. The sensational book went through nine editions and was used by early abolitionists to make their case against the practice that had become an important part of the American economy. "African slavery could be brutal, but seldom did African masters hold life and death power over their slaves," say James Oliver Horton and Lois E. Horton, noting that slavery in America was "ultimately a more devastating institution than that known in Africa."[4]

Also, the slave trade was used as a tool for spreading Christianity and Islam. Slavery in Muslim Mali dated to the fourteenth century. Pope Alexander VI granted Portugal the right to conquer land and enslave Africans from the Azores to West Africa. Six nations most responsible for using the Atlantic slave trade to foster economic interests were said to be Portugal, Spain, the Netherlands, France, Britain, and the United States. These nations used slave labor to plant and harvest sugar, tobacco, cotton, and indigo and to mine precious metals. Key figures in the Atlantic slave trade were Prince Henry the Navigator, of Portugal; Christopher Columbus, the Italian navigator, who brought five hundred Native American slaves on his second voyage from the Americas; and Sir John Hawkins of England, who was knighted in 1562 by Queen Elizabeth I for his pioneering slaving success in Sierra Leone.

Although the plantations of the American South were the main markets and users of slaves, the North gained perhaps the greatest profits from the trade. Boston; New York; Newport, Rhode Island; Perth Amboy, New Jersey; and other Atlantic ports were the most active U.S. slave-trading centers, with Philadelphia close behind. Historian Hugh Thomas asserts that on the eve of the Revolution, the slave trade "formed the very basis of the economic life of New England."[5] Even after slavery was outlawed in the North, vessels from New England continued to carry cargoes of Africans to the American South. Some 156,000 slaves were brought to the United States between 1801 and 1808, almost all carried on ships that had sailed from New England ports where slavery recently had been outlawed. Nor was the U.S. government innocent in the abhorrent traffic. "Long after the U.S. slave trade officially ended, the more extensive movement of Africans to Brazil and Cuba continued," historian Douglas Harper writes. "The U.S. Navy never was assiduous in hunting down slave traders. The much larger British Navy was more aggressive, and it attempted a blockade of the slave coast of Africa, but the U.S. was one of the few nations that did not permit British patrols to search its vessels, so slave traders continuing to bring human cargo to Brazil and Cuba generally did so under the U.S. flag. They also did so in ships built for the purpose by Northern shipyards, in ventures financed by Northern manufacturers."[6] Harper goes on to say:

> Slavery in the North never approached the numbers of the South. It was, numerically, a drop in the bucket compared to the South. But the South, comparatively, was itself a drop in the bucket of New World slavery. Roughly a million slaves were brought from Africa to the New World by the Spanish and Portuguese before the first handful reached Virginia. Some 500,000 slaves were brought to the United States (or the colonies it was built from) in the history of the slave trade, which is a mere fraction of the estimated 10 million Africans forced to the Americas during that period. Every New World colony was, in some sense, a slave colony. French Canada, Massachusetts, Rhode Island, Pennsylvania, Virginia, Cuba, Brazil—all of them made their start in an economic system built upon slavery based on race. In all of them, slavery enjoyed the service of the law and the sanction of religion. In all of them the master class had its moments of doubt, and the slaves plotted to escape or rebel.[7]

"The effects of the New England slave trade were momentous. It was one of the foundations of New England's economic structure; it created a wealthy class of slave-trading merchants, while the profits derived from this commerce stimulated cultural development and philanthropy," observes Thomas.[8]

All of the original thirteen U.S. colonies had slaves, and slavery was legal for two hundred years in the nation. Slavery was given official sanction in 1787 at the Constitutional Convention of the United States in Philadelphia. A federal fugitive slave law was the main enforcement tool of what became known as "the peculiar practice"—slavery. South Carolina delegates Pierce Butler and Charles Pinckney inserted a clause in the Constitution that prevented slaves from gaining freedom by escaping into states where slavery was not legal. The government was obliged to deliver up escaped slaves like convicts, or, as Connecticut's Roger Sherman observed, like horses. Delegates wrangled over the future of slavery but by 1808 finally agreed that the United States would cease its transatlantic slave trade. After that date American vessels no longer traveled to Africa to seek human cargo but continued a domestic "coastwise" slave trade between U.S. ports. Although an act passed on 2 March 1807 prohibited slave trading in the United States, an exemption allowed the coastwise trade. Vessels over 40 tons were allowed to transport slaves if duplicate manifests were made describing each Negro. Strangely, vessels under 40 tons carrying slaves were subject to a fine of $800 per slave. Historian J. C. Furnas observed how slaveholders began early to protect their labor source: "Congress agreed to join Britain in suppressing the brutal and cunning slave trade, but Southern influence hamstrung the navy when it came to enforcing the law."[9]

Rebecca Yamin, a contemporary researcher on the status of slavery in early Philadelphia, found by examining tax records, constables' household censuses, and other records that about one of every twelve Philadelphians on the eve of the American Revolution was enslaved, and about one of every five white households contained slaves. Deborah and Benjamin Franklin, therefore, were not unusual in owning human property in pre-Revolutionary Philadelphia.[10] George and Martha Washington owned more than one hundred slaves at Mount Vernon and also reportedly owned eight or nine slaves while they lived in Philadelphia from 1790 to 1800 and attempted to conceal the slaves with a hidden passageway into their house.[11]

Because of the visibility of slavery's horrors and injustice, people of principle took active notice, and the abolition movement took root and flourished in centers of trafficking, especially Philadelphia. As the world's model democratic republic emerged, slavery inevitably would be affected. "Before the American Revolution, slavery was not a problem; after the American Revolution there was never a time it was not a problem," commented Harvard's Bernard Bailyn. Aaron Fogelman is even more emphatic when he says, "The most important thing the American Revolution did for slavery was to end it."[12] Of course the Revolution only started the process of recognition of human rights, and the end did not come for eight decades and until a terrible war was needed to write its epitaph.

Nearly half of all those enslaved were transported to the New World from 1700 to 1808 by British and American slave ships. Author Marcus Rediker states, "We know that the slave ship was the instrument of history's greatest forced migration." Even though he was "outraged" by the "dark and disturbing story" during his research, Rediker called the slave ship an instrument of globalization, vital to Europe's development and conquest and the growth of capitalism through development of plantations and, ultimately, empires. "The greatest accumulation of wealth the world had seen was not possible without the slave ships," writes Rediker.[13] The experience with slavery in New England was even more dramatic and ironic than that of Philadelphia. Although New England was important in the abolition movement, more than one thousand slaving voyages left Rhode Island ports alone, returning with more than one hundred thousand slaves. Prestigious Ivy League Brown University only recently acknowledged that its Brown family cofounders funded the university with money earned by trading and exploiting African slaves. However, one of four brothers, Moses Brown, notably became active in the abolitionist movement and opposed his own brothers in a lawsuit against the practice.[14]

In the aptly named Congo Square, at the heart of Philadelphia, slaves were auctioned, bartered, and condemned to lives of misery while at the London Coffee House at Front and Market streets, pipe-smoking burghers sipped coffee, chatted about local politics, and bemusedly watched the spectacle. In the peak year of 1762, about five hundred African slaves were imported to Philadelphia. Later, Scotch Irish and German immigrants dominated the arrivals, and the traffic from Africa slowed. After the Gradual Emancipation Act of 1780, public slave sales were not as frequent, but in 1810 the Negro population of Philadelphia exceeded ten thousand, about 10 percent of the city's total.

Even though the slave trade was part of America's economic lifeblood, Philadelphia's Quaker community joined with free Negroes to establish a resistance network headed by the Free African Society and Mother Bethel African Methodist Episcopal Church that coordinated with antislavery organizations and Vigilant Committees to help the enslaved. The Quaker sect, formally called the Religious Society of Friends, had embraced equal rights for women, religious minorities, and racial minorities since the 1640s when it was founded in England. However, Quaker settlers so desperate for labor to clear land suppressed their moral objections and quickly purchased the first 150 African slaves imported by the British into Philadelphia in 1684.

Philadelphia, only fifteen miles north of the Mason-Dixon Line, became a hub of abolitionist defiance. While other states were debating slavery, free Africans and Quakers were influencing local opinion. "The city would lead the world in anti-slavery activities, taking their protest to London and igniting the British abolitionist movement," says historian Rodney Stark. However, America would lag behind Britain in abolishing slavery, because its slave owners had more centralized political power than possessed by

British masters in the East Indies and other remote slave-populated colonies.[15] Thus, a Briton, William Wilberforce, rather than an American, as should have been the case, became the recognized pioneer of the world anti-slavery movement.

Why James Birney Sr. left his family's comfortable home in the Irish village of Cootehill and came to Philadelphia remains a mystery. His father, John Birney, was a prosperous farmer and miller, a church vestryman, and a magistrate who was influential in local government.[16] Rumors were that the son's leaving had something to do with the arrival in Ireland of some of Lord Cornwallis's British Royal troops after their defeat by the colonials under Gen. George Washington at Yorktown, Virginia, in 1781.

The Birneys were an admixture of nationalities from restless parts of the world and times when power-mad rulers called on their followers to sacrifice all for specious causes. A Birney family history rhapsodizes: "The highland surname Birney has been prominent in adding weighty influence to an already monumental image. From the sea swept Hebridean islands and the mountainous western coast of Scotland, this surname has emerged as a notable family whose history is romanticized by the skirl of the bagpipes, the brandished sword, the tartan kilt and the highland games." Three of Birney's French/Scottish ancestors were part of Oliver Cromwell's British "New Model Army" that invaded Ireland in 1649 and massacred the Irish at Drogheda and Wexford. After most of Cromwell's soldiers had returned to England, some of the feisty clan, then known as McBirnie, stayed on and were granted lands of the native Catholic Irish. When they defied the lord protector's decrees against consorting with Catholics and mated with Irish lasses, they in turn felt English oppression.[17] Religious warfare, which was endemic in Ireland, may have been another factor prompting James Birney Sr. to immigrate to America. He was an Anglican who was constantly contending for power, influence, and money with Scots-Irish Presbyterians and the more populous, although less powerful, Catholics. County Cavan had been ruled for centuries by the O'Reilly clan, whose expert cavalry and warlike Gaelic hordes had rebuffed the Normans and the English until the rebellions of the early 1600s. The clan's military tradition, and the Irish love of freedom, would carry over to the new land. Another immigrant from Cavan to America, half a century after James Birney Sr. came to America, was Philip H. Sheridan, who would lead Union cavalry in the Civil War. Among General Sheridan's cavalrymen was the great-grandson of the senior Birney, Capt. James G. Birney IV.[18]

Birney obtained a supply of dry goods at a reduced price on credit from his employer and in 1788 trekked across the Allegheny Mountains to

Kentucky County, Virginia, and set up a store. After several trips back across the mountains to Pennsylvania, with an armed party sleeping with their rifles and driving packhorses and mules, the enterprising Birney prospered in his storekeeping enough to buy land for a plantation. In the next five decades of his life, Birney would see the slavery issue become the nation's obsession and would watch his son, James Gillespie Birney, transformed from a compliant slaveholder like himself into a pariah in the South—a radical abolitionist. The son displayed the exceptional courage to combat the system that encircled him and was the basis of economics supported by church, state, and society at large.

In 1790 James Birney Sr. eloped with Martha Reed, daughter of John and Lettice Wilcox Reed. Reed, also an immigrant from Ireland, had come to Virginia about a decade earlier "and had already become a man of social prominence in Danville by the time James Birney arrived," writes historian Richard Brown. Perhaps it was the fact that Birney had arrived in Danville only two years before and was barely getting established in business that led John Reed to oppose the marriage at first. His opposition was short-lived, however, perhaps because of his son-in-law's Irish background and the fact that he was a gentleman and proved to be a good businessman. Brown contends the senior Birney had come to America as an indentured servant, a statement for which no verification exists and is today denied by family members.[19]

A Reed and Birney family history expansively states:

> John Reed, an Irish gentleman of great elegance and nobility of character came from Ireland to Virginia, and there married a Miss Wilcox. They moved as early as 1779 thereabouts to Kentucky. They had a son and a daughter. The son became distinguished and was sent as Senator from Mississippi. The daughter married James Birney, a man who led but never followed; who possessed great qualities of leadership whether shown in financial ability to attain success, or beyond commercial or agricultural acquirement, in his magnetic power to guide and influence all who came within the pale of his personal acquaintance.[20]

The elder Birney was described by grandson William Birney as "a very positive man; morally and physically courageous in meeting the numerous emergencies of frontier life, full of generous impulses; easily excited by meanness or disingenuousness; strong in his personal attachments; quick in his resentments; and frank, bold and vehement in asserting a right or declaring an opinion." William further described his grandfather as "a Conservative, with Federalist tendencies. He admired Calhoun for his intellect but detested his theories. For General Jackson he cherished an antipathy that amounted to rancor, and the feeling prepossessed him against the general's personal and political friends."[21] The father's antipathy to Calhoun and Jackson was not only embraced by his son, James G. Birney, but would also prove fatal to his promising political career later in Alabama.

In Kentucky both Birney Senior and John Reed prospered and mingled socially on good terms with the local gentry, including many descendants of the English aristocracy. However, not being members of the militia, they were not eligible to participate in the constitutional conventions that started in 1784, although clergymen were invited. Despite the fact they were slaveholders themselves, the Irishmen thought it was time the practice so foreign to their heritage was ended. Their opposition to slavery began in 1792, during the last of ten Kentucky constitutional conventions in Danville in dating back to 1784, through a surrogate, "Father" David Rice, a traveling Presbyterian pastor known as "The Apostle of Kentucky." That was the same year James Gillespie Birney was born. As an adult he was the first leader of the political abolitionists, carrying on a crusade through his lifetime, waving the banner of Father Rice's main precept—that slavery violated the natural law and the laws of God. Rivers of ink and blood would flow and hundreds of thousands would die before the nation that proclaimed itself the freest in world history would finally resolve that issue over the next century and three-quarters. The agony over the issue of equality for all would suffer through the Civil War, Reconstruction, and post-Reconstruction oppression of black men and women until the passage of the Civil Rights Act of 1964.

CHAPTER 2

Birthing Kentucky
and a Birney

Nothing to fear, nor to be feared.

—BIRNEY FAMILY MOTTO

AFTER THE REVOLUTIONARY WAR, VIRGINIA GAVE BIG CHUNKS OF ITS western lands to former soldiers, but Tories also moved in from the Carolinas and Pennsylvania along Boone's Trace and the Wilderness Road, setting the stage for long-term conflicts that persisted through the Civil War days. Kentucky County was so far from the capital at Richmond that government control was hard to assert, and the seat of justice was too far distant to be of practical value to the frontier populace. It was a situation that George Rogers Clark, "Conqueror of the Old Northwest," had warned about in 1776. Clark had suggested a radical idea: Kentucky should declare independence and align with a foreign power. Ultimately, the maverick settlers of the isolated region would attempt to resolve differences over land, boundaries, debts, taxes, and use of the Mississippi as much as slavery, in ten constitutional conventions before leaders could agree.

When James G. Birney was born in Kentucky in 1792, the ink had been dry for less than two decades on the masterpiece of Thomas Jefferson and Benjamin Franklin, the Declaration of Independence. George Washington was in the third year of his eight-year presidency. The Treaty of Paris finally separating the infant nation from Great Britain had been signed just nine years before. And the Kentucky constitution, which perpetuated slavery, was soon to be adopted despite the efforts of Birney's father and grandfather, along with the Presbyterian missionary Rev. David Rice, to guarantee equality. The watershed year 1792 also saw the formation of the political party system in the United States with the Federalists uniting behind Alexander Hamilton and John Adams and the Republicans adhering to Thomas Jefferson. However, no political party would seriously address the issue of the abolition of slavery until James G. Birney reached manhood and led the Liberty Party nearly five decades later.

James G. Birney was said to have been born "in a large brick mansion" in Danville, perhaps an exaggerated description of a humble house on North Third Street, about halfway between Main and Broadway. But local historian Calvin M. Fackler theorized he may have first seen light in a less grandiose setting—in an apartment above the Birney & Gillespie Company store. One of the early business partners of James Birney Sr. was David Gillespie, whose name was adopted by his parents as the lad's middle name upon his birth in 1792. Little else is known of David Gillespie except that he must have been successful in business, since he donated a substantial $150 to the proposed location of the Kentucky Academy in Danville while James Birney Sr.'s contribution was $50. A brother-in-law of Birney also had the name Gillespie, but the Kentucky Gillespie is considered the source of the middle name of his son. Gillespie's name lived on and gained a modicum of fame as the middle name of a two-time presidential candidate and political philosopher of the movement that led to the Republican Party.

Despite his father's wealth, the boy's life was not without travail. At age three he stood in knickers, lace collar, and tears, looking plaintively at his infant sister, squirming in the arms of their grandmother, as they peered into the grave chiseled into the layered, muddy brown shale that was characteristic of the soil of Mercer County, Kentucky. The mourners backed away slowly, afraid to accept the brutal truth: the children's mother, Martha Reed Birney, was dead, taken by a frontier plague in the prime of motherhood. "Oh, Lord, your spirit works in mysterious ways; we are your servants, it is your will," the minister droned, voice trailing off in the wind.

A distraught James Birney Sr. gathered himself after Martha's burial, searched his soul, and asked himself, "Who will raise the children?" After much prayer and reflection, dismissing the idea of another wife immediately, he dealt with the family emergency by summoning his sister Margaret Doyle,[1] a childless widow, to frontier Kentucky from the ancient homeland of County Cavan, Ireland. The ship, like the one that bore him a dozen years before from Dublin to Philadelphia, was long weeks in coming. Finally the coach came over the mountains from Lexington, only a short carriage ride away. The matronly lady had last seen her brother as a beardless lad of sixteen years of age, bent on escape from Cavan and adventure in a new land across the sea. Now he was a hale, strapping, confident fellow of twenty-eight years, a respected member of the Danville aristocracy, a land-holder and business entrepreneur bent on making his fortune from hemp, the favored product of the central Kentucky area.

Mrs. Doyle, who came from Ireland to care for young James and his infant sister, Anna Maria, called "Nancy," became the matriarch of the Birney home; her innate maternal skill quickly calmed the children's fears over the loss of their mother despite her strange Irish brogue and simple old country foods and superstitions. The fond memory of Aunt Doyle inspired James's son William Birney to recall later, "Dear old lady! How vividly I remember her venerable figure, with the shawl, spectacles, knitting and prayer book!" Mrs. Doyle would read to young James the sermons of Reverend Rice, who was one of the new state's leading antislavery advocates. Later, two more Birney sisters from Cavan, Mrs. Gillespie and Mrs. Whelan, immigrated to Kentucky with their husbands and children, so James and Nancy were instantly equipped with a ready supply of friendly cousins as playmates and schoolmates.

Birney's father and his grandfather John Reed had attempted at the 1792 Kentucky constitutional convention "to prevent the tragedy of allow-ing her to enter the Union with the curse of slavery perpetuated within her borders." The irony is that Birney Senior and Reed, along with their Kentucky constitutional colleague Reverend Rice, and many of the early antislavery advocates, continued to hold and exploit slaves, apparently as a bow to conventional social mores. That situation certainly led to conflict in the younger Birney's mind about the nature of American society. As a boy, Birney had gone with his father and Aunt Doyle to hear the antislavery preaching of the apostate Baptist Rev. David Barrow, a Revolutionary War veteran who, realizing slavery was contrary to the laws of God, had freed his slaves. In 1806 Reverend Barrow was expelled by the North District (Bap-tist) Association, resulting in the formation of the Emancipation Baptist churches, which excluded slaveholders or denied them the right of commu-nion. The far-reaching implications of this movement deserve consideration in that the father and stepmother of Abraham Lincoln, early settlers in Kentucky, where Lincoln was born in 1809, were Emancipation Baptists. Thomas Lincoln was baptized into the Little Mount Separate (meaning "antislavery") Baptist Church in 1809, the year future president Abraham was born, and Thomas and his second wife, Sarah Bush Johnston Lincoln, the stepmother of President Lincoln, were members of the Little Pigeon Creek Baptist Church, which also adhered to antislavery principles.[2] Rever-end Barrow published pamphlets against slavery that were widely circulated.

Asa Barrow, grandson of the minister, writing in 1933, amplified: "The expulsion of Barrow resulted in the withdrawal of ministers and churches from nearly every association in Kentucky and in the formation of Emancipation Baptist Churches, which were organized in September 1807, at New Hope Meeting House, Woodford County, into an Association under the name Baptized Licking-Locust Association, Friends of Humanity. When Thomas Lincoln, the president's father, left Kentucky he carried with him a church-letter from a church that was a member of Baptized Licking-Locust Association, Friends of Humanity."[3]

Certainly young Abraham was influenced by his father's and stepmother's antislavery views even though he never formally joined any church. His Emancipation Proclamation issued during the Civil War conformed with the antislavery side of the question of perpetual servitude in the Salem Association of Baptists and other Emancipationist branches of the sect. One of Reverend Barrow's Emancipation Baptist acolytes, Dr. James Priestly, was James G. Birney's tutor for two years in the Birney home in Danville. At Transylvania University in Lexington, Birney also came under the influence of an instructor named Robert Hamilton Bishop, an opponent of slavery who preached to Negroes and established Sabbath schools for them. Then, perhaps most influential of all, six-year-old Birney developed a boyhood friendship with Michael Matthews, a four-year-old slave given to him by his grandfather, John Reed. The friendly relationship between young Birney and Michael would continue throughout their lives. Birney freed Michael, at age forty, and his family in 1834. Betty Fladeland observed, "Slavery was confusing to James Birney, but he accepted it. His slave Michael and he had grown up as playmates; but because he was white, he was free, while Michael, who was black, was a slave and had to do his bidding."[4]

Michael's burning eyes, defiant posture, and brave demeanor bespoke more mature wisdom and recognition of his special life situation. Well-placed bravado was a quality Birney came to admire in his fellow humans early in life. The trait perhaps attracted him because of his Irish heritage, evident in his father and grandfather, both of whom had found the courage to escape English oppression in the old country and had come to America as immigrants. The boys—one a white aristocrat and the other a black slave—had chased each other in friendly play through the barnyard, around trees, and over fencerows on the plantation. Michael's bone-smooth ebony skin shone glossy with perspiration in the Kentucky sun. Curly black hair covered his perfectly round head, notable for its ridges above steady eyes topped with bushy brows reminiscent of Oriental children. A ready smile creased his face, providing a channel for sweat droplets running down his cheeks and landing on the sandy soil of Woodlawn, Birney's manorial estate and hemp plantation in the central part of the state. Slavery laws in Kentucky had been adopted from Virginia, the mother state from which it split in 1792, the year of Birney's birth. Under the law any white master could force a slave to work dawn to dusk at any job. For disobedience or any minor offense the master had the legal power to whip, maim, or even kill a slave. That was not to happen here. Instead of the usual master-slave relationship of subservience, Birney and Michael became friends. The fateful bonding that occurred would ultimately help Birney to realize the evils of slavery and to participate in leadership of a political movement that eventually led to a revolutionary change in the social structure of the nation.

Dr. Priestly wrote to Birney's father, outlining the studies the young Birney had mastered and giving recommendations for his future education, noting his high regard for the boy's character, which he observed had been molded under "uncommon influences." It would take more than half his lifetime, but those uncommon antislavery influences finally resulted in a fundamental change in the way Birney viewed the accepted societal scheme that black men and women should always be slaves subservient to white masters. Those influences, plus intelligence, a sense of philanthropy, righteous religion, and enlightened patriotism, all combined to create this dramatic shift.

Abolitionist minister Beriah Green, in a sketch of Birney's life for the 1840 presidential election, recalled an incident from Birney's boyhood that was indicative of his character. At age thirteen, while swimming with a cousin and another boy, the cousin, a poor swimmer, panicked and pulled Birney underwater. The companion shouted for Birney to let his cousin go and save himself. Instead, Birney encouraged and assisted the floundering youth. Birney commented later that it never entered his mind to abandon the boy, actions that drew admiration from Reverend Green, who alluded in the sketch to Birney's strong character and sterling qualifications for high office. In Green's opinion the swimming incident showed Birney's concern for others, those in danger and also those of any color under threat of injustice. "His friends remember how valiantly, even when a schoolboy, he struggled against tyranny, and how boldly he would tell the truth, even when it exposed him, as expose him it did."[5]

The philosophy underlying America's widespread belief in white racial supremacy was polygenesis, the theory that blacks and whites were separate branches of the human race. Rev. Samuel Stanhope Smith, president of the College of New Jersey (later Princeton University and referred to as such hereafter) from 1795 to 1812, was the nation's leading proponent of monogenesis, the opposing theory, which held that all men are descended from the same branch. Smith's viewpoint on the common genesis of all men was reflected in the political career of one of Smith's students at Princeton from 1808 to 1810, James Gillespie Birney. "Dr. Smith taught his pupils that men are of one blood, and that slavery is wrong morally and an evil politically, but that there is no remedy except in voluntary manumission," James G. Birney's son William Birney wrote in 1890. Smith, despite his preaching against slavery, also was a slaveholder. He postulated the incredible dichotomy that may have infected many in the founding generation, maintaining "that citizens acquire slave property under the sanction of the laws, and can not equitably be compelled to sacrifice it; that property rights of all kinds should be held sacred. What free people would allow their legislature to dispose in the same manner of any other portion of their property?" William commented, "This sophistry appears to the modern reader wretchedly bald; but it had its effect in 1810. Imagine a youth saturated with it for two years and a half by a venerated preceptor!"[6] The issue of property rights as a bar to ending slavery may also have influenced the founders of the nation whose wealth, and that of their fellow aristocrats, depended on their slave "property."

Birney would take a vastly different course than most of his friends and neighbors from Kentucky who also attended Princeton. His roommate, Joseph Cabell Breckenridge, was of a respected Kentucky family that became a pillar of the Confederacy while Birney, of course, led the political movement that evolved into the antislavery Republican Party. The university was a nonsectarian institution, although it had ties to Presbyterianism that, through Reverend Rice and others, connected it to the Birney family. On the other hand, Harvard University in Massachusetts trained Puritan ministers, and Yale University in Connecticut was connected to Congregationalism. Southern parents had concerns about abolitionist influences their offspring might encounter, but half the elite slaveholders attended eastern or northern schools, including about a third at the Ivy League Harvard, Yale, or Princeton. "But virtually all the planter'nabobs recognized the value of formal educational training and went to great lengths to ensure that their offspring, both male and female, received the highest quality of instruction that money could buy," writes contemporary author William Kauffman Scarborough, who documented the lives of cotton, rice, hemp, and tobacco tycoons.[7] Despite their slave country heritage, young Birney and Breckenridge were among the Southern aristocrats to receive the advantages of higher education in the more liberal East. But the way each inclined later in life was vastly different.

Kentucky County, Virginia, stood at the confluence of the New West and the Old South, regions from which two historical themes sprang to dominate the nineteenth century: expansionism and slavery. Kentucky was the first territory into which large waves of white settlers flowed. Historians have observed that none of the territories of the trans-Appalachian West inspired the American imagination more than Kentucky. And perhaps nowhere did slavery persist more doggedly than in the state carved from Virginia.

The earliest pioneers in Kentucky built small log forts as defense against constant and vicious Indian attacks. James G. Birney's grandfather John Reed had a fort at Reed's Station in Mercer County, and Abraham Lincoln's ancestors lived about fifty miles west in the fort at Hughes Station. Rev. John Dabney Shane interviewed some of the pioneers and commented, "Their heroic personal combats, desperate sieges, and fierce pursuits of, and raids against, their skilled and powerful enemy are surpassed by nothing in history; and their epic deeds continued until the Federal Government assumed the defense of the Indian Frontier." Mrs. Sarah Graham described one "Abraham Linkhorn" (later Lincoln), the grandfather of the president, and how he was captured by "spy Indians" who made him run the gauntlet and kept him captive for about eighteen months. Abraham Lincoln the first, the grandfather, owned four hundred acres of land at Long Run in Jefferson County. At about age forty-two, with his wife and five children, Lincoln purchased his land in March 1780 and later probably lived within the fort built on that land by Morgan Hughes, called Hughes Station. The death of the grandfather in May 1786 is described as follows: "Abraham Lincoln with his three sons, Mordecai, Josiah and Thomas, was busily engaged in the field putting in a crop of corn. Without warning they were attacked by two or three Native Americans. The father was killed at the first fusillade." Thomas, age ten, the father of Abraham the second, the sixteenth president of the United States, survived by taking shelter in a cabin. How Thomas survived is further described: "An Indian despising the ability of Mordecai's marksmanship stepped out of the thicket to secure the scalp of the paleface [and, presumably, that of his younger brother Thomas]. Mordecai from within the cabin took aim at a silver pendant on the breast of the Indian and brought him down. Josiah had reached the fort at Hughes Station and warned the settlers, who started in pursuit of the redskins." After his death the widow of Abraham Lincoln the first and the children moved about thirty miles north to Nelson County, where he had relatives.[8]

Obviously history would not have seen the Great Emancipator lead the nation in a civil war if the Native Americans had succeeded in killing

Thomas Lincoln in that fateful battle. A baby boy was born to Thomas Lincoln and Nancy Hanks on 12 February 1809. He was named Abraham after his paternal grandfather. Carl Sandburg observed that Dennis Hanks, brother of Lincoln's mother, had said "he'll never come to much" as the infant screamed into life after delivery by the local "granny woman."[9] Thankfully for the nation, the gloomy prediction by Hanks was dead wrong, although predictable given the circumstances of Lincoln's birth on the frontier in virtual poverty. A boy whose father was saved from death by a brother's sure shot and courageous pioneers sallying forth from a log fort to protect him became, against all odds, the nation's protector and freedom's champion. It was, as Reverend Shane grandiloquently stated, "surpassed by nothing in history."

The accepted social scheme in this frontier community was outlined by Danville historian Maria T. Daviess in reviewing Kentucky's "sanguinary battlefield, where the Indians and whites contended for possession." She pontificated the creed widely embraced in the South: "The whites triumphed; they are undoubtedly the sons of Japheth, and if there be any truth in the theory that the Indians are the lost tribe of Israel, then for more than a hundred years has been fulfilling the prophesy uttered thousands of years ago, 'that God shall enlarge Japheth and he shall dwell in the tents of Shem, and Ham shall be his servant.'"[10] Ham, of course, was the biblical designation for Negroes. The Hamitic myth, postulating that Ham, one of Noah's sons, had fathered the peoples of Africa, was used by Europeans to justify the slave trade. The biblical myth had transmuted the ancient enemies of the Jews to the enemies of the descendants of the English Cavaliers, who now were exporting their beliefs, as well as their avaricious descendants, into the wilderness of western Virginia known as Kentucky County.

Kentucky must have reminded the elder Birney of County Cavan in Ireland, with its undulating land, low round hills, lakes, and nearby mountains. That region in the midsection of the country where the Birney plantation was located the natives knew as "Ka-ten-tah-teh," a Wyandot Indian name meaning "land of tomorrow." The landscape does appear futuristic, with reliefs of one hundred feet to more than two hundred feet and the divide between the Kentucky and Salt and Rolling Fork rivers with elevations up to one thousand feet. The hills swoop along southeast through verdant forests of red spruce, balsam fir, and mountain ash and run headlong into the Allegheny Mountains, rising to the clouds.

The elder James Birney's success and wealth, derived from business and farming, was so great that his son would be vaulted to the status of the nation's elites, sent to the best schools and universities, and financially aided to become a lawyer like other landed gentry in the nation. The main difference between the younger Birney and his father, and most other Southern aristocrats, was that he would not bow to the conventional wisdom that slavery was good or, as his father apparently believed, an unhappy situation that had to be tolerated to maintain social stability. His sister, Anna Maria, and her husband, John J. Marshall, state representative and senator and judge of the Louisville circuit court, would never disavow slavery; he was a cousin of John Marshall, secretary of state under President John Adams and later one of the most influential chief justices of the U.S. Supreme Court. One descendant of Birney's sister would deny that anyone in the family except one recalcitrant cousin ever supported slavery.[11]

Birney Senior made his fortune as a hemp planter and processor of hemp for rope, and his bagging and business enterprises were highly successful. In order to become so enriched so quickly, slaves necessarily were at the heart of his agricultural enterprise. Slavery was an economic necessity and accepted practice in Kentucky, and Birney was more interested in financial gain than in sociology. The cultivation of hemp, especially, required the use of heavy manual labor to break the stalks, and since it was an extremely "dirty" crop, male slaves were used almost exclusively in its harvesting and processing. "None but our strong able Negro men can handle it to advantage," said a plantation owner quoted by University of Kentucky author James F. Hopkins in 1951, who amplified: "A Lexingtonian stated in 1836 that it was almost impossible to hire workmen to break a crop of hemp because the work was 'very dirty, and so laborious that scarcely any white man will work at it.' Without hemp, slavery might not have flourished in Kentucky, since other agricultural products of the state were not conducive to the extensive use of bondsmen." Hopkins added, "It is a significant fact that the heaviest concentration of slavery was in the hemp producing area. Among the slaves most in demand in Kentucky were those who were able to work in manufacturing establishments where hemp was turned into bale rope and bagging, but the agricultural skill which most contributed to the value of the Negro was the ability to hackle [comb] hemp fiber in preparing it for market."[12] Record books show that in 1824 there were about forty slaves on the senior James Birney's hemp plantation, surrounding a mansion called Woodlawn, in Danville, Kentucky.

William Birney reported in his 1890 biography of his father that his grandfather, James Birney, had branched out from storekeeping and presidency of a bank to a hemp-bagging factory and ropewalk in Danville "from which he accumulated a small fortune."

During the War of 1812 he was a contractor on a large scale for furnishing supplies to the Western army. For many years he was reputed to be the richest man in Kentucky, and one of the most cordial in his hospitality. His estate at Woodlawn, the front gate of which was but a short half-mile from Danville, was as beautiful as blue-grass slopes, noble forest trees, and good taste in landscape could make it. Woodlawn was the home of twenty-odd slaves. They were never punished or sold, being regarded as held for their protection as well as his convenience. All the harsh features of slavery were toned down. The overseer was obliged to manage without the whip, and got along peacefully with the slaves if not profitably for the owner. Most of the Negroes had been born on the estate, and they looked upon their master with mingled fear and affection. It must be admitted, however, that they took the farming and rope-spinning life easily; they were almost as lazy as the fifteen to twenty pure-bred mares and colts that roamed through the rich pastures, costly pets of the owner.[13]

William Birney's idyllic picture of slave life on the Birney plantation is no doubt glamorized and its burdens minimized, especially given Hopkins's description of the hand labor required to operate a ropewalk such as the one Birney owned. The ropewalk was a long, narrow building six hundred to eight hundred feet in length, the Kentucky version about half the length of similar structures in New England. Hopkins described the laborious process of making rope from hemp, which appears not only physically arduous but requiring a high skill and intensity. William Birney's comments about the laziness of the slaves thus seems incongruous when regarding the facts of the agricultural enterprise as well as the manufacturing process required to make rope out of hemp.

Events had occurred earlier that were to frame the destiny of James G. Birney and his sons. In 1793 a fugitive slave law was adopted by Congress, following the lead of the founders, making it illegal for anyone to help a slave escape or give refuge to a slave. Federal law also allowed slave owners, their agents, or their attorneys to seize fugitives in free states and territories. About the same time, a law was passed by the infant United States Congress, dominated by Southerners, that affected the trend of race relations in the nation for decades: blacks were barred from serving in the U.S. military.

Reverend Rice had identified Thomas Jefferson's "sin," that, though apparently bravely proclaiming universal freedom in the Declaration of Independence, left a loophole in the Constitution for slavery to be perpetuated by providing that those persons "held to Service or Labour . . . shall be delivered up." In Rev. Rice's address to the Kentucky constitutional convention in 1792, he called for a corrective change in the U.S. Constitution.

Contemporary author Matthew Mason, referring to Jefferson's 1785 *Notes on the State of Virginia,* points out that "many abolitionists had nothing but disdain for Jefferson's conclusion that slavery was for the time being a necessary evil given the obstacles to emancipation," charging that "selfish greed" was at the basis of slavery's continuation.[14] Slavery historian Dwight Lowell Dumond commented, "Anyone with more than a superficial knowledge of American history knows the Southern claim that slaves were property based in the common law, . . . that slavery could be abolished only by a state constitutional convention and was lawful wherever it had not been so prohibited."[15] The concept of slavery as sin was described by Presbyterian and other theologians as part of a curse that should be considered by Christians much the same as poverty, sickness, disease, or death. This theme had been stated earlier by Reverend Rice and later was embraced by James G. Birney. Rice had his 1792 Kentucky convention speech, titled "Slavery Inconsistent with Justice and Good Policy," printed in pamphlet form the year James Gillespie Birney was born. Slavery was unjust and immoral because it violated God's natural law of human freedom, the cleric declared, asserting: "All men are equal under God; one should not be compelled to obey another." Rice contended that slavery was bad policy for the community because it bred idleness and weakened political virtue. Property laws in humans were invalid because they were contrary to the laws of God. Forty-six years after his birth, James G. Birney, as corresponding secretary of the American Anti-Slavery Society, would have Father Rice's speech, with his own notes added, reprinted as a pamphlet and distributed in Kentucky and throughout the South.

Rev. David Rice, called "the father of Kentucky Presbyterianism," was descended from Thomas Rhys, a Welshman who immigrated to the colony of Virginia in the late 1600s, and his son, David Rice Sr. Future minister David Rice Jr. was born in 1733. A wiry young man well above average height, although not of robust frame, young Rice could handle a team of oxen, was handy with an ax, and was used to frontier hardships. His father allowed him to raise and sell a hogshead of tobacco each year to pay for his schooling. Father Rice's early influences came from education by Presbyterian ministers inspired by the "Great Awakening" that later also enveloped James G. Birney and many abolitionists. Rice was a protégé of the Reverend Samuel Davies, who became the president of Princeton University in 1759. After graduating from Princeton in 1761, Rice studied divinity with the Reverend John Todd and in 1762 was licensed by the Presbytery of Hanover in Virginia, later becoming the moderator of the presbytery. He was believed to have been the author of the famous petition for religious liberty to the Virginia House of Burgesses.[16] Father Rice's influence against slavery was never very effective during his lifetime, but it was multiplied significantly by his acolyte James G. Birney through his long crusade.

When the vote was taken in the Kentucky constitutional convention on the provision regarding slavery, Reverend Rice had already resigned from the body for unknown reasons, and the six other ministers (three Baptists, John Bailey, George Smith, and James Garrard; two Presbyterians, James Crawford and Benedict Swope; and a Methodist, Charles Kavenaugh) were on the losing side of a twenty-six to sixteen vote. Even among the sixteen dissenters who favored emancipation, the majority were slaveholders. The constitution contained two important slavery provisions barring the legislature from passing laws for the emancipation of slaves without consent of their owners and allowing immigrants to bring slaves into the state. A phrase suggested by influential Carlisle attorney George Nicholas—"all men, when they form a social compact, are equal"—was adopted. It was a blunt and telling distinction. Since slaves (and free Negroes) had not been involved in the formation of the constitution (and thus had not formed a social compact), they were not equal and were not entitled to the protection of the Bill of Rights, Kentucky historian Lowell Harrison concluded. In future years that phrase would be an oft-cited defense of state's rights that reserved the power of the people to alter, reform, or abolish their government.[17] Thus, the continuance of slavery born in Virginia was chiseled into the compact of the new state that finally, after prolonged agony, after ten constitutional conventions, in 1792 emerged from the womb. Kentucky became the fifteenth state of the Union, following antislavery Vermont, which had been admitted the year before. Thereafter states would be admitted by twos, one slave and one free, a pattern basically followed until the Civil War. The Kentucky constitutional convention had failed to purge the sin of slavery and, seven years later, when the constitution was revisited, would compound the evil by retaining the pro-slavery provision and disenfranchising free Negroes as well.

Politics was one of the diversions of frontier life, and Danville, Kentucky, was prominent among the tiny, scattered communities. William recalled visits to his grandfather from the famous politician Henry Clay, Speaker of the House of Representatives, of nearby Lexington, and, "worse still," having to read Clay's speeches aloud to the old man. Clay, one of the giants of American politics, was elected Speaker at age thirty-three when he entered the House, served five terms in the Senate, sought the presidency five times, and was on the ballot three times. Ironically, Clay's last desperate try for the presidency, in 1844, was foiled by about fifteen thousand votes in New York for the Liberty Party candidate, James G. Birney. It was the first time a third-party candidate had determined the outcome of a presidential election.

Upon graduation from Princeton in 1810, Birney spent about a month with a party of friends escorting Henry Clay during his canvass for a seat in Congress. Birney admired the tact and kindness of Mr. Clay, and he remained for many years thereafter an admirer, friend, and political supporter of that noted orator and legislator. At that point Clay was advocating emancipation of slaves and their relocation to Africa, so young Birney certainly absorbed some of that philosophy. Later, Clay's stand on slavery was typical of many politicians; he spoke against it while backing legislation that perpetuated it, such as the admission of Missouri and Arkansas to the Union as slave states and the Compromise of 1850, which included a fugitive slave law. The political careers of Birney and Clay were to meet again in a fateful way in the future; however, in the light of history, their reputations would diverge. Clay, an oratorical spellbinder from Lexington, would be recognized as one of the nation's greatest legislators of all time while Birney's political efforts would be misunderstood and denigrated both during his lifetime and afterward.

Birney studied political and moral philosophy and logic and became a talented and effective debater at Princeton. Despite a high life that included being suspended twice for coming to class intoxicated, he graduated with high honors. Although he had achieved academic success, Birney needed seasoning, his father decided. He would not be allowed to stay in Kentucky, racing horses, drinking, and gambling with the fast set while leisurely reading William Blackstone's Commentaries on the Laws of England, standard manual for American lawyers despite the Revolutionary rift and independence of the colonies. Training for public life would involve the law and required a cultural and intellectual environment far from frontier Danville. Before the year 1810 was out, young Birney was sent to Philadelphia to study law with the noted Alexander J. Dallas with serious purpose but looking and acting like the wealthy Southern aristocrat that he was. Birney was fortunate in having both the means to indulge his cultural tastes and the proper family and educational background to be admitted to the best social circles of the day. With a team of thoroughbreds and a smart carriage as well as a generous allowance from home, Birney lived like a carefree wealthy gentleman.

The next three and a half years Birney spent as a student in the office of Dallas, a celebrated lawyer and U.S. district attorney for Philadelphia. Dallas was as active in politics as in law and was a friend of the nation's political elites like Thomas Jefferson, James Madison, and James Monroe. Vice President Aaron Burr sought refuge at Dallas's home after the duel in 1804 that resulted in the death of Alexander Hamilton, the former secretary of the treasury. Besides cultural, legal, and political influences, Philadelphia presented another face for Birney to experience: abolition, a nascent movement led by a religious sect. The Friends, or Quakers as commonly known, who abhorred war and cultivated peace among mankind, also openly opposed the practice of slavery. They were the first abolitionists, and their message of compassion was only faintly heard above the screams of slaves in agony for about two and a half centuries.

In May 1814, Birney, age twenty-two, had completed his law studies, passed the bar examination, and returned to Danville to practice law. He was a different person from the arrogant, pleasure-bent young slaveholder who had gone to Philadelphia several years before; the seasoning his father had sought had occurred, but the influence of Quakers and other abolitionists had created a man with a set of morals that were different from those of his father and most Southerners of the time. Young Birney was on a path to intellectual development and maturation of attitudes that would put him among figures like William Wilberforce of England and Daniel O'Connell of Ireland, champions of freedom for all. His Philadelphia experience led to an unintended consequence his father had not foreseen and would take his son on an unexpected and dangerous path in public life—as a leader of the movement for the abolition of slavery. In Danville the newly minted lawyer began to harvest the fruits of wealth and privilege, being named to represent the bank his father had established in 1806 with two friends. Much to his father's delight, he joined the Masonic order and within three years was Grand Senior Warden of the Grand Lodge of Kentucky. And he made important political connections. In 1815, when Henry Clay was a delegate to the peace conference at Ghent, Belgium, Birney carried on Clay's campaign for reelection to Congress by stumping for the "Great Compromiser" in Mercer and surrounding counties.

On 4 February 1816, his twenty-fourth birthday, James Gillespie Birney married Agatha McDowell. Vivacious, intelligent Agatha was a favored daughter of a favored family of the South. Wealth begat wealth, and social distinctions were finely drawn. Although not a descendant of English aristocracy like the McDowells, James Gillespie Birney was a handsome, likable young man, scion of a wealthy family, graduate of Princeton, lawyer of talent and promise, and a Christian gentleman in the best Southern tradition. He had so many good attributes that the McDowells, devout Presbyterians, could overlook the choice of a church in a prospective bridegroom like him. So, too, could James Birney Sr., a devout Episcopalian, accept the religious difference in such a mate for his only son.[18] So at age twenty-four

James G. Birney stood steady and confident in black frock coat and was wed to Agatha, daughter of the federal district judge for Kentucky, William McDowell, another Danville aristocrat.

The McDowells' background was similar to that of the Birneys in that they came from Ulster in Ireland, but they were more socially prominent members of the landed Virginia aristocracy with royal ties from England. William McDowell was the son of Samuel McDowell, a Revolutionary War patriot, one of the first trustees of Danville, appointed by George Washington as the first marshal of Kentucky. Agatha's grandfather Samuel McDowell had been a commander at the Battle of Guilford Courthouse, a member of the Virginia House of Burgesses, and a member of the convention to send delegates to the Continental Congress to vote for independence. Samuel presided over the first ten constitutional conventions that finally achieved statehood for Kentucky.[19]

Birney's wealth, created by bootstrapping in frontier business and agriculture, was comparable to that of the McDowells but had not come tied with a blue ribbon. There were no royal land grants on the Birney side. On the other hand, eighteen-year-old Agatha, a vision in hoop skirts, her pretty face topped by curls and ringlets coiffed by tittering Negro body servants, was a member of one of the most socially prominent families in Kentucky. She was the fourth of seven children of Judge McDowell and Margaretta Madison, called "Peggy." According to family and regional histories, she was the favorite niece of Kentucky governor George Madison and a cousin of President James Madison. Young Birney's marriage to such a well-connected Southern belle put him in elite political as well as social company. The marriage took place while Madison's presidency was in its last year. In the tradition of wealthy Southern families, the wedding gifts included several household slaves given by both families. The region's elites were secure in their power, bolstered by slave numbers, which had controlled the nation for much of its existence. Jim Tracy, a McDowell family historian, explains Madison's tolerance of slavery: "Like Washington and Jefferson, he would come to hate the institution of slavery, but required the system to maintain an aristocratic life style. This was the attitude even in Kentucky where slaves were treated more on a family basis. The whip was never used."[20]

Birney and Madison's family connection through marriage took on additional philosophical and political significance. The diminutive, intellectual Madison had helped frame the Bill of Rights and had made a major contribution to the ratification of the Constitution by collaborating with John Jay and Alexander Hamilton in writing *The Federalist Papers*. There was another tie: Alexander J. Dallas, Birney's law mentor in Philadelphia only a short six years before, was secretary of the treasury in the Madison administration then in office in the new capital of Washington, District of Columbia. Philosophical ties between President Madison and young Birney also extended to the American Whig Society, an exclusive literary and social group founded by Madison, Aaron Burr, Philip Freneau, and Henry Lee to which Birney was admitted when he was a sixteen-year-old student at Princeton. This group was more than just a casual campus social club; its influence was enormous on its members and, ultimately, on society through their later political activities.

The American Whig Society began on 24 June 1769. The term "American Whig" was taken from a series of essays by a new trustee of the college, William Livingston, who would become first governor of the state of New Jersey. It followed ancient principles of British political and religious dissent that later were inherent in the Revolution and the founding documents of the American republic. Livingston was one of the principal members of the first Congress in 1774, and in 1787 he was a delegate to the convention that formed the U.S. Constitution. The Whig Society, and its companion organization, the Cliosophic Society, organized about the same time. According to Alexander Leitch, the societies "were the main focus of undergraduate life for much of the nineteenth century. Elaborately organized, self-governing youth groups (though often receiving advice from alumni and faculty) they were, in effect, colleges within colleges. They constructed and taught their own curricula, selected and bought their own books, operated their own libraries (often larger and more accessible than that of the college itself), and developed and enforced elaborate codes of conduct among their members. Their libraries afforded undergraduates easy access to the world outside; their debates trained generations to consider the great public issues of the day, from slavery to American expansion, from women's rights to the dismemberment of the union."[21]

With a host of liberal influences, especially that of the Whig Society, the reality of the unthinkable heresy of eliminating slavery came over the young Mister Birney: he became an advocate first of colonization, the return-to-Africa movement, and then gradually became a supporter of the abolition of chattel slavery of African bondmen. As the growth of the cotton economy demanded more and more cheap manpower, pro-slavery attitudes hardened and any opposition to slavery caused inflammatory reaction. Even in the face of growing public support for slavery, Birney more boldly asserted his ideas. Not only was he braving the rising tide of public sentiment, but he also was in constant danger, and threats were leveled on his life wherever he went. Ironically, it was Birney, the ultimate Southern aristocrat, who was motivated to help the nation fulfill its democratic promise. His affinity to Madison in a psychic fellowship through the Whig Society as well as the family relationship were no doubt factors in his eventual dedication to the equality of all Americans.

Notably, several national political leaders in the struggle over slavery had Kentucky connections: President Abraham Lincoln, Confederate president Jefferson Davis, and Senator Henry Clay all were born or lived at one time or another within one hundred miles of the Birney home in Danville. Two leaders born in Kentucky would personify the character of the West and South: Lincoln and Davis, respectively. Lincoln was the populist leader of the newly empowered democratic republicans of the frontier, Davis the stalwart conservative defending slavery and the aristocratic white supremacist tradition of colonial days. They would rise to direct battle in the Civil War and win undying fame. Clay, too, has been a subject of numerous laudatory historical accounts. However, few writers have seen fit to mention James G. Birney's accomplishments in laying the political groundwork for the most massive shift in public opinion in the nation's history, from a pro-slavery to an antislavery consensus.

CHAPTER 3

Roots of the Conflict over Slavery

The abolition of slavery was neither an accident nor a miracle; it was a result of evolution.

—WILLIAM BIRNEY

JAMES G. BIRNEY'S PROGRESS FROM SLAVEHOLDER TO ABOLITIONIST would proceed much like the nation would address slavery—excruciatingly slowly and with many missteps. At the root of his personal conflict lay the inexorable facts: slaves were property according to the laws of most states, and slavery apparently was sanctioned by the Bible. The wording of the Declaration of Independence, the United States Constitution, and the Bill of Rights did not clearly state that slaves were individual citizens who were to be free. Jefferson's pertinent phrase in the Declaration of Independence was "all men are created equal." The loophole parsed out of the seemingly inviolable statement was that some men remained free, and others were slaves owned by others as a condition of their life after being born, or "created." The effect was much the same as the statement in the Kentucky constitution granting freedom to "*all men, when they enter into a state of society.*" Jefferson had used the same phrase in the Virginia Bill of Rights, adopted on 12 June 1776. Slaves, of course, did not enter into a state of society. This differed from the Massachusetts constitution of 1780, drafted by John Adams, which declared without qualification, "all men are *born* free and equal." Thus, the unparalleled idealism of some of the founders was not truly fulfilled in the compromise crucial to the formation of the Union. Without that compromise there would have been no Union to preserve.

Only the Apostles of Equality, Birney and his fellow abolitionists, the Republican Party, and Abraham Lincoln and the Union Army ultimately assumed the power of preservation of the Union and were successful only after the Civil War.

By the time young Birney graduated from Princeton in 1810, the slave population of the North had fallen by a third, from 40,000 to about 27,000, but had increased by more than 40 percent, from 717,000 to almost 1,200,000 in the South. Kentucky's slave population had multiplied by nearly seven times, to 80,000, from 1790 to 1810. The increase was a direct consequence of the need for more slaves sparked by the invention of the cotton gin by New England mechanical wizard Eli Whitney about the time young Birney was born. The gin, a saw-toothed contraption of bird-cage wire and slotted metal, enabled a slave to clean fifty pounds of cotton a day instead of one pound with the hand method. Just before Birney's birth and Whitney's invention, in 1791 cotton production was a mere 140,000 pounds in the United States. By the time Birney was eight years old, in 1800, about the time he was given his personal slave, Michael, by his grandfather Reed, the cotton output of slaves in the South using the new machinery had multiplied 250 times, to about 35 million pounds a year. That change led to the growth of the plantation system and, as author Ira Berlin has postu-lated, to the development of the slave society from the previous situation of societies with slaves.[1]

The perpetuation of slavery required violence, enforced by local militia as well as civilian slave patrols and by slave owners and their whip-wielding overseers. Violence to control slavery correlated with an equally violent Southern code of honor imported from Ireland and Europe. The Code Duello enveloped gentlemen in its grip and involved an elaborate series of challenges and personal combat—dueling with pistols, or rifles or shotguns at greater distances. None of the Birneys was known to be involved in a duel, or even to be challenged to a duel, although the younger Birney's life was threatened many times for his abolitionist views. He was a harsh critic of the barbaric practice, as were such prominent Americans as George Washington and Benjamin Franklin. It seems clear in retrospect that atti-tudes of Southern leaders like Henry Clay, John C. Calhoun, Jefferson Davis, and others, such as Alabama "Fire Eater" William Lowndes Yancey, created personal hatred toward political rivals and even helped convert a sectional dispute to war. Future president Andrew Jackson in 1806, then a major general in the U.S. Army, shot and killed Nashville attorney Charles Dickinson after Dickinson's father-in-law had lost ten thousand dollars on a horse race to Jackson and the attorney had cast aspersions on the general's premature wedding to Rachel Robards, a much-gossiped-about scandal. "A gentleman of this period could demand satisfaction from another gentleman for any grievance, either real or imagined, and the man who refused to accept a challenge was regarded as a coward of the lowest degree who hardly deserved to live," wrote Kentucky historian J. Winston Coleman Jr. "Under this vicious code of honor, personal differences were settled with pistols, often resulting in the death of one or both of the parties. Early attempts were made to suppress this 'pernicious practice,' but public opinion sustained it and, as a result, the law merely winked at the affray and the press said very little. The best excuse was that the duel prevented informal brawls and street fights, and gave personal encounters an atmosphere of gentility. All too often, however, the wrong man died; the trickier eye or the quicker shot, won out."[2]

The need to institutionalize violence to control the slaves flawed the South's ability to maintain equilibrium when political winds blew against it and even contributed to the inability to maintain the national solidarity needed to win a war. Citing "an addiction to violence in many parts of the country," slavery historian Elbert Smith commented, "A people who had spent so many years shooting Indians and animals and who had written the right of every individual to bear arms into their national Constitution found violent personal conflicts easy to forgive if the antagonists had a theoretically even chance to kill or maim each other. Judges and juries alike were remarkably lenient to the victors of fatal encounters, and in numerous states dueling itself was still legal."[3]

However, the Code Duello impinged on some members of the Birney family. Noted Kentucky politician Henry Clay, a neighbor from Lexington, challenged Humphrey Marshall, fellow member of the Kentucky legislature and son of James G. Birney's sister, to a duel in 1809 that resulted in both receiving minor wounds. To avoid the law, the pair went across the Ohio River at Shippingport, above Louisville, on the Indiana shore. The dispute, recalled a historical report, was "to settle with pistol and ball what they had started with oratory back in the statehouse at Frankfort." Three shots were fired by each man, Clay wounding Marshall slightly above the navel on the first exchange. On the second round Clay's pistol misfired and Marshall's shot went wild. Then Marshall wounded Clay in the thigh, ending the affair. "In about two weeks, the Master of Ashland returned to his public duties in the House, and he had demonstrated a bravery under fire which in no wise detracted from his public popularity."[4]

Humphrey Marshall was the son of John J. Marshall, nephew of famed Supreme Court Justice John Marshall, and Anna Maria Birney, the sister of

James G. Birney. Humphrey Marshall was a West Point graduate, Mexican War veteran, member of Congress, and minister plenipotentiary to China. When sectional warfare arose in 1861, Humphrey Marshall opposed secession but reluctantly joined the rebellion and became a Confederate brigadier general. In 1841 John J. Marshall defaulted on a debt he owed Birney, but during the presidential election campaign of 1844, he defended his brother-in-law from political attacks in a letter to one James Loughead published in the *Signal of Liberty,* a Michigan abolitionist newspaper.

Noting that the duel in 1804 between former secretary of the treasury Alexander Hamilton and Vice President Aaron Burr had turned public opinion in the North against the practice, contemporary writer Jim Gannam comments: "Southerners were much slower to give up the dueling tradition, in part because the defense of personal honor was much more important in the aristocracy that thrived in the plantation culture. It took the carnage of the Civil War to end the practice of dueling south of the Mason-Dixon. The abolition of the plantation system and the downfall of the aristocracy closed the book on the Code Duello. The new merchant class that rose in the South after the war was disinclined to risk life and fortune for sacred honor."[5]

James G. Birney's opposition to dueling may have come from the realization that the violent culture of dueling, systematized by the Code Duello from his father's homeland of Ireland, was at the root of the brutality of slavery and was causing Southerners to adopt a dangerous and overconfident strain of aggression. He was keenly aware of the sectional differences in population and industrial capability, having spent considerable time in the North, perhaps more than the average Southern slaveholder. This led Birney to predict the terrible conflict of the Civil War far in advance of its actual explosion, a warning that went entirely unheeded especially by the minions of the slave culture who were intoxicated by their own power and that of their region. Bertram Wyatt Brown, whose latest book on the subject is titled *Southern Honor: Ethics and Behavior in the Old South,* sees the "darker aspects" of the code carrying gentlemen to "silent acquiescence" when the call for secession arose. "It was the threat of honor lost, no less than slavery that led them to secession and war," he says.[6] Elbert Smith theorized that "a traditional indifference to violence also helped keep both Southerners and Northerners unaware of the frightful extremities a military solution of their difficulties would reach. Southerners really believed their boast that any of their number could whip ten Yankees, and this notion contributed not a little to their incredibly light-hearted and optimistic approach to the question of war."[7] The Code Duello, the basis of the Southern code of honor, was as much a plague to the freedom of the nation as was the stream of captured African natives. They, too, were immigrants, but not by choice. The two plagues interfaced explosively as the South and North grappled with their consequences.

James G. Birney quickly and fearlessly joined the volatile political discussion that was heating up over slavery. Birney was elected to the Kentucky state legislature in 1816 "virtually without opposition," his son William later observed. A twenty-four-year-old lawyer, Birney quickly established himself as unafraid to challenge the slaveholding majority on issues about which he believed he was right. He sponsored a bill to incorporate the Danville Academy and to prohibit the circulation of private notes as currency. As a patriotic gesture he supported a joint resolution commemorating Andrew Jackson's victory at New Orleans, although he would later, in Alabama, oppose Jackson. Then his early indoctrination by abolitionist preachers, Princeton teachings by Dr. Smith, and Quaker influences from Philadelphia arose. Commenting on a bill requesting neighboring states to pass laws against aiding fugitive slaves, Birney protested, "Shall the State of Kentucky do what no gentleman would do—turn slave catcher?"[8] That kind of talk was not popular in Danville—or anywhere in Kentucky, for that matter—so Birney quickly decided a move was in order for his family. Besides, he had been rejected for a post on the faculty of Centre College, despite the fact that he was one of the sponsors of legislation establishing the Danville college; his political career obviously had been compromised by his antislavery stand. Birney, however, was not yet ready to stand shoulder-to-shoulder with the Quakers barring the gates to the slave pens. His path to abolitionism would require more trials—farther south, in Alabama. And it would require several more plateaus of action, including a futile period working to persuade Negroes to emigrate to Africa.

Several years before the arrival in Philadelphia of the Irish immigrant James Birney Sr., in 1783, Pennsylvania had adopted gradual emancipation. Slaves born after 1780 were to be freed upon their twenty-eighth birthday. While the elder Birney was in Philadelphia in 1787, the Northwest Ordinance was adopted banning slavery in the vast territories ceded by Virginia, and the U.S. Constitution was ratified providing that a slave would be counted as three-fifths of a man in allocating seats in the House of Representatives, even though bondmen could not vote. That historic provision gave the slaveholding South a numerical advantage in Congress over the more antislavery North without any fear that their Negro power base would vote to defeat their aims. Even free Negroes were barred from voting and were not part of the three-fifths count. This corrupt structure perpetuated decades of Southern rule and helped to continue slavery until a terrible war was fought that finally ended it in 1865. Some modern observers see the compromise on the three-fifths rule as an attempt by the founders to limit Southern power. They note that a full count of all male Negroes would have made the political imbalance even greater.

James G. Birney's transition from slaveholding, to advocating colonization, to full-fledged abolition was complicated by the confusing messages of Dr. Smith, Benjamin Franklin, and other leaders as well as the strong social strictures around him. But Birney's strong sense of morality and humanitarianism that led him to the antislavery cause won out, even though it cost him much of his fortune along with his favored position as an aristocratic politician in Southern society.

National leaders for years had made a great show of planning for the end of slavery. On 1 January 1794 the first convention of delegates from the abolition societies met in Philadelphia under the leadership of Dr. Benjamin Rush, signer of the Declaration of Independence, member of the Continental Congress, and surgeon general of the Continental Army. The minutes refer to the session as "The American Convention for Promoting the Abolition of Slavery and Improving the Condition of the African Race." Virginia and Maryland societies were represented along with Connecticut, New York, New Jersey, Pennsylvania, and Delaware, and Joseph Bloomfield of New Jersey was elected president of the convention. Twenty-two delegates were on hand for the first meeting. It took several meetings for the group, until 7 January, to agree on resolutions petitioning Congress, the state legislatures, and the people of the United States to pass laws prohibiting the slave trade and the fitting out of vessels for the trade in ports of the nation. Minutes of the proceedings were sent to Granville Sharp, a British abolitionist and chairman of the London Society, to the Speaker of the U.S. House of Representatives, state legislatures, and for publication in newspapers in each state. Twenty-four conventions were held between 1794 and 1829. Antislavery societies from eleven different states, also including Rhode Island and Tennessee, were represented at various times, and other states sent communications but no delegates.

After the 1821 Missouri Compromise, which allowed for the expansion of slavery, emancipation became the primary goal of the group, which adopted memorials also recommending education of the slaves before freedom was granted. The American Convention opposed the deportation of Negroes to Africa and urged local abolition societies to set up schools for free Negroes to prepare them for citizenship and membership in society.[9] Abolitionists of the American Convention who later became prominent members of the American Anti-Slavery Society (AASS) provided the transition from the American Convention to the AASS, which was formed in 1831. These included Benjamin Lundy, Arnold Buffum, and Abraham L. Pennock, a Quaker merchant whom Birney had known in Philadelphia during his law studies. All were in attendance at the twenty-fourth and last convention, held in Washington, D.C., in 1829. Another member was Thomas Earle, of Pennsylvania, who became Birney's Liberty Party running mate in 1840. In a committee report Earle said that a proposal "to reduce slaves to the condition of the serfs in Poland and Russia, fixed to the soil, without the right on the part of the master to remove them," was unlikely to receive public support. Earle's report stated that abolitionists had been unable to convince slaveholders "that there is less pecuniary profit in the employment of slave labor, than in that of freemen," and concluded "gradual abolition is the only mode which at present appears likely to receive the public sanction."[10] But of course even gradual abolition was not likely to be approved by a Congress weighted in favor of Southern slaveholders by the three-fifths rule.

Birney made numerous antislavery acquaintances in Philadelphia, including Pennock and other Quakers and a free Negro sailmaker, James Forten, and absorbed more of a sense of the egalitarian, liberal East as well as abolitionist influences. Forten was active in the early antislavery campaigns, and in 1800 he led a drive that petitioned Congress to emancipate slaves and criticized the Pennsylvania legislature for barring free black men and women from other states.

In 1811 the abominable murder of the "slow" slave boy George by Isham and Lilburne Lewis, nephews of Thomas Jefferson, occurred in Kentucky. It is an incident later documented by Birney and his associate Rev. Theodore Weld. The case created little sensation despite its horrific details or the celebrity of the participants. Lucy Jefferson, sister of the president, and Col. Charles Lilburne Lewis were the parents of Lilburne and Isham. The two brothers murdered the family slave forty miles south of the James Birney hemp plantation at Danville, Kentucky, and about sixty miles south and east of where two-year-old Abraham Lincoln was growing up with his father, hardscrabble farmer Thomas Lincoln, and mother Nancy Hanks Lincoln in Knob Creek, Washington County, Kentucky. Nineteen-year-old James Gillespie Birney was in Philadelphia at the time, reading law. It is hard to imagine that the Lincoln and Birney families never heard of the Lewis incident at the time it occurred, but evidence of such knowledge has not surfaced in historic literature or news reports. The seventeen-year-old George was slain by the Lewis brothers for the "crime" of breaking a piece of crockery. The family slaves were gathered in a meat house to witness the "punishment" as a warning against slacking in their work. One of the Negroes was then forced at gunpoint to chop George's body to pieces, by some accounts, first at the feet, then the legs and arms, while the pitiful lad screamed for merciful beheading: "Massa, start at the other end of me!" The brothers then stuffed the body parts into a fireplace to hide their crime. Soon after the horrific deed, however, the New Madrid earthquake, said to be the most violent in history east of the Rocky Mountains, shook the Danville area, uncovering George's body for all to see. Lilburne's drunken response to his brother's cries of alarm was, "It's only the devil in hell, rejoicing over having got hold of George!"[11] After being caught, the murderous brothers' subsequent attempt at double suicide failed when a musket misfired. Isham, the survivor, escaped from prison and was one of eight U.S. soldiers to die in the Battle of New Orleans during the War of 1812.

The facts of the murder, although not suppressed, were muted. A news item appears in the *Kentucky Gazette* of 12 May 1812; the trial is listed in the Livingston County Court records for the years 1811–1814; William Courtney Watts recounts the story, although with names changed, in an 1897 book titled *Chronicles of a Kentucky Settlement;* and a letter with details of the crime, written by Rev. William Dickey in 1824, was published by Rev. John Rankin in his *Letters on American Slavery* in 1833. Not a word of the scandal is mentioned by Jefferson in any of the thousands of letters he left upon his death in 1826. It was left to James G. Birney and Rev. Theodore Weld to make the world aware of the mayhem in Weld's earth-shattering exposé in the book *American Slavery As It Is: Testimony of a Thousand Witnesses,* published in 1839 by the American Anti-Slavery Society, with Birney as corresponding secretary.

The case of George has surfaced periodically over the years, and a new shock wave hits Americans until it, too, dies out. But the horrendous facts still linger over the history of the nation and cloud the legacy of Jefferson, one of its most revered founders.

Besides his own efforts to sway public opinion against slavery, Birney collaborated with Rev. Theodore Weld in distributing antislavery literature throughout the West in the mid-1830s.

In an agonizing gradual fashion the nation began to confront slavery. Newspaper publisher Horace Greeley observed that from the settlement of the Missouri Compromise in 1821 to 1835, Northern people, "busy, usually prosperous," mainly ignored slavery. Greeley wrote in his autobiography, "What use in parading a conviction which can have no other effect than that of annoying your proud and powerful neighbor?"[12] During most of that time, Greeley was a young man serving as an apprentice on a Vermont newspaper while Birney was a slaveholding planter and lawyer in Alabama, so neither was in position to reflect accurately on Northern political sentiment. But Birney's alarm about the effects of slavery on the South began to grow with the ripple effects in Alabama of the execution of Denmark Vesey and twenty-nine other black men after a failed rebellion in South Carolina in 1821. Slave codes were tightened all over the South as a result of the unrest and fear of more uprisings.

Then in 1830 William Lloyd Garrison began to publish his antislavery newspaper, the *Liberator,* from Boston. Its abolitionist propaganda prodded the South into even more fury. Modern writer Wendy McElroy comments:

> In a sense, *The Liberator* was badly timed. "Walker's Appeal," a pamphlet recently published by a free black, had panicked the slave states. This pamphlet flaunted black superiority and called for insurrection in the South. As a direct result, in 1830, North Carolina passed a law to prohibit slaves and free blacks from reading and writing. All blacks emancipated after 1830 were ordered to leave the state within 90 days. On August 31, 1831, a Virginia slave named Nat Turner instigated a slave revolt in which a slave owner and his family were killed. Eventually, the victims of Turner's band exceeded 50. The South exploded with fear and rage, with many blaming Northern abolitionists, especially William Lloyd Garrison.[13]

The Turner revolt reignited the uproar and a new wave of reprisals was launched. Southern reaction to the slave revolts only convinced the antislavery forces of the brutality of slavery and strengthened their resolve to end the practice.

Religion was playing an increasingly large role in the willingness of ordinary citizens to oppose slavery. A hellfire-and-damnation preacher, Charles Grandison Finney, was stirring up the East, preaching reform to great crowds in upstate New York, and the spirit of the great revival known as the "Second Great Awakening" spread across the country from 1800 to 1835. It was a time when a comet's tail was said to have swept the nation, driving everyone a little mad. Reverend Finney exhorted Christians not only to believe in the Lord but also to seek salvation through good deeds, a concept foreign to religious groups in America until that time. "Unlimited freedom had been granted religious expression, no matter how eccentric it might be."[14] All major Protestant denominations, except Episcopalians, embraced revivals and reform. Theodore Weld, Gerrit Smith, Elizabeth Cady Stanton, and the Tappan brothers, Lewis and Arthur, all became disciples of Finney, foreshadowing their collaboration with Birney, who also had caught the reform fever.

A great sectional conflict was shaping. In the late eighteenth century, while Southern states passed more laws to support slavery, many states in the Northeast began to pass laws abolishing slavery. But the antislavery movement really got its impetus from the Second Great Awakening. "The first half of the nineteenth century saw such a flurry of sectarian activity in New York . . . that the area earned for itself the name of 'Burned Over District,'" Emerson Klees writes, adding, "The anti-slavery crusade became the principal reform movement, thrusting aside, at least temporarily, the temperance and women's rights movements. The Second Great Awakening, with its camp meetings, itinerant preachers and interdenominational missions, reached its peak in this area between 1825 and 1837." The economic boom resulting from the construction of the 364-mile-long Erie Canal from Albany to Buffalo was a pathway for the Second Great Awakening. As upstate New York's population grew because of the canal, this economic growth spread to Ohio, Michigan, Illinois, and other Midwestern states, sweeping along with it the religious and reform fervor of the immigrants.[15] The reception to the reform movement was vastly different in the South. Historian Carl N. Degler observes, "Reformers found an uncongenial atmosphere south of Mason's and Dixon's line, because it was well known that reformers interested in temperance, women's rights, international peace, and so forth, frequently maintained close ties with abolitionists."[16]

Petitioning by abolitionists had pressured Parliament to free slaves in the British colonies in 1833, so abolitionists who began to seriously organize about that time in the United States adopted the same tactic with Congress. However, there was a great difference: although there was little slavery in Britain itself, the abolitionists in the United States were confronting an entrenched system that used slavery as the basis of political power as well as for economic purposes. Julian P. Bretz, an early historical analyst, noted: "Anti-slavery men thought they saw in the South a combination of pro-slavery interests, which, with the aid of Northern politicians, dominated the national government. This aggressive force they called the slave power, later the slavocracy, and still later, marking commendable progress in invective, the cottonocracy."[17] Birney, with a clear-eyed focus, agreed with Garrison that the goal of their radical movement should be an immediate and uncompensated end to slavery. They were polar opposites, however, on how the end would come. Garrison and his supporters wanted a new government disallowing slavery from the start. The Constitution was illegal, they contended, because it denied freedom to black men and women. If the South would not outlaw slavery, Garrison argued, the North should secede and create its own country. Other members of the American Anti-Slavery

Society saw Garrison's views as too radical. Even though slavery was wrong, the Constitution had created a legitimate government under which the people had the right to end oppression. Rather than tearing the nation asunder, Birney and the non-Garrisonian abolitionists focused on electing politicians who would outlaw slavery within the existing framework of government.

In 1834 Birney had stated that slavery was incompatible with a republican form of government, and he was among the first abolitionists to advocate political action in contrast to Garrison's "moral suasion" and non-voting strategies. After the party's second resounding defeat, in 1844, a rift developed among the abolitionists, prompted by Chase and the Ohio group of anti-Garrisonians, including Gamaliel Bailey and Joshua Giddings, who suggested a nonpartisan league or merger with Democrats. Michigan's *Signal of Liberty* observed that the Liberty Party of Ohio did not expect or wish to be a permanent national party. "A more important movement was one started by Birney to transform the Liberty party into a general radical reform party. The 'one idea' had proved too narrow; if the platform should contain planks pledging the party to all kinds of reform, many men favoring one or more of these might come in who would otherwise be unable to do so. This movement began in Michigan with a letter from Mr. Birney, and a circular sent by Guy Beckley and Theodore Foster of the *Signal of Liberty* to all the leading Liberty newspapers in the country, requesting co-operation in bringing the party to broaden the platform."[18] Birney was convinced that inevitably all antislavery advocates would gather under one big political tent. Birney's motivation to free slaves was mainly along religious and humanitarian lines while other leaders focused on the economic costs to the North. Slowly and against heavy opposition, the antislavery snowball began to roll in the free states, pushed into motion by Birney and the political abolitionists. Eventually, a quarter century later, it would turn into a Republican juggernaut. Their efforts, however, came at a high price.

James G. Blaine, onetime Republican candidate for president, observed: "In the early days of this agitation, the Abolitionists were a proscribed and persecuted class, denounced with unsparing severity by both the great political parties, condemned by men of the leading churches, libeled in the public press, and maltreated by furious mobs. In no part of the country did they constitute more than a handful of the population, but they worked against every discouragement with a zeal and firmness which bespoke intensity of moral conviction."[19] Birney had advocated political action but at first avoided partisanship, instead urging the abolitionists to apply pressure on all parties. He wrote in the *Philanthropist* his ideas of political responsibility, which included attempting to influence Congress to adopt antislavery legislation and refusing to back candidates who would in any way contribute to the continuance of slavery or condone mob action against abolitionists. He shaped a resolution embracing those ideas and presented it to the Ohio Anti-Slavery Society's convention, which supported it in 1837. Birney reported back to Dr. Gamaliel Bailey in Cincinnati that abolitionists were united about the necessity of political action. On a trip east Birney visited John Quincy Adams and William Ellery Channing, encouraging the former to continue the fight on petitions and urging the latter to come out with a letter to Clay against the annexation of Texas. These initiatives were both successful: Adams took the lead against the "gag rule," and Channing's letter to Clay may have influenced Clay in his early opposition to the acquisition of Texas, a move that may have been fatal to his political fortunes.

Historian Carl Schurz pointed out that the Nat Turner rebellion in 1831 and the emancipation of slaves in the West Indies in 1833 by the British Parliament "gave the agitation of the Abolitionists a new significance" and "made the slaveholders keenly sensible of the hostility of public opinion in the outside world, and increased their alarm." The combatants sharpened the weapons at hand for the mounting battle. "The slave power found it necessary to assert to the utmost, not only its constitutional rights, but also its moral position," Schurz wrote. "Abandoning its apologetic attitude, it proclaimed its belief that slavery was not an evil, but economically, politically, and morally a positive good, and 'the cornerstone of the republican edifice.'" The slaveholders were facing a foe wielding the thunderbolts of the Lord, who would not easily retreat. "They imperiously demanded of the people of the North that the abolitionists be silenced by force; that laws be made to imprison their orators, to stop their presses, to prevent the circulation of their tracts, and by every means to put down their agitation. They said that, unless this were done, the Union could not be maintained."[20]

After abolitionists flooded Congress with petitions demanding the abolishment of slavery in the District of Columbia, Sen. John C. Calhoun had stormed out of the Senate in March 1836 in blustering anger when his initial attempt for a gag rule was rejected. William Lee Miller states: "After rejecting Calhoun's plan on March 16, the Senate devised a curious, complex, and obscure delaying procedure. It would vote not on whether to receive the petition itself—this would dignify the petition—but on whether to accept the question of receiving the petition. This indirect method produced enough confusion to provide political cover for all members regardless of position. It was a classic example—a quarter century before the Civil War—of postponing the inevitable."[21] Aiming to placate Calhoun and furious Southerners, Northern Democrats supported the adoption of this devious trick. The situation appeared to be hopeless for abolitionists. Their entreaties would not even be considered, and one of their main strategies would be nullified. But then a new champion came forward: Rep. John Quincy Adams, a Massachusetts Whig, who responded to the gag rule in the House of Representatives on 25 May 1836, arguing that the Constitution guarantees citizens the right "to petition the government for a redress of grievances." Adams, son of John Adams, the second president, was a diplomat early in his career. After becoming the sixth president of the United States, he was ousted by Andrew Jackson with Southern pro-slavery backing in 1828. Adams had retired to his home in Braintree, Massachusetts, until he was surprisingly drafted for a House seat in 1830. Called "Old Man Eloquent," he was to devote the last years of service in Congress as well as the last years of his life to preserving civil liberties, including an eight-year campaign that finally ended the gag rule.

Abolitionists, led by Birney as a leader of the AASS, stepped up their antislavery petition drives, in the session of 1837–1838 sending more than 130,000 petitions asking Congress for the abolition of slavery in the District of Columbia. As the antislavery campaign mounted, Southern members of Congress in turn stepped up their defense of the practice. In succeeding Congresses, Southern members escalated the conflict by adopting even more Draconian strictures against petitions. "Most senators wanted this irritating issue to disappear," according to a Senate source. "They feared that Calhoun's proposal to bar the Senate door to these petitions would inadvertently benefit the small and regionally isolated anti-slavery movement. Overnight, the troublesome enemies of slavery could be transformed into noble champions of civil liberties."[22] Adams tried various parliamentary tactics in continued attempts to read slavery petitions to the House, but each time he was foiled by the gag rule. Antislavery sentiment finally gained momentum, and more Northern congressmen supported Adams's position against stifling the right to petition. In 1844, on Adams's motion, the House at last rescinded the gag rule. A valiant campaigner to the end, Adams died of a stroke on the House floor in 1848.

Horace Greeley, in his autobiography, explained his antipathy toward third parties: "I clung fondly to the Whig party, and deprecated the Abolition or Third Party movement in politics, as calculated fatally to weaken the only great National organization which was likely to oppose an effective resistance to the persistent exactions and aggressions of the Slave Power." He further expanded on his suspicions of the Liberty Party, no doubt focusing on the motivation of Birney, saying, "I have little faith in third-party movements—which are generally impelled by an occult purpose to help one of the leading parties by drawing off votes from the other."[23] Greeley may have been voicing the specious charge made during the 1844 campaign that Birney was in league with the Democrats. Birney, of course, was a supporter of neither Clay nor Polk, both of whom were slaveholders and at least tacit supporters of the status quo. It could be fairly said in light of the passage of time that Birney and the Liberty men were making their own statement against slavery with no political connivances in mind.

While the abolitionists saw a conspiracy by the slavocracy, their opponents in turn conceived their own threats of subversion, as noted by historian David Brion Davis: "On a different level of continuity, the Federalist image of French Illuminati foreshadowed later anti-abolitionist fantasies. Like the agents of the French Revolution, the abolitionists were supposedly the tools of a foreign power—in this case England; operating from secret cells, they deluded the public with subversive propaganda and plotted the destruction of religion, private property, and the family." Just as the advocates of slavery could justify that practice, which was maintained only by violence, they also could rationalize violence against the abolitionists, Davis notes, "Since both the Illuminati and abolitionists relied on the cunning manipulation of words to overthrow the social order, it was claimed they had forfeited the protection of civil liberties."[24]

Positing how these attitudes escalated to more dangerous actions and, eventually, civil war, Dumond observed: "Men allowed their hatred of abolition to weaken their reverence for the majesty of the law. They forgot that principles of free inquiry and protection, to be secure, must be sustained independently of the opinions expressed and of the persons requiring protection. They allowed the will of the majority to become the criterion of right and wrong, and mob violence to undermine the foundation of civil government. Slavery and free discussion were incompatible, but the attempt to suppress the latter served mightily to hasten the former's destruction."[25]

At age twenty-eight, as a member of the Illinois legislature, on 3 March 1837 Lincoln joined with Dan Stone, another representative from Sangamon County, to protest pro-slavery resolutions that had been passed by the state legislature while at the same time disapproving of abolitionists and stating a policy of noninterference with slavery in the states that was to persist until the Civil War. "They believe that the institution of slavery is founded on both injustice and bad policy; but that the promulgation of abolition doctrines tends rather to increase than to abate its evils," Lincoln said. "They believe that the Congress of the United States has no power, under the constitution, to interfere with the institution of slavery in the different States. They believe that the Congress of the United States has the power, under the constitution, to abolish slavery in the District of Columbia; but that that power ought not to be exercised unless at the request of the people of said District."[26] It was one of Lincoln's first public declarations against slavery, modified and muted as it was, but nonetheless courageous for the time, since the slave power was engaged in a massive campaign to stamp out any opposition.

Late in 1837 Calhoun restated his "compact theory" of government, asserting the states had entered the Union to gain security against domestic and foreign threats to its domestic institutions; therefore, the federal government must prevent attacks on slavery, or the Union could not be preserved. Under this theory, abolitionism would be outlawed. But, thanks to Adams, the antislavery crusaders were still hoping to get their views considered. Better yet, the movement for political action was gaining speed, aided by the intransigence of the slave power that was aimed at subverting constitutional protections.

Constitutional outrages were evident even in the shadow of the nation's capital. Georgetown, in the District of Columbia, passed a law prohibiting any free black person from taking the *Liberator,* Garrison's abolitionist newspaper, from the post office on pain of a twenty-dollar fine or thirty days' imprisonment. As the pro-slavery forces were becoming more aggressive, in January 1838 Birney sent a tract titled "Why Work for the Slave?" from the AASS offices in New York to Calhoun and other members of Congress from Southern states. In the tract Birney offered to provide information "cheerfully"; in response he received a list of fourteen questions from Rep. Franklin H. Elmore and apparently a committee of slaveholding representatives, although Birney thought Calhoun himself was likely the source of the queries. While the abolitionists had been petitioning and questioning the slave power legislators for years without reply, in March Birney responded in a gesture of goodwill with full details of the operations of the AASS. In his request Representative Elmore warned that the information would, "if deemed expedient, be freely used."[27] Birney explained frankly that the aims of the antislavery societies were "the re-animation of the Republican principles of our Constitution" and the "establishment of the Union on an enduring basis," while admitting that Congress had no power over slavery in the states, according to Fladeland. Although the correspondence on both sides was civil, cautionary notes were added by the abolitionists: "The societies would continue to try to influence Congress to abolish the slave trade, end slavery in the District of Columbia and the territories, and prevent its extension." Thus Birney laid out the flash points for the Civil War more than a quarter century before they came to a head. Birney concluded, "If the South chose to dissolve the Union on this ground, it would bring only ruin upon itself. The Southern people should be informed of the storm gathering over their heads." All the abolitionists asked was for access to the popular mind, Birney pleaded. Of course that was exactly what the slave power was worried about and was not inclined to provide. Twenty-five thousand copies of the correspondence were published by the AASS.[28]

Perhaps the most important publishing initiative undertaken by the AASS under Birney's leadership was publication of Rev. Theodore Weld's book *American Slavery As It Is* in 1839. The book details incidents of slave mistreatment, maiming, and murder compiled from twenty thousand Southern newspapers. Weld had purchased the contents of the New York Reading Room from 1837 to 1839, including many newspapers from the South. With his wife, Angelina Grimke, and her sister, Sarah, who had grown up in a slaveholding family in South Carolina, Weld scrutinized the papers for documented evidence of abuse of black men and women as reported in the press in slaveholding regions. (Modern military intelligence calls the process used by the Welds "content analysis." From minor reports a pattern of behavior and activity is revealed.) The reports were credible and explosively persuasive, at least to Northerners, since they came from the heart of the slave South as documented by news reports and advertising by slaveholders, speeches by Southern members of Congress, and statements and writings by prominent slaveholders. Historian J. C. Furnas called Weld's book "a hair-raising compilation of atrocities and barbarously phrased advertisements for runaways that remained the keystone of antislavery propaganda for the duration."[29] And Dumond commented, "It is a book of horrors. It is as close as history can come to the facts, because it was compiled from the statements of men who knew slavery, who had come North because they could not witness its cruelties and remain silent, and who were now in a position to speak freely."[30]

The book was the first telling salvo in the abolitionist war of words. One hundred thousand copies of it were sold in its first year. Monique Prince of the University of North Carolina Library describes the book as follows: "It was designed to portray the horrors of American Slavery through a collection of first-hand testimonials and personal narratives from both freedmen and whites. The book describes the slave diet, their hours of work and rest, clothing, housing, privations and afflictions. It also includes pro-slavery arguments that the authors refute. *American Slavery As It Is* was widely distributed and was one of the most influential of the American antislavery tracts."[31] Thus, Weld and the Grimke sisters, collaborating with Birney as publisher through the AASS, built on the works of earlier antislavery writers and publishers with intensive field research that irrefutably laid out evidence of the evils of slavery. For reasonable readers with open minds, the book was powerfully convincing. With that foundation laid, the abolitionists' attention could be turned to doing something about slavery through the political process, a seemingly insurmountable task.

Noted historians Bruce Catton and William Catton described how Birney accomplished his goal of establishing abolition as a political initiative: "Birney was not cut from the harsh, sharp-edged pattern that a consistently bad press had succeeded in stamping on most workers in the abolition movement. Calm and judicious, he seemed to radiate 'the utmost candor, a simple, earnest intent in pursuit of truth, a quick conscience, perfect fairness—the traits of a mind that could not be partisan.' To be sure, Birney was thenceforth partisan enough in the antislavery cause, but he always avoided the angry covenant-with-death fulminations of William Lloyd Garrison and never laced his zeal with intemperance or hysteria."[32] Another writer, J. C. Furnas, observed about the abolitionists, "Few of them—some of the Quakers and J. G. Birney seem to have been exceptions—got into Abolitionism simply through encountering the problem of slavery and determining to do away with the horrible thing."[33]

Birney's view of the Constitution was at the root of the political abolitionist movement. Although he undoubtedly formed the opinion earlier, his thoughts were stated in a "Whig Journal" published in an 1845 book: "Such parts of the Constitution as are opposed to the law of God, to common justice, to humanity, to good morals, I reject as no part of that instrument. The Constitution of the United States is a Constitution of Government. Governments have no right to ordain what is immoral or unjust. Morals and Justice, make the only allowable basis of government. There is no other basis. Government is intended to secure natural rights—to enable those who are subject to it, to perfect their happiness, and make themselves, in all good and proper things, what they are capable of being made. Injustice is opposed to the object of all rightful government, and can never constitute one of its elements."[34] The concept was diametrically opposed to the doctrine of John C. Calhoun and others who held that slavery was a positive good with a biblical basis and was protected by the Constitution and therefore should be upheld by the U.S. government. In Birney's eyes the question of slavery was one of good versus evil, right versus wrong—a religious, moral basis that was unassailable. The editors of the *American Whig Review* commented that Birney's interpretation "opens an entirely new chapter in political and moral philosophy," since he "means to execute [the Constitution], not as *it is,* but as he thinks *it ought to be.* Truly this may be called by way of distinction *the conscientious age.*"[35]

A monumental clash of ideologies was shaping, opposing sides were marshaling forces, and events of the next quarter century would guarantee that the nation would never be the same.

CHAPTER 4

Trapped in the Golden Circle

The Cherokee Nation, then, is a distinct community, occupying
its own territory, with boundaries accurately described,
in which the laws of Georgia can have no force.

—U.S. SUPREME COURT CHIEF JUSTICE JOHN MARSHALL

THE GREEN MEADOWS AND PINEY WOODS OF FRONTIER ALABAMA IN the early 1800s offered great profit to settlers if they owned slaves, planted cotton, and were good managers. James G. Birney qualified on the first two counts, but he failed miserably on the third. He was too sympathetic, too softhearted while successful plantation owners and their whip-wielding overseers were hard drivers of their slaves. But being a softhearted humanitarian was not Birney's only problem in Alabama.

After the War of 1812, as Alabama historian Virginia Van der Veer Hamilton has observed, a folk migration broke out, rivaling the California Gold Rush that came decades later. It was a biblical-like exodus from more populous states created by "Alabama Fever."[1] And the young Birneys had caught the fever. It was a land of plenty, where farmers boasted of corn that grew so fast they could feed their own razorback hogs, scarcely ever have to buy meat, and have enough corn left over to brew up vats of moonshine. The jug stashed in the barn was always full, even though drinking didn't exactly fit with the more temperate admonishments of their Methodist or Baptist faiths.

The cavalcade of rickety horse-drawn carriages and wagons piled with furniture jolted on muddy roads and corduroy causeways heading south from Kentucky to Alabama. The conveyances carried a stream of immigrants seeking opportunity in the virgin territory of the Tennessee Valley.

One of the jolting wagons contained exuberant James G. Birney, twenty-six, glad to be free of the social strictures of Danville; Birney's boyhood slave and companion, Michael; and Michael's wife and three children. Several other wagons carried two dozen family slaves of all ages—from two-year-old toddler Polly, to Tom, a white-thatched forty-four-year-old, worn from years of work in the fields—who Birney intended would be the foundation of a successful cotton plantation. They were the lucky ones being able to ride. A British traveler cited by Hamilton told of seeing nearly a thousand foot-weary slaves along a trail to Montgomery and chained coffles shuffling perhaps twenty-five miles a day into Huntsville under the lash of a slave trader from Mobile.[2]

It was spring 1818 when Birney moved to Alabama seeking a fresh place to settle his family and escape the disapproval he was facing in Danville. He had committed a cardinal sin: showing sympathy for slaves by opposing a fugitive slave law as a member of the Kentucky state legislature. The slavery-saturated white social structure immediately rose up like an angered dragon and blew its hot breath on the infidel who dared raise a spear against it. There was no defense except to flee, and Alabama was seen as ideal to begin anew. Fertile land could be had for as little as $1.25 per acre, and compliant slaves to work it were plentiful. After the land was purchased, Birney returned for his pretty, delicate wife, Agatha, and son, James Jr., not yet one year old. They arrived in the autumn of 1818 in a new carriage purchased for him by his brother-in-law John Marshall for $400. Fatherly advice was given in a letter from James Sr. from Danville: "It is a neat, light comfortable little carriage and I think very cheap; Mr. Marshall ought to be indemnified and the payment of his note with gratitude when it is fully due."[3]

The family hemp business, in which young Birney had become a partner with his aging father, who then was fifty-one, was a major source of his finances for a time. Noting that Gratz and Brothers had paid $1,800 for cordage, his father wrote, "Half this sum will be due to you and you may apply to your use that amount of the last of the sales of rope which may be made by you, or should it so happen that funds cannot be raised in time for your purpose from that source you may draw on me at sight or direct the payment of that sum in any way which will be most agreeable to you."[4]

But the rope business was in for a readjustment. Russian cordage and sail duck were considered superior to domestic supplies, being produced through the more difficult and expensive method of "water rotting" the fibers, according to James F. Hopkins. Russian cordage became scarce during the turmoil of the Napoleonic wars, so the U.S. government began to solicit Kentucky growers to produce those materials, and the elder Birney, using the American "dew rotted" method, was a major supplier, along with Lexington neighbor and wealthy legislator Henry Clay. However, the hemp cordage business declined precipitously at the end of the War of 1812, and from 1815 on the U.S. Navy bought only rope of Russian manufacture until in 1838 it established its own ropewalk and began producing cordage at the Charlestown, Massachusetts, Navy Yard.[5] Many Kentucky growers had abandoned the trade when government orders fell, and judging from the correspondence between Birney and his father, the profitability of hemp production was severely reduced by the loss of the major government market. The fact that he could no longer count on heavy subsidies from Kentucky through sales of cordage was no doubt among the factors that worsened young Birney's financial difficulties in Alabama.

However, with a theological degree from Princeton and a law degree from Philadelphia as well as brief experience as a state legislator in Kentucky, Birney was poised to become self-sufficient and one of the most important men in the new state formed soon after he arrived. Alabama historian Willis Brewer described him as follows: "In appearance he was short and stout, with handsome and expressive features, and polished manners. His mind was of a high order, and his capacity as a writer and speaker was considerable."[6] Alabama joined the Union in December 1819 as the twenty-second state. It was a slave state, balancing free Maine, which came in a few months later in 1820.

The influx of settlers to frontier Alabama even attracted a curious President James Monroe. The president, accompanied only by a military aide, showed up unannounced in Huntsville on 1 June 1819 as part of a Southern tour, staying at Andrew Jackson's favorite haunt, the Green Bottom Inn. Birney was one of probably a hundred prominent citizens at a dinner for the president, presided over by Birney's friend and political collaborator Clement Claiborne Clay. Among twenty-one toasts made at the dinner for the visiting chief executive, the nineteenth was most prophetic about the future of the nation: "To the people of the territories west of the Mississippi— When their numbers entitle them, may they be admitted to the Union with no other restrictions than those prescribed by the Constitution."[7] The eerily prophetic toast appeared to be a direct reference to the looming argument over the extension of slavery into the territories that was beginning to divide the nation.

Biographer Fladeland described Birney's attitude toward slavery during the early 1800s: "Owning slaves was consistent with his views at the time. Although he had been exposed to anti-slavery views since childhood, he had not yet arrived at the point where he recognized his individual responsibility in the matter. Like so many of the Southern planters, including Washington and Jefferson, he deplored the evils inherent in the system but continued to practice it while hoping for its gradual extinction."[8] Much like his mentor at Princeton, Dr. Stanhope Smith; his idol, James Madison; his political ally from Kentucky, Henry Clay; and many others in the generations from the founding of the nation to the Civil War, Birney could not justify replacing the sacred American principle of property rights with the rights of people to be free. Despite the brave words of the Declaration of Independence, declaring the equality of all men, slavery was enshrined in the Bible and—as many believed at the time—in the U.S. Constitution.

While seeking a frontier Eden opened up by the U.S. victory in the War of 1812, the Birneys actually were entering a frontier maelstrom of epic proportions. Whites were wresting away the lands of Native American tribes, including the Creeks and Cherokee, with little regard for ancient property rights. Birney had acquired 235 acres of prime land in Madison County, Alabama, near the Tennessee border, for about ten dollars an acre. Local settlers boasted the land was so fertile that even in bad times a planter there could become wealthy. But wealth could only be created on a cotton plantation stocked with hardworking slaves, and at that point in his life, Birney was no less guilty than any other Southern planter in exploiting that human resource. After the War of 1812, trade revived and cotton was in great demand. According to Alabama historian Thomas Jones Taylor: "Slave labor became the most profitable of all occupations. A large number of slaves were brought into the county and they soon were equal in number to the whites, and the slave owners made money rapidly. With lands making a hundred dollars worth of cotton to the acre, with the cheapest labor system in the world, no part of the Union offered a better investment of capital than in Madison County."[9]

Frontier Alabama eventually would be where Birney's dramatic transformation from traditional Southern slaveholding planter to antislavery activist took shape. That transformation, which so alarmed his pro-slavery neighbors and colleagues, plus the deaths of three small children, would guarantee that the family's stay in Alabama would end as an unhappy experience for the Birneys.

In his first few years in Alabama, Birney was a leader in the organization for statehood as a member of the first state legislature in 1819. Immediately he asserted his antislavery sentiments, applying them even more forcefully than he had in Kentucky. Although he was not a member of the constitutional convention, he did secure a provision empowering the legislature to bar importation of slaves to be sold and allowing emancipation if slave owners agreed or were compensated. More vitally, the clause required owners to treat slaves humanely, including providing food and clothing. According to Alabama historical sources, Birney's initiative also provided: "For any crime more serious than petit larceny a slave was entitled to a trial by jury. Any person dismembering or killing a slave was to be subject to the same punishment as that which would be meted out if the crime were committed against a white man. The only exception was in case of a slave insurrection."[10]

Birney's son William, who was born in Alabama in 1819, the year after the family arrived, grew up there and many years later recalled at that time in the South every lawyer was a politician, and most were also planters. Huntsville pioneers Clement C. Clay, Arthur F. Hopkins, and Reuben Chapman all followed those occupations, prospered, and held important positions in state government. Clement Comer Clay was a state legislator who collaborated with Birney on antislavery initiatives, later becoming governor of Alabama and a U.S. senator; Hopkins became Birney's law partner and later was chief justice of the Alabama Supreme Court and a U.S. senator; and Chapman served in Congress for twelve years and was governor of Alabama from 1847 to 1849. Hopkins also was active in evangelical Protestant reform movements stressing religion and temperance and was founding president of the Alabama Colonization Society and owned slaves, much like Birney. When Birney asserted antislavery views, Hopkins diverged, opposing emancipation because he believed that without the restraint of slavery, black men and women would become "miserable vagabonds and hapless paupers." His former law partner, Birney, by contrast, became a radical abolitionist and led the political movement that aimed to end slavery. Scholars recently have advanced the theory that the cotton boom and emerging market economy necessitated the expansion of slavery, which "made the South an increasingly distinctive region antagonistic toward the free labor economy of the North."[11]

The would-be Southern planter Birney soon found that the twenty-four household slaves he had brought from Kentucky were inadequate and unsuited for heavy plantation work, so he needed to bolster his slave roster with hands more experienced in cultivating and harvesting cotton. The available bondmen included his personal slave and friend, Michael, now about twenty-four years of age; two house slaves he had obtained from his father-in-law, Judge McDowell; ten from his father; and eleven who had been born of family slaves. He bought nineteen Negroes more experienced in fieldwork for $13,495, making a total of forty-three bondmen available for labor at an average price of $710 each. Ten of Birney's slaves who traveled with him to Alabama were obtained from his father, although there is no record of a purchase price and no indication of their last names. Michael's last name, Matthews, is known only because it was on the deed of manumission filed in the Mercer County Courthouse by Birney in 1834. Surnames of slaves, along with a short description, were listed in 1839 when Birney freed his father's twenty-two slaves; perhaps by then he had matured somewhat in his sensibilities toward bondmen, reflecting a change in attitude since 1824.

One slave, Jesse, born in 1795, had been the property of Birney's grandfather John Reed, who had purchased him in 1798 when Birney was three years old. Notes in the plantation record book show that Jesse died at age twenty-six on 30 October 1821. The record book also shows that Birney purchased male slaves from five states around the South: Tom, $600, from John Dodd of Kentucky; Billy Banks, forty-one, $500, from J. C. Richardson of Kentucky; Sam, twenty-six, $720, from Jarrett Ficklin of Kentucky; Hartwell, twenty-six, $875, from Will S. Jeffries in Virginia; Jerry, twenty-six, $900, from W. G. Bowers of North Carolina; Little Ben, sixteen, for $405 from Joseph Sykes in Tennessee; Charles, sixteen, $500 from William Hogan in Kentucky; Luke, fifteen, $500, from E. Hardy in Virginia; Moses, fourteen, $400, from N. Harris of Kentucky; Isham, seventeen, $800, from S. Chapman of Alabama Territory; and George, eighteen, $595, from Thomas Pope of Alabama. The women included the oldest, Judy, forty-one, acquired from his father; several six-year-olds—Mary, Margaret, Caroline, and Betsey—all apparently born on the plantation in Alabama; two-year-old Polly, born on the Kentucky plantation of his father; three women who cost $600 each: Amy, thirty-one, purchased from Dodd; Daphne, twenty-nine, also acquired from Bowers; and Biddy, twenty-seven, purchased from John McChord of Kentucky. Viney, twenty, and Silvia, sixteen, were purchased from Pope for $525 and $450 respectively.[12]

Birney's slaves were deficient for their intended labor in one major way: they had never seen a cotton field. "Cotton culture requires skilled labor unceasingly applied in some form for at least eleven months in the year," William Birney observed. "It admits of no awkwardness in the use of the hoe, no negligence in keeping the weeds from the plants, no clumsiness in picking, no ignorance in the processes of ginning and baling. Kentucky farm hands that had never seen a cotton field could not at once be made profitable operatives in one. During the years 1820, 1821, and 1822, Mr. Birney became embarrassed in his financial affairs. Owing to his frequent absences from home, the inexperience of his slaves in the methods of cotton culture, and his repugnance to severities in plantation management, his cotton crops had not proved profitable."[13] Politics took Birney away from the plantation at Triana, a small town 13 miles southwest of Huntsville, much of the time, and the cotton crops no doubt suffered from want of closer supervision of the slaves. The plantation record book indicates a complete failure of the cotton crop in 1821.

The year 1821 apparently was one of depressed economic times as a letter from Birney's father indicates times were tough in Kentucky. "Is bale rope worth anything with you; how would it exchange for good cotton?" he writes. The senior Birney also informed his son that John Marshall, his sister's husband, was in dire financial difficulty. "With regard to Poor Mr. Marshall he is entirely gone. In 1819 I loaned him bank stock and cash to the amount of $17,000; besides I endorsed a note he passed to Joshua Barber for $1,800 which of course I had to pay. I took from him at the same time a deed of trust on all his Negroes, household furniture and one tract of land on the Kentucky River in the value of property that must ruin him completely."[14]

About the same time Birney heard from his father-in-law, Gen. William McDowell, from Bowling Green, Kentucky. McDowell had been considering moving to Alabama to be near his daughter and the growing family and wrote, "My anxiety to go to your country still continuing, yet I can see no chance to sell my land here, times are very tough and money as scarce as it ever has been. I therefore trust you will not (if it is necessary for you) omit selling the quarter section you designed for me."[15]

Some of his personal pursuits at the time added to the financial problems. Like Henry Clay and John C. Calhoun in the South, and Northerners like Daniel Webster, the younger Birney followed the fashion of gentlemen politicians of the day by devotion to the gaming table, playing for high stakes, and laying wagers on horse races. In Birney's case gambling led to disaster. Several heavy losses at the tables, added to his failures as a planter, compelled him to mortgage his plantation and slaves. Unwilling to sell his slaves, he resolved never to bet again and to pay off the mortgage upon his property by the more active practice of the law.

At the same time he was beginning as a cotton planter, James G. Birney was involving himself in Alabama politics. The legislature was meeting in the city of St. Stephens, on the Tombigbee River about 220 miles south of Huntsville. The territorial legislature in 1818 was a small body, William Birney, whimsically noted. "The Senate consisted of a single member, who united in himself all its offices. His name was Titus, and it was his humor to go punctiliously through all the forms of legislation, discussing bills sent up from the House, putting them to vote, signing them as Speaker, countersigning them as clerk, and forwarding them with due formality to the

Governor." Birney collaborated with two old Kentucky friends, Sen. John J. Crittenden and Henry Clay, then Speaker of the U.S. House of Representatives, to obtain passage of the enabling act in Congress that set the place of the constitutional convention at Huntsville. Thus, Birney was able to attend almost every session of the constitutional convention even though Clement Comer Clay was the convention delegate and Birney was the state legislator from Madison County. "His liberality and humanity, too, have left their traces in the sections of the Constitution which relate to slavery," wrote his son.

Under Birney's influence, the Alabama constitution also included the following provision, first in a slave state: "Any person who shall maliciously dismember or deprive a slave of life shall suffer such punishment as would be inflicted in case the like offense had been committed on a free white person, and on the like proof; except in case of insurrection of said slave." Georgia had adopted such a clause in 1798, but nullified it with the exception "Unless such death should happen by accident in giving such slave moderate correction." William Birney reckoned, "Such deaths were not uncommon in Georgia; but as no master was ever tried, convicted and hanged for the murder of his slave, all the deaths, to use the constitutional phrase, must have 'happened by accident.'"

The section on slavery in the Alabama constitution adopted under Birney's sponsorship empowered the legislature to pass laws to emancipate slaves with compensation to their owners. The Alabama legislature freed 203 slaves by petition during its first eleven years of existence, from 1819 to 1829, an average of eighteen per year.[16] Sponsorship of that provision in the constitution was perhaps Birney's greatest contribution toward ameliorating slavery within the existing system in the South. Alabama authors have pointed out that the legislature freed seventeen slaves in its first session, while Birney was a member, and continued to free them for the next ten years, while Birney was still a resident. Slaves sometimes were allowed to purchase their freedom or were rewarded for long years of meritorious service to a family or some heroic act or because the planter knew the slaves were his own children.[17] After the Nat Turner revolt in Virginia in 1831, however, requests to the legislature for manumission became less frequent. Shortly after that time a discouraged Birney left the state, convinced that slavery would never be eliminated by Southerners themselves.

Birney's slave roster was made in 1824 just after he turned the plantation over to an overseer and moved fourteen miles south into Huntsville to resume his law career in hopes of improving his finances. The slave capital was used for collateral—human flesh mortgaged, as it were—at a bank to obtain direly needed cash. Unpaid loans he had made to cover losses from gambling on horse racing and failure of the cotton crop in 1821 were the subject of a circuit court suit by a creditor in 1823. The plantation record book shows only one profitable transaction on the plantation: the sale in 1819 of Kitty, a sixteen-year-old slave, for $800, a neat, quick $200 profit, since she had been acquired for $600 that same year.[18] At that point Birney was no different from any other Southern slaveholder—selling slaves for profit. He was still about fifteen years away from becoming an abolitionist. The record also noted the death of Susan, an infant slave, age one and a half, who died in 1823; she was the same age as Birney's daughter Margaret, who had died the year before. The Birney household would suffer three such losses of children in their own family during their Alabama sojourn. Besides the early deaths, the fourteen years in Alabama were trying times for the family financially and emotionally. In 1824 Birney resolved to fight his personal demons by swearing off drinking and gambling and dedicating himself to practicing law. Even more important, Birney, the profligate aristocrat, would seek redemption in defending Native Americans and later Negroes in the antislavery cause.

Birney's abortive attempt at becoming a rich planter with a few dozen unskilled slaves on a relatively small tract of land was pitiful: by contrast, future Confederate president Jefferson Davis's wealth was created by the one thousand slaves of his brother and guardian, Joseph Emory Davis, on five thousand acres of delta land in Mississippi, placing the Davis brothers among the richest Americans; and bombastic, Falstaffian Howell Cobb, another rebel leader, had a similar number of slaves that enriched him through his Georgia plantation.[19]

When Birney moved to Huntsville in 1823 the city was already a commerce center for the nearby states of Tennessee, Virginia, and Georgia. The population of about two thousand was growing, and "the beauty and healthfulness of Huntsville had attracted a number of men of fortune and leisure. General [Alabama's first U.S. senator, John William] Walker lived in a house resembling the Parthenon; it looked down on the town from a height on the east. Ex-governor [William Wyatt] Bibb and other planters occupied costly mansions. It gave a warm welcome to James G. Birney, who had already gained a high standing as a lawyer by his occasional practice on the circuit," Birney's son William observed.[20]

Birney was a strong advocate of justice for all as postulated in the Constitution. Prior to his defense of Native Americans, Birney, as state solicitor (prosecutor) of five populous Alabama counties in the years 1823–1827, sued a "lynch club" that had been controlling justice as they saw fit with murderous initiatives. Despite threats that he would be the target of the lynch club, Birney faced the vigilantes in Jackson County, arranged a change of venue to Madison County, and won damages for the son of a lynched counterfeiter.[21] The lynch club disbanded, and Birney had won a great victory, according to local observers. Rev. Theodore Weld also noted in *American Slavery As It Is* that Birney had won an indictment against a white man who had slain an escaping Negro. "Here was an example of the kind of offense Birney had insisted on having covered in the slavery clause of the Alabama constitution, that a white man killing or dismembering a slave was just as guilty as if the crime were committed against another white man." However, public sentiment prevailed against extradition of the culprit from Tennessee.[22]

Birney's early political stances were similar to those stated by Abraham Lincoln in his first campaign speech in 1832, including adherence to the Whig Party and steadfast opposition to Jacksonian Democrats. William Birney wrote: "From the date of his anti-Jackson speech in the Alabama Legislature of 1819, Mr. Birney had been identified with the national party [Whigs] that favored a protective tariff, internal improvements and a liberal construction generally of the Constitution. . . . In 1828 he was nominated as one of the electors on the Adams and Rush ticket for Alabama. He spoke . . . attacking the politics of Jackson and Calhoun as fatally dangerous to maintenance of the Union."[23]

Birney's solicitude for Native Americans, which led to his involvement in the abolitionist movement on behalf of blacks, made him unpopular, but his opposition to Andrew Jackson was even more shattering to his political career. His complaint that the government had spent "forty millions of dollars" on the Florida War, prosecuted by Jackson, aimed mainly at exterminating fugitive slaves in Florida, may have cited an exaggerated cost, but his opposition was based more on humanitarian than economic reasons. In 1819 Jackson, already sniffing about for the White House, came to Huntsville for the fall horse races, part of a national tour de force testing the presidential waters. He stayed several weeks to build an Alabama political base, although he was already well known in Huntsville, visited there frequently, and attended meetings of the Huntsville Masonic Lodge. Early historian Edward Chambers Betts reported that Jackson, "who acquired vast areas of Madison County lands," also was partial to the hostelry of the Old Green Bottom Inn, where, "as legend has it—General Jackson raced his horses and fought his cocks."[24]

Alabama was strong for Jackson, who had fought and won battles on its soil, saving its citizens from Indian massacres, as they believed, "and he was the hero of New Orleans!" and had saved their land and homes from British invaders. Col. Howell Rose, a state representative from Autauga County, proposed a resolution of tribute to the gallant general in the Alabama legislature. Alabama historian Albert James Pickett commented about Rose: "He was ardent in his attachment to Jackson, and was the first to propose resolutions approbatory of his valuable services to the State performed during the late Creek and Seminole wars. Colonel Rose introduced joint resolutions of this character, together with one inviting the general to a seat within the bar both of the House and the Senate on all occasions when it should be his pleasure to attend those bodies, which were adopted. Colonel Rose, at the head of a committee, waited upon Jackson, with a copy of the resolutions, to which the latter replied in a letter full of the liveliest gratitude."

Representative Birney would have none of it, Pickett wrote. "To him, the general appeared a contemnor of the law, a headstrong and violent man, who, in hanging Arbuthnot and shooting Ambrister, in April, 1818, had disregarded evidence and crowned the long series of brutal deeds which proved his unfitness to wield power. He not only voted against Colonel Rose's resolution, but also gave his reasons in a calm and forcible speech. From that date his election to political office in Alabama was impossible, and he did not again become a candidate."[25] Alexander Arbuthnot and Robert Ambrister were British traders who had collaborated with the Seminoles in Florida in a war Birney considered immoral. Jackson considered them enemies and, after the pair was captured in battles, summarily ordered their executions. In a strange twist of history, Birney's son William would return to Florida during the Civil War, and afterward during Reconstruction, to fight not Native Americans but former Confederates and help to end a slavery system Jackson had supported.

Birney's "conversion" from a dissolute life and move into Huntsville in 1823 led him to a renewed interest in religion, education, and other social movements that followed Reverend Finney's lead. Birney joined the newly reform-minded Presbyterian Church, becoming active in temperance, free public education, higher education, Bible and tract societies, and Sunday schools. His energy, now that he had shaken drinking and gambling, seemed endless. Birney seemed intent on personally forging a new, more philanthropic nation, and he was destined to move as though afire, beginning with religious and social reform activities prompted by the Great Awakening, to representing the Indians, to working for colonization of Negroes in Africa, then to gradual abolition of Negro slavery, and finally to the pathfinding politics of the immediate abolition of slavery.

Birney's style of leadership bordered on the fanatical, especially as concerned alcohol, since it had led to his earlier downfall. The rights of Native Americans and Negroes would come later. Having kicked demon rum, Birney wanted everyone else to become a teetotaler, too. "Once converted to a principle himself, he became impatient with others who could not or would not admit its truth," historian Thomas McAdory Owen observed. When an ordinance he had promoted to ban the sale of intoxicating beverages to be consumed on premises was challenged by the local press, Birney, as president of the board of trustees (in effect, mayor) of Huntsville, asked the public for a confidence vote. He won the vote, and a temperance movement was started, headed by his law partner, Arthur Hopkins. Fladeland points out that this was almost a century before the acceptance of recall as a function of government and an expression of voters' rights.[26]

Birney also concerned himself with the education of youth, especially poor children, sponsoring the establishment of a primary school. Children under age twenty-one who "by poverty are unable to get any education" were listed in a census taken by the assessor, and Birney, as mayor, appointed a committee that arranged financing through a property tax and private donations and opened the school in early 1830. He also got the University of Alabama to admit a proportionate number of students without charge, a plan similar to one proposed for the University of Virginia by Thomas Jefferson.[27]

Birney's feelings toward Native Americans was replicated in his relations with Negroes, even though he was still a plantation owner whose success depended on diligent work by the slaves, who sometimes required discipline. William Birney recalled an incident during the family's Alabama days: "The manager of the farm chafed a good deal under the prohibition of the use of the lash on the servants. On one occasion he sent the writer, who had been at the farm hunting ducks and squirrels, which were numerous, a note stating that Jack, a Negro, must be whipped. My father was much troubled by this note, but sent me to tell the manager that if Jack would not behave himself he should send him at once to his master. In speaking with me about the matter he said: 'It is hard to tell what one's duty is toward these poor creatures; but I have made up my mind to one thing—I will not allow them to be treated brutally."[28] It was one thing to be a benevolent master to his own slaves and quite another to launch a campaign to free all the slaves, about three million at this point in the nation's history. However, Birney never thought on a small scale; once convinced a particular course was right, he was fervent, undeterred, and willing to brave anything and give up everything to achieve his goal.

Birney's son William said his father organized a gradual emancipation society in Kentucky in late 1830 when he was on his way home from a recruiting trip for faculty and officers for the University of Alabama, about to be established at Tuscaloosa, of which he was a founding trustee. Oliver W. Davis, biographer of David Bell Birney, observed the historic implications of that trip: "During his visit North, James G. Birney, actuated by a liberality of spirit which at that time was seldom found among men living south of Mason and Dixon's line, attended anti-slavery meetings in Philadelphia, New York and Boston. By the arguments he heard advanced, he became convinced that it was the duty of every slaveholder to give his slaves every opportunity of going to Africa, and he returned home a strong Colonizationist." A few years later Birney made a second trip north and became an emancipationist.[29] Birney may have had some discussions about emancipation in 1830, but the organization of the Kentucky Society for the Gradual Relief of the State from Slavery was not effected until he returned to Danville from Alabama in 1833.

On the trip north for the University of Alabama, Birney was in Boston for the celebration of the two-hundredth anniversary of its founding, 17 September 1830. As a Southern gentleman and a slaveholder, an article in the *Nation* magazine later observed that "all doors were open to him. He met [Senator Daniel] Webster and [Harvard Professor George] Ticknor, he called on President [Edward] Everett at Harvard."[30] Birney secured Rev. Dr. Alva Woods, a Rhode Island Baptist clergyman, as president and Henry Tutwiler as professor of ancient languages for the university. Reverend Woods had been president of Transylvania University in Lexington, Kentucky, where Birney had once attended. Two mathematics professors, a professor of chemistry, and one of English literature were recommended by Birney. Some other offers were declined either because the professors were committed to other universities or because they did not wish to make homes in the South. He also recruited teachers for the Huntsville Female Seminary.

An act of Congress in 1818 set aside a township in the territory of Alabama for establishment of a "seminary of learning." First president Reverend Woods wanted to emulate Harvard, which he had attended, with knowledge of classical Greek and Latin as admission requirements. With such high standards, and with students coming from the raw frontier, not surprisingly less than 10 percent of the student body of about one hundred graduated in some of the early years.[31]

Birney is not listed in the university's catalog or archives. Abolitionist Samuel J. May offered the following explanation: "When the report reached Alabama that Mr. Birney had become an immediate Abolitionist, had renounced the Colonization Society, and had liberated his slaves, most

of those who had formerly known and honored him there united in expressing very emphatically their displeasure, and declaring their contempt for
his new fanatical opinions. The Supreme Court of that State expunged his
name from the roll of attorneys practicing at its bar. And at the University
of Alabama, of which he had been a most useful trustee, several literary
societies of which he had been an honorary member, hastened to pass resolutions expelling him from their bodies. These acts convinced him of their
hatred, but not of his error."[32] However, Alabama Historical Society reports
from 1905 explain that Birney was never officially a trustee of the University of Alabama, that he was commissioned by Alabama governor Gabriel
Moore, and that he was paid a total of $900 to find the president and fac-
ulty members.[33]

Abolitionist propaganda such as Garrison's *Liberator* abolitionist newspaper and Walker's Appeal pamphlet prodded the South into even more
fury than had been stirred up by Adams's defeat of Clay in 1824. As a direct
result, in 1830, North Carolina passed a law to prohibit slaves and free blacks
from reading and writing. All blacks emancipated after 1830 were ordered
to leave the state within 90 days. After the 1831 Virginia slave revolt, the
South exploded with fear and rage, with many blaming Northern abolitionists, especially William Lloyd Garrison."[34] The Turner revolt reignited the
uproar and a new wave of reprisals was launched. Southern reaction to the
slave revolts only convinced the antislavery forces of the brutality of slavery
and strengthened their resolve to end the practice.

William Birney had perceived the defeat of Clay by John Quincy Adams
on a vote in the House of Representatives in 1824 as a turning point in North-
South relations. He wrote that the concept of the "Solid South" had been
formulated in the Missouri struggle over slavery in 1820–1821. After that,
he opined, "the nation went fast asleep on the slavery question; the subject
was not discussed at the South because of the danger to life, or at the North
because of apathy." He further observed, "From the election of Adams to that
of his successor [Jackson], in 1828, all means were employed to fire the Southern heart." He cited Adams's view of Jackson's victory in 1828, saying, "In this
instance the slave states have clung together in one unbroken phalanx, and
have been victorious by means of accomplices and deserters from the ranks of
freedom." Birney also noted that Southerners were alarmed by a survey taken
by the Manumission Society of North Carolina showing that in 1825 three-
fifths of the people of that state were "favorably disposed to the principle of
emancipation." Pointing to the fact that the survey was taken in forty-five different localities, he theorized, "It may be safely taken as a sure guide to public

sentiment not only in North Carolina but in Tennessee and Virginia." It was an early instance of public opinion polling that is so prevalent today in judging voters' attitudes on issues.

William Birney saw the Southern campaign that elected Jackson in 1828 as a vast conspiracy to spread slavery, charging, "[John] Calhoun . . . candidate for the Vice Presidency on the Jackson ticket, was secretly engaged in undermining the Union!" He contended that Calhoun was "earnestly in favor of the acquisition of Texas and the extension of slavery westward, and is generally credited with being the first to suggest the brilliant scheme afterward incorporated in the creed of the 'Knights of the Golden Circle,' the creation of a slaveholding empire, including the Southern states, Texas, Mexico and Central America." Southern leaders, seeing the tariff on cotton as lifting the North to prosperity and sinking the South to ruin, also advised "an attitude of open resistance to the laws of the Union."[35] It was clear, grand strategy—or not—that Southerners were marshaling to repel any challenge to slavery that might come from the North.

James G. Birney had been surprised when the Alabama legislature on 13 January 1827 passed a bill he promoted prohibiting sale of slaves. The act levied a $100 fine for each slave brought in illegally and provided other penalties including imprisonment. Citizens could bring in slaves for their own use but could not hire or resell them for two years. Birney's joy at the bill's passage was tempered by the legislature's adoption, at the same session, of a bill disapproving of actions of several Northern states proposing emancipation of slaves. It was clear that the Alabama measure had passed because of fear of the rapidly growing Negro population, not because of antislavery sentiment. "One of the first effects in Alabama of Jackson's election was the repeal, January 22, 1829, of the law of 1827 [drafted and promoted by Birney], which prohibited the introduction of slaves into the state for sale or hire," William Birney wrote. "The inauguration was promptly followed by measures calculated to bring about the acquisition of Texas."[36] These developments, coalescing around positions on slavery, set the stage for the issue of Texas to become crucial in the careers of Henry Clay and James G. Birney, as well as impacting the future of the nation in the presidential election of 1844.

During the sixteen years Birney spent in Alabama, colonization was fast becoming the fashionable idea among elites seeking a way to deal with the growing numbers of slaves and freedmen, especially in the South. At the urging of Rev. Theodore Weld, who came to Huntsville to lecture in 1832, Birney finally decided that colonization might be an important first step to break the logjam leading to the eventual emancipation of slaves.

CHAPTER 5

Defending the Cherokee, Launching Abolition

Exceptionally tragic was the removal of the Cherokees from the Southeast to Indian Territory during the late 1830s. It was such an ordeal that Cherokees subsequently named the journey Nunna daul Isunyi; literally, the Trail Where We Cried; it has become known in English as the Trail of Tears.

—RUSSELL THORNTON

THE TERRITORY OF ALABAMA WAS ESTABLISHED IN MARCH 1817 ON lands east of the present state of Mississippi. Just about that time James G. Birney and William Love, a fellow member of the Kentucky legislature, traveled to the territory to see if Alabama was the land of opportunity equal to their dreams. Convinced by his brief visit, Birney returned with his slaves in the spring of 1818 and went back that autumn to bring his wife, Agatha, and young son James Jr. to their new home.

Birney quickly found that prejudice against the Native Americans surpassed that aimed at Negroes. The Cherokee, in addition to being viewed as enemies, were refusing removal, a process to which other tribes had agreed. White vituperation against the Cherokee may have had a moral basis dating to the early days on the frontier. Fundamentalist Christians must have recoiled in horror when confronting what British lieutenant Henry Timberlake called a "barbarous nation" and "hospitable though savage." The early Cherokee were described as an attractive people, and their olive skins were stained with indelible dyes in varied artistic patterns. The males were muscular and athletic, said to be larger than men of other tribes, and most of the women were tall and perfectly formed, with delicate feet and hands.

In the manner of some African and island tribes, the Cherokee went to great lengths to achieve a distinctive look by contorting their ears with ritualistic self-torture. "Their ears were slit and stretched to an enormous size, causing the persons who had the cutting performed to undergo incredible pain," writes historian Albert James Pickett. "They slit but one ear at a time, because the patient had to lay on one side forty days for it to heal. As soon as he could bear the operation, wire was wound around them to expand them, and when they were entirely well they were adorned with silver pendants and rings."[1]

More than two decades before the Birney family arrived in Alabama, the Cherokee had established five towns along the Tennessee River, where they lived until their removal by the U.S. government in the late 1830s. When the War of 1812 broke out, the hostilities enveloped these towns and settlements of other tribes. Half of the Creek nation and some of the Cherokee had joined Andrew Jackson to put down a rogue faction of Creeks called Red Sticks. Inspired to take the war path by the Shawnee chief Tecumseh, the rogue Creeks destroyed Fort Mims at the junction of the Alabama and Tombigbee rivers, killing several hundred whites and alarming frontier settlements. Jackson and his militiamen from Georgia, Alabama, and his home state of Tennessee ended the Creek uprising with the Battle of Horseshoe Bend in 1814. Terms of the Treaty of Fort Jackson included cession of 25 million acres of land in Alabama and Georgia. General Jackson and his men then went on to defeat the British at New Orleans in 1815.

Some accounts say the Cherokee tribe had come from the eastern part of the nation to the South; others say they originated in the Great Lakes region. They were driven out of Virginia by British settlers and, after some disagreement with tribes from the North, relocated on the Little Tennessee River. Another branch of the tribe originated in northern Georgia and northwestern North Carolina. Powerful and warlike but mercurial, the Cherokee alternately allied with the English and the French, leaving both as enemies. Smallpox, which infested the Native Americans from a slave ship that docked in Charleston, South Carolina, reduced them to about four thousand persons by 1740. Lieutenant Timberlake lived among the Cherokee for several months and documented their lifestyle in *Timberlake's Memoirs,* published in London in 1765. He took three Cherokee leaders to London to meet King George III, a trip that itself became a saga. He was accompanied by Sgt. Thomas Sumter of the Virginia Militia.[2]

According to Timberlake, some Cherokee marriages lasted for life, especially if children resulted, while other unions survived only a few months, and some individuals married three or four times a year. Tribal members were fond of interminable entertainments like dancing and ceremonial pantomimes and were given to excess in eating, drinking, and gaming. They were extremely superstitious, abandoning settlements they considered haunted by witches. Timberlake described funeral practices as strange; sometimes they merely threw the corpse into the river, but they would pay a white man if he buried the body. Other accounts were that they buried the bones only after the corpse had decomposed for months in log enclosures. Amazon-like war women, who had distinguished themselves in battle in their younger days, were given the title of "Beloved" and wielded power by the waving of a swan's wing, being able to "deliver a wretch condemned by the council, and already tied to the stake."[3] Alabama historian Virginia Van der Veer Hamilton observed academically that the Native Americans of the South "practiced burning at the stake in about the same ratio that whites practiced lynching." Some Native American traits set them drastically apart from whites, she noted, calling them "economic communists" since land was owned by the tribe in common. "Men, having no temptation to acquire wealth, enjoyed leisure to lounge in the sun, joke, gamble and play games."[4]

No doubt many of the habits and customs of the Cherokee were repulsive to white settlers, and the extremely proud tribe in turn despised lower-class Europeans and would deal only with military officers, so peace between the races was problematic. In addition, most of the Cherokee had allied with the British in the American Revolution, and white memories were long and abiding. Thus the social factors were in place for one of the great pogroms of early America, the displacing of the tribes from their native lands and the epic Trail of Tears to exile in the land that would become Oklahoma. Other than the missionaries; James G. Birney; the eminent attorney William Wirt; Supreme Court Chief Justice John Marshall, a distant relative of Birney's by marriage; and, amazingly, Henry Clay, few whites were sufficiently courageous to try to assuage the injustice and agony they were to suffer.

The Cherokee Nation was formed by a loose alliance of northern and southern bands. They attempted to assert independence against Georgia and Alabama, which were seeking their removal so that their lands could be opened to white settlement. Andrew Jackson had dealt the cruelest blow: even though some of the Creeks, and the Cherokee, had fought alongside American troops when they defeated the Red Sticks, Old Hickory had turned on his allies and presided over theft of their lands and, when he became president in 1829, dictated their demise or exile to Indian Country. Historian H. W. Brands observes, "Jackson believed there would be no peace for the Indians east of the Mississippi. This was a harsh prediction, but history allowed no other." States would not tolerate creation of other states within their boundaries, Jackson thought, so he denied the appeals of the Cherokee and Creeks who had sought tribal autonomy in Georgia and Alabama.[5] The idea that Jackson was rewarding expansion-minded frontier voters who had put him in office by allowing them to take Native American lands was not part of the discussion. Through the Indian Removal Act, U.S. troops drove the people of five Indian nations from the lower South to Indian Country, opening 25 million acres to white settlement and cotton cultivation. Besides the Cherokee and Creeks, other displaced tribes were the Choctaw, Chickasaw, and Seminole.

Clay opposed Jackson as early as 1819 in the debate in Congress on Jackson's part in the Seminole War in Florida. "Failing to recognize the regional shift in power, Clay continued to ally himself with the northern and eastern elite," wrote Rickey L. Hendricks in 1986. "His reaction to Jackson's Indian Removal bill in 1830 and his Senate 'Memorial' for the Cherokee in 1835 also reveal this alignment. Each instance illustrates the confrontation between the old style politics and the new and shows how Clay failed to represent a national consensus on the Indian issue. Neither the eager frontiersman nor the acquisitive land speculator was swayed by his concern for the constitutional, humanitarian, and international legal aspects of Jackson's actions against the Indians." Clay also supported a motion to censure Jackson and in a speech called him "a military despot," charging him with "inhumanity and the unconstitutional usurpation of civilian control of the military," thus aligning himself with Birney in that regard. Jackson "refused to equivocate," Hendricks notes, defending the execution of two Indian chiefs with the statement, "We have on the statute book a perpetual declaration of war against them . . . their color was sufficient evidence of the right of disposing of them as justice required." Jackson favored the "cultural extinction" of the Indians, according to Hendricks.[6] Clay's continuing alliance with a declining constituency perhaps cost him the presidency, Hendricks theorized. He concluded that Jackson had united the mobile and turbulent society of the 1830s behind a militant expansionism.

Birney had turned down the Cherokee when they approached him in 1824 to be their legal counsel. "After his conversion, this bothered him," says Fladeland. "Could he, in good conscience, refuse to help this long suffering people?" In 1826 Birney accepted, even though "prejudice against the Indians was violent, and public opinion was clamoring for the opening of their valuable lands to white settlement and the removal of the Indians to lands west of the Mississippi."[7] According to his son William, Birney's actions on behalf of the natives were diverse:

He caused missionaries to be sent and schools to be established among them; he encouraged them to cultivate farms, build houses and open roads; he aided an educated Indian, who had invented an alphabet for the language, to start a Cherokee paper; he defended them in their property rights and brought to punishment some of the authors of the outrages upon their persons; he counseled them to peace and good behavior; and, most surprising of all, he succeeded in introducing, quietly and without opposition, several Indian girls into the Huntsville Female Seminary. It was said they were the daughters of chiefs. They attended the Presbyterian Church, and were reputed to be wards of Mr. Birney. Two of them I remember as beautiful. The Indians visited Huntsville from time to time for the sale of pelts, nuts, blow-guns, bows and arrows, and game, and they never failed to pass by my father's house and leave for him some token of their gratitude.[8]

The Cherokee had decided to emulate white ways and institutions in efforts to retain their land; they established a unique language, a body of laws, cities, churches, courts, newspapers, and all the trappings of civilized society. The loose sexual practices of primitive days were cast aside. The Cherokee became one of the most advanced of Indian nations. In 1827 they established a constitutional government asserting sovereign nation status as a basis to resist removal. But the old hatreds remained. The Georgia legislature's angry response to Cherokee defensive measures was to extend its power over the Cherokee in the state. The state annexed Cherokee lands and set up a scheme to distribute it to whites and abolished the Cherokee government. Even though about 90 percent of Indian lands had already been ceded to whites since the early 1700s, the settlers, and the government, wanted it all. Contemporary writer Mary Hershberger comments:

Andrew Jackson's request to Congress in December 1829 for federal monies to remove Southeast Indians beyond the Mississippi River generated the most intense public opposition that the United States had witnessed. In six short months, removal opponents launched massive petition drives that called on Congress to defeat removal and to uphold Indian rights to property. To block removal, author Catharine Beecher [daughter of noted preacher Rev. Lyman Beecher] and Lydia Sigourney [a poet], organized the first national women's petition campaign and flooded Congress with anti-removal petitions, making a bold claim for women's place in national political discourse. The experience of opposing removal prompted some reformers to rethink their position on abolition and to reject African colonization in favor of immediatism.[9]

Gold was found on Cherokee land in 1830—the same year the Indian Removal Act was passed. Lotteries were staged to give Cherokee land and gold rights to whites. Cherokee were not allowed to conduct tribal business, contract, testify in courts against whites, or mine for gold. Caught in the dispute were two New England missionaries, Samuel Worcester, a Vermonter, and Eliza Butler, who also was a physician, both with the American Board of Commissioners for Foreign Missions. The pair of missionaries refused to bow to a new Georgia law barring them from the Cherokee Nation without permission. The state militia arrested Worcester, Butler, and nine other missionaries. Their conviction and sentence of four years in prison at hard labor prompted an appeal to the U.S. Supreme Court. In the majority opinion Chief Justice John Marshall wrote that the Indian nations were "distinct, independent political communities retaining their original natural rights" that had been acknowledged by the treaties with the United States.

Supporting Cherokee claims for protection against the state of Georgia, Birney wrote to Clement Comer Clay, fellow member of the Alabama Territorial Legislature, then an Alabama congressman, on 26 April 1832, saying, "when they seek justice, let justice be done tho' the heavens fall," borrowing a phrase from Judge Lord Mansfield in the famed *Somerset* case that freed slaves in England, although not in the British colonies, in 1772. At the same time, however, Birney believed the Cherokee would not receive justice and, before the crisis came to a head, should "sell their country to the U.S." and agree to remove to Western reservations "to preserve the union—to save the country."[10] Here Birney referred to the decision of the Supreme Court in the case of *Worcester v. Georgia*.

Even though the Cherokee had representation by William Wirt, the most noted trial lawyer in the country, and the Supreme Court had ruled for them, with Chief Justice Marshall declaring the laws of Georgia "repugnant to the Constitution" and "null and void," they were still faced with removal at the hands of Andrew Jackson.[11] Supposedly, Jackson had said, "John Marshall has made his decision; let him enforce it now if he can." Wirt came to the Cherokee at a very perilous time, since they had little money after President Jackson and his cronies changed how the United States had agreed to pay the Cherokee their annual annuity for prior treaties. Secretary of War Lewis Cass, a former Michigan territorial governor, opted to pay the Cherokee individually rather than as a tribe, a move that undermined the tribe's financial stability. Wirt had to depend on donations from sympathetic Northerners in his representation of the Indians.

Then occurred one of the most brutal periods in American history, akin to the removal and massacre of the Sauks from Illinois about the same time.

In the case of Illinois it was the Black Hawk War, in which both Abraham Lincoln and Jefferson Davis were involved as young soldiers, and in the South it was the Trail of Tears. Between 1830 and 1850 about one hundred thousand American Indians in Illinois, Missouri, Michigan, Georgia, Alabama, Louisiana, and Florida were forcibly moved west by the U.S. government. Many were treated brutally by the U.S. Army, some forced to walk in chains, along the one-thousand-mile westward trek. An estimated thirty-five hundred Creeks died in Alabama on the agonizing journey. Dr. Butler estimated the total Georgia Cherokee deaths at four thousand, approximately one-quarter of the entire Cherokee Nation. Theda Perdue and Michael D. Green relate that in later years, "In one Kentucky town, a local resident asked an elderly Indian man if he remembered him from his service with the United States Army in the Creek War. The old man replied, 'Ah! My life and the lives of my people were at stake for you and your country. I then thought Jackson my best friend. But ah! Jackson no serve me right. Your country no do me justice now!'"[12]

In his letter to Clement C. Clay, Birney seemed to be angling for a government appointment to mediate the Indian situation: "I cannot but believe that if they were relieved from all suspicion of unfairness or coercion by the appointment of men to treat with them in whom they had full confidence,—of men who acknowledged their right under our laws and treaties with them to the uninterrupted possession of their country, that they could be persuaded of the utter impracticability of remaining where they are under existing circumstances—and, therefore, of the propriety, in consulting their own happiness, of a removal." If a treaty with Georgia could be effected in a few months, Birney ventured, then the government could release the missionaries Worcester and Butler, thus diffusing the standoff with Georgia in which the Supreme Court mandates were being disobeyed. It was a gesture that, even if it had reached Jackson's attention, was sure to be in vain. Despite being a member of Congress, Clement C. Clay lacked the clout in Washington to intervene, especially in view of Jackson's stated intentions for removal "to separate the Indians from immediate contact with settlements of whites, free them from the power of the states, enable them to pursue happiness in their own way and under their own rude institutions."[13]

Clement C. Clay had befriended and encouraged Birney by earlier sending him fifty-five dollars for the American Colonization Society, a small portion of which was to go for the *African Repository* newspaper. But there is no recorded response by Clay to Birney's pleas regarding the Cherokee. Fladeland reflected, "Birney felt that the trouble between the Cherokees and Georgia and Jackson's refusal to co-operate with the Supreme Court threatened the Union. He was practical enough to see that might would make right on the question of Indian removal, but he thought that the desired end could be accomplished by persuasion rather than by force if someone in whom the Cherokees had confidence were appointed to deal with them."[14] Birney's apparent desire to mediate the crisis went unnoticed, and the removal of the Cherokee beyond the Mississippi to Indian Country aroused anger within him against what he saw as a heartless government.

Historians and legal scholars Garrett Epps and Gerard N. Magliocca recently have identified the defense of Native American Indians as the beginning of the abolitionist movement that led to the Fourteenth Amendment to the U.S. Constitution. Magliocca wrote: "The removal of the Cherokee Tribe by President Andrew Jackson was a seminal moment that sparked the growth of the abolitionist movement and then shaped its thought for the next three decades on issues ranging from religious freedom to the antidiscrimination principle. When these same leaders wrote the Fourteenth Amendment, they expressly invoked the Cherokee Removal and the Supreme Court's opinion in *Worcester v. Georgia* as relevant guideposts for interpreting the new constitutional text. What the traditional narrative misses is that the abolitionist movement was largely born from the ashes of Worcester. A fresh examination of the primary sources demonstrates that it was the injustice of the Cherokee Removal that helped convince a generation of activists to become abolitionists and expand human rights."[15] Epps wrote, "Viewing the Fourteenth Amendment in its totality, it is not too much to say that without it, the United States would not be today what we call a democracy."[16]

Magliocca gives credit to William Lloyd Garrison; Theodore Weld; the Grimke sisters, Angelina and Sarah; along with Birney and others as the initiators of the Cherokee removal movement. However, only Birney was in the South defending Native Americans as a lawyer from 1826 until he left Alabama in 1833. Garrison and the others may have voiced support for their cause, petitioned and editorialized about it, but Birney was actually in the arena. However, he was long gone from Alabama when the removal began in 1838. The U.S. Army marched the remnants of the Cherokee "sovereign nation" along with the Chickasaw, Creeks, Choctaw, and Seminoles, making up the "Five Civilized Tribes," more than seven hundred miles to Indian Territory. Eventually most of the tribes ended up on reservations there in what was then considered worthless land. When white settlements expanded or oil was found on the land, even those original reservations were reduced in size and the Indians further marginalized. Indeed, the heavens had fallen, but there was little justice for Native Americans, as sought by Birney and like-minded others, in the unforgiving skies over Oklahoma.

CHAPTER 6

The Colonization Debacle

To have the ship ready to receive the emigrants, to have its sails unfurled,
to display before their eyes the solemn act of returning to their sorrowing
mother children now rejoicing in hope, would it seems to me move hearts of
stone and melt them into tears.

—JAMES G. BIRNEY

SENDING BLACK MEN AND WOMEN BACK TO AFRICA WAS AN IDEA
that had been around for more than half a century before it was embraced
by James G. Birney in 1832. There was a reason it had not caught on: it
would involve wealthy Americans divesting themselves of their fortunes,
or a substantial portion of their wealth, and paying extra to send the slaves
back to their homeland. In the end, few of the New World plutocrats were
willing to do that; but it was a brave idea that made the founders and others
believe they were grappling with the problem of slavery.

There were mixed opinions about colonization: some abolitionists
opposed it, thinking it would strengthen slavery by removing free Negroes,
who were considered a source of agitation among the slaves. Others saw
immigration to Liberia as a chance for black people at last to be fully free,
in their own country under their own laws. Another school of thought was
that colonization was a way to defuse sectional tensions that were rising
every year. Most black men and women were, like Birney's friend James
Forten and his compatriots in Philadelphia, wary of the idea, noting that the
backers of colonization were almost all prominent slaveholders.

Birney at the time was serious about the colonization movement, whose
first president had been his wife's relative James Madison. It turned out to
be a way station on his ascent to abolitionism, but the plan in reality was a

deluded idea and became a costly mistake. Birney had given up a lucrative law practice in Huntsville with an income that had reached $4,000 a year to accept the offer of Charles Carroll, president of the Washington, D.C.–based American Colonization Society (ACS) at a salary of $1,000 annually plus traveling expenses. On 1 August 1832 Birney was named agent of the ACS for the South Western District, including Tennessee, Alabama, Mississippi, Louisiana, and the territory of Arkansas.[1] Ralph R. Gurley, ACS secretary, handled the communications with Birney in Carroll's name. Birney's sincerity in the cause of colonization is evident in a letter to Gurley: "To have the ship ready to receive the emigrants, to have its sails unfurled, to display before their eyes the solemn act of returning to their sorrowing mother children now rejoicing in hope, would it seems to me move hearts of stone and melt them into tears."[2]

Meanwhile, Birney began more seriously contemplating escaping the distress that being in the midst of slavery had on his conscience. His Alabama neighbors also were signaling greater hostility against the man they recognized as a traitor to their principles. Even his benevolent leadership of the religious tract and Bible societies came into question in letters to the editor of the *Huntsville Democrat* by a writer using the pseudonym "Justin Martyr." Rural Baptists had adopted an "anti-mission" mentality and were displaying sectarian hostility against Presbyterian reformers. Birney and another writer called "Veritas" responded to charges that the Presbyterians must have been profiting from their outreach. "A great cultural gulf separated the pious merchants and professionals of Huntsville's Presbyterian Church from the rural Baptists and Methodists of Madison County," writes Alabama historian Daniel S. Dupre. "Worse yet, some grew suspicious of the real motivations of colonization agents, a fear reinforced by Birney's embrace of immediate emancipation in the mid-1830s."[3]

Birney was considering a move to Jacksonville in the free state of Illinois, near Lincoln's home west of Springfield. He was attracted by the beauty and fertility of the land, the apparent intelligence of the population, and the hopes for foundation of a college perhaps to be headed by Edward Beecher. Beecher's brother was the famed abolitionist preacher Henry Ward Beecher, and his sister was Harriet Beecher Stowe, who would later write the antislavery novel *Uncle Tom's Cabin*. Birney's father, seeing fears of slave uprisings growing in Kentucky, too, agreed that such a move north might be best "to save all his children from destruction."[4] Those children included sons William and David, who later would cross paths with Lincoln and play important roles in the Union Army in the Civil War. From Huntsville, Birney wrote to Gurley:

I have not yet abandoned an intention which had almost ripened before I undertook the agency in which I am now engaged to remove to Illinois that I might rid myself and my posterity of the curse of slavery. My mind is ill at ease upon the subject of retaining my fellow creatures in servitude. I cannot, nor do I believe any honest mind, can reconcile the precept "love thy neighbors as thyself" with the purchase of the body of that neighbor and consigning him and his unoffending posterity to a slavery, a perpetual bondage degrading and debasing him in this world and almost excluding him from the happiness of that which is to come. Should I remove from this state, I shall send all the slaves I own to Liberia.[5]

As it turned out, Birney neither moved to Illinois nor did he send his slaves to Liberia. He moved back to Kentucky and freed his slaves, who remained after his stay in Alabama, then continued his crusade in Ohio, New York, and Michigan.

Birney's intentions in supporting colonization were not aimed at removing black people from the nation because they were a problem, as Henry Clay and others believed. With the urging of Rev. Theodore Weld, he finally decided that colonization might be an important first step toward the eventual emancipation of slaves. Whereas some people considered colonization a moderate movement, others believed it was a radical approach to the problem of slavery. The idea had fervent backers like Madison, Jefferson, and Clay, who saw it as the only solution to an almost insoluble problem, and at the same time had fierce opponents like the Negroes themselves, who by this time considered themselves Americans, albeit marginalized ones, and many abolitionists, who considered it an attempt to defuse the campaign for emancipation.

The colonization issue had come into focus in the community of those most affected in 1817. On 15 January 1817 Negro men of all descriptions with all manner of dress seemed to come from all directions as they filed into the Bethel AME Church in Philadelphia in response to a call by James Forten and other black leaders to discuss colonization. It was a cold, windy, snow-driven night, causing many to stomp their feet and shiver against the chill. Among the smiles and nods of greeting were grimaces of concern, giving foreboding of the topic of the day. The comers included mariners, day laborers, hairdressers, domestic servants, bakers, tailors, teamsters, caterers, carpenters, musicians—the lot making up much of the free black middle class of the city. Joining the throng were unmistakable members of the lower class, fugitive slaves, and refugees from the revolution in St. Domingue, faces pinched with trepidation about their fate in America.

The colonization movement was being promoted by Paul Cuffe, a free black ship captain and Quaker convert from Massachusetts. Cuffe was working with the sponsor of the movement, Rev. Robert Finley, of Basking Ridge, New Jersey. Finley was a hard-driving Presbyterian pastor and conducted a large, popular boys' school in addition to pursuing his passion for colonization. He later was elected president of the University of Georgia but died within months of taking office.

On 21 December 1816, Reverend Finley gathered a distinguished group at the Davis Hotel in Washington, D.C., with Henry Clay presiding. Also on hand were such luminaries as James Monroe, Daniel Webster, Andrew Jackson, Francis Scott Key, and Bushrod Washington, a Supreme Court justice and nephew of the nation's first president. The group met again a week later and adopted a constitution for the new ACS and began raising money to send black immigrants to West Africa. "Thomas Jefferson expressed interest in helping free persons of color set up a colony in the American West as early as 1777, and the Virginia legislature urged the federal government to secure land in Africa for that purpose in 1801 and again in 1816.[6] Reverend Finley's new organization aimed to fulfill those legislative goals.

The original purposes of the ACS were to rid the United States of an "undesirable population"; to plant a nucleus of Christian Negroes in Africa as a means of civilizing that continent; to place the colonists in an atmosphere more congenial to the development of latent talents than existed here; and to some degree hasten emancipation. Dumond commented, "Its great strength—prejudice against free persons of color—was, in the end, its undoing." The majority of Southerners, he wrote, "were anxious to rid their communities of a disturbing element—an element for which there was no provision in the social system they were rearing, which was a constant source of irritation and a threat to the security of society." In the North, Dumond continued, "the theory of biological inequality and racial inferiority of the Negro was seldom questioned. Black codes and colonization bore a close relationship, and were supported, principally, by the social aristocracy."[7]

The formation of the ACS and the accompanying campaign by whites to ship members of the Negro race to Africa is what prompted the stream of black men to the church in Philadelphia. In all, nearly three thousand crowded into the church, where several black ministers exhorted the group to favor immigration of their race to Africa. "However, when Forten called for those in favor to say 'yea,' not a single voice was heard. When he called for those opposed, one tremendous 'no' rang out that seemed 'as it would bring down the walls of the building.'" The angry group also adopted a resolution: "Whereas our ancestors (not of choice) were the first successful cultivators of the wilds of America, we their descendants feel ourselves entitled to participate in the blessings of her luxuriant soil . . . We will never separate ourselves voluntarily from the slave population of this country; they are our brethren by the ties of consanguinity, of suffering and wrong."[8] A few years after Birney left Philadelphia, Forten helped form the Convention of Color, a group that opposed resettlement of freed slaves to Africa but urged their relocation in Canada. That was where the Underground Railroad eventually took many of them.

Had Birney stayed in contact with his friend Forten after he left Philadelphia in 1814, it might have saved him considerable trouble, since Birney became an advocate of the flawed idea of colonization and spent many tortuous months in the effort. Forten would have told him, based on his experience in Philadelphia in 1817 and later, that Negroes were almost universally against the idea and that it would be all but impossible to induce many of them to emigrate to Africa.

Thomas Jefferson, in his autobiography, had this contradictory opinion of the disposition of black people, which seemed to support colonization: "Nothing is more certainly written in the book of fate than that these people are to be free. Nor is it less certain that the two races, equally free, cannot live in the same government. Nature, habit, opinion has drawn indelible lines of distinction between them. It is still in our power to direct the process of emancipation and deportation peaceably and in such slow degree as that the evil will wear off insensibly, and their place be *pari passu* filled up by free white laborers."[9] Madison was said to have had similar opinions, along with Lincoln, who in 1860 used Jefferson's words almost exactly when discussing colonization.

Historian Philip Shaw Paludan says that Lincoln, as president, used colonization as a smokescreen for advancing equality. He quotes another historian, Stephen Oates: "Every time [Lincoln] contemplated some new antislavery move he made a great fuss about colonization." But Lincoln and his party knew that colonization was a logistical impossibility. Lincoln's colonization strategy, it seemed, followed Birney's idea that it was the first step toward emancipation and a way to get people thinking about a change in the status quo. As one Republican politician wrote privately, "Colonization is a damned humbug but it will take with the people."[10]

Colonization was a favorite idea of many white leaders, and Birney at first embraced it enthusiastically. This was some fifteen years after the movement had been launched, and white leaders were still deluding themselves that it could be made to work. Birney was encouraged by Henry Clay, who introduced him by a letter to Josiah Polk, colonization agent in the Southwest.

When Polk came to Huntsville in early 1830 on an organizational mission, he met with Birney and town leaders. Money was being raised statewide, and Birney took note of some initial public enthusiasm when a meeting on colonization at the Presbyterian Church attracted a crowd of one thousand. But the suspicion that abolitionism was behind the movement lurked in the shadows. Birney's friend and early collaborator Clement Clay, who had stated that charge in a speech printed in the Democrat, rescinded the statement after Birney complained, but the damage had been done to the movement, and to Birney as well.[11]

Testimony that American political leaders were at sea over slavery is shown by a letter Speaker of the House Henry Clay wrote in 1831 to John Switzer of Frederick County, Maryland, who had questioned his stated support for emancipation of slaves: "Slavery is undoubtedly a manifest violation of the rights of man. It can only be justified in America, if at all, by necessity. That it entails innumerable mischiefs upon our Country I think is quite clear. It may become dangerous in particular parts of the Union. But the slaves can never, I think, acquire permanent ascendancy in any part. Congress has no power, as I think, to establish any system of emancipation, gradual or immediate, in behalf of the present or any future generation. The several states alone, according to our existing institutions, are competent to make provision on that subject, as already intimated."[12] The letter confirms Clay's dedication to Southern state rights ideology leading to his reluctance to seek a solution, even though he considered slavery "a manifest violation of the rights of man." As political observers later were to point out, statesmanship demanded more and Clay was found wanting. Clay remained an advocate of colonization, a difficult and costly process that Birney was soon to find totally unworkable.

In the year and a month Birney spent as agent of the colonization society, from 23 August 1832 to 24 September 1833, he continually confronted charges that the organization was comprised of Northern extremists or abolitionists and was causing restlessness among slaves. He toured the states of Tennessee, Alabama, Mississippi, Louisiana, and Arkansas and had some success seeking donations of funds and slaves or freemen who wished to emigrate to Liberia. In New Orleans he chartered the brig *Ajax* at a cost of nearly $5,000 and was able to put 150 immigrants aboard for the long trip to Africa on 20 April 1833, although 29 died of cholera along the way. His idea that the expedition would excite popular support was a total failure, as the people of New Orleans were apathetic. On top of that disappointment came cruel personal blows; within a month an epidemic of scarlet fever took his five-year-old son, Arthur Hopkins Birney, and daughter Martha, three.

By June 1833 he was distraught, warning Gurley that appeals for colonization funds was causing alarm among Southerners in Congress who opposed any thought of legislation that might touch on slavery. A few months later he resigned from the ACS and immediately began a new approach: gradual abolition of slavery.

According to Dupre, "The polarized atmosphere of the 1830s left little room for the middle ground of gradualism. Madison County, and the rest of the South, grew more militant in defense of slavery, more unwilling to consider the merits of moral reform. James Birney too abandoned the elusive goal of voluntary emancipation and emigration." Declaring the colonization movement "dead," Birney left Alabama for Kentucky in 1834. "The following year he cut himself off from his former life by freeing his slaves and formally denouncing colonization, embracing instead the abolitionism that would sustain a long career and bring him national fame."[13]

Within a few years the atmosphere had drastically changed. Kentucky historian Lowell H. Harrison writes: "Garrison's 1831 publication of *The Liberator* signaled the emergence of a much harsher attack upon slavery and slaveholders. Kentuckians who had never owned a slave joined their slave-holding neighbors in resenting the vitriolic attacks that Garrison and others poured forth in their papers and speeches. Warned by John C. Calhoun that the South's position was a minority one and that the region would have to present a united front to its enemies, Southerners became less tolerant of dissent and dissenters. Only ten years after Benjamin Lundy found more antislavery societies in the South than in the North, not a single one existed below the Mason-Dixon line."[14]

James M. Gifford puts the issue into perspective, citing the author of a history of the Old South: "Clay's attitude, according to Clement Eaton, illustrated the ambivalent feelings of most white Southern supporters of colonization. Twisted and confused, many like Clay, Thomas Jefferson, and the youthful John C. Calhoun were sympathetic to gradual and eventual emancipation, but at the same time 'believed that if the slaves were freed and remained in the South a race conflict would follow and Southern civilization would be destroyed.'" Gifford cited several Southern correspondents who had speculated that Clay was using his presidency of the American Colonization Society for the political purpose of gaining popularity in the North, a campaign initiative that proved to be of questionable value. Clay, who became ACS president in 1836, served the society even after his death in 1852, the *African Repository and Colonial Journal* noted in 1855, in that the society sold blank membership certificates previously signed by Mr. Clay for thirty dollars each as a fund-raising scheme.[15] Connection with celebrity seems to have been the main motivation for the purchases of these certificates, since at that point in history the colonization movement was nearly as dead as Mr. Clay. But the abolition movement was beginning to have new life.

In 1853, however, one prominent Southerner responded to the old message of the colonizationists. Robert E. Lee, then superintendent of the U.S. Military Academy at West Point, New York, freed many of his slaves and offered to pay expenses for those who wanted to go to Liberia. Among 261 black men and women who sailed from Baltimore on the *Banshee* were former Lee slaves William and Rosabella Burke.[16] William became a Presbyterian minister in 1857, thus conforming to one of Birney's ideas about providing missionaries to the Africans.

The American Colonization Society hung on, by 1867 having transported an estimated thirteen thousand free blacks to Liberia. Many blacks were willing to go to Liberia after the Civil War, but by then the irritant of free blacks in a slave nation had been dissipated by emancipation and there was scant financial support for colonization. Likewise the goal of sending blacks to Liberia was no longer an ACS priority, and the society's main aims involved educational and missionary efforts. At the urging of the ACS, Liberia declared itself an independent nation in 1847. Amazingly, the ACS survived nearly 150 years and was not formally dissolved until 1964, when its records were turned over to the Library of Congress.

CHAPTER 7

Birney's Epiphany

Altho' I am in the midst of enemies . . . and am often much perplexed,
yet altogether I have never had so much peace—never before have I felt
God to be a Help so present . . . Let my soul magnify the Lord!

—JAMES G. BIRNEY

BIRNEY WAS NOT YET AN ABOLITIONIST IN THE EARLY 1830S, BUT recent events and his maturing attitudes had convinced him to escape the culture of slavery as soon as possible and to embrace the rising crusade against the practice. Besides the hostility his Alabama neighbors were showing toward him for his liberal attitudes about Negroes, there were other confirmations that slavery would not go away on its own, as his former Kentucky neighbor, political ally, and idol Henry Clay had predicted.

Within a few years, freedom of speech became impossible in the South, and Birney was forced to leave Alabama to save himself and his family and continue to pursue his obsession with ending slavery. While still in Alabama, Birney courageously—some might say recklessly—challenged the slave power on several fronts. He "not only advocated the tariff but took issue with the South Carolina nullifiers and the slavery extensionists," his son William recalled. "In numerous speeches delivered in different parts of the State, he exposed the sophistries of the resolutions of 1798, pointed out the dangers of attempting to control national politics in the interest of a single pecuniary interest, and warned the slaveholders not to invite a national discussion of slavery by attempting to extend it over new States in Texas, thus destroying the balance of power between the North and South. He appealed to them not to repeat the agitations of the Missouri controversy; not to awaken the sleeping lion; and he developed and illustrated the suggestions made by Henry Clay in his Lewisburg speech in 1826."[1] In that speech Clay had asserted that the Constitution "confers no authority to interpose between the master and the slave," but that an insistence of the South on the rule of slavery would lead to disunion, warning, "The slaveholding states cannot forget that they are now in a minority, which is in a constant relative diminution, and should certainly not be the first to put forth a principle of public action by which they would be the greatest losers."[2]

In opposing the resolutions of 1798 and 1799, Birney was among those firing the first verbal shots of the ongoing philosophical battle that eventually ended in the Civil War. Jefferson had written the "Kentuckey resolves," as he called them, in virtual secrecy in response to the Alien and Sedition Acts, and they were adopted by the Kentucky legislature without his knowledge. James Madison wrote the Virginia resolutions in 1798 and 1799—also carried out clandestinely—claiming, as did the Kentucky doctrine, the right of states to reject federal power not specifically described in the Constitution. The resolutions were opposed by Northern states, which held that the judiciary, rather than the states, should make decisions on constitutionality. The resolutions later formed the basis of Southern contentions of the right of states to nullify federal actions they considered unconstitutional—such as seceding from the Union.

Birney's old Princeton roommate, Joseph Cabell Breckenridge, corresponded with the reticent Jefferson in 1821 about reports in the press that had imputed a role by his father, John Breckenridge, in crafting the Kentucky document.[3] Jefferson admitted to Joseph Cabell Breckenridge that he wrote the resolutions and kept silent when questioned about the elder Breckenridge's possible role in writing them. A Princeton University analysis of the confusing issue concludes, "Although the porous documentary record is largely to blame, a thorough understanding of Jefferson's resolutions has also been impeded by the fact that even some of his strongest advocates, for reasons having to do with the sectional conflict resulting eventually in secession and civil war, have been loathe to embrace his authorship of the document—especially that portion of his eighth resolution that dealt with nullification."[4]

Noting that mob violence increased after the election of Jackson in 1828, William Birney commented, "Freedom of speech was not unknown at the South during and before the period [the decade ending in 1830] in question." However, the Nat Turner slave insurrection in 1831 "caused a panic," and "the defeat of the nullifiers, in the winter of 1832–'33, turned all their activities into the agitation of slavery, for the purpose of creating a sectional feeling as a basis for a future separation of the States. Hostility to Northerners was fomented, and vigilance committees were formed, the chief duty of which was 'to hang abolitionists' on short shrift. In this work the Jackson and Clay men vied with the nullifiers; and before the end of 1835 the South was terrorized into silence, and thoroughly organized to support the claims of the slave power."[5]

Contemporary author Chris Morris summarizes how Birney gravitated toward abolition from a start in other moralistic crusades. "James G. Birney, the future abolitionist, played a prominent role in these debates. His leadership in the local Bible and tract societies, Sunday school, and temperance society helped win him election as mayor, an office he used to close down dram shops and enforce Sabbatarian restrictions. But Birney always pressed too hard to win much political success, although that did not deter him. His commitment to self control and moral order led him down the path to abolitionism, a journey that would require his leaving Madison County and the South. Birney was exceptional, but instructive nevertheless because he viewed slavery in terms of moral order."[6]

The message was clear, and emerging abolitionist Birney began more seriously contemplating escaping the distress that being in the midst of slavery had on his conscience. The fires of abolition were smoldering in his soul at the same time the slave power's resentment against abolitionists was heating up in the South. Birney was still living in pro-slavery Alabama even as he began to launch a war of words against the churches and ministers who supported the status quo. After working as an agent for the American Colonization Society for about a year, he realized the futility of his effort and resigned, switching immediately to the formation of the Kentucky Society for the Gradual Relief of the State from Slavery. "There are many like myself who look upon it as impracticable to arouse the South sufficiently to make it the means of ridding us of Slavery," he wrote.[7] He compared colonization to the Indian removal then under way by President Andrew Jackson's administration.

As was the case with Michael Matthews, his black slave friend, Birney was concerned about the welfare of the Negroes, both slave and free. In 1831 Birney had written to authorities in New Kent, Virginia, inquiring about the status of a free biracial man of his acquaintance named Foster Balkins. The New Kent clerk, John D. Christian, replied by saying that although Balkins had been "born free," he had "forfeited his freedom" by being convicted of larceny, detailing, "It is considered by the Court that the said Foster Balkins receive Thirty nine stripes on his bare back . . . and that he be sold as a slave and transported and banished beyond the limits of the United States in the manner prescribed by Law." The clerk further informed Birney that "Balkins was carried to the penitentiary, where he was duly sold," and enclosed a copy of the 1825 Virginia law dictating a grand larceny charge for theft of goods valued at ten dollars or more supporting the state's action. The law also gave the state power to execute any banished person who returned to Virginia.[8] The fact that the State of Virginia itself was engaged in the sale of slaves—to foreign parties, no less—undoubtedly distressed Birney, who could not even bring himself to order the whipping of an unruly slave.

Flames of freedom burst in Virginia in the spring of 1831, when Nat Turner fomented a slave revolt that killed dozens of whites. And in Huntsville, Alabama, the home of thirty-nine-year-old lawyer and planter James G. Birney and his family, warmth was on its way, but it was very different from the soft breezes of Southern weather. It was a fire that had been kindled in the hearts and minds of slaves in hovels, pens, and hidden backwoods camps. A spirit of liberty was sparked by hope of change, word of which had crackled through the slave quarters and leafy retreats. Freedom was in the air: Mexico had barred further importation of slaves into Texas territory, and the British had freed slaves from the schooner *Comet* after the vessel was wrecked on a voyage from Virginia to New Orleans. A servile insurrection in Jamaica fueled the fires even higher. Fear of more revolts galvanized whites to defense and made conditions much worse for all black people. Reverberations spread across America. Birney became increasingly concerned for the future of the South as more laws controlling slaves were passed, curfews were tightened, whippings and torture stepped up, and slave patrols increased to deter escapes. Songs of freedom soon turned to wails from the slave quarters. The slave power's reaction had unintended effects: it convinced many neutral observers of the evils of slavery and incited the radicals who wanted to end slavery immediately to greater efforts.

Both Abraham Lincoln and Birney would feel the same spirit that affected the slave community. Besides the slave revolt in Virginia, a flatboat trip to New Orleans where he saw slaves auctioned in 1831 marked Lincoln's growing awareness of the evils of slavery. That same year James G. Birney started on the path to becoming an abolitionist with a tentative first step—in support of the colonization movement—the mad scheme of sending willing blacks back to Africa. Although colonization was a flawed cause, it would lead Birney to abolition and to the wider road of politics as the first antislavery presidential candidate, antedating Lincoln by twenty years, blazing the path that none had dared to tread.

The Turner revolt was the only notable slave uprising in the United States from 1820 to 1860, authors George M. Frederickson and Christopher

Lasch observed, comparing it to "a millenialist peasants' revolt."[9] Huntsville residents were paralyzed by fear of slave revolts. There was another, allied bedevilment: abolitionist newspapers like William Lloyd Garrison's newly issued *Liberator,* copies of which quickly found their way south from Boston, which Southerners felt incited rebellion.[10] In fact it was said that Garrison made sure his paper was sent to Southern editors, further riling the citizenry with his printed bombast.

The man who eventually succeeded Birney as the antislavery standard-bearer, Lincoln, did not live where many slaves were kept, but his restless spirit and willingness to try almost anything took him to slave country. It was an improbable trip that very nearly did not happen. Lincoln encountered a hard-drinking frontier entrepreneur named Denton Offutt who wanted to promote a flatboat trip down the Mississippi River to New Orleans, hoping for good profit from a load of live hogs, dressed pork, and corn. He needed a boat and crew, and Lincoln was caught up in the fantasy. The project seemed a will-o'-the-wisp idea, since the group had no vessel, and, even if it had, the Sangamon River, a tributary of the Mississippi that led to New Orleans, was blocked by a milldam. Ever optimistic and enterprising, Lincoln chopped trees on government land, coaxed boards out of rusty saws at an old mill, built a crude flatboat eighty feet long and eighteen feet wide, and marshaled his cousin John Hanks and his foster brother, John D. Johnston, for a crew. As the freshets rose in mid-April, the trio launched their ark and were happy to wave good-bye to their whiskey-soaked sponsor. They were able to cross the milldam after Lincoln drilled a hole in the boat, offloaded some of the live hogs, and shifted pork barrels and hogsheads of corn to free the impaled craft.

Lincoln, the young, carefree, wide-eyed laborer, as yet had not formed firm opinions about slavery. Of Quaker ancestry, his father, Thomas Lincoln, had been troubled by the caste system in Indiana, which placed slave owners at the social pinnacle and free laborers, regardless of color, at the base; young Abraham no doubt absorbed some of his father's attitudes. But when the boat and crew reached New Orleans, the future president was aghast when he witnessed a slave auction. It was a life-changing event. As biographer Henry C. Whitney, a contemporary of Lincoln's, wrote: "Lincoln saw the institution of slavery in its most revolting and reprehensible aspects. Nothing was more common in those days than the traffic in slaves, and New Orleans was the greatest slave market in the Union. One could not walk extensively in the streets without being an involuntary witness to the horror and infamy of the institution." Lincoln was revolted to see humans advertised, displayed, described, bought and sold like animals. Whitney reported: "Lincoln saw an octoroon girl [one-eighth black] offered for sale on the auction block. As the auctioneer dilated on her physical perfections to the lecherous crowd of tobacco-chewers and whiskey-blossomed sots congregated in the market, and these passed ribald jests on the subject, the young Northerner was sickened by the scene, and hastily withdrew from it, prophetically remarking to Hanks: 'If I ever get a chance at that thing, [slavery] I'll hit it hard.'"[11] It was an amazing statement by a self-educated young laborer whose chances of achieving enough political power to strike at the ingrained institution of slavery appeared remote at that point in his life. It also was confirmation that deep within the heart and mind of the easygoing Lincoln lurked the soul of a reformer, much like James G. Birney, with intense concern for his fellow man.

Actually, Lincoln had real reason to dislike and suspect Negroes. Biographer Carl Sandburg noted that on his first flatboat trip to New Orleans, while tied up for the night at a plantation below Baton Rouge, nineteen-year-old Lincoln had been attacked by seven black men with theft and murder on their mind. Lincoln and Allen Gentry, son of the boat's owner, James Gentry, of Pigeon Creek, Indiana, awakened to the nighttime danger and fought off the attackers with clubs. Lincoln suffered "a gash over his right eye that left a scar for life," wrote Sandburg.[12]

New Orleans was the headquarters for sale of slaves. Slaves bred in Kentucky and other Southern states ended up there, at the outflow of the Mississippi, the busiest Southern port. Presumably these "excess" slaves would be sold and shipped to buyers in Virginia, Texas, the Caribbean, or other labor-hungry places. Confirmation of Lincoln's antislavery attitude is contained in a letter he wrote to his friend Joshua Speed, who was of an opposite opinion typical in the South. "You say that sooner than yield your legal right to the slave—especially at the bidding of those who are not themselves interested, you would see the Union dissolved." The letter also reveals Lincoln's belief that the government had no power to end slavery, a belief that was consistent until his hand was forced by the Civil War:

> I also acknowledge your rights and my obligations, under the constitution, in regard to your slaves. I confess I hate to see the poor creatures hunted down, and caught, and carried back to their stripes, and unrewarded toils; but I bite my lip and keep quiet. In 1841 you and I had together a tedious low-water trip, on a Steam Boat from Louisville to St. Louis. You may remember, as I well do, that from Louisville to the mouth of the Ohio, there were, on board, ten or a dozen slaves, shackled together with irons. That sight was a continued torment to me; and I see something like it every time I touch the Ohio, or any other

slave border. It is hardly fair for you assume that I have no interest in a thing which has, and continually exercises, the power of making me miserable. You ought rather to appreciate how much the great body of Northern people do crucify their feelings, in order to maintain their loyalty to the Constitution and the Union.[13]

The mixed-race girl Lincoln saw being auctioned in New Orleans, the ill-fated Foster Balkins sold out of the country by the state of Virginia, and a little biracial girl later rescued by Birney with her slave mother in Tennessee were not uncommon types. Civil War diarist Mary Boykin Chestnut, wife of James Chestnut Jr., U.S. senator from South Carolina, noted the "phenomenon" of white slaves and commented, "Like the patriarchs of old our men live all in one house with their wives and concubines, and the mulattoes one sees in every family exactly resemble the white children— and every lady tells you who is the father of all the mulatto children in everybody's household, but those in her own she seems to think drop from the clouds, or pretends so to think."[14] Mrs. Chestnut expressed what most Southerners, and Northerners too, were loath to discuss: the sexual exploitation of female slaves by lustful, opportunistic masters. "Regardless of the legal criteria established for being a white person, it is a fact that many white people remained enslaved under the *partus* rule," Lawrence R. Tenzer writes. Numerous accounts of white slavery appeared in abolitionist newspapers distributed throughout the North. Tenzer notes: "As Southern power grew . . . many publications, abolitionist and otherwise, which addressed white slavery started to include political commentaries as well. The abolitionist press was a powerful force and had impact because of the size of the abolitionist movement. In 1838 James G. Birney who was the corresponding secretary of the American Anti-Slavery Society observed that the organization had 1,300 chapters with about 109,000 members."[15] Antislavery politics increasingly emphasized the threat of slavery to Northern whites, who soon realized that chains could hold all races if the slave power decreed, according to A. D. Powell, an author specializing in mixed race issues.[16]

When the American Anti-Slavery Society was founded in Philadelphia in 1833, under Garrison's leadership, Birney was still involved with the colonization movement. The society's statement of purpose, however, was in line with his thinking on the subject of slavery: "We have met together for the achievement of an enterprise, without which that of our fathers is incomplete; and which, for its magnitude, solemnity, and probable results upon the destiny of the world, as far transcends theirs as moral truth does physical force."[17] The goal, of course, was completing and fulfilling the promise of freedom and equality for all as postulated in the Declaration of Independence and the Bill of Rights. Birney was losing faith in colonization and, after his move back to Danville, wrote to Ralph Gurley, "I do not believe that anything effectual can be done South of Tennessee." Regarding slavery, the planters of the South, Birney observed, "are determined not to have touched in any way. It is my sincere belief that the South, at least that part of it in which I have been operating has, within the last year, become, very manifestly, more and more indurated upon the subject of Slavery. The large planters (I speak generally, allowing exceptions) think that the self-evident principle that all men are created equal is about as ridiculous nonsense as was ever published. They are as blind to the natural rights of their Slaves, as the whites of the West Indies were."[18]

In addition to his own efforts to sway public opinion against slavery, Birney collaborated with abolitionist missionary Reverend Weld in organizing abolitionist "apostles," distributing antislavery literature throughout the West in the mid-1830s and in book publishing through the American Anti-Slavery Society, for which Birney served as corresponding secretary. As a theology student at New York's Oneida Institute, Weld had promoted the virtues of manual labor, temperance, and moral reform. He turned his earnest, appealing face, framed by curly dark locks, to the antislavery front in the early 1830s. His antislavery initiatives culminated in the Lane Seminary debates in Cincinnati in February 1834. The event—a revival-like forty-five hours of protest lectures, two and a half hours a night, over eighteen days, by a former slave, slaveholders, and Southerners—illuminated the brutality of slavery and flashed like lightning into the abolitionist movement, igniting a new wave of zealous advocates. Two questions were debated, each for nine nights: (1) "Ought the people of the slaveholding states to abolish slavery immediately?" and (2) "Are the doctrines, tendencies, and measures of the American Colonization Society, and the influence of its principal supporters, such as render it worthy of the patronage of the Christian public?"

The long-term effect of the debates was powerful, both in public awareness of slavery and in the fact that the revival concluded not only that slavery was a sin requiring immediate abolition but also that colonization, the movement to send blacks back to Africa, was wrong. After attending the debates, Birney met with Lane students that spring and became convinced to abandon colonization and declare himself an abolitionist. The British Parliament had abolished slavery in its colonies in 1833, and Birney was deeply influenced by the British antislavery authors whose books he had in his library. Even more telling about his inspiration was his response in 1829 to a question posed by the Greene Academy Cliosophic Society in Huntsville about "illustrious names to rouse you up to noble action." Birney's reply was recorded as, "Go to the Gardiners, the Wilberforces, the Clarksons," citing those and other British antislavery advocates as examples for young Southerners to emulate.[19]

Weld formed a group known as the Seventy Apostles that fanned out to spread the gospel of abolition across the nation through preaching and organization. Because of the gag rule blocking congressional consideration of abolitionist petitions, the group's publications were aimed at convincing the public of slavery's evil. The message was spread through receptive press organs, pamphlets distributed through friendly groups, pulpit oratory, and meetings resembling the revival sessions of Reverend Finney. As a member of Weld's executive group, also comprised of other prominent abolitionists, and an informal adviser to Mrs. Stowe on the support of slavery and involvement in the practice by preachers and the church establishment, Birney was a major influence on the grassroots campaign for public opinion. While Garrison railed in print in Massachusetts, Birney was patiently helping to provide the facts about the horrors of slavery to the mass of the public in the West, believing that the intransigence of the nation's statesmen and legislators would only be overcome by public pressure in an unprecedented campaign.

Birney especially targeted churches and ministers, as he realized the powerful hold they had on the attitudes of the people of the South, as well as the North, toward Negroes. Slavery historian Conrad J. Engelder observed, "The main point of difference between the pro and anti-slavery theologians was one of approach. Defenders of bondage stressed the numerous specific references to it in Holy Writ for their support while the anti-slavery leaders emphasized the general precepts of Christ. This different approach was the major factor in the inability of noted scholars from the North and South to reach an understanding as to the Bible's position toward Negro servitude."[20]

Birney collaborated with Lane students in disseminating copies of his "Letter to the Ministers and Elders of the Presbyterian Churches in Kentucky." In the letter Birney appealed to the clergymen on moral grounds like a fire-breathing evangelist, noting that slavery "has *always been,* and is *at this day* maintained by a violence that is utterly at variance with the mild spirit of the gospel." Slavery's effects on blacks, Birney wrote, "stupify and benumb the mind . . . and of course prepare them for hell." In the whites, he asserted, the practice creates "*indolence, diabolical passions, deadness to the claims of justice* and the calls of *mercy* . . . it rather prepares them for the sentence of the *damned* than for the invitation of the *blessed.*" Birney continued, "Does it not seem passing strange that a monster of such hideous mien should have been received within the very midst of the church of God?" He concluded, "If then slavery be characterized by *violence, oppression, injustice*—by tendencies to the ruin of the souls of both master and slave—why should you hesitate to say *it ought to cease* AT ONCE?"[21] Copies of the Birney letter were mailed to ministers of all denominations throughout the Mississippi Valley. The *Huntsville Southern Advocate* of 7 October 1834 pronounced his project incompatible with the security of whites and the happiness of the blacks and accused him of being unconcerned about racial amalgamation.

When Birney resigned as vice president of the American Colonization Society of Kentucky, a recent report observes, "He wrote a widely distributed open letter explaining his new opposition to colonization as stemming from its parallels with the recent removal act. Birney pointed out to his readers 'the very great resemblance this case bears in its most prominent features to that of the Indians who have been moved upon, in nearly the same measure to consent to leave their lands within the limits of several of the states.'"[22] This, therefore, marked Birney's epiphany, his conversion from a weak position against slavery based in colonization to full-throated abolition. After years of tentative and ineffective opposition to slavery, his soul truly was ready to "magnify the Lord." Birney's conversion from supporter of colonization to abolition was made public in his organizational efforts for a Kentucky Anti-Slavery Society. In a letter to Lewis Tappan, he reported obtaining more than twenty-five signatures of brave souls willing to sign their names to the society's roster but identified only a bare handful of abolitionists of his knowledge in Kentucky, including two professors at Centre College. At a meeting on 19 March 1835 in Danville, attendance at which was hampered by bad weather, some twenty-two people signed the constitution of the new organization. Professor James M. Buchanan of Centre College was named president; Birney was appointed vice president and delegate to attend the AASS's second anniversary meeting in May.

At the second anniversary meeting of the AASS, on 12 May 1835 in New York, Birney was chosen as one of the vice presidents and appointed to a committee, along with Arnold Buffum and Joshua Coffin, to lobby for repeal of laws upholding property rights in humans and to another to distribute Bibles to homes of black men and women, a project for which the society would allocate $5,000. A wider goal was for Birney to lead expansion of the abolitionist movement in the slave states and coordinate with northern branches of the AASS. Showing that his embrace of abolition was maturing with volatility, Birney offered a resolution calling for concentration of the "whole moral power of the free states" toward the extermination of slavery.[23] In a keynote speech delivered in a large Presbyterian church, he anticipated the direction the nation would eventually take with a call for Northern action to "help the South in a final solution to the slavery problem," because foreigners were judging the entire nation, North and South alike, "for this evil so contrary to the magnanimous and noble-spirited ideals of our country." Eventually the blacks held in bondage would so outnumber the whites that military force would be required to prevent a servile insurrection. He warned prophetically that when the slavery issue came to a head, it would "burst over the land with tremendous and devastating violence."[24] Even more prophetic was a statement he included in a letter: "If Virg'a be not detached from the number of slaveholding states, the slavery question must inevitably dissolve the Union, and that before very long."[25]

In a short period of time, from 1833 to 1834, Birney had gone from a colonization backer, to a cautious gradual emancipation position, to a supporter of immediate emancipation. The political and personal implications of his new stand were quickly to be realized. News of Birney's antislavery activities and collaboration with Northerners already had reached the South and struck at his home in Danville: Birney's father had received an anonymous letter warning of a plot to seize his slaves, threatening fatal consequences if resistance were mounted. Despite the threatening situation, Birney returned to Danville and immediately and publicly challenged an intractable minister who, although he had declared himself against slavery, had continued to own slaves. The fact that two public debates with the churchman had created a standoff among witnesses who took opposing sides of the issue was instructive to Birney, who reported the outcome in a letter to Gerrit Smith. Birney's deeply felt and religiously based emotions over his settlement on a course of action regarding slavery also were revealed: "Altho' I am in the midst of enemies . . . and am often much perplexed, yet altogether I have never had so much peace—never before have I felt God to be a Help so present . . . Let my soul magnify the Lord!" He continued, again anticipating the coming conflict and its intensity: "Immediate emancipation will have to be sustained by the comparatively poor and humble. The aristocracy created and sustained by Slavery, will be 'ugly enemies.'"[26] In light of the Civil War, the "poor and humble" could be characterized as ordinary farmers and workingmen who made up the bulk of the Union Army while the "aristocracy" would represent the leaders of the Confederacy, along with non-slaveholders in their thrall, many motivated by a desire to perpetuate the slave culture. It was an amazingly perceptive insight twenty-six years before the war would begin. The preordination of the conflict was inherent in the prejudices of the people.

In a letter to an influential British clergyman, Birney informed him the abolitionists were "laboring zealously to banish Slavery, and the spirit of Slaveholding from our American churches; not only with a view to their purification, but as . . . an indispensable preliminary, to the extermination of Slavery from the whole land." He cited "prejudice against color which is cherished to a deplorable extent in nearly all the Protestant churches even in the free States of the Union."[27] Religious historian C. C. Goen, remarking on the targeting of churches by the abolitionists, noted that "on the Northern side, evangelical abolitionists made no secret of their conviction that the antislavery crusade was of one piece in church and nation." The Methodists, Baptists, and Presbyterians, "increasingly agitated by disputes over slavery, sundered into northern and southern factions long before political rupture, thus opening the first major cleavage between slaveholding and free states; and that the denominational schisms portended and to some extent provoked the crisis of the Union in 1861."[28]

Abraham Lincoln was elected to the Illinois state legislature as a Whig in 1834 and, of course, as a first-term state legislator could have made little impact on national affairs, or slavery. In his second term, beginning in 1836, he began to oppose Southern attempts to influence Illinois legislators to condemn abolitionists about the same time Birney was engaged in his battles with the pro-slavery mobs in Cincinnati. Although it was a slow start, it marked the beginning of a skein of initiatives that ultimately would lead to formation of the Liberty, Free Soil, and Republican parties and Lincoln's election as the first antislavery president of the nation. Whitney, in his biography of Lincoln given the perspective of a law partner, provides what he describes as "an understanding of the political and social bias of his neighbors and neighborhood." Southern Illinois was populated mainly by settlers from the slave states, Whitney noted, "so that the Yankees and Abolitionists were as much *below par* in southern and central Illinois as they were in Kentucky or Missouri." As Birney had asserted, churches were the root as well as the spreading branches of this flowering prejudice that supported evil. Whitney instructs as well as entertains with mock back-country lingo, alluding to a character from Dickens, the Reverend Mister Chadband, a pompous, hypocritical clergyman who fails to practice what he preaches: "A Chadband of the 'hardshell' order thus exclaimed in a sermon: 'The overwhelming torrent of free grace *tuk in* the mountings of *Ashy,* the isles of the sea, and the uttermost ends of the *yearth*. It *tuk in* the Eskimo and the *Hottingtots;* and some, my dear *brethring,* go so *fur* as to suppose it *tuk in* them *air* poor, benighted *Yangkeys;* but I don't go that *fur!*"[29] While Birney was imploring the Lord to "magnify my soul" in opposing slavery, the mass of preachers of all denominations were "hardshell Chadband" types, as described by Whitney, who supported the status quo and the system of slavery.

When the Birneys left Alabama in 1833, traveling with Agatha and James were five boys: James III, sixteen; William, fourteen; Dion, ten; David, eight; and eighteen-month-old George. They left behind three small graves in the Huntsville cemetery. The graves are not marked, supposedly because the Birneys feared they would be desecrated.[30] The graves were for Margaret, who died in infancy in 1822; Arthur, taken by scarlet fever at age five in 1833; and daughter Martha, three, who died within a month of Arthur, also of the fever. Agatha had given birth to nine children in seventeen years, and six were living. Almost constant childbearing and the worrisome fact that her husband had failed both as a planter and as a politician had worn on Agatha. She was ill and was fated to live only until 1839.

CHAPTER 8

Saving the South from Destruction

I believe the condition of Slavery to be altogether un-Christian, and, therefore, that its tendency is to the ruin of us as a people.

—JAMES G. BIRNEY

BIRNEY FELT BY MOVING BACK TO DANVILLE HE WOULD HAVE A BET-
ter chance to launch the antislavery crusade that was becoming his consuming obsession now that it was apparent that there was little support, either white or black, for colonization. In May 1833 he began writing a series of essays on colonization to the newspapers in the South. The essays stressed that colonization was both patriotic and benevolent and would remove a rapidly growing evil—free people of color—thus approaching a pro-slavery position. Also, black American colonists could become missionaries to convert Africa's millions to Christianity, he posited. Birney denied that the American Colonization Society was dominated by abolitionists, claiming accurately that it had been organized by slaveholders for their benefit. In fact, abolitionists such as William Lloyd Garrison were opposed to the movement, he noted.

The fifteen essays were printed by both the *Huntsville Democrat* and the *Southern Advocate,* and some were reprinted in other papers. The abolitionist opposition was stated by Nathan Green, a Tennessee law professor and one of Birney's correspondents: "The Emancipationists say, the Colonization Society is but making fast the chains of slavery on the blacks in the U.S. and therefore they oppose it."[1] On the advice of friends Arthur Hopkins and Dr. Thomas Fearn, Birney scrapped the fifteenth essay, which pointed out that

Rome had fallen because of corruption created by slavery. According to the *African Repository and Colonial Journal* (the ACS organ), he stopped writing the series voluntarily, not because of complaints or refusal by publishers.

Although not for want of effort, Birney's success at colonization was lagging. On 24 September 1833 he wrote from Huntsville to Ralph Gurley, saying, "Kentucky, I would trust, will offer a better field for operations than that in which I have been laboring." The intransigence of ministers was, as always, a nagging concern. "I have been greatly disappointed at the insensibility of the religious community on the subject of Slavery," Birney wrote. "So far from sending their slaves to Liberia the greater part are not slow to justify Slavery, in our circumstances. They say, if the relation of Master and Slave be in itself immoral, it would have been condemned by the Savior,—and the apostles would not have given instructions for regulating the conduct of those who were placed in it."[2]

Birney decided he would find new apostles, who would have a different view valuing equality. Fladeland summarized Birney's state of mind at that time regarding slavery. "Birney was not yet an abolitionist when he left Alabama," she writes. "He was not fully convinced that slavery was a sin, which must, therefore, be completely given up. He found himself unable to answer satisfactorily the Southern defense of slavery on Biblical grounds. He was still a colonizationist, though, it is true, he had begun to doubt that colonization could be a final solution to the problem; and he was still of the opinion that in Alabama and Mississippi, where blacks would eventually outnumber the whites, free Negroes did constitute a real problem."[3]

It was becoming clear that the strategy of the colonizationists—as Gurley stated, "to get the humane and pious of the South deeply and earnestly engaged in plans and measures tending to the abolition of slavery"—was an abysmal failure. It was also clear that this group of people, including Birney and others in the American Colonization Society, was eminently concerned about the feelings of fellow Southerners who so coveted their slaves and were hoping to avoid a great sectional collision over the practice. Of course history has proven the improbability of that hope. There was to be no quiet amelioration of the conflict. The intransigence of the South was having the perverse effect of frustrating honest peacemakers like Birney and driving them to their only hope to initiate the process leading the end of slavery: the cause of immediate emancipation.

Birney wanted to return to Danville, as his father wrote, "to save his family from destruction." He was determined to publish a newspaper that would help the South understand the dangers of slavery and lead the region toward abolishing the practice. It was the only solution for the South,

Birney had said in written and spoken statements. He resigned from his post as agent for the American Colonization Society, bought farm property adjoining his father's plantation in Danville, and moved to Kentucky, hoping the future would be brighter for the cause of slave and slaveholder alike. In early 1833 the wagon bearing the reformer and his family rolled into Danville, welcomed by warm greetings from relatives and friends. Surely, the elder James Birney hoped, he would now forget the insane scheme of colonization that had consumed him recently and would conform to the views accepting slavery that were prevalent in the community. Rather than conforming to the existing system of slavery, the younger Birney had the opposite opinion, considering Danville the best location in the country for taking a stand against slavery.

A letter to Gurley dated 11 December 1833 confirmed that Birney had given up most hope for colonization: "The subject of Colonization is most favorably received in this State—but there are many, who like myself look upon it as impracticable to arouse the South sufficiently to make it the means of ridding us of Slavery. I believe the condition of Slavery to be altogether un-Christian, and, therefore, that its tendency is, to the ruin of us as a people."[4] He had been involved in the colonization effort for just over a year since accepting the agency position in August 1832. Gurley, just returned from a two-month fund-raising trip, was hoping that colonization would "save the country from the most terrible convulsions that [have] ever threatened it," but also was losing faith, noting by return mail, "without some clear evidences that the South does intend at some time, and that not very remote to abolish slavery, our cause cannot [continue] as a barrier in the way of inconsiderate and fierce anti-slavery measures."[5]

Now Birney took the next step up the ladder toward abolition and turned his attention more forcefully to gradual emancipation, an effort that had been started and had languished. He wrote a tome titled: "Constitution and Address of the Kentucky Society for the Gradual Relief of the State from Slavery," which was signed by circuit judge John Green, the organization's secretary. The title indicated the group's tentative approach, calling for society members to emancipate their slaves at age twenty-five and, "if a female, her offspring with her." The society's constitution declared immediate emancipation "probably impossible" while posing a goal of preparing black men and women for freedom in the future. Of course, full-throated abolitionism was the ultimate step, still a half score of years away for Birney. A Kentucky historian reported that in 1834 he revived the "gradual relief" organization from the nine members who attended the first meeting to between sixty and seventy members, including many women.[6]

Birney was "much vilified and abused about Danville" but still gathered the courage to debate slavery with Dr. John C. Young, president of Centre College, before members of the school's literary societies. When the young men rejected abolition by a vote of 22 to 20, Birney was distraught, thinking "the state's youth were being corrupted." After his forty-four-page "Letter on Colonization" to the Reverend Thornton J. Mills, corresponding secretary of the Kentucky Colonization Society, was published by the *Anti-Slavery Reporter* in New York, declaring his futility with that movement and shift to abolition, the antislavery forces sprang into action. Birney charged in the letter that the "consent" of the free people of color to emigrate was being extorted by "proscription, prejudice and scorn," calling it "a solemn farce, a refinement of inhumanity." He invoked the Declaration of Independence and railed against the "anti-republican tendencies of slavery," asserting the practice was "against the very essence of our government." Fladeland summarized the importance of the letter, saying, "Here, for the first time, was a native Southerner, himself a former slaveholder, not of the poor-white, have-not class, but of the aristocracy, and one who had firsthand acquaintance with the workings of the Colonization Society, coming out strongly, directly, and with no reservations against slavery and against colonization."[7]

Birney's letter was sent to several newspapers; it was rejected by the editor of the *Western Luminary* of Lexington, who claimed he was an abolitionist but feared repercussions, and the editors of the *Lexington Intelligencer* printed it only as an advertisement, disavowing responsibility for its content. Weld and his Lane Seminary colleagues collected $100 to distribute a thousand copies through the West and Southwest, sending them with theology students going home for the summer. The son of Rev. John Allan, Birney's old pastor in Huntsville, was to carry the letter home and gather names and addresses with the goal of distributing eight thousand copies in the Mississippi Valley. In New York Elizur Wright, secretary of the American Anti-Slavery Society, wrote to Weld that he was "electrified by that noble letter of Birney." He wrote to 110 antislavery societies and hoped that one hundred thousand copies of the letter would be printed and spread throughout the East.[8] Suddenly, Birney was a nationally known abolitionist, celebrated by antislavery supporters and soon to be widely vilified by the defenders of slavery. Now was the time to take even more drastic action: freeing his slaves.

On the sultry morning of 2 June 1834, a determined, businesslike James G. Birney assembled his family and slaves in the living room of their new home in Danville for a ceremony of manumission: a fancy term meaning legally freeing slaves. Friends were arriving in carriages, and quill pens and an inkwell sat ready beside a sheaf of paper on the dining room table. Outside, the still-wet Kentucky bluegrass was speckled with yellow blooms called hoary puccoons in those parts, surrounded by heart-shaped leaves like shamrocks, along with violet wood sorrel and wild strawberry. The day began to take on a sparkle, like those rare times that inspired the human heart with hope for a better future. The chief figure was, of course, Birney, the only son and heir of plantation owner James Birney Sr. The younger Birney stood five feet nine inches tall and carried himself with the almost regal bearing bestowed by wealth and being "to the manor born." The son of an Irish immigrant who had arrived penniless in Philadelphia had become an American frontier aristocrat because of the riches and privilege created in large part by slave labor. An aquiline head and sparse gray hair in Napoleonic style crowned his sturdy frame. Deep-set brown eyes flashed with gravely tempered outrage at any offense he considered an affront to the American democratic ideals as he saw them. Birney was not a duelist like family friend Henry Clay and many other prominent Southerners, but he fearlessly stood his ground, especially on issues involving justice. As the family motto proclaimed, "Nothing to fear nor to be feared."

Birney's boyhood companion was the other principal figure in the room, Michael Matthews was now about forty-years-old, strong, well-formed, and intent. As a four-year-old, in 1798 he had been a gift to the six-year-old Birney. His family now stood at his side: his wife, Sarah, thirty-two; daughters Mary, seventeen, and Betsy, sixteen; son Edwin, fourteen; and a little biracial girl Birney had adopted, age six. Witnesses to the ceremony were Birney's friends Joshua Fry Bell, a prominent Danville storekeeper, and William Miller, another friend and neighbor. The Matthews family and the little biracial girl were to be officially given their freedom by their master. It was a rare, but not unheard of, occurrence in the South. By Kentucky law the deeds of emancipation included bonds with sureties to indemnify the state and county against bad conduct or pauperism on the part of those who were manumitted. Birney's deeds also contained his statement that slavery "was inconsistent with the Great Truth that all men are created equal, upon which I conceive our Republican institutions are founded—as well as with the great rule of benevolence delivered to us by the Savior Himself that in all things whatsoever ye would that men should do unto you do ye even so to them." The deeds were filed in the Mercer County Courthouse, in Harrodsburg.[9]

Over his adult years, Michael unfortunately had shown a fondness for strong drink, and Birney, who had struggled with the same demon, had extracted a temperance pledge from the about-to-be-freed slave. It was for his own good, and that of his family, Birney thought. Besides, he was investing in Michael and was hoping his faith would be justified. The new freedman was paid a free laborer's wages, plus interest, for all the years he had been a slave. The funds were invested for him in a livery stable in Louisville. Edwin was apprenticed to a Cincinnati blacksmith, and one of the daughters was placed as a housemaid. The little girl stayed with the Birney family, was educated in Cincinnati, and when she came of age was taught to be a seamstress. To Birney's relief, Michael proved sober and industrious and prospered in the livery stable business. His success was one confirmation that black men and women could take their places in society and a refutation of the widespread belief, in both North and South, that they not only were inferior but incapable of caring for themselves. Birney's investment in Michael was a great risk, but one he felt he must take, especially realizing that he had exploited the man all of his life.

Who was this strange master who freed and paid his slaves? And what motivated him to this unusual humanitarian act? The act of freeing his own slaves was illustrative of Mr. Birney's character that also led to his perilous quest to end slavery through the political process. It is an inspirational tale of the pursuit of the American promise of freedom by a man whose determination and principles helped change the nation's history.

For a decade the South had solidified a defensive front against abolitionist sentiments and was about to go on offense. After John Quincy Adams had defeated Birney's friend Henry Clay for the presidency in 1825, John C. Calhoun had marshaled political forces to fortify and perpetuate slavery in the "Golden Circle" of the solid South. At first the most inflammatory issue was not the horrors of slavery of African captives in the United States; it was whether slavery could even be mentioned in print, conversation, or—incredibly—on the floor of the U.S. Congress. With Birney's friends conducting a massive campaign to publicize a letter revealing a prominent Southerner to be a hated abolitionist, Birney was at the eye of the hurricane, and his safety and life were threatened.

In August 1835 Lewis Bond, postmaster of Clinton, Mississippi, felt compelled to write Birney a letter that was both a warning against his intent of publishing an abolitionist newspaper and a revelation of sectional sentiment: "You certainly Sir are blinded and know not the injury that the abolitionists are doing to the good cause both of Christianity and the peace of this union. Already has the fire kindled in the hearts of the Southern states against the Northern abolitionists to such a flame as to become quite jealous of the whole people of the North in this affair. What motive can you possibly have in view in the publication of your journal other than that of stirring up the Negroes in rebellion against the whites?"[10]

From Glasgow, Kentucky, John Jones, who was acting as an agent for the proposed newspaper, to be titled the *Philanthropist,* wrote to Birney, saying, "There are so many HORRID and GHOSTLY rumours and stories afloat in this region concerning the treasonable, seditious, and incendiary sayings and doings of the Abolitionists that the very name has become a term of reproach; and many would gladly, no doubt, see them all hung up. Nearly all believe, and very many hope you will not be permitted to publish your paper."[11]

One rare instance of support was evidenced in Danville in 1835. A proslavery mob there was thwarted from murderous intent against Birney by the bravery of a valiant young man named Joseph J. Bullock, who "when a crowd was gathering mounted a box and declared that no attack should be made unless the assailants were ready to march over his dead body and those of many others. When Birney rode up the street a few minutes later, not a hand was raised against him."[12] The valiant Bullock later became a Presbyterian minister and served as chaplain of the U.S. Senate from 1879 to 1883.

Birney wrote to fellow abolitionist Gerrit Smith at Peterboro, New York, pouring out his soul about the death of three of his children and his life, referring to his drinking and gambling habits a decade previously in Alabama. "Our third child was a daughter," he wrote. "She was taken away whilst I was rapidly pursuing the road to Hell. The affliction hardened me much and, added fuel to the ferocity of my heart against Him whose consolations I proudly scorned." He told of his determination to move to Cincinnati and called for abolitionists to leave the slaveholding states or "all is lost." The letter contained a jeremiad:

> Our high professions, of freedom as a nation—our unparalleled religious privileges—our obdurate perseverance in the sin of oppression—the exorbitant claims of the South on the liberties of the free states—demanding every thing that has heretofore been deemed precious to them should be surrendered, in order that the Slaveholder might be perfectly at ease in his iniquity—all I say indicate that repentance is far off, if at all to be expected, and that God will avenge himself of a Nation like this. It is as much as all the patriotism in our country can do, to keep alive the spirit of liberty in the free states. The contest is becoming—has become,—one, not alone of freedom for the black, but of freedom for the white.

Birney concluded the letter by informing Smith that the Danville postmaster "has determined to become my intellectual caterer. He is beginning to withhold my papers."[13] It was a further confirmation that freedoms of the whites, freedoms promised in the Constitution, were being limited because of the clash between the politics of abolition and the slave power.

Desperately perplexed by the slavery problem, Birney decided to make one more attempt to persuade the political leadership in the nation to address the issue. He would visit Henry Clay, his old collaborator who had helped him with state legislative matters fifteen years before when he was in Alabama. Clay had spoken against slavery as a young legislator in 1799, and Birney reasoned that perhaps it was time to renew the acquaintance and ask Senator Clay to use his legendary skills and avoid the crisis Birney could see looming. Riding horseback to meet Reverend Weld on the Cincinnati Road north of Georgetown, Kentucky, to talk over plans for Birney's involvement in the American Anti-Slavery Society, Birney stopped to sound out Presbyterian ministers on slavery. He found the first churchman too timorous to challenge the system and prayed for two hours with another, who had been known as a missionary among the Cherokee. Birney was convinced the minister would free his four slaves when he returned to Alabama. Passing through Lexington, site of the Clay estate, Ashland, Birney wrote a note and was granted an impromptu meeting with the senator, who had just returned from Washington. Fladeland described the legislative paragon of Lexington: "Clay, in his fifty-seventh year, was Kentucky's most famous son and one of the men to be reckoned with in the legislative halls of the nation. His suave, affable manner blended well with the quiet beauty of Ashland."[14]

Clay no doubt had been alerted about Birney's plans to publish an abolitionist newspaper when the pair last met in early September 1834. Fifteen years older than Birney, Clay had been in public service since he was twenty-six. He was born in Hanover County, Virginia, in 1777, came to Lexington as a young lawyer, and was immensely popular. He had served two short terms in the senate, had been Speaker of the House of Representatives, helped negotiate the peace treaty with Great Britain in 1814, served as secretary of state under John Quincy Adams, and had twice been a candidate for president, in 1824 and in 1832. He was elected Speaker of the House six times, brokered the Missouri Compromise in 1820–1821, and helped diffuse South Carolina's nullification crisis in 1833.

Birney at this point was a forty-two-year-old lawyer and failed planter who had served short terms as a Whig in the Kentucky and Alabama legislatures. Although he had campaigned for Clay in an 1815 congressional campaign in Kentucky and in the presidential campaign of 1824 as well as supporting the Adams ticket in 1828 in Alabama against Jackson when Clay was secretary of state, winning a letter of praise from Clay, the pair had had no contact since. Now Birney had been publicly identified as an abolitionist, a hated class in the South; Clay certainly had noticed and was ready when Birney arrived at the Ashland estate in Lexington for a seven o'clock breakfast meeting. Birney had indicated in his note, sent the night before, the subject that he wanted to discuss—the slavery issue, of course. Birney could hear Clay's statements from his early speeches ringing in his ears:

- "We must have freedom for all men. Slavery is an evil which must be ended."
- "George Mason and Jefferson were right; it is hypocrisy to claim our rights as free men while holding other men as slaves."
- "Slavery is ruinous to all, whites as well as Negroes, since it encourages arrogance and sloth in our young people."

"Clay was ready with his answer and did most of the talking for about an hour, but before much of it had passed, Birney knew he had nothing to hope for in the way of support," Fladeland writes. "He was hearing a glib politician rationalize his action, or lack of it, with the same, well-worn excuses." Birney wrote in his diary after the breakfast with Clay, September 16: "He said that slavery in Ky, was in so mitigated a form as not to deserve the consideration of a very great evil—that men's interests in property had been found an insurmountable barrier to gradual emancipation then, in '99—that now, they were more formidable—the case was hopeless by any direct effort, and was to be left to the influence of liberal principles as they should pervade our land."[15] Clay's hard-featured wife, Lucretia, perhaps appearing so because of perpetual anxiety over Henry's habitual gambling and carousing, served breakfast. Out of deference to her sensibilities, there was no political talk during the long, polite meal.

The trio gazed out across a sloping lawn, where, like an English country seat, the Clays had transplanted a glorious profusion of mountain trees and shrubbery—dogwoods, redbuds, and hollies cut through with walks and gardens. Rows of straight blue ash trees fronted a savanna pasture the Clays called a park; and on the rear lawn was a "pleasure area" for social events, a large, smooth lawn from which animals were barred. After the leisurely breakfast meeting, the pair ambled along the estate's Henry Clay Walk and the Locust Walk, where many of the Great Compromiser's most famous speeches were inspired and composed in his head. Under a delicate interlacing of foliage amid the tall pines and broad-leafed catalpas, Norway spruce, and sugar maple, on the serpentine tanbark trails, the young reformer and the elder statesman jousted with ideas and words like knights with clashing lances, elegant yet deadly in purpose and consequence.

"Slavery is so mild a form here in Kentucky, James, that it scarcely can be termed evil," the senator observed calmly. Birney recalled that he had heard that Clay had continued to buy and sell slaves and that slave life at Ashland had never changed, despite the master's political protestations. "Birney realized there was no point to be gained by further argument," Fladeland observed. "The man talking to him, it was now apparent, was a man with no conscience in the matter, someone who seemed 'never to have gone beyond the mere outer bark of the subject.' And that outer bark was his own political skin. This was the last time Clay and Birney were to meet. As Clay shook hands with his departing guest that morning, little did he dream that James Gillespie Birney was one day to stand between him and his highest aspiration, the Presidency of the United States."[16]

Birney, saddened, rode off slowly to the east, his mind trying to justify the intransigence he had just encountered, trying to shake off the disappointment he felt in an iconic figure of the national government, a family friend and political collaborator to whom he had looked for inspiration as a young man dreaming of a glorious career in politics. The pulsating sun was nearing its heights of midday, haze and clouds blown off and standing clear in the bright blue sky. Birney thought," the heavens are my beacon," as he gazed hopefully upward and headed down the road that led over the rise alongside acres of azure grasses to the crossing where Reverend Weld was waiting.

Later Birney endorsed Clay's response to his hastily written invitation of the night before the fateful meeting, saying, "I breakfasted with Mr. C. and had an hour's conversation with him on the subject of emancipation. I found him, according to my conceptions, altogether wrong—and that he had gone very little beyond the standard of vulgar reflection on the subject." He wrote further in his diary, "The impression made upon me, by this interview was that Mr. C. had no conscience about the matter, and therefore, that he would swim with the popular current, the current which presented a smooth surface to the outward eye, but which hid the deepening chasm underneath it."[17]

Clay's description of slavery in Kentucky as mild is belied by the brutal murder in 1811 of the slave George by the nephews of Thomas Jefferson (see chapter 3), many contrary reports by slaves themselves, and by the experience of abolitionists like Calvin Fairbank, who served a total of seventeen years and three months in Kentucky prisons for aiding slaves to escape. Fairbank's recollections to Levi Coffin included accounts of flogging amounting to thousands of stripes administered on a regular basis by brutal jailers in Frankfort. Fairbank finally was pardoned by the lieutenant governor in April 1864.[18]

Birney had resigned from his post as agent for the American Colonization Society, bought property adjoining his father's plantation in Danville, and moved to Kentucky, hoping the future would be brighter for the cause of slave and slaveholder alike. Freeing Michael Matthews and his family was an important step in realizing that hope. But the dream that leaders like Clay would recognize the need for equality was soon rudely ended. Pressure from neighbors soon was applied on the abolitionist living in the midst of nonbelievers. "Wherever Birney went," Fladeland comments, "in Danville or neighboring towns, he had come to expect to be lectured to by old friends, to be 'roundly abused' by others. Even groups of ladies accosted him on the street to assail him verbally. There was no chance now that his hope of an appointment to the faculty of Centre College would materialize; parents would refuse to send their sons to an institution where they might imbibe such dangerous ideas as he held."[19]

A group of pro-slavery townsfolk had pooled funds and purchased the local weekly newspaper, ironically called the *Olive Branch,* to keep Birney from publishing his abolitionist doctrines. The decision to move from his birthplace and home of Danville was heart-wrenching. We can only imagine the family's agony as the wagon rolled down the main street of Danville, the burning, hateful eyes of neighbors boring in upon them from all around. It was a gorgeous October 1835, the warm and mellow autumn day contrasting with the cold hearts of those who were overjoyed to see the Birneys go. The sad traveling troop's trek would lead north about one hundred miles to Cincinnati, where, although it was across the Ohio River into land covered by the Northwest Ordinance, which barred slavery, even more perils from the white advocates of slave power would await them.

CHAPTER 9

The Tar and Feathers Agenda

*Public Meeting—A meeting of the citizens of Cincinnati opposed
to the course now pursuing by those individuals composing Abolition
and Anti-Slavery societies. Jan. 22, 1836, at the Court House.*

—BROADSIDE PUBLISHED AND DISTRIBUTED IN CINCINNATI

A GRIM-FACED DELEGATION BANGED ON THE DOOR OF BIRNEY'S home on Race Street in Cincinnati. Birney opened to find Mayor Samuel W. Davies, City Marshal James Saffin, and Charles Hammond, the editor of the *Cincinnati Gazette,* staring him down. The vicious glares and stiffly folded arms told Birney this was not a welcoming committee. Birney's plans to publish an antislavery newspaper had instantly aroused the ire of the proslavery citizens of Cincinnati, and the delegation of officials was responding to their concerns. Cincinnati's ties with the South were strong because of commercial ties, personal friendships, and family connections. Slave-bound Kentucky was just across the Ohio River, and Cincinnati residents had learned to be wary of escaped slaves using the Underground Railroad to traverse Ohio and slip into Canada through Detroit.

Cincinnati, settled mainly by Revolutionary War veterans who were granted lands, was a town used to dealing strictly with lawbreakers and mavericks. A local historian, Rev. Charles F. Goss, observed, "At first the [court] sessions were held in the barrooms of the various taverns, of which there were, from the first, a plenty. In front of one of them (that of George Avery) stood the instruments of justice—a pillory, stocks, whipping post and, at times, a gallows."[1] Some of Kentucky's slave laws had been adopted in Cincinnati as well. Perhaps some of Birney's opponents wished the equipment of discipline and punishment still remained so that they could use them on him. Reverend Goss explained the state of public mind in the city and noted that only five years before Birney had arrived, the outright murder of black men and women by mob violence was accepted practice:

> Cincinnati lay so near to the South [of which it was and is the natural gateway] that slaves were forever escaping into it for refuge, and free blacks found it a convenient place to make their homes. As early as 1829 it was discovered with apprehension that there were 2,258 colored people residing within the city limits. So great was the antipathy felt toward what seemed at the time an undesirable element that mobs formed and assailed the negroes whenever they could be attacked with impunity. So many were killed or wounded in these melees that more than half the number of these unfortunate creatures fled from a situation so full of peril, and those who remained were naturally the lowest and worst.

Saffin, who had just succeeded the aptly named Jesse Justice in the marshal's post, was no ordinary hired policeman. Fees for arrests and successful prosecutions enriched him up to $25,000 a year.[2] The hostile trio quickly and directly made known its purpose. They complained of the "incendiary" nature of a broadside titled "Declaration of Sentiment of the Cincinnati Anti-Slavery Society" and warned Birney that violence was imminent because of his plans, stated in the handbill, to publish a newspaper promoting the abolitionist cause. Birney stated his firm intention to assert his rights and politely turned the tables, stressing that the city authorities could, and should, suppress any threatened mob action.

The *Cincinnati Whig* headlined an article on 21 December 1835 "ABOLITION PAPER," which read: "We perceive by a notice in the *Christian Journal* that James G. Birney is about to commence his abolition paper at New Richmond, Clermont County. Finding that his fanatical project would not be tolerated at Danville, Ky., nor in this city, he has at length settled himself on the border of Kentucky and so near Cincinnati as to make the pestiferous breath of his paper spread contagion among our citizens. We deem this new effort an insult to our slaveholding neighbors and an attempt to browbeat public opinion in this quarter. We do therefore hope, not withstanding the alleged respectability of the editor, that he will find the public so inexorably averse to his mad scheme that he will deem it his interest to abandon it."

His father was not a nonresistant, William noted in his biography of his father. Birney locked the doors, and he and his sons placed about forty muskets and double-barreled shotguns at strategic places in the house for protection.[3] "So the Birney family was to live for almost two years, with the ever present apprehension of danger hanging over them," Fladeland wrote. "Any noise in the street, any sign of commotion, might be the indication that the posts of defense must be taken. It was enough to shake anyone's nerves, and Mrs. Birney, far from well and again pregnant, was in a constant state of worry. Her chronic cough and recurrent fever had begun to give unmistakable signs of tuberculosis."[4]

To ease the pressure from the pro-slavery forces, Birney judiciously decided to publish the *Philanthropist* in New Richmond, Ohio, a small town about twenty miles up the Ohio River from Cincinnati. Location of the press required Birney to spend long hours on horseback to and from Cincinnati, but he was willing to make the effort to defuse the opposition and improve family safety. The first issue, dated 1 January 1836, diplomatically invited discussion on both sides of the slavery controversy. However, there was to be no collaborative discussion of this volatile topic between abolitionists and pro-slavery forces.[5] A mob gathered in New Richmond not to threaten Birney, but to protect him. This friendly mob was in response to reports that a boat had been chartered at Cincinnati "to bring up a party of pro-slavery men whose avowed purpose was to destroy *The Philanthropist*," states a historical source. "Lawless men from Kentucky and other places threatened to destroy the office, and the abolitionists and personal friends of the editor of *The Philanthropist* rallied to defend the paper. At the signal of danger a meeting was held in the old market-house of the village, which was addressed by Caleb S. Walker and other friends of freedom, and the most emphatic assurance given Mr. Birney that they would stand by him, though it might require the sacrifice of life and property. Happily, better counsel prevailed and the boat did not leave Cincinnati, but all that night the friends of a free press patrolled in front of the newspaper office to protect it from possible assault."[6]

Townsfolk in Cincinnati now were even more aware of Birney's abolitionist activities and were galvanized in opposition. A meeting was held on 22 January 1836 in the Hamilton County Courthouse to rally the anti-abolitionists. A week later the *Philanthropist* reported on the comments of Col. Charles Hale, who attended the meeting: "He was happy in his graphic description of his going to the house of Mr. Birney, to warn him, though a stranger, of the public indignation with which he would soon be visited if he did not desist from publishing his paper, and from lecturing about slavery in this city. The manner in which he related the circumstances of his being found by Mr. B on the steps of the door on opening it for admission, with one of the biggest and blackest [Negroes] he had ever seen in the whole course of his life—and Mr. B's treatment of him and the [Negro] drew forth no small merriment and applause."[7] Editorials in the *Cincinnati Republican* said Birney's newspaper was aimed in "the unholy and unpatriotic cause of abolition," charging that Birney's intent was "dissolution of the Union." Placards were posted on street corners calling a meeting in the courthouse to suppress the City Abolition Society and the abolitionist newspaper. Leading citizens lending names to the call included the editor of the *Whig, Post,* and *Republican* newspapers, the city's postmaster, two former members of Congress, two candidates for sheriff, and judicial and congressional candidates. Runners were sent to foundries and machine shops to drum up workingmen; plans were laid for the mob to visit the antislavery printing office, the bookstore where antislavery pamphlets were sold, and Birney's house.

Birney's son William, then seventeen, was an eyewitness to the mob action and later, long after the Civil War, attested in a biography to his father's heroism in personally confronting danger. He marched into the courthouse shoulder to shoulder with his father through the angry gang of slavery defenders. William later recalled, "An immense crowd of people was already there. The approaches were thronged; men stood on the windowsills and looked through and talked in groups in the yard. Inside every place was filled, from the judge's bench to the gallery. We made our way with difficulty to the foot of the steps leading to the bench." Col. Charles Hale, of the local militia, an illiterate livery stable keeper and ward politician, "made a most inflammatory harangue against Mr. Birney, charging him with amalgamation, incendiarism and treason to the Constitution of his country." As his son described it, Birney was accused of making Cincinnati the base of intrigues to overthrow the Constitution and plunge the South into the blood-reeking massacres of a servile insurrection. "The roughs cheered him wildly, and, at the close of his peroration, were ready to rush to the work of destruction," William wrote.

What occurred next is a crystallized moment in time as Birney spoke: "Mr. President, my name is Birney. May I be heard? My personal character and my cause have been unjustly attacked. May I defend them?" The irate stableman and his cohorts moved toward Birney amid cries of "Kill him!" "Drag him out!" "Tar and feather him!" However, a few opposing shouts of "Fair play" and "Hear him out" were raised. "In the height of this tumult, Surveyor-General R. T. Lytle, the recognized chief of the anti-abolition movement but a man of generous and chivalrous temperament, sprang to the judge's bench and by gesture demanded silence," the younger Birney recalled. Lytle said, "'My friends, hear before you strike. Don't disgrace our city and our cause before the nation. I oppose abolitionism but I honor a brave man, and Mr. Birney tonight has shown himself the bravest man I have ever seen.'" By a large majority the group approved a motion to allow Birney to speak, and he held his critics spellbound for three-quarters of an hour, William reported.

Birney cleverly aimed an opening declamatory ploy at the venerable Hale, an aging military man with flowing white hair. One day Colonel Hale had arrived at his door, William said, accompanied by a colored man. "Both were strangers to him, and, supposing they had come together, he had invited them to enter. The colored man applied for employment and was dismissed. He left it to the gallant colonel to explain why he came with such a companion. The tables were turned on the colonel, and the crowd laughed at his discomfiture and would not hear his explanation." Birney sagely asserted the South would gain representatives in Congress by emancipation of the slaves through the two-fifths of the Negro population not covered under the apportionment scheme of the Constitution. "In a magnificent appeal he developed the grand object of the Constitution to secure the blessings of liberty to ourselves and our posterity," William wrote. "To the charge of hostility to the national Constitution, he answered by a noble vindication of that instrument. He denied that it contained any compact with slavery or any guarantee or even any mention of it; claimed that the nearest approach to a recognition of it was the stigma placed upon it in the denial of congressional representation to two fifths of a certain class of population, and that the South would gain and not lose in the number of its members of Congress by emancipation." William concluded, "His triumph was complete. The subsequent efforts of orators to excite the crowd were fruitless. As my father left the courtroom the crowd made way respectfully for him, and he was neither followed nor molested on his way home."[8] In Fladeland's words:

> Birney was not usually an eloquent or impassioned speaker, but that night in the courthouse, facing a mob against which he had no protection except his power of persuasion, delivered a more eloquent plea for the cause of the slave than ever he had as a lawyer defending an accused man before the bar of justice. Further attempts to rouse the mob to the previous pitch were unavailing. When Birney and his son walked out, the men respectfully made way for them. Mob action had once more been averted, but the fact that respectable men of high standing in the community would even participate in such a procedure was to Birney a realization filled with mournful solicitude for the cause of liberty.[9]

At home on Race Street, with the shotguns and muskets at every window, William recalled his father saying, "Though nearly all of that crowd will go home quietly, the little band led by Hale means mischief and may be down on us tonight." Birney posted William at an upstairs bedroom window as a lookout while he went downstairs to console a distraught Agatha. William concluded, "There was never a time when he would have refused or neglected to defend his wife and children." The night passed without incident, and for several months following the great mob meeting at the courthouse all was quiet in Cincinnati.[10]

In the spring of 1836 Birney, tired of the long round-trip horseback rides carrying newspapers from New Richmond, moved his office to Cincinnati. His new printer, Achilles Pugh, was a fearless Quaker who "shared Birney's opposition to slavery," according to Ohio historian Henry Howe. "Mobs twice attacked the A. H. Pugh Printing Company's office. Many white Cincinnatians opposed Birney's views. Many of these people were former slaveowners and believed that African Americans were inferior to whites. Other whites believed that slavery was morally wrong but feared that, if slavery ended, African Americans would flood the North, depriving whites of jobs."[11]

Meanwhile, Birney, a Masonic member in Kentucky, played majoritarian politics when he joined an anti-Catholic discussion led by Alexander Campbell that also involved Charles Hammond, editor of the *Cincinnati Gazette,* the only local editor who defended his right to publish antislavery views.[12] After nearly six months of relative calm, Birney was feeling optimistic that tolerance was taking hold in Ohio, and perhaps in Kentucky too. William later observed: "Anti-slavery publications were openly sold in Cincinnati; the City Anti-Slavery Society held frequent meetings. Mr. Birney lectured in the city and its suburbs; his well-known figure still attracted attention in his daily walks in the streets, but respect and curiosity were more marked than ill-will. To outward seeming, the enslavement of the press in the Queen City of the West had been defeated. But the snake was only scotched, not killed; it was to regain its venom and vigor in the heats of the following July. Then the excitement of the presidential campaign would be at its height and the city hotels and boarding houses would be full of sojourning slave-holders."[13]

Suddenly came another pro-slavery explosion. Vandals broke into Pugh's printing office, tore up copies of the *Philanthropist,* and dismantled the printing press. Broadsides were distributed headlined "ABOLITIONISTS BEWARE." It was a warning to Birney to stop publication. The message on the broadside read:

> The Citizens of Cincinnati, embracing every class, interested in the prosperity of the city, satisfied that the business of the place is receiving the stab from the

wicked and misguided operations of the abolitionists, are resolved to arrest their course. The destruction of their press on the night of the 12th Instant, may be taken as a warning. As there are some worthy citizens engaged in the unholy cause of annoying our southern neighbors, they are appealed to, to pause before they bring things to a crisis. If an attempt is made to re-establish their press, it will be viewed as an act of defiance to an already outraged community, and on their heads be the result which will follow.

A copy of the broadside reprinted in the Birney Letters was annotated: "Stuck up on the corners of the streets just before the mob of July 1836."[14]

Shortly thereafter Birney received a letter from an unknown person purporting to be a "friend of Abolitionist," signed "Alpha," claiming that the culprits who had destroyed his newspaper press were a trio from Covington, Kentucky. The letter, sent to the *Philanthropist*, said, "Sir there is a band organized for to take you prisoner if you set your feet on the Kentucky side. For to tar and feather you. I would give you warning not to come over on our side."[15] Before the printer would continue, the executive committee of the antislavery society had to give him a $2,000 guarantee to indemnify his property. The opposition offered a one-hundred-dollar reward for Birney, calling him "a fugitive from justice," who "in all his associations is black, although his external appearance is white." Again, the threatening missive apparently came from across the Ohio River, being signed "Old Kentucky."

When Birney's press was dumped into the Ohio River, the Cincinnati mob, frustrated by failure to find Birney, who was on a speaking tour, raged destructively through Negro homes. "The crowd then rushed to the houses, one after another, of well known abolitionists, whose absence saved them from the hand of violence," recalled Beriah Green. "But Mr. Birney was the special object of the Bedlam-vengeance which had now broken loose. Hands, as cowardly as cruel, were eager to seize upon him, and drag him away to the tribunal where Lynch Law, with its gallows-ropes and bowie knives, clamors for the best blood in the veins of the republic. He was, however, as a gracious Providence would have it, at a considerable distance from the city, aiding the friends of Freedom in their philanthropic exertions."[16] Cincinnati historian Clara Longworth de Chambrun observed: "*The Philanthropist . . .* roused political passion to such an extent that it brought about the first serious riots known to the town. A mob dismantled the office on Main Street where the paper was printed. In turn the rioters were assaulted by the rough Negro elements of Church Alley. Before the disorder could be quelled, some forty persons were wounded and several killed. Judge Walker wrote in his journal at this time: 'The tendency is truly alarming. If the friends of order do not rally against the mob spirit in every form, our American experiment fails.'"[17]

Mob violence roused the civic ire of fair-minded rival editors and, Birney felt, ironically won thousands to the cause. Although the Cincinnati editors never joined Birney and Illinois minister Elijah Lovejoy, another Northern abolitionist editor, in opposing slavery, they found common cause with the abolitionists in defense of freedom of speech and the press, which were traditional constitutional domains. However, many Cincinnati residents, alarmed by how pro-slavery mobs had treated Birney, began to sympathize with him and look more closely at the issue. Abolitionist books thrown out of windows by the mob were picked up, taken home, and read; some readers actually were converted to abolition. Birney wrote in his *Philanthropist* that the action of the mob had won people to the cause by the thousands where only tens had been added before.[18] One of his sympathizers, Harriet Beecher Stowe, began penning letters to newspapers in his defense. Her antislavery fervor and literary efforts would intensify over sixteen years, finally gushing out in her emotional novel, *Uncle Tom's Cabin.*[19]

Printer Pugh proved to be stalwart in the cause of abolition. After Birney's departure from Cincinnati for New York in August 1837, Pugh continued publication of the *Philanthropist,* with Gamaliel Bailey as editor. Pro-slavery mobs partially destroyed Pugh's press again in 1841. "Each time Pugh quickly had the *Philanthropist* back on the streets," states Charles T. Greve in a history of Cincinnati.[20] It took Pugh, with legal representation in one case by Salmon P. Chase, later Lincoln's secretary of treasury and Supreme Court justice, two years to win two suits against the vandals, being awarded only fifty dollars in one in 1838 but $1,500 in damages in a suit concluded in July 1839. Pugh continued publishing the abolitionist newspaper in Springboro, Ohio, but later returned to Cincinnati and operated one of the city's most successful job-printing firms. In 1838 the *Philanthropist,* then edited by Bailey, editorialized against the "especially notorious" practice of taxing black men and women for schools they could not send their children to.[21] Birney's newspaper was published until 1847, thus becoming one of Ohio's longest-running abolitionist publications.

Lincoln's treasury secretary, the magisterial, ambitious Chase, was born in New Hampshire in 1808, a year before Lincoln's birth. He was, in contrast to the self-educated Abe, formally and highly educated. His later background, however, was more parallel to Birney's. Chase was an 1826 Dartmouth graduate while Birney had been graduated from Princeton in 1810. Chase had studied law under U.S. attorney general William Wirt while Birney's legal tutelage was in Philadelphia under Alexander J. Dallas, later James Madison's secretary of the treasury. Although Chase was not an abolitionist, he had defended Birney against Cincinnati rioters protesting publication of the *Philanthropist.* "It was this incident which brought Salmon P. Chase to stand openly with the abolitionists when his own sister [Abigail], the wife of Dr. Colby, took refuge in his house during the riots," Chase historian Albert P. Hart recounted.[22]

In an intense consultation twenty-four hours before a trial in 1837, Birney and Chase reviewed the legal and constitutional aspects of the Fugitive Slave Law as applied in Ohio. Birney helped Chase write a speech in defense of an attractive young octoroon slave, Matilda, a maid in Birney's Cincinnati household, who had been grabbed by slave catchers while she was on an errand. The slave catchers were posing as agents for the girl's "owner," said to be her father, Larkin Lawrence of St. Louis, Missouri. Despite Chase's able defense, the judge returned Matilda to the fraudulent agents, who hustled her aboard a boat to New Orleans to be sold at auction. Compounding this cruel injustice, Birney was indicted under an 1804 Ohio law for harboring a Negro fugitive. Found guilty and fined fifty dollars, Birney, with help again from Chase, appealed the conviction on grounds that were to frame pre–Civil War arguments against slavery for more than two decades: They maintained Birney was not guilty because Matilda was no longer a slave the moment she stepped on the free soil of Ohio. Although the Ohio Supreme Court exonerated Birney on a technicality that he had not knowingly harbored a fugitive slave, the free soil principle in the Ohio constitution was later upheld by the court in another case defended by Chase partnering with Birney's son William.[23]

Birney and Chase both articulated the "Higher Law" doctrine that was later used by Abraham Lincoln and William H. Seward in their 1860 campaigns for the Republican presidential nomination. "In one sense there are laws by which even the makers of the Constitution as well as the legislators are bound—those rules of right existing in the public mind prior to the Constitution," Birney said to the judiciary committee of the New York legislature on 5 March 1840.[24] Chase made a similar argument in an address to the Liberty Party convention on 9 December 1841 in Columbus, Ohio.[25] "In particular, Chase made the argument that Lincoln and others adopted, linking the anti-slavery natural rights philosophy as expressed in the Declaration of Independence to the Constitution," notes historian John Niven.[26]

Birney followed the Negroes who had fled Cincinnati in the face of violence. In the spring of 1837 he moved to New York, where he was named corresponding secretary of the American Anti-Slavery Society. Birney's job was to conciliate the growing factions in the movement. The well-known

Quaker poet and abolitionist newspaper editor John Greenleaf Whittier, of Massachusetts, who was more than ten years younger than the forty-five-year-old Birney, was to have been second choice had Birney not accepted. Whittier was an early ally of William Lloyd Garrison, although he himself was convinced of the futility of moral action without political initiatives. His split with Garrison was complete when in 1839 he became one of the founders of the abolitionist Liberty Party.

By 1837 Birney's name was familiar to all who were interested in abolition, either for it or against, especially since he was an ex-slaveholder. The Cincinnati riots had spread his notoriety, and his *Philanthropist* was one of the leading antislavery newspapers. Birney was lecturing widely and was considered one of the nation's outstanding authorities on legal and constitutional issues surrounding the slavery issue. Michigan educator and historian A. D. P. Van Buren reflected on Birney's influence on the antislavery movement: "It was thus that in the winter of 1837–38 he visited every state capital from Maine to Ohio and Michigan in which a legislative body was in session. In Massachusetts and Pennsylvania he was instrumental in having enacted laws which gave fleeing slaves a trial by jury; Connecticut repealed her black laws, and nearly every other state visited, passed resolutions demanding the right of petition, and expressed opposition to the admission of Texas with slavery. Anti-slavery societies were formed everywhere east and west, and unpaid agents and lecturers traversed the country scattering books and pamphlets and challenging in debate. The anti-slavery leaders soon saw their disadvantage in not having representation in Congress."[27]

Soon John Quincy Adams was elected, along with William Slade, of Vermont; Benjamin Wade and J. R. Giddings, of Ohio; John P. Hale, of New Hampshire; and Seth M. Gates, of New York. "With such men as these in the front and the determined efforts of statesmen to strengthen their lines," commented Van Buren, "the great battle was fully on in 'the repeal of the Missouri compromise' measures, and never again settled until the surrender of Appomattox."[28]

The difficulties the abolitionists faced were exacerbated by attitudes of important politicians like Henry Clay who feared public unrest and attempted to dissuade Birney and other leaders. Aaron Burr, Revolutionary War hero and former vice president under Thomas Jefferson, who had supported emancipation in New York in 1784, visited Garrison in Boston sometime in 1831–1832. Burr, now a seventy-six-year-old New York lawyer, had been discredited over his grandiose schemes and the dueling death of Alexander Hamilton and now tried to dissuade Garrison from publishing his *Liberator,* an abolitionist newspaper that had only recently gone into publication, "skillfully setting forth the hopelessness of my object, the perils to which I should be subjected, the dangers of a general emancipation of the slaves, the power and spirit of the slave oligarchy, etc., etc. Yet I do not remember that he undertook to argue the rightfulness of slavery—his aim being, rather, to convince me both of the folly and danger of attempting to struggle with the Slave Power for its overthrow."[29] Thus, even one of the founders of the nation was still unwilling to oppose slavery, apparently convinced it was a futile effort, reflecting a concerted opinion that abolitionists would face in most parts of the nation.

LIBERTY NOMINATIONS!

Election One Day, Tuesday, Nov. 5.

"We hold these truths to be self-evident: that all men are created equal: that they are endowed by their Creator with certain unalienable rights: that among these are Life, LIBERTY, and the pursuit of Happiness."

FOR PRESIDENT,

JAMES G. BIRNEY,
OF MICHIGAN.

FOR VICE PRESIDENT,

THOMAS MORRIS,
OF OHIO.

FOR ELECTORS.

ARTHUR TAPPAN, State Electors.
ASA B. SMITH,

1 Joseph Hudson,	8 Richard Aldrich,	15 Jabez Parkhurst,	22 Josubua Copeland,	29 E. Wilbert Priddo,
4 Peter Shaffer,	9 Peter Roe,	16 Jesse Smith,	23 Charles G. Case,	30 Henry E. Badger,
3 James Kennedy,	10 Jonah Ford,	17 George Thomas,	24 George S. Kessale,	31 Constant B. Allen,
4 Lewis Halleck,	11 Alfred Peck,	18 Basil Kimball, Jr.	25 Samuel E. Unsworth,	32 Gideon Durkee,
5 Horace Dresser,	12 Ezekiel Baker,	19 Perley C. Kevin,	26 John M. Robinson,	33 Henry Brewster,
6 Dexter Fairbanks,	13 George W. Dorsor,	20 John Blair,	27 Alexander Purdy,	34 Basil Atwood
7 Selleck V. St. John,	14 George Sherman,	21 James Mercereu,	28 Samuel B. Pierce,	

FOR GOVERNOR,

ALVAN STEWART,
OF ONEIDA COUNTY.

FOR LIEUT. GOVERNOR,

CHARLES O. SHEPARD,
Of Wyoming County.

FOR CONGRESS,

ISAAC PHELPS,
OF AURORA.

FOR CANAL COMMISSIONERS,

Noadiah Moore, Nathaniel Safford, Cha's A. Wheaton, Lindley M. Moore.

FOR SENATOR,

JOSEPH PLUMB,
OF ERIE COUNTY.

FOR ASSEMBLY,

ASA WARREN, Eden.
ELEAZER BANCROFT, Lancaster.
NATHAN B. THORP, Buffalo.

Election of 1844 Liberty Party broadside from New York.

Mathew Brady photograph of Maj. Gen. David Bell Birney (center, bearded) and II Corps staff. Maj. Fitzhugh Birney is left of his brother.

James G. Birney was an 18-year-old law student in Philadelphia when this watercolor miniature on ivory was painted, attributed to Benjamin Trott. It is the only known image of the future Presidential candidate in his early years.

A mature James G. Birney, was depicted in this engraved portrait, believed to have been used in the 1844 Presidential election campaign, now in the Huntsville, Alabama, Public Library.

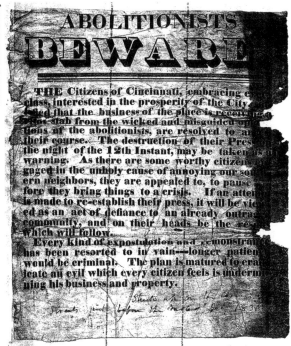

Inflammatory flyer posted on street corners in Cincinnati during anti-abolition riots in 1834.

ABOLITIONISTS
BEWARE

THE Citizens of Cincinnati, embracing e___ class, interested in the prosperity of the City ___ed that the business of the place is recei___ ___at stab from the wicked and misguided op___ ___ions of the abolitionists, are resolved to a___ their course. The destruction of their Pres___ the night of the 12th Instant, may be take___ warning. As there are some worthy citizen___ gaged in the unholy cause of annoying our so___ ern neighbors, they are appealed to, to pause ___ fore they bring things to a crisis. If an atte___ is made to re-establish their press, it will be vie___ ed as an act of defiance to an already outra___ community, and on their heads be the res___ which will follow.

Every kind of expostulation and remonstra___ has been resorted to in vain—longer patien___ would be criminal. The plan is matured to era___ icate an evil which every citizen feels is underm___ ning his business and property.

By virtue of his six years as U.S. Minister to The Hague, Judge James Birney, son of the philanthropist, was featured in this steel engraved portrait in the 1894 Biographical History of Prominent Men of the Great West.

James G. Birney with respects of the Publisher

THE

AMERICAN CHURCHES,

THE BULWARKS

OF

AMERICAN SLAVERY.

BY AN AMERICAN.

THIRD AMERICAN EDITION,

ENLARGED BY AN APPENDIX.

NEWBURYPORT:
PUBLISHED BY CHARLES WHIPPLE.
1842.

James G. Birney's personal copy of his pamphlet criticizing churches and ministers for supporting slavery.

Capt. James G. Birney IV was a 19-year-old lieutenant in the Michigan cavalry perhaps on leave or detached duty when this photograph was taken in New York. Along with a photo of his wife, Mary D. Deuel of New York, the photo was part of an album of the U.S. Colored Troops who served on the Texas frontier after the Civil War. Birney was an officer with the 9th U.S. Cavalry.

Lee Oskar Lawrie's striking bronze sculpture in a niche at the granite Pennsylvania State Memorial at Gettysburg in tribute to Maj. Gen. David Bell Birney. It is one of eight such likenesses honoring key generals in the pivotal battle although the monument is misidentified as James Gillespie Birney, his father.

James Birney Sr. is depicted in full color oil painting by an unknown artist. The painting hangs in the hallway at Woodlawn, the former Birney estate in Danville, Kentucky. The stately, pillared onetime Birney home is now owned by a non-profit group serving children.

Brig. Gen. William Birney, seated right, with staff during five month summer Florida campaign in 1864. Photo reportedly was taken in Jacksonville. Other officers are identified as Capt. Lewis Ledyard Wild, Lt. Quartermaster D.V. Purington and another lieutenant identified only as Boteler.

The Philanthropist.

First issue of anti-slavery newspaper The Philanthropist, published by James G. Birney in New Richmond, Ohio, on January 1, 1836. The publication immediately stirred opposition in nearby Cincinnati.

Fitzhugh Birney as a young first lieutenant in the 23rd Pennsylvania Infantry, serving under his brother, David Bell Birney, then a lieutenant colonel.

Carte de visite of Maj. Gen. David Bell Birney from Matthew Brady photo.

Lower Saginaw, now Bay City, was a few speculation buildings along the east bank of the Saginaw River in frontier east central Michigan when James G. Birney and his family arrived in 1841. Birney's home is third from left and law office is building with pillars, right rear.

Engraved by P. Reason.
A Colored Young Man of the City of New York. 1835.

Mr and Mrs Birney
Very dear friends
We expect to be united
in the sacred relation of husband and
wife on the 15th of the present month at
the residence of Mrs Front. No 3. Belmont Row
Spruce Street above Juniper— And most
affectionately invite your presence and prayers
on that occasion— precisely at 8 O'clock

Theodore D. Weld
Angelina E. Grimké—

Philadelphia May 1st—38

Personalized invitation to Birney and his wife Agatha to wedding of Theodore Weld and Angelina Grimke, prominent abolitionists. Note engraving at top with notation: "A Colored Young Man of the City of New York, 1835" There is no indication the Birneys attended, Agatha being ill.

PART 2

The Republicans

CHAPTER 10

Lincoln's Prophet

There was James G. Birney, who did more, perhaps, for the abolition of slavery in the United States than any other man.

—PAXTON HIBBEN

BIRNEY WAS "LINCOLN'S PROPHET"—HIS CANDIDACY IN 1840 FORE-casting the antislavery position the nation would take by electing Lincoln in 1860. In quick succession Birney had lost his father and his wife, Agatha, both of whom died in 1839, but he was no more deterred by personal problems than by almost universal political opposition. Nevertheless, it took a public show of animosity from an old friend, perhaps, to push Birney into a hopeless third party presidential campaign.

The clash with Henry Clay over slavery may never have propelled Birney into a run for president, especially one that would put him at odds with his former friend and collaborator, but for Clay's volatile reaction to abolitionist agitation and personal enmity toward Birney. Apparently anxious to continue dialogue with Clay and perhaps gain his support for antislavery initiatives, Birney wrote the senator in 1838, enclosing a copy of "Emancipation in the West Indies," by James A. Thome and J. H. Kimball, two of the Lane Seminary rebels. He also enclosed a pamphlet titled, "Correspondence Between the Hon. F. H. Elmore and James G. Birney," which had been published by the American Anti-Slavery Society, for which Birney served as corresponding secretary. Clay responded with a letter dismissing the West Indies study as "far from conclusive on the question of African slavery in the U.S." He made the point that the situation in England was different, that Parliament had the power to emancipate the slaves, "whilst with us the power of emancipation is exclusively possessed

121

by the slave states." Referring to the decision in Kentucky against a constitutional convention to reconsider slavery, Clay opined that it "was mainly produced by the agitation of the question of Abolition at the North." The state was rapidly advancing toward gradual emancipation, Clay wrote, but was thrown back fifty years by the abolitionists. He denied ever favoring immediate emancipation but rather declared he had been for gradual emancipation like that in Pennsylvania, by which all born after a specified day were to be free at age twenty-eight. "I do not complain of your opinion that the election of a Slave holder to the Presidency would be a public calamity, so far as it may be supposed to affect me. I have never yielded my consent to be a Candidate for that office, since the last election; and late events indicate a strong probability that, if I were a Candidate, your wishes are likely to be gratified. But I think that your justice, on reconsideration, must lead you to question of the propriety of a rule which would have deprived the Country of the services of Washington, Jefferson, Madison & Monroe in the highest executive office, and of Marshall in the highest judicial office." Although commenting in the letter to Birney that his remarks were not for the public press, Clay delivered a speech with similar content on the senate floor as debates on the right of petition were under way in February 1839. Historian Joseph H. Borome observed that his speech was "replete with strictures on the abolitionists and on abolition. Then the following year Birney ran for the Presidency on the out and out abolition ticket."[1] Thus Clay perhaps agitated an opponent and predicted his own defeat over the issue of slavery that occurred in 1844, a defeat caused by the abolition votes Birney gained in New York.

Birney always spoke like a prophet and not a statesman, some leaders of the antislavery movement said. Skeptics of his electability included wealthy New York merchant Lewis Tappan, a stiff Calvinist with wild ideas like intermarriage as a solution to racial problems; Ohio abolitionist newspaper editor Gamaliel Bailey; and reformist Judge William Jay of New York. The trio was less than impressed with Birney's approach to politics and reluctant about his nomination as the standard-bearer of any new party.[2]

Less than half the antislavery men favored political action, and several state branches of the AASS, notably New York, Ohio, and Michigan, had voted against it. Nevertheless, hot-blooded organizers Alvan Stewart, Myron Holley, and Gerrit Smith wouldn't stop trying. When the AASS met in Cleveland on 23 October 1839, Myron Holley proposed two resolutions, one for independent nominations if necessary and a second that stated, "That when existing parties directly oppose or purposely overlook the rights of the slave it is time to form a new political party." Both were defeated, mainly through the work of the Ohio contingent and Bailey, then editor of the *Philanthropist,* which was still being published in Cincinnati.[3]

Finally the society split over the issue, with Garrison's nonvoting wing keeping the name American Anti-Slavery Society and Lewis Tappan and the political abolitionists, mainly from New York, forming a new group called the American and Foreign Anti-Slavery Society. The split in the society between Lewis Tappan and the conservatives and Garrison and his radicals led to the formation of the Liberty Party. Other leaders of the conservative Liberty wing were Arthur Tappan, brother of Lewis; the immensely wealthy Gerrit Smith; Judge Jay; and Salmon P. Chase. The party sought to broaden its base by inviting all those drawn to "Republicanism," forecasting the name of the new party that would be formed in the mid-1850s and would immediately become a major force in national politics. The Liberty tent also was optimistically thrown open to delegates from slave states, including Kentucky and Virginia, where few antislavery advocates existed and even fewer would have the courage to openly associate with the radical abolitionists. However, the abolitionists considering a break from the existing political parties, again led by Holley, persisted at another meeting on 13 November 1839 in Warsaw, New York.[4]

In Warsaw, Birney had been nominated as the new party's candidate for president, with Dr. Francis LeMoyne of Washington County, Pennsylvania, a "conductor" on the Underground Railroad, to be the vice presidential nominee. Lewis Tappan and Judge Jay considered Birney politically inexperienced and agreed that "Birney's canvass will render abolitionists contemptible in the eyes of politicians & perhaps in their own."[5] Birney declined the Warsaw nomination, not only doubting it was the right time for independent action but also suspecting the leaders might really want as their candidate the better-known Judge Jay, fifty-five-year-old son of Chief Justice John Jay, or U.S. senator Thomas Morris, who hailed from New Richmond, Ohio. While Judge Jay sat on the local bench in Westchester County, New York, he was a nationally known reformer, had helped establish the New York Anti-Slavery Society, was a founder of the American Bible Society, headed the American Peace Society, and was a strong opponent of colonization.

As the 1840 election approached, abolitionists were in a sea of uncertainty about how to proceed with their agenda. Easterners also were nervous about forging ahead with a new political party. Henry Stanton, in a letter to Birney dated 21 March 1840, expressed fears about independent nominations, noting that a thousand subscribers, mostly Whigs, had canceled subscriptions to the *Massachusetts Abolitionist,* published by the anti-Garrison crowd.

Another convention, this one at Albany, New York, on 1 April 1840, again nominated Birney—and this time he accepted. Thomas Earle, a forty-five-year-old Philadelphia lawyer and newspaper editor, was the vice presidential nominee. He had lost favor with Democrats by advocating Negro suffrage, and after drafting a new state constitution that included voting rights for blacks, his efforts were spurned by the Pennsylvania constitutional convention in 1837–1838, which restricted the vote to whites. The only issue on the Liberty Party platform was the end of slavery, and Birney's acceptance letter was in fact the platform of the new organization. "He accepted the nomination of the Liberty Party," Dumond observed, "because he was convinced that only a new political party could effectively challenge the domination of the 'slave power' and bring about the emancipation of the slaves."[6] Replacing one pro-slavery president with another would, in Birney's view, merely postpone the sectional crisis.

In his long platform letter to Liberty Party leaders, consenting to his nomination, Birney outlined his views, lamenting that opposition candidates Martin Van Buren, the Democrat, and William Henry Harrison, the Whig, were "pledging their honor not . . . to disturb . . . a system which wrests from ONE SIXTH of our native countrymen their personal liberty—robs them of the rewards of their labor,—scoffs at their right to the pursuit of happiness and sells them as beasts in the market." He complained that "a large proportion of the Whig Abolitionists have decided to support General Harrison," and ruminated, "they will do so, not because his 'bowing the knee to the dark spirit of Slavery' is altogether objectionable to them . . . but they think there are other interests of the country of primer importance than the immediate abolition of slavery."[7] It was a classic example of preaching to the choir, but perhaps Birney felt he needed to reinforce his philosophy in the minds of his supporters. He excoriated Van Buren "for the low and deranged condition of the monetary affairs of the country, for the last three years," blaming the president for "consenting . . . to become the instrument of the Slave Power." Birney had special vituperation for the Florida War, saying, "Nearly $40,000,000 has already been expended in this enterprise, the object of which [to break up a refuge for runaway slaves], is useless to us as a nation, as the manner in which it has been conducted is disgraceful to our honor."[8]

The Second Seminole War, 1835–1842, considered the most prominent of three such actions, was the most expensive of the many Indian wars and lasted longer than any war involving the United States.

The federal government had been established to uphold the principles of the Declaration of Independence, respect the doctrine of human rights and equal justice, and promote the security of life and liberty, according to Birney. Protection was needed for the rights of individuals to promote their own happiness, he said. The new Liberty Party embraced these ideas without having a coherent plan about how to get them adopted by the voters of the nation. Independent nominations, apart from the dominant parties that were considered subservient to the slave power, apparently were considered sufficient. Birney would not even remain in the country before the 1840 election, apparently since campaigning was not the traditional way of seeking public office.

Birney's main prophecy, noted Dumond, was that there would never be a solid union if the North continued to adhere to republican principles and the South persisted in slaveholding despotism. The danger was that if the South failed to recognize the superior resources of the North, if the more powerful section was stirred to action, "the reign of the conquerors would be over." Dumond commented: "He was saying the same thing that Seward and Lincoln said in their 'Irrepressible Conflict' and 'House Divided' speeches twenty-five years later."[9] Thus Birney predicted exactly what would happen in 1854 with the formation of the Republican Party leading to the start of the Civil War in 1861; it was not an opinion entirely original with Birney, since Henry Clay had alluded to the dangers to the South of attempting to maintain slave power over the country in his Lewisburg, Virginia, speech in 1826, and Birney had amplified that stance soon afterward.

Clay, who felt his time was right, arrived confident at the Whig convention in Harrisburg, Pennsylvania, in December 1839. However, he was a member of the Masonic order, and anti-Masonic sentiment, combined with the feeling among Whigs that he had made too many enemies over the years, led to the failure of his nomination. Gen. William Henry Harrison was nominated with 148 votes to Clay's 90 and 16 for Gen. Winfield Scott. John Tyler was nominated as Harrison's vice presidential candidate. Meanwhile, President Martin Van Buren was unanimously renominated by the Democrats but with no running mate.

Ironically, while Birney was in the British Isles neglecting to campaign in the United States, the election of 1840 marked the first of the more aggressive campaigns featuring slogans, songs, and campaign promotional paraphernalia. The hysteria created by Harrison supporters was orchestrated around the slogan "Tippecanoe and Tyler, Too," recalling the battle that Harrison had won against the Indians in 1811. Using the symbols of log cabins and hard cider, the Whigs used hype to portray Harrison, who had been an uninspired military leader, as a great war hero. At the same time, the Whigs tore into Van Buren with the negative slogan "Van, Van, is a used up man!" They also portrayed the plain-living president as having aristocratic habits such as drinking fine French wines and opulent living, an image that was effective political theater but was actually far from the truth. Overriding all the hype was the major issue in the election: the economy that Harrison promised to stimulate. Showing the early effects of negative campaigning, Van Buren was so "used up" by the Whigs that he even lost his home state of New York. Suddenly, campaigns had become a huge part of the American presidential political scene, and the absent Birney was hopelessly left behind. However, in Philadelphia the Liberty Party did distribute ballots invoking Birney's name along with the Declaration of Independence: "Fellow Citizens, Enclosed You Will Find a Ticket for Electors of President and Vice President of the United States: It is a Ticket Pledged to Carry Out the Doctrines . . . Life, Liberty and the Pursuit of Happiness . . . Throw off your Allegiance to the Slave-Power, and Bear Your Testimony Against It This Day, by Voting the Enclosed Ticket, For President: James G. Birney, of New York, For Vice President: Thomas Earle, of Pennsylvania."[10]

Even though there were an estimated 70,000 members of antislavery societies, Birney received only 7,453 votes in the 1840 presidential election. The Liberty canvass was greatly flawed, mostly because an insufficient number of Liberty ballots were distributed, and abolitionist voters assumed the candidates had withdrawn. Even in Massachusetts and Ohio, states with the most abolitionists, Birney received less than 1 percent of the vote. The puny vote for the Liberty Party was illustrated by the turnout in Medford, Massachusetts, a Boston suburb. J. C. Furnas reported that the only three votes in Medford for Birney were from George L. Stearns, a wealthy Boston merchant who was married to a niece of "lady abolitionist" Lydia Maria Child; a local carpenter; and a watchman at the oil mill, an eccentric who loved to drink linseed oil.[11]

Prophets, as history has proven, are often voices crying in the wilderness, and that was Birney's fate as well. Unfortunately, neither the North nor the South was ready to listen to the prophet in 1840. Despite his stated efforts to "save the South," events were set in train that would lead to its destruction. That year not only marked the first antislavery campaign for the presidency, but it also was the year that Abraham Lincoln's fervor for higher political office began to boil, according to his law partner, William Herndon, who was quoted as saying, "Mr. Lincoln told me that his ideas of something burst in him in 1840."[12] Presidential politics undoubtedly would have been part of Springfield, Illinois, social talk in those heady political days. Lincoln, who was highly aware of politics even as a young man, undoubtedly knew about Birney and his abolitionist aims in running for president. The two men had a common relative by marriage, Ninian W. Edwards, governor of

Illinois, whom Birney had criticized for failing to take a stand against slavery in discussion of a proposed Illinois state constitutional convention in 1824. Lincoln had served in the Illinois legislature with the governor's son, also named Ninian W. Edwards, a fellow member of the "Long Nine," a group of Whigs so named because of their larger stature. Whatever Lincoln thought of Birney's futile quest to end slavery through a third-party presidential bid, twenty years later Lincoln would become the fifth antislavery standard-bearer as a Republican in a presidential race.

Birney's 1840 "campaign" in the British Isles after the first World Anti-Slavery Convention, held in London, extended to a speaking tour that sought to establish greater understanding of the evils of American slavery and support from Britons for abolition in America. It was an effort that perhaps had long-term effect. Birney traveled with Henry Stanton and his new wife, Elizabeth Cady Stanton, an aggressive leader of the women's suffrage movement, as part of an American delegation of forty. Birney's travels in England, Scotland, and Ireland were the subject of brief notes that survive in a small notebook with a brown cover. Scribbled in pencil and faded with the years, the notes mainly indicate the stops, along with a few mentions of the individuals he met and, in some cases, reflections on the places where he spoke at antislavery meetings. The Clements Library archives also include a copy of the ticket purchased in advance from the Great Western Steam Ship Company, offices at 35 Prince Street, Bristol. According to the ticket information, Birney paid forty-five guineas for round-trip fare and sleeping berth ("No. 3") and one guinea steward's fee for passage on the *Great Western* from New York on the voyage commencing on 7 May 1840. The ship actually left 11 May and landed at Torquay on 1 June.[13]

Elizabeth Cady Stanton's *Reminiscences,* published in 1898, gives insight into Birney's personality, character, and attitude at the time. "James G. Birney, the anti-slavery nominee for the presidency of the United States, joined us in New York, and was a fellow-passenger on the *Montreal* for England," she recalled. "He and my husband were delegates to the World Anti-slavery Convention, and both interested themselves in my anti-slavery education. They gave me books to read, and, as we paced the deck day by day, the question was the chief theme of our conversation."[14]

Birney no doubt believed he was doing the right thing by making the pilgrimage to a nation where slavery had been ended by governmental action. The humanitarian aspect was paramount in Britain, where Parliament had passed the Abolition of Slavery Act in 1833. The measure was a culmination of years of work by abolitionists led by William Wilberforce, who died soon after the act was adopted. The British measure was significant in that:

- All slaves under the age of six were immediately freed;
- Slaves over age six were paid wages for one-quarter of the time they worked, then freed after four years;
- Slave owners were paid a total of 20 million pounds compensation for "losing" their property.

Birney was not a supporter of women's suffrage, a prime motivation of Mrs. Stanton, supported by Garrison and others. The twenty-two-day voyage gave the group long hours to become acquainted. "Mr. Birney was a polished gentleman of the old school, and was excessively proper and punctilious in manner and conversation," wrote Elizabeth Stanton, recalling an incident when she said, "'Well, what have I said or done to-day open to criticism?'" Birney replied, "'You went to the masthead in a chair, which I think is very unladylike. I heard you call your husband "Henry" in the presence of strangers, which is not permissible in polite society. You should always say "Mr. Stanton." You have taken three moves back in this game.'" She also made a personal observation about the forty-eight-year-old Birney: "At this time Mr. Birney was very much in love with Miss [Elizabeth] Fitzhugh of Geneseo [New York], to whom he was afterward married. He suffered at times great depression of spirits, but I could always rouse him to a sunny mood by introducing her name."[15] Birney's feelings also may have been governed by seasickness, from which he suffered greatly during the long voyage. Elizabeth Stanton recorded a memorable trip by stagecoach through picturesque villages. At Exeter the party was enchanted by the tones of an organ reverberating in the twilight at the cathedral. The group reached London on 4 June, roomed at Queen Street, and launched into six days of sightseeing at attractions that have continued to draw tourists to this day: St. Paul's Cathedral, the British Museum, Tower of London, Windsor Castle, St. James Palace, Westminster Cathedral, and the Houses of Parliament.

Controversy loomed immediately. The "woman question" caused a division, Mrs. Stanton observed, writing: "as the Garrisonian branch maintained the right of women to speak and vote in the conventions, all my sympathies were with the Garrisonians, though Mr. Stanton and Mr. Birney belonged to the other branch, called political abolitionists. To me there was no question as important as the emancipation of women from the dogmas of the past, political, religious, and social. It struck me as very remarkable that abolitionists, who felt so keenly the wrongs of the slave, should be so oblivious to the equal wrongs of their own mothers, wives and sisters, when, according to the common law, both classes occupied a similar legal status."[16]

The World Anti-Slavery Convention began on the twelfth of June in

London's Freemasons' Hall. The female contingent at the convention was not admitted as delegates, had no voice, and was seated behind a curtain "for twelve of the longest days in June," recalled Elizabeth Stanton. In sympathy with the shunned women, the Garrisonians refused to participate. Garrison biographer Henry Mayer explained the schism over the "woman question." "Birney, Tappan, and others feared that Garrison would use the women's vote to dominate the organization and fasten his other heretical ideas upon it," Mayer wrote. "On the woman question, as with nonresistance, Garrison symbolized the possibility of a more thoroughgoing social transformation than the conservative abolitionists were prepared to accept. In order to suppress or purge the socially disruptive Garrison, they realized, they would have to bar women."[17]

Birney was elected a vice president of the convention and met the Liberator of Ireland, Daniel O'Connell, and their mutually congratulatory confrontation was duly documented by the *London Sun* on 25 June 1840. The fearless, well-known O'Connell was nearing the end of a long and courageous battle for the freedom of the Catholic people in Ireland. The speeches of Birney, a former slaveholder in the world's leading slave nation, at the conference, were well received, and as a result he was invited to address crowds in many locations in the British Isles. This gave him the chance to spread the message of abolition on a wider stage. Stanton reported that Birney made a great impression on the British. "By his solid and varied attainments, rich fund of information, courtesy, candor and fine debating powers, he inspired confidence in his statements and reflected credit upon his country."[18] Stumping vigorously like a typical politico in England, Scotland, and Ireland and soliciting support for the abolitionists from the Irish leader O'Connell, Birney was forthright in revealing the brutality of slavery and received wide press coverage of his talks. He had been making strong use of his inside knowledge in efforts to persuade Americans to oppose slavery and followed the same strategy to inform Europeans of its evils.

An important aspect of his trip came in Birney's meeting with O'Connell, the Irish populist leader who became known as the "Father of Irish Freedom." Elizabeth Stanton described the Irishman as "a tall, well-developed, magnificent-looking man, and probably one of the most effective speakers Ireland ever produced. He had all Wendell Phillips' power of sarcasm and denunciation, and added to that the most tender pathos. He could make his audience laugh or cry at pleasure."[19] O'Connell had supported the American female contingent in their efforts to gain entrance to the convention in a letter declaring "mind has no sex" and calling the exclusion "a cowardly sacrifice of principle to a vulgar prejudice."[20] However, that opinion did not keep O'Connell from collaborating with Birney, who did not want the focus of abolition to stray to other areas of inequality.

Ironically, the Protestant Birney, descended from a soldier whose army under Cromwell came in the 1600s to subdue the Irish, and the Catholic O'Connell, whose County Kerry family had been impoverished by the British Penal Laws, contrived perhaps the most unusual petition ever presented from a foreign land to the people of the United States. Birney solicited the Irish leader's promise that he would prepare an address to the Irish people of America on the subject of slavery. As a Member of Parliament, O'Connell had been a leader in the slavery emancipation movement in the British empire in 1833 and was determined that America should follow that lead. Nearly two years earlier, Elizur Wright originally had broached the idea of an address to the Irish in America in a letter to O'Connell, but it was Birney's follow-up that would ultimately bear fruit. Wright had written that O'Connell "could do great service to the slave" by sending an "address to the Irish portion of our population, giving plainly your views on slavery. They will listen to you."[21] However, O'Connell had not acted on the request and did not until Birney's visit and plea.

Famed British antislavery leader Thomas Clarkson had briefly been chairman of the convention, and Birney and the Stantons met with him at his home in Ipswich. Also present were some of the key figures of the age, including Lady Byron, the Duchess of Sutherland; Lord Morpeth; and Lord Brougham. Birney presented the latter with an elaborate inkstand from the Pennsylvania Anti-Slavery Society that had been carved from the wood of Pennsylvania Hall, which had been destroyed by a pro-slavery mob. They met with antislavery author Harriet Martineau, and "as we were obliged to converse with her through an ear trumpet, we left her to do most of the talking," Elizabeth Stanton recalled, commenting, "She was not an attractive woman in either manner or appearance, though considered great and good by all who knew her."[22]

Birney didn't return to New York from Bristol, England, until 24 November 1840—too late to vote for himself. The results of the election were predictable: William Henry Harrison's rollicking log-cabin, hard-cider "Tippecanoe and Tyler, Too" campaign put him and John Tyler in the White House with 1,275,612 votes to incumbent Martin Van Buren's 1,130,333. The issue of race had begun to surface before the election when the Whigs abandoned Henry Clay, who was considered unacceptable to many Northern voters because of his ownership of slaves. The Democrats hadn't even made a formal nomination for vice president because of the party's embarrassment over the incumbent Richard M. Johnson, who was married to a biracial woman and defended racial intermarriage. But as the shunning of Johnson and the low vote for Birney showed, most voters were far from ready to embrace abolition or even moderate their racial prejudices. However, the 1840 election was a vital incremental step forward for the antislavery movement. Neil A. Hamilton, a modern analyst, declares, "Despite Birney's loss, the ideas of the Liberty Party lived on when it merged with the Free Soil Party in 1848, whose members eventually joined the Republican Party."[23]

Support for Birney was weak even in Vermont, where, although it had little contact with the South, the state legislature had sent antislavery petitions to Congress in 1837 and 1838, and women were said to have donated their jewels to help finance the antislavery cause. "In June, 1840," R. L. Morrow wrote of the situation in Vermont, "a small group of workers chose a slate of electors which favored Birney for President. Their campaign was not important or decisive. Attacked by the Whig papers as being tools of the Locofocos, attacked by the Van Buren papers as being tools of the Whigs, and attacked by the Voice of Freedom as unwise, it is not surprising that the Birney slate polled but 319 votes throughout the state."[24] The Locofocos were a Democratic reform faction branded as erratic and unpredictable by the appellation, which meant a type of sputtering Spanish match. The matches and candles had been used by the splinter group when Tammany Hall party regulars shut the lights off during a dispute in an attempt to end a nominating meeting in 1835.

The heaviest vote for Birney and Earle was in New York, with 2,809, followed by Massachusetts at 1,618 and Ohio with 903. New Hampshire came in with the highest percentage, 1.45 percent, with 872 votes of a total vote for president of 59,956. Pennsylvania polled 340 votes for the Liberty ticket, but the percentage vote of 0.12 was among the three lowest, the others being Delaware with 13 votes, 0.12 percent, and New Jersey with 69 votes, 0.11 percent. Birney's future home, Michigan, gave him 321 votes of 44,350 cast, Illinois came in with 160 votes of 93,175 total, and Rhode Island polled 42 Liberty votes of 8,621 cast. Strangely, Birney received no votes in Indiana, Maine, or Connecticut, and of course he was shut out in the South, not even being on the ticket in the remaining eleven states, including his birthplace of Kentucky and Alabama, where he had spent fifteen years and had been a state legislator, mayor of Huntsville, deputy attorney general, and one of the founders of the University of Alabama.

O'Connell, fulfilling Birney's request, took two years but did prepare an appeal, published in the Ann Arbor, Michigan, *Signal of Liberty* on 6 April 1842, titled "ADDRESS FROM THE PEOPLE OF IRELAND, to their Countrymen and Country-women in America!" The appeal was accompanied by a statement of the goals of the Liberty Party, reflecting Birney's effort to have immediate impact on political thought. Calling slavery "that foul blot upon the noble institution and the fair fame of your adopted country," O'Connell asserted, "But for this one stain, America would, indeed, be a land worthy your adoption; but she will never be the glorious country that her free constitution designed her to be." The Irish leader called on Irish Americans to unite with the abolitionists "never to cease your efforts, until perfect liberty be granted to every one of her inhabitants, the black man as well as the white man. We are all children of the same gracious God; all equally entitled to life, liberty, and the pursuit of happiness. . . . Aid him to carry out this noble declaration, by obtaining freedom for the slave. Irish men and Irish women! *treat the colored people as your equals, as brethren.*—By all your memories of Ireland, continue to love liberty—hate slavery—CLING BY THE ABOLITIONISTS—and in America *you will do honor to the name of Ireland.* [Signed by] DANIEL O'CONNELL, [Father] THEOBALD MATHEW, and SIXTY THOUSAND *other inhabitants of Ireland.*"[25]

Actually, the address was prepared by two Dublin Protestant abolitionists, James Haughton and R. D. Webb. Author John F. Quinn explains, "O'Connell, who had been too busy campaigning for office to draft a letter of his own, was happy to sign it. The other famous signer was Father Theobald Mathew, who was then leading a phenomenally successful temperance campaign."[26] O'Connell's nationwide network of repeal wardens had obtained the impressive number of sixty thousand signatures. The letter was brought to the United States by Charles Lenox Remond, a free black abolitionist who had been lecturing and fund-raising in Ireland. When Remond arrived in Boston, he presented it to his friend and mentor William Lloyd Garrison, who was confident it would break the Irish immigrants' alliance with Southern slaveholders and Northern Democrats. The newspaper explained what happened when the address was presented in a public forum and commented:

> The Irish address was read and exhibited at Faneuil Hall, Boston, in the presence of thousands. The politicians and some of the Catholic clergy became alarmed and efforts have been used to suppress it, impeach its authority and prejudice the Irish against it. Bishop Hughes of New York in the *Courier and Enquirer* declares his decided impression that it is not authentic and declares it the duty of every naturalized Irishman to resist and repudiate the address with indignation. The natural feelings of the Irish heart must respond to the claims of liberty. Although Bishop Hughes claimed that the sacerdotal vows prohibit priests from taking any active part in politics, a large number of Catholic clergy signed the address.[27]

The *Signal of Liberty* also published the "Objects of the Liberty Party": jury trials for all citizens, the elective franchise for citizens of color, the right to be heard in national councils, abolition of slaveholding and slave traffic in the Federal District [District of Columbia], end of slavery in Florida (a free land), end to legalized vessels carrying slaves from state to state, repeal of the 1793 Fugitive Slave Act, alteration of the Constitution, alteration of the three-fifths rule for representation in Congress, end to free states paying for military actions to aid slave states, no addition of slave states, government efforts to procure foreign markets for surplus agricultural products of free states such as cotton, tobacco and rice. The newspaper concluded, "We do not ask Congress to abolish slavery in the States—we wish it to be confined to the States— and the more strictly the better. We ask our national Government to have nothing to do with slavery."[28]

Garrison had promoted the Faneuil Hall rally well and the audience was estimated at five thousand, including fifteen hundred Irish. Contemporary author Brian Dooley observes, "At the meeting, a grateful Garrison compared slaveholder claims that the slave was incapable of looking after himself with England's claim that Ireland was unfit for self-government." The turnout of the Irish at an abolitionist meeting was remarkable, since "there was already widespread suspicion among Irish Americans that the Protestant abolitionists were anti-Catholic."[29]

The controversy over the address from O'Connell and supporters reflected the division of opinion of Irish in America over slavery. On one hand, they feared the threat posed by free black men and women to jobs of the Irish, which on the other hand, clashed with the traditional Irish spirit of freedom and revulsion against oppression, formed by experiences with the English in their native land. However, the O'Connell letter was a powerful message to the Irish nationwide, since doubtless many of the signers had relatives who had immigrated here. A huge blow to the O'Connell initiative came when Archbishop John Hughes of New York rejected the stance taken by the address, doubting that the signatures of priests were valid, since clerics supposedly were bound not to participate in politics, and "declared it the duty of every naturalized Irishman to reject it with indignation."[30] However, in a major triumph for the followers of Birney's abolitionist philosophy, Hughes eventually reversed his opinion and his support grew into important backing for the Union during the Civil War.

The archbishop's change of position in support of abolition was not entirely unexpected. Although he initially equivocated about the O'Connell address, Hughes was said to have written antislavery poems as a young man.[31] In 1829, during a Friends of Ireland banquet celebrating Catholic emancipation in Ireland, the recently ordained Hughes had dedicated a sermon to O'Connell and compared the hardships of Irish Catholics to the trials of African slaves.[32] Hughes's influence was further described by Thomas F. Moriarty: "At the outbreak of the Civil War, although not an abolitionist, he boldly sustained the Union cause, and was in frequent communication with William H. Seward, Secretary of State, to whom he offered useful suggestions on the conduct of the war."[33] Hughes did more than just sustain the Union cause. His diplomatic mission to the court of Napoleon III at the behest of Secretary Seward perhaps helped dissuade that monarch from recognizing the Confederacy, according to some observers, and Hughes received thanks in a personal letter from President Lincoln. Actually, by his mission to France, Hughes became one of the Union's most successful diplomats, marshaling the power of the Catholic Church in a major Catholic country on behalf of freedom. The refusal of France to recognize the Confederacy cannot be underestimated, since it perhaps helped to influence England to withhold its recognition as well.

Although abolition was primarily a Protestant movement, it was infused with vitality from Catholic sources like O'Connell in Ireland and Archbishop Hughes in New York. Author Brian Dooley observes, "Bostonian Wendell Phillips, who succeeded Garrison as president of the American Anti-Slavery Society, conceded that it was O'Connell who gave the abolitionists their first lessons in the techniques of non-violent mass agitation."[34] Southerners were irate and relentless against the opposition. Upon receiving a mass mailing of the proceedings of the World Anti-Slavery Convention, slave power advocates offered a reward of $500, dead or alive, for the head of Congressman Seth Gates, of Leroy, New York. Gates had committed the "sin" of using his congressional postage frank to mail the proceedings across the South, violating the Calhoun gag order forbidding even the mention of slavery on the floor of the House.

The sparse support received by the abolitionist Liberty Party in 1840 was a grave disappointment to the idealistic Birney, but in retrospect it was a vital way station on the road toward a political revolution of immense proportions that would be headed by Lincoln in 1860.

CHAPTER 11

Henry Clay's Nemesis

Surely the occasion for a third party in politics is sufficiently obvious and stirring. The necessities which demand it reach down to the very foundations of Human Nature, and are as imperious as the authority of Heaven.

—BERIAH GREEN

JAMES GILLESPIE BIRNEY HAS BEEN BLAMED BY POLITICIANS AND historians for the defeat of Henry Clay in the 1844 presidential race, a factor that perhaps more than any other led him to be castigated while he lived and ignored after his lifetime. Birney's contribution to the progression of anti-slavery philosophy and voter sentiment has been pushed aside by emotions over candidates and by long-standing anti-abolitionist attitudes related to political strategies of the Republicans.

According to many historians, it is clear that the proposed annexation of Texas was the major issue in the 1844 election. It also marked the high-water mark of the Whig Party, which died in 1852, the same year as Henry Clay. A Northern historical commentator said of Clay, "He was the favorite leader of the Whigs; they were downcast over his defeat and their hatred of the abolitionists was more intense than ever."[1] According to some observers, Clay caused his own defeat by initially departing from his traditional pose of compromiser to a more aggressive stance against the proposed annexation of Texas. He seemed to panic after realizing that stance might cost him Southern votes, and he made things worse by waffling on the issue in two letters declaring that annexation might be acceptable if war could be avoided. By his indecision, he no doubt made Northerners doubt his fitness for the high office. James Polk, on the other hand, played to voters' emotions on the Texas issue. Polk's political message portrayed the Lone Star standing alone against the antislavery Mexicans and the ever-rapacious British, eager to thwart U.S. expansion. That message was embraced by voters, who nearly a decade earlier had been enthralled by the martyrdom of Texans at the Alamo in the ultimately successful Texas Revolution. Finally, the rich and spacious Texas territory still could be had if Americans rose to the challenge. Polk's emotional message convinced more voters than did Clay's parsed intellectual arguments and skittishness about possible war. Critics said that Clay, five times an unsuccessful candidate for president, often lost votes by too clearly defining his stand on the issues. However, in this case it may have been his lack of clarity on where he stood on Texas. The election was decided by only 39,490 popular votes of 2.7 million cast, a margin that nevertheless produced a decisive 170 to 105 victory in the electoral college. George M. Dallas, Birney's classmate at Princeton and the son of his legal mentor in Philadelphia, Alexander Dallas, was Polk's vice president. The surname would live on in the name of one of the largest Texas cities.

The intent of the South regarding Texas, although it seems clear and long settled, remains open to some debate. There were ninety-five Southerners and only ten Texans, mostly colonists of Mexican descent, at the Alamo when it fell to the Mexican army in 1836. A South Carolinian, William Barret Travis, and a Kentuckian, Jim Bowie, contested for leadership of the approximately two hundred Alamo defenders. Southern designs on new areas for expansion of slavery may have been a prime motivation for involvement of the Southern adventurers, some historians and political analysts conclude. "Soon after the close of the war with Great Britain [1815], the emigration of slave-holders to Texas had been encouraged by Southern politicians, with a view to the ultimate seizure of the country," wrote William Birney. "In 1819, an armed invasion of Texas from the Southwest had been prevented by the United States Government. Between 1825 and 1829, five insurrections had been attempted by colonists, who were acting, the Mexican Government believed, with the connivance of Joel R. Poinsett, of South Carolina, the United States Minister to Mexico. After the accession of Jackson, the demonstrations of Mr. Poinsett became so marked that in August, Mexico demanded his recall because of his intermeddling with her internal affairs."[2] "The Texas controversy released demons that were never again pushed back into the bottle," states Joel H. Silbey in a book on the events leading to the admission of Texas to the Union. "What began in the controversy over annexing Texas proved to be crucial in framing a long process that culminated, a decade later, in a profound reorganization of American politics and then in Southern secession and the Civil War—crucial in ways that earlier sectional crises had never reached."[3]

Birney gained about fifteen thousand votes in New York; a switch of about five thousand votes from Birney would have put Clay in the presidency instead of Polk, who had been considered a weak candidate. However, the evidence seems to point more to Clay's shifting positions on Texas rather than to Birney's incursions as the cause of Clay's defeat. On 17 April 1844 he had written to the editors of the *National Intelligencer*: "Annexation and war with Mexico are identical. Now, for one, I certainly am not willing to involve this country in a foreign war for the object of acquiring Texas. I do not think that Texas ought to be received into the Union, as an integral part of it, in decided opposition to the wishes of a considerable and respectable portion of the confederacy. I think it far more wise and important to compose and harmonize the present union, as it now exists, than to introduce a new element of discord and distraction into it."[4] In an attempt to distance himself from the abolitionists, he had later written another letter critical of his nephew, Cassius M. Clay, an antislavery activist who was campaigning on his behalf, and in a third letter he wrote that the Texas annexation might be acceptable if it could be done without war. Clay's ownership of slaves and his uncertain position on the annexation of Texas did not sit well with many voters. Thus, when one of the most popular politicians in American history failed in his third and final election attempt for the presidency; the loss had to be blamed on something other than Clay himself, and Birney was the obvious scapegoat.

Birney's campaign in the election of 1844 consisted merely of a speaking tour of the East from the middle of October until early November, financed by the Liberty Party. Copies of Birney's portrait were sold at one dollar each, eight dollars a dozen, or fifty dollars a hundred. Elizur Wright wrote an "Ode to Birney," and his eleven-year-old son composed a "Birney March." Fifty thousand copies of the *Liberty Almanac* carried an antislavery message into homes. After making thirteen stops in Massachusetts, Birney spoke at New Haven, Connecticut, where his son James III was an active antislavery Congregational minister. Birney drew a large crowd at Albany and spoke in New York at upstate Peterboro, home of abolitionist Gerrit Smith, his brother-in-law, and in Rochester, New York, and Detroit on his way back to Saginaw, Michigan. Wright, reporting that Birney had infused new life into Massachusetts abolitionism, effusively described him as "the finest specimen of the glorious, erect, reasoning animal" and compared him to George Washington with glowing praise, saying, "Should he die this day, he has achieved more for the liberty and welfare of his country than all the presidents or all the candidates for the Presidency, that have lived since Washington died."[5] However, such extravagant praise would not have much effect on the hearts and minds of the American voting public, which was still basically supporting the system of slavery. But the issues of 1844 and Birney's Liberty Party candidacy did succeed in sharpening the opinions of men in both the Whig and Democratic parties who were grappling with slavery.

The issue of Clay's dueling was raised during the 1844 presidential campaign by the abolitionist newspaper *Signal of Liberty,* which commented:

> Mr. Clay had not the sympathies of the people on the subject of dueling. Mr. Clay was known to be a duelist. All his duels sprang out of his public life—from words spoken in debate by adversary. The constitution guaranteed to every one that he should not be held to account for language spoken in Congress, Mr. C disregarded this—and held men responsible, not however to the laws of this country, but to the code of Honor,—a code not known to law, in violation of it and not sanctioned by the great mass of the people. There was much palliation for Mr. Clay in the circumstance of his life—also in the provocation he at times received; still if he could not control his passions into obedience to the law while in his country's service, Mr. Birney did not regard him as a safe person to be entrusted with the government.[6]

Support for Birney came from an unlikely source: his slaveholder brother-in-law John J. Marshall of Louisville, who wrote to the *Boston Morning Chronicle* in a letter reprinted in the *Signal of Liberty* on 14 October 1844: "Any doubt as to Mr. Birney's devotion and sincerity to the cause he has espoused is folly—is preposterous. He would have been unfortunate indeed to have refused home, friends, relations and fortune, for an opinion, and to have achieved a doubtful recognition from the advocates of that opinion. Mr. Birney is well known to me. A man of more pure morality, more honest principles, and of warmer heart, does not exist." Marshall was a judge and author of *Marshall's Reports* on Kentucky legal decisions. The *Signal* commented: "We have no expectation that the advocates of Mr. Clay will retract their slanders, on this or any evidence. Their policy is too well settled to allow of any such magnanimity. But the extent of our circulation, and that of other Liberty papers, enables us to do much more than we formerly could to repel their falsehoods."[7]

According to Dumond, "The great question of the terms on which anti-slavery men would unite for political action was clarified by the campaign of 1844. . . . Birney was deluged with questions about his views on the tariff, a national bank, the disposition of the public lands, a Sabbath observance, the Masonic Lodge, and the principles of democratic government."[8] At a campaign address in Pittsburgh, Birney strongly rejected the idea of admitting Texas to the Union: "On this ground, were there no other, I should say we cannot receive Texas as a slave territory. We have no right to continue chains which we have no right to forge, or to impose."[9] A host of petty disputes led the Liberty Party to lose votes, including charges that Birney was really a tool of the Democratic Party in coalition with the radical reform group known as the Locofocos, that he was secretly a Catholic, that he was being paid to sympathize with black men and women, that he was the candidate of British abolition societies, that he was a Mason, and that he had sold slaves in Alabama to make money. The latter charge was true, even though the sales had been completed before Birney became an abolitionist and even before he worked for colonization. Garrison even got the Massachusetts Anti-Slavery Society to adopt a resolution condemning Birney for his stand against the nonvoting "no human government" advocates. The infamous "Garland Forgery," a letter purporting to tie Birney to the Democrats, was published in five states just before the 1844 election, so Birney had no chance to refute it. Democrats in Saginaw County, Michigan, had nominated Birney for the state legislature, and he accepted as representing his duty to the people even while denying he was a Democrat, which further confused the issue. William Birney later estimated that the forgery cost several thousand votes in Ohio alone.[10]

The nearly ninefold growth in the presidential vote for Birney over four years—from 7,453 in 1840 to 62,103 in 1844—reflected growing abolitionist sentiment in the nation. New York led the Liberty polling with 15,814, scaling down to Rhode Island with only five votes, a loss of 37 votes from four years previously. In between were Massachusetts, 10,815; Ohio, 8,082; Maine, 4,839; New Hampshire, 4,161; Vermont, 3,894; Michigan, 3,638; Illinois, 3,433; Pennsylvania, 3,152; Indiana, 2,108; Connecticut, 1,943; and New Jersey, 131. The vote indicated the level of antislavery sentiment in the thirteen states where Liberty votes were cast, up from eleven in the previous polling. Maine was the greatest gain, having had no Liberty votes in 1840 and 4,836 in 1844; Connecticut went from no votes in 1840 to 1,943; and Indiana recorded 2,106 in contrast with none in 1840. There were no votes for Birney and Morris in twelve other states, all of them in the South except Delaware, where only thirteen Liberty votes were cast in 1840 anyway. The Ohio vote may have been helped along by Birney's running mate, the sixty-eight-year-old Thomas Morris, a former Democratic U.S. senator who had served about fifteen years in the state legislature and was popular among abolitionists. Morris was from New Richmond, the

Cincinnati-area town where Birney had first published the *Philanthropist* and where townsfolk had guarded against threatened slaveholder attacks on the press. After six years as a senator, the Democrats replaced Morris in 1839 because of his stand against slavery. He died soon after the election, on 7 December 1844.

"The stubborn refusal of many deeply religious antislavery men in New York, Michigan and Indiana to support a Kentucky slaveholder [Clay] whom they considered immoral helped keep New York, Michigan and Indiana out of the Whig column,"[11] writes Michael F. Holt. The abolitionist vote brought antislavery politics to an even higher plateau than it had reached in 1840, even though vote totals in both elections were statistically insignificant. According to some observers, the election unleashed forces toward an inevitable conflict that had been building since the founding of the republic. The result of the election still reverberates. "Election of the militant expansionist, James K. Polk, was nothing less than a summons to the battlefield of all available pro-slavery and anti-slavery forces," Dumond commented, "because, war or no war, the South was determined to have Texas—for Texas divided would counterbalance a goodly number of free states—and was determined to have California, perhaps everything north of the Rio Grande. Suddenly, the issues of a bank and a protective tariff seemed less important. Polk's expansion policy and certainty of a rush of settlers to a vast new national domain brought principles, politicians and governmental policies to a crisis from which there was no escape."[12] Evidence that the issue of Texas was the monumental question of the era was the fact that the election drew a remarkable 80 percent of eligible voters compared with about 56.5 percent in both 1836 and 1832.

The question remains: why did Clay at first oppose the annexation of Texas? In 1837 Unitarian theologian William Ellery Channing proclaimed opposition to the annexation of Texas in a letter to Henry Clay in which he stated, "the Texas revolution was not justified by grievances against Mexico and that its real causes were land speculation and proslavery expansion aims."[13] Channing feared the annexation of Texas would result in war with Mexico, which it did, and war with Britain, which it did not, and lead to fracture of the Union, which of course it helped along. Perhaps Clay was influenced by Channing's letter and wrote his first letter in good conscience out of concern for the Union; then political considerations became paramount, prompting his shifting position and leading to his downfall.

Some influential Texans favored slavery, according to some historical reports, and author Eugene Barker has cited several references indicating a connection between the slavery question and the revolution: "In a Fourth of

July address intended to stir up the colonists to resistance R. M. Williamson, a prominent radical, declared that the Mexicans were coming to Texas to compel the Texans, among other things, to give up their slaves. . . . In a letter of 21 August 1835, Stephen F. Austin said, 'Texas must be a slave country. It is no longer a matter of doubt.' . . . On 28 August the radicals issued a circular in which they quoted H. A. Alsberry, who had recently returned from Mexico, as saying that the Mexicans boasted that they would free the slaves of the Texans and set them against their masters."[14] Travis, Williamson, and Bowie were the most active early warmongers, according to Barker. Travis was an erstwhile lawyer and sometime slave catcher who, it was said, had abandoned his wife, son, and unborn child in Alabama. Barker's own evidence of pro-slavery agitation by Austin, Travis, Bowie, and Williamson belies his claim that "slavery played no part in precipitating the revolution." Likewise, Clay's waffling belies the claim that as president he would have avoided the war with Mexico, defused the slavery issue, and so avoided the Civil War.[15]

The anti-Birney campaign began during his political career. After the 1844 presidential election, in which Birney's fifteen thousand votes in New York denied the presidency to Henry Clay, Horace Greeley reportedly ordered that Birney's name never again appear in his *New York Tribune.* Greeley wrote in his autobiography that he had been an active campaigner for and "loved" Harry Clay and asserted that New York had been lost to Mr. Clay because fifteen thousand anti-Texas votes were thrown away on James G. Birney.[16] Regarding Greeley's alleged order that Birney's name never again appear in his newspaper, William Birney cited as authority one Robert Carter, a *Tribune* sub-editor. Evidence that Birney was made the scapegoat for Clay's loss came with Greeley's statement in the *Tribune* during the Civil War when he wrote, "It has long been his decided conviction that but for Mr. Clay's own unfortunate and sadly perverted letters to Alabama, with regard to the annexation of Texas, his election could not have been prevented."[17]

In the autobiography Greeley charged that "illegal votes" were cast for Polk in both New York and Louisiana that were costly to Clay. But certainly Birney and his campaigners were not guilty of voter fraud on Polk's behalf. In "A Tribute to James G. Birney," an unknown Detroit author asserted, "Can Mr. Greeley be so simple minded as to suppose that those 15,000 votes would have been cast for Mr. Clay, even if he had not written a letter that his warmest friends could not help execrating?" The commentator noted that Greeley, in an article for the *New York Independent,* "takes pains to say as to Mr. Clay, that although oratory was popular at the time of delivery, yet that he failed to ally himself with any great moral question that would render his fame lasting. Perhaps Mr. Greeley, in his forthcoming work, giving a history of the struggle for freedom in America, may advance so far as to admit that Mr. Clay never evinced statesmanship in his treatment of the subject of slavery. Certainly it is true, and can be demonstrated that for twenty-four years he made no progress in grappling with the problem."[18] The unknown writer, obviously writing during the Civil War, concluded:

> Between the upholding of those principles on which the government was founded, and the mere party triumph of Mr. Clay, which will history decide to have been the most important? If the Anti-Slavery men of 1844 were wrong, then the Republican party of 1864 is entirely wrong! The Liberty party warned the nation twenty years ago of the very calamity that is now upon it. Instead of accepting their warning, the multitude have mocked, scoffed and contemned their predictions. The nation is now paying the penalty in the loss of millions of money, and of thousands upon thousands of invaluable lives. That freedom and slavery cannot flourish together, and form a lasting union is now as apparent to reasoning men, as is the astronomical fact to men of science, that the earth moves. Yet there was a great readiness in this republic of boasted light and knowledge to persecute James G. Birney for uttering the former sentiment, as there was Galileo, centuries ago, for asserting the latter.[19]

Continuing the political and journalistic attacks on Birney, the *New York Times* ran an uncomplimentary, and incorrect, obituary almost cheerfully announcing Birney's death in 1852. The "obituary" was really editorial comment. Referencing the 1844 election, the *Times* noted:

> The issue of the contest rested upon Texas annexation; and the distrust of Mr. Clay's views upon the subject induced Mr. Birney and his friends to continue in the field, notwithstanding their opposition to that measure, and the fact that Mr. Clay would certainly be defeated by their course. The election of Mr. Polk and the consummation of annexation, were consequently attributable to this ill-judged policy. Of late, it is said, Mr. Birney had altered his views with reference to the Slavery question. A pamphlet urging upon the colored population of the United States the policy of emigration to the West Indies or Liberia, is, we are told, now in press at Cincinnati, and evinces an entire abandonment of his earlier extravagances. The fact may serve as consolation for the loss of the author.[20]

Birney was very much alive and would not die for five more years, but the comment showed a bias against him that would manifest itself increasingly in the historiography.

An unknown historical commentator, who perhaps was Republican senator Isaac P. Christiancy from Michigan, summarized:

> In the presidential campaigns of 1844, 1848 and 1852 the Whigs voted the Whig ticket and the Democrats voted the Democratic ticket with undeviating regularity, although vital issues growing out of slavery and its aggressions were forming in the public mind, and the only thing they agreed upon was dislike of the abolitionists. The last appearance of the Whig Party in a national campaign was in 1852. In 1844 the abolition vote for James G. Birney defeated Henry Clay in the state of New York and lost him the presidency. He was the favorite leader of the Whigs; they were downcast over his defeat; and their hatred of the abolitionists was more intense than ever. Already the anti-slavery movement was gathering force, though generally condemned. Soon thereafter came the great political upheaval of this century; the Republican Party was organized in 1854, and all the Whigs, the Free Soil Democrats and the abolitionists became Republicans.[21]

Although Birney's candidacy undoubtedly caused the defeat of Clay and the election of "Young Hickory," James K. Polk, both Clay and Polk were slaveholders, so the course of the nation probably was not altered much, if at all, by the outcome. Clay had displayed his dedication to property rights in men in his last meeting with Birney in 1834, and there was no indication he had changed his position in the following ten years.

Had Clay become president, faced with pressure from fellow slaveholders, there is little to support the idea he would have resisted annexation of Texas and expansion of slavery.

The fierce approbation of Whigs like Horace Greeley and others against Birney—which persisted into the Republican era and buried him in historical irrelevance—appears to have been misplaced as well as patently unfair.

Meanwhile, the Mexican War gave a platform to a young congressman that was his first opportunity to gain positive notice. During his lone term in Congress, from 1846 to 1849 (he had promised to serve only one term and not seek reelection), Abraham Lincoln questioned President Polk on the causes of the Mexican War. Polk had sought to justify the war on grounds it was waged only to repel invasion and avenge killings of Americans on our soil. Lincoln introduced a series of resolutions asking the executive to inform Congress,

> "(1) Whether the spot on which the blood of our citizens was shed, as in his message declared, was or was not within the territory of Spain, until the Mexican revolution; (2) Whether that spot is, or is not, within the territory wrested

from Spain by the revolutionary government of Mexico; (3) Whether that spot is, or is not, within a settlement of people, which settlement has existed ever since long before the Texas revolution, and until its inhabitants fled before the approach of the United States army." The resolutions, which contained five other questions, were supported by Mr. Lincoln in the first speech that he made in Congress, but they were tabled. His frequent use of the word "spot" in the resolutions and speech gave him the nickname of "Spot Lincoln."[22]

The nation, and the world, would have to wait more than a decade, but much would be heard from "Spot Lincoln" beginning in 1860.

CHAPTER 12

Uncle Tom Comes Alive

*Charles Sumner said that if "Uncle Tom's Cabin" had
not been written, Abraham Lincoln could not
have been elected President of the United States.*

—BETTY L. FLADELAND

DESPITE THE APPARENT FUTILITY OF THE EFFORT, THERE WAS AN
important outcome to James G. Birney's abolitionist activities: his battles
with the mobs in Cincinnati provided some of the inspiration to Harriet
Beecher Stowe to write her monumental 1852 book, *Uncle Tom's Cabin.*
Mrs. Stowe's biographer, Joan Hedrick, explains how Mrs. Stowe was influenced by Birney's trials when both were living in Cincinnati: "During the
anti-Birney agitation, Harriet wrote to [her husband] Calvin, 'For my part,
I can easily see how such proceedings may make converts to abolitionism,
for already my sympathies are strongly enlisted for Mr. Birney.'" Her distress
was heightened when her uncle John Hooker agreed to become part of a citizen's committee that intended to suppress Birney's abolitionist publishing,
those violent activities being endorsed by most of the Cincinnati newspapers. Hooker, a lawyer, was married to Harriet's aunt, Isabella Beecher. After
Birney's press was destroyed and thrown in the Ohio River by a mob, Mrs.
Stowe was moved to begin writing letters, using the pseudonym "Franklin,"
to the *Cincinnati Journal* in Birney's defense. According to Hedrick, this was
the start of Mrs. Stowe's antislavery career.[1]

Henry Louis Gates Jr., author of *The Annotated Uncle Tom's Cabin* with
Hollis Robbins, notes another connection between Birney and Mrs. Stowe
and her family, the Beechers: "Birney had known Lyman Beecher since their
days in Boston and had promoted Harriet's early literary endeavors." Gates

also notes that Harriet had been reluctant to voice her opinions in 1836 and that her brother, Henry Ward Beecher, had edited her letters to the *Cincinnati Journal*.[2]

As a resident of Cincinnati, across the Ohio River from slaveholding Kentucky, Mrs. Stowe had close opportunities to experience the effects of slavery. Her father, Dr. Lyman Beecher, had been the president of Lane Theological Seminary, where the wellspring of an antislavery campaign was begun by nine evenings of debates over eighteen days initiated by students led by Rev. Theodore Weld in the spring of 1834. The debates were about whether the people of the slaveholding states should "abolish slavery immediately" or support the American Colonization Society. Half a century later one of the former Lane students, Rev. Huntington Lyman, of Cortland, New York, recalled the student "rebels" and the debates as well as their influence. "James G. Birney, a slaveholder and secretary of the Kentucky Colonization Society, whose conscience had been awakened, appeared at the seminary," Lyman wrote. "The enlightened students took him in and expounded unto him the way of God more perfectly. Every day brought its advance."[3] Harriet was no doubt disappointed in her father's lack of courage in the face of negative public reaction to the debates. "A revival spirit swept the campus; students experienced a personal conviction of the guilt of slavery and were converted to the idea of abolition," recalled historian Fladeland. "Excitement grew so intense that President Lyman Beecher, fearful of repercussions against such radicalism, tried to discipline the students for introducing seditious ideas into the college."[4]

A former slave from Arkansas, James Bradley, who had bought his own freedom, was a member of Lane Theological Seminary's first class of forty students, and Dr. Beecher had written to Arthur Tappan stating his views on admitting Negro students: "'We have taken,' he says, April 23, 1833, 'no order on the subject, as none is needed, and I trust never will be. Our only qualifications for admission to the seminary are *qualifications* intellectual, moral, and religious, without reference to color, which I have no reason to think would have any influence here, certainly never with my consent.'"[5] The seminary's open admission policy was all the more notable since sons of slaveholders from the South were among its students. The powerful effect of the debates showed as one slaveholding scion, "who had come to the seminary relying upon the hire of his slaves to carry him through his theological course, went home and emancipated his slaves and put himself to expense for their benefit," recalled Lyman.[6] Despite his willingness to admit black students to the seminary, Lyman Beecher's fear of offending the local establishment showed he had backslid since 1820 when he preached antislavery sermons during the debate on whether Missouri should be admitted as a slave or free state. But at the time of the Missouri antislavery sermons, he was in Litchfield, Connecticut, insulated from Southern disfavor, and in 1834 he was in Cincinnati, which was vastly more affected by the slave power.

Theodore Weld emerged as a titan from the debates, revealing his complete grasp of the subject of slavery as he held the floor for nearly eighteen of the total twenty-two and a half hours of the discussions. Reverend Lyman recalled: "His speech was a thesaurus, giving the origin, history, effects, both upon the despot and the victim, of slavery. When the debate ended, it was found that we were prepared to take decided ground. We were for immediate emancipation by a most decisive majority."[7] If Lyman's recollection was correct, Weld's domination of the debates would have been a marvel; he would have spoken for more than 90 percent of the time the sessions lasted, or at least two hours each night. Later commentators would observe that the Lane debates were more like antislavery rallies.

The fire of conversion also consumed James A. Thome, a wealthy student from Augusta, Kentucky, whose father, Arthur, operated a flour mill with slave labor. Thome was invited to speak at the annual meeting of the American Anti-Slavery Society in New York and "made a very powerful impression upon the public mind," wrote Garrison in the preface to a pamphlet reprinting the speech. Thome posed a thesis later followed up by Mrs. Stowe: "Come and tell us what shocking scenes are transpiring in our own families under the cover of night. Go with us into our kitchens and lift up the horrid veil; show us the contamination, as it issues thence and wraps its loathsome folds about our sons and daughters."[8]

That was exactly what *Uncle Tom's Cabin* did, weaving the naked facts about slavery into a novel of life in the South "among the lowly." Readers got to know the characters of Eliza, Uncle Tom and Aunt Chloe, George Harris, Pearl, and Little Jim Crow, contrasted with slave owners Mr. and Mrs. Shelby, the slave dealer Haley, and the slave driver Simon Legree. Dramatic tableaus like Tom's being sold down the river and Eliza's escape across the river on ice floes were powerful images that quickly became part of the American literary and emotional lexicon. Negro figures who demonstrated sympathetic feelings toward family members and Christian affinity created intimacy and understanding in a way no other medium could have among white readers. The fact that "Tom shows" continued for decades after the Civil War demonstrates the overwhelming interest and appeal of the story to Northern whites, most of whom had little close experience with Negro culture. The fact that the novel is set in Kentucky, described by the narrator as a place where "perhaps the mildest form of the system of slavery is to be seen," and where quiet agricultural pursuits "makes the task of the Negro a more healthful and reasonable one," recalls the temporizing attitudes of Sen. Henry Clay in his conversations with James G. Birney about slavery.[9]

The Garrison pamphlet also contained the letter of another student, Henry B. Stanton, summarizing the debates and faculty efforts to suppress free discussion of slavery. Stanton also reported on an informal poll on colonization taken by one student who found Negroes almost universally opposed to leaving the country, confirming the experience of Birney's Negro friend James Forten in Philadelphia nearly twenty years earlier. The same pamphlet included a letter from one of the nation's leading clergymen, the Reverend Dr. Samuel H. Cox, attacking the American Colonization Society. Dr. Cox, invoking the name and courage of Wilberforce in England, spoke for "peaceful abolition" with the assertion, "I assume it as practically certain that the blacks and the whites, or the African and European races of men, are to exist together on this continent—till the morning of the resurrection; and also that slavery cannot co-exist with the descendants of these two races, cannot exist at all, much longer. It must certainly be destroyed—and we all *know* that."[10] Thome's father, who had disowned his heretical abolitionist son, quickly recanted and even emancipated his own slaves.

When the Lane trustees, alarmed by the pro-slavery reaction, issued Draconian laws abolishing antislavery societies and banning public communication among students "without leave of the faculty," the students revolted and quit the school. In a deserted brick tavern five miles away, "we set up a seminary of our own and became a law unto ourselves," Lyman wrote. "It was desirable that we remain near to Cincinnati for a season, as we were there teaching in evening schools for the colored people of that city."[11] Lane was finished as a school when most of the students moved to Oberlin College, another Ohio institution, to complete their religious education the following year. The debates and the pro-slavery reaction had wrecked the Lane Seminary, but the series of events in Cincinnati set the stage for the next acts in the epic drama starring Birney, Weld, and especially Mrs. Stowe. Oberlin became the nation's first and only fully integrated college campus, admitting both women and blacks. The Oberlin Anti-Slavery Society was established by students and faculty who joined the abolitionist Liberty Party and, later, the antislavery Free Soil and Republican parties. Oberlin's antislavery zeal spread north to the University of Michigan, as well as east to Dartmouth, Williams, and other colleges.

Thome, the young former slaveholding Kentuckian, was one of thirty-one Lane students who went to Oberlin. After graduation, Reverend Thome became one of the agents of the American Anti-Slavery Society whom Weld called the "Seventy Apostles" after a biblical group spoken of in the gospel of Luke 10:1–12. In 1836 Thome was sent along with J. Horace Kimball to the West Indies to report on the effects of emancipation on the Negroes after the experience of three years of freedom. The result was a report that Weld rewrote and Birney published in a widely circulated book through the society proving that Negroes could be self-sufficient without the need for an apprentice system or other preparation for freedom.[12] The apostles were sent out across the nation to spread the gospel of abolition and to change public attitudes about slavery and the capability of Negroes through religion, journalism, and an early version of mass marketing through pamphlet distribution and verbal persuasion. "In the Anglo-American world the success of the abolitionist movement turned on its ability to rally public opinion to its cause," writes R. J. M. Blackett. "In fact, it can be argued that abolitionists were the first to recognize the extent to which public pressure, organized and sustained over time, could influence government policy."[13]

However, despite the progress of the abolitionist organizations, in light of the Compromise of 1850 and a new fugitive slave law, orchestrated by Henry Clay, Birney was rapidly losing faith that the movement could succeed in producing freedom for slaves. In his diary entry of 27 November 1851, he recounted a visit to his son James III in Cincinnati:

> James read part of my plan showing what the colored people under their circumstances ought to do [move to Liberia] but it appears to have been relished very little. That they will ultimately be forced out of the country and that they will in the end find it best to go to Liberia, I have no doubt. Passion may postpone it for a time, but reason will confirm it as the best thing that they can do. The fact that we have reduced to the most abject condition millions of those amongst us—that we have deprived of freedom and its attendant enjoyments, those whom we declared inalienably entitled to them by the very words which we first spoke on organizing our national independence; the fact that while the slaveholders, like the soldiers of the camp, hold the slaves in bonds and make them work for nothing, we, of the free states, stand as their sentries.[14]

However, neither Birney nor anyone else could have predicted the effects of Harriet Beecher Stowe's emotional novel about slavery that was soon to be published. The Harriet Beecher Stowe Center states: "All of Lyman [Beecher]'s children carried out Lyman's commitment to their religion, but in a new way. They thought of God as much more loving and forgiving, and believed that the best way of serving God was to take action in society to make a better world. . . . Harriet was one of eleven brothers and sisters, many of whom became famous reformers."[15]

Calvin E. Stowe was a professor at Lane when Harriett Beecher met and married him. Five of their six children were born in Cincinnati. The Fugitive Slave Act that was passed by Congress in 1850 made it a crime for citizens of free states to aid runaway slaves and stoked Harriet's passion to write the book. Calvin moved the family to Brunswick, Maine, where he taught at his alma mater, Bowdoin College, and Harriet wrote most of *Uncle Tom's Cabin.* Fladeland reported that Mrs. Stowe kept Weld's book, *American Slavery As It Is,* "in her work basket by day, and slept with it under her pillow by night, till its facts crystallized into *Uncle Tom's Cabin.* "[16]

Mrs. Stowe's novel was serialized in a weekly abolitionist newspaper, the *National Era,* published in Washington, D.C. Boston book publisher J. P. Jewett took notice of high public interest in the series and shaped it into a book in March 1852. The book was an immediate sensation, selling ten thousand copies the first two weeks, three hundred thousand copies the first year, and three million copies by the start of the Civil War. In 1862 Lincoln met Mrs. Stowe, supposedly with the famous words, "So you're the little woman that wrote the book that started this great war," a statement made in jest but containing more than a grain of truth. She became a popular author and an internationally acclaimed celebrity for *Uncle Tom* and lesser novels that flowed from her pen over more than half a century. Stowe's novel was instrumental in awakening the abolitionist cause. The book in today's literary parlance was a "blockbuster" bestseller and a powerful influence in sharpening debate, explaining the evils of slavery, solidifying opposition of a confused Northern public, and goading Southerners to increasingly indignant denial and retaliation. Thus was Birney's courageous antislavery stand in Cincinnati in the mid-1830s amplified through stages in the escalating duel of words that burst into civil war in 1861. The book also was a best seller in England, Europe, and Asia and was translated into sixty languages. The *National Era,* on 15 April 1852, quoted the *Congregationalist:* "We conceive, that in writing *Uncle Tom's Cabin* Mrs. Harriet Beecher Stowe has done more to diffuse real knowledge of the facts and workings of American Slavery, and to arouse the sluggish nation to shake off the curse, and abate the wrong than has been accomplished by all the orations, and anniversaries, and arguments, and documents, which the last ten years have been the witness of."[17]

As would be expected, Southern reaction to the novel was vehement and copious. Mrs. Stowe received daily hate mail postmarked from the South, but the most obnoxious was a package with a severed black ear, believed to be that of a slave. The *Charleston Mercury* commented with sarcastic sexual overtones: "Now we shall be in dread that Aunt Harriet Beecher Stowe will some of these days lead down into the sunny cotton fields of the South, a host of Massachusetts young women, armed with broomsticks, to rescue from captivity the dark skinned George Harrises, whom she has so elegantly described in *Uncle Tom's Cabin,* as more beautiful, brave, gallant, liberal, intelligent, and moral than their masters." Chivalrous men had been replaced with women "who had seized the lance," in the *Mercury* writer Edwin De Leon's view. The *Mercury* also made a startling admission about why abolitionist exertions had failed to warm the cold heart of the slave power: "The incessant assaults on slavery, made by the North on the South for the last twenty years, have undoubtedly tended to increase rather than diminish the evils of slavery. Slaveholders have considered it necessary to adopt more stringent precautions than before. And the education of slaves has been circumscribed or prohibited, lest learning to read and write, they should be excited by incendiary papers, and be able to concoct plans of insurrection. The intercourse of slaves with each other, has been restricted for the same reason."[18]

From the time of its publication to the Civil War, twenty-seven proslavery works were written in response to Stowe's novel, Thomas F. Gossett points out. Some of these works defended the plantation as a good place, and others attacked the North for its treatment of the working class ("white slaves"). A common theme was depicting blacks as happy in slavery and/or unfit for freedom. None of these opposition works rivaled the overwhelming success of Stowe's book, but some were moderately popular.[19] A Michigan historian commented:

> Every great movement has its bible—is voiced in literature. Some one gives utterance to the formative sentiment of the time when great historic upheavals come and hastens their culmination. Thus, Harriet Beecher Stowe's undying story, weaving the actual incidents of life among the lowly and the oppressed into the attractive form of a novel, became at once, on its appearance in a book, the gospel of the anti-slavery dispensation. It stirred the hearts of men and women to their depths, and profound convictions of the moral wrong and political degradation of slavery broke the crust of conservatism and destroyed that reverence for the compromises of the constitution upon which manhunting and man-stealing rested for more than half a century.

The commentator called Mrs. Stowe's work "a book that still lives because in portraying a great wrong it appealed to the moral natures of men and women at a crucial period of American history and is as perennial as the desire for liberty and immortal as human rights.[20]

Mrs. Stowe used Birney's pamphlet *American Churches: The Bulwarks of American Slavery*, regarding the pro-slavery stand of churches and ministers, in her *Key to Uncle Tom's Cabin* issued in response to Southern criticism. As Southern reaction to the book mounted, Rev. Leonard Woolsey Bacon, on behalf of Mrs. Stowe, wrote Birney at Saginaw on 28 December 1852 for permission to use his work. "Mrs. Stowe's book is likely to bring the facts upon the whole question of Slavery into far wider notice than they have ever before received," Bacon wrote, "and she must expect, in a corresponding degree to find her statements controverted and denied. Can you furnish sufficient verifications of the principal facts and quotations from your work? And will you allow Mrs. Stowe to refer to you, generally by name, as having in your possession evidence to substantiate the statements in the pamphlet?"[21] On 12 January 1853 Birney wrote to Mrs. Stowe, addressing her as "Respected Madam," noting that he was "feeling very confident that in your hands the Key will give additional force to the onset made many years ago on the 'sum of human villainies.'" Here Birney was no doubt referring to Reverend Weld's *American Slavery As It Is*. Birney mentions his former slave Michael Matthews and writes, "The Key will be most needed by those who are strangers to Slavery, but by those who have been in the house it is meant to open and who have long abided in it—as I have been from a very early age, till I was more than forty-two years old." That would have been about 1836, when Birney left Kentucky for the last time.

If there was any error in the book, Birney commented, it was too much of the *couleur de rose*. He went on to excoriate slaveholders as "uninformed, ignorant, boorish," asserting, "Is it not the tendency of Slavery to make them even more so? If it is, the Slave States—remaining such—must be a perpetual clog on the free states in their generous aspirations to a higher measure of refinement and civilization."[22]

As a member of Weld's executive group, also comprised of prominent abolitionists, and informal adviser to Mrs. Stowe on the support of slavery and involvement in the practice by preachers and the church establishment, Birney was a major influence on the grassroots campaign for influencing public opinion about slavery. However, even in the face of spreading humanitarian emotions, facts, best-selling books, and public pressure in an unprecedented campaign, the intransigence of the nation's statesmen and legislators about slavery would not be overcome peacefully.

CHAPTER 13

Michigan's "Wonderful Revolution"

*Oh, shame! Who then are these free people,
among whom one is not allowed to hate slavery?*

—GUSTAVE DE BEAUMONT

MICHIGAN IN THE 1840S WAS AN UNLIKELY PLACE FOR THE START OF a revolution that would shake the civilized world by ending slavery, which had persisted for two centuries in America. The state was remote and sparsely populated with scattered crude frontier settlements. In prehistoric days, groups of Paleo-Indians had subsisted by hunting mastodon, musk ox, giant bison, elk, moose, caribou, and wooly mammoth. Roaming the peninsula were saber-tooth tigers and huge wolves, along with beaver, bear, and small game like deer and rabbits in what had once been a giant lake gouged into the land by glaciers. The French, who had kept black and native slaves at their far-ranging forts, had fought the British for years in the "Beaver Wars," finally surrendering in 1760. The state was so remote and populated with so many natives that the British had determined that if they won the Revolutionary War, they would make it their Indian Country. Fur-bearing animals were so numerous and profitable that the British refused to abandon the state after they lost the war in 1783.

Incomprehensibly, Michigan continued to be governed as a province of Canada for thirteen years until the Jay Treaty finally allowed the Stars and Stripes to be raised over Fort Detroit on 11 July 1796. Even at that, British traders could not be controlled and continued to bribe the Indians to obtain beaver, otter, mink, marten, fox, and other animals until Congress passed an act forbidding the fur trade by foreigners in 1816. The state was slow to grow, primarily because U.S. Army survey crews had marked their maps of the land with the word "uninhabitable" because of its numerous swamps. Because four of the five Great Lakes surround and isolate Michigan, it was not until the Erie Canal in New York opened in 1825, opening a pathway from Albany to Buffalo on Lake Erie, that Michigan's population began to grow. The newcomers included egalitarian, independent easterners and foreign immigrants who knew nothing of slavery and rejected the authoritarian social ideas that were prevalent in the South. Thus was the way prepared for Michigan to be the wellspring of what Lincoln later called "a rebirth of liberty."

Michigan had been only a little more supportive than the rest of the country of New Yorker Birney's Liberty Party candidacy in 1840, giving him only 321 votes, less than a quarter of 1 percent of the total state vote for president of 43,969. His 7,453 votes nationwide amounted to just .03 percent of the total vote of 2,411,187. The nation, even in the North, was far from ready to seriously consider a candidate who advocated abolition of slavery.

Distressed after receiving tepid support for his antislavery message and achieving poor results in the election of 1840, Birney sought a place of exile but also one that offered opportunity to profit in land and recoup losses incurred down South. He had invested in land in Ohio and Indiana and considered moves to each of those states, along with Illinois. Then his old friend from Princeton, Dr. Daniel Fitzhugh, a physician, member of the New York legislature, and land speculator, not only interested him in land in Michigan but also in his sister, Elizabeth, a thirty-eight-year-old spinster. Birney had first met Elizabeth while visiting Gerrit Smith, the wealthy upstate New Yorker and leading abolitionist who was married to Elizabeth's sister. Birney and Elizabeth married in early 1841, and along with four of his six children, they moved to Saginaw, Michigan, in 1842.

Michigan was wilderness; French writers Alexis de Tocqueville and Gustave de Beaumont had visited Saginaw in July 1830, finding little but a few Indians, mosquitoes, and snakes, as they wrote in their famous report, *Democracy in America*. The Frenchmen were lawyers studying the American penal system for the monarch Louis-Philippe. Their nine-month trip broadened their study and report to a comprehensive social commentary that included Tocqueville's conclusion: "The most formidable evil threatening the future of the United States is the presence of the blacks on their soil. The greatest American tasks—and failures—have been in expressing the solicitude, what solicitude there is, of the conquering white race toward people of color."[1] Beaumont later wrote the novel *Marie; or, Slavery in the United States,* a social critique about the condition of slaves in Jacksonian America. In it he explored "the reconciliation of American democratic ideals with racism and slavery." When he and Beaumont arrived in America, the country was experiencing a unique three-pronged upheaval: the abolitionist movement was developing even as the cotton economy was demanding more slaves, and President Andrew Jackson was pushing a more aggressive policy of Indian removal.

Beaumont underestimated the reaction of pro-slavery forces to the abolitionists, Gerard Fergerson writes in a new introduction to the 1999 reprint of Beaumont's novel. The story takes the star-crossed couple, the "tragic mulatto" Marie and her lover, Ludovic, a French visitor (perhaps Beaumont himself) to Michigan on their futile quest to marry. Marie's brother George is killed when he joins with Native Americans and escaped slaves to resist Indian removal by the government aimed at easing westward expansion. When Marie dies from a strange fever in Michigan, Ludovic retreats to the woods in grief. The novel cautions against mob law and racial persecution and tyranny by the majority. It was a little-noticed insight comparable to the comprehensive analysis about America that made Tocqueville famous. Fergerson notes a telling assessment by Beaumont, who wrote, "the laws of the United States guarantee an equality which is not found in reality." Fergerson points out that a "sanitized" version of Tocqueville's *Democracy* was widely distributed while *Marie* went through five editions and won literary awards in France but was unknown in the United States. He comments, "This is not to mention that between 1831, when Beaumont first arrived in the United States, and 1958, which marked the appearance of the first English translation, interracial marriages were illegal in virtually every state in the south."[2]

The status of race relations in the United States and other factors reported in *Democracy in America* were reviewed 150 years later by Richard Reeves, a former *New York Times* reporter and syndicated political columnist, who was commissioned by the publishing firm of Simon and Schuster to retrace the Frenchman's steps for a book published in 1982 titled *American Journey: Traveling with Tocqueville in Search of Democracy in America.* Reeves concluded that "the Republic and federalism are both collapsing in the face of more and more democracy—and Americans are better and happier for that." Reeves reported that a leading black governmental and business leader in Detroit, William Beckham, said that racism in the United States was "personal and institutionalized and nothing is ever going to change that." He also noted that Tocqueville had interviewed Charles Carroll, infirm at ninety-five, the last surviving signer of the Declaration of Independence and reputedly the richest man in America. Carroll's Maryland estate of thirteen thousand acres was worked by about three hundred slaves.[3] It was Carroll who had signed James G. Birney's commission as agent of the American Colonization Society in 1832. Carroll would die later that year.

Settlement of Michigan accelerated with the westward movement sparked by construction of the Erie Canal from Albany to Buffalo, New York, in 1825. Settlers, land and timber speculators, and opportunity seekers took ship from Buffalo to Detroit and found their way into the heavily wooded interior, mainly going by small vessel around the "thumb" of the state, which juts into Lake Huron. By the time Birney and his family settled in Lower Saginaw in 1842, easterners had begun to trickle into the Saginaw Valley, which ranges north about 60 miles from Flint, about 50 miles north of Detroit. After Saginaw it was about 150 miles through the wilderness to the Straits of Mackinac, which marks the end of the peninsula; all of that vast territory was part of Saginaw County. When Tocqueville and Beaumont reached Saginaw, its remoteness was proven by the fact they were forced to backtrack 150 miles and go north again by water from Chicago to reach Mackinac Island, a historic fur-trading and military site in the straits between Lakes Huron and Michigan.

Because of the influence of New England immigrants, who often opposed slavery, Michigan was a more welcoming place for abolitionists and liberal thinkers like Birney. Quakers had welcomed black men and women to Cass and Lenawee counties in the southwestern part of the state. Many free black pioneers as well as slaves fleeing the South settled in Detroit, a major station on the Underground Railroad to Canada just across the Detroit River. "Since practically all the early settlers came from non-slaveholding states they had very little first-hand knowledge of the institution of slavery," wrote Floyd B. Streeter. "Imbued with the spirit of equality prevalent on the frontier, many of the early settlers disliked the social stratification existing in the South and failed to see that somehow there might be a racial and social adjustment between the whites and Negroes in that section."[4]

The earliest known public example of antislavery sentiment in Michigan was in 1807 when Michigan territorial attorney general Elijah Brush, acting under the Fugitive Slave Act of 1793, began court proceedings to return nine fugitives to slaveholders who had moved to Canada. "Upon hearing of Brush's petition, several Detroiters swore that they would prevent, by violence if necessary, any slave's forced return to Canada," writes Michigan legal scholar David Chardavoyne. In an ironic twist on traditional Southern punishment, Detroiters led by tavern keeper and justice of the peace Richard Smyth, threatened to tar and feather the judge and the slave-holders if the slaves were returned. Chief Justice Augustus B. Woodward held that "the common law recognized no inherent right to recover slaves, that the recapture provision in the Northwest Ordinance applied only to slaves fleeing from another state of the Union and that the petitioners, by choosing to relocate to Canada in 1796, had abandoned any protection for their 'property' afforded by the Jay Treaty between the United States and Great Britain."[5]

The path from Kentucky to Michigan was well worn in the War of 1812, fomented by Henry Clay, John C. Calhoun, and about two dozen war hawks in Congress. Over intense opposition in Congress and across the nation, Clay and the war hawks prevailed. "I trust I shall not be presumptu-ous when I state that I verily believe that the militia of Kentucky alone are competent to place Montreal and Upper Canada at your feet," Clay said. Perhaps inspired by Clay's bravado, many regiments of Kentucky militia traveled to Michigan to fight the British. Michigan writer Ralph Naveaux estimates the number of Kentucky troops engaged in the war at more than 15,000; some 1,200 were killed and 3,740 wounded, a casualty rate of about 30 percent.[6] Nine Kentucky counties were later named for participants in the Battle of the River Raisin in that war.

By the 1820s activities to aid escaped slaves that later became known as the Underground Railroad were common in Detroit. Michigan's conflicts with Kentucky slaveholders began in 1828 when a slaveholder's successful court action was frustrated by dithering state officials, and in 1833 Kentuck-ians who had arrested two former slaves were attacked by black Detroiters. The secretary of war, former territorial governor Lewis Cass, sent a company of federal troops to keep order.

In abolition pioneer Levi Coffin's memoirs, he chronicled incidents demonstrating the attitude of Michiganians of the time regarding slavery. When a heavily armed party of Kentuckians headed by a minister raided Calvin Township of Cass County on the night of 16 August 1847, intent on capturing free blacks and returning them to bondage, about two hundred whites from Cassopolis, led by blacksmith Bill Jones, rescued the blacks and arrested the Southerners for kidnapping. A similar rescue occurred in 1848 near Marshall, Michigan, involving Adam Crosswhite, a lone fugitive.[7] Although raids by slaveholders into free states were virtually nonexistent elsewhere, those raids by Kentuckians in 1847–1848 into southwestern Michigan "captured the interest and indignation of Americans north and south." Again, the invasions by slaveholders aroused white citizens to vio-lence in defense of the former slaves. When another Kentucky raiding party into Cassopolis, led by lawyer Francis Troutman, was indicted for kidnapping and returned empty-handed, "Kentucky newspapers exploded with indignation at the 'Cassopolis Outrage.'" The Kentucky legislature adopted a resolution deploring the actions of Michigan citizens on behalf of escaped slaves and "directed Kentucky's representatives in Congress to push for stronger fugitive-slave legislation that would impose 'the severest penalty for their violation that the Constitution of the United States will tolerate.'"

In September 1849 came an even more inflammatory incident: nine men from Boone County, Kentucky, kidnapped the slave family of David Powell, who had escaped two years previously. Stopped by an Indiana posse, the arrival of several more posses from Cass County, Michigan, led to a Wild West–type showdown with drawn pistols in South Bend, Indiana. A judge freed the Powells, who were escorted to Detroit and across the river to freedom in Canada.

The Kentucky resolution "increasing penalties for hindering recapture of a fugitive slave and requiring all federal officers to assist owners to recapture fugitive slaves" led to the infamous Fugitive Slave Act of 1850,[8] noted Chardavoyne. Kentucky senator Henry Clay, James Birney's former associate, with whom he had split over slavery in 1834, was the architect of the Compromise of 1850 that included the Fugitive Slave Law. Criminal trials and retrials and civil suits over the Kentucky raids continued into the early 1850s and helped create more antislavery feeling in Michigan. "Like so many other apparent victories of the slave states in the 1850s, such as the Kansas-Nebraska Act of 1854, the Dred Scott decision and the crushing of John Brown's raid on Harper's Ferry," Chardavoyne observed, "the Fugitive Slave Act of 1850 proved, in fact, to be a key factor in hardening the resolve of the non-slave states." The South used the Michigan cases "as examples of northern intransigence and as excuses for enacting stricter fugitive slave laws, while in Michigan they became symbols of the possibilities of moral resistance to slavery by private citizens, 'practical abolitionism.'"[9]

Birney made frequent use of the cooperative press in Michigan, writing many antislavery and constitutional theories that were published. The city of Jackson was the home of the original organ of the abolitionists, the *Michigan Freeman,* a newspaper replaced in 1841 by the *Signal of Liberty,* published in Ann Arbor by Guy Beckley and Theodore Foster. An immigrant from Rhode Island whose father of the same name had been an early U.S. senator, Foster wrote to Birney in 1845 commenting that a coming edition of the *Signal* would contain four columns of his "Bible argument," with more to come. Birney's letters contain frequent correspondence with the publishers regarding his writings, and one letter mentions his preference for the Republican nominee over the Whig, as the appellation of the forthcoming Republican Party was beginning to emerge.

Abolitionist influences in Michigan began before Birney's arrival but reflected his influence from the start of his political career. The Michigan State Anti-Slavery Society was formed in 1836 in affiliation with the American Anti-Slavery Society. "Members initially eschewed the idea of forming an independent abolitionist political party. In 1840, however, the leadership of the state body reconsidered its position, endorsed James G. Birney for president, and encouraged abolitionists in Michigan to nominate their own candidates for local, state and national offices." The circulation of the *Signal of Liberty* had reached about nine hundred by the time of Birney's arrival in Michigan in 1842 and is believed to have risen to about two thousand by the mid-1840s. Most of its subscribers were cash-crop farmers, artisans, or professionals; thirty-five to forty-nine years old; born in New England or New York; and affiliated with the Presbyterian or Congregationalist churches and having evangelical leanings, according to an extensive analysis by John W. Quist of Eastern Michigan University. "It is likely that the world views of many abolitionists were shaped by the revivals of the Second Great Awakening," much like Birney, whose main difference from his new neighbors was that he was a native of the South. The majority of subscribers lived in the southeastern part of the state, with the counties of Washtenaw (315 subscribers) and Oakland (103) dominating the list. The political power of the Liberty Party in Michigan was rooted mainly in the influence of the *Signal of Liberty,* according to Quist, and in 1845, despite support from the newspaper and the embryo party, Birney polled only 7.6 percent of the vote, 3,023 votes, for governor. The previous year the Liberty men had turned out 3,639 votes for Birney in his bid for president, amounting to 6.5 percent of the total state vote.[10]

Birney investigated the Michigan land Dr. Fitzhugh had recommended and wrote to his brother-in-law in Mount Morris, Livingston County, New York, on 19 November 1841, "So well convinced am I that Lower Saginaw will be a place of some importance, that I have made up my mind—Elizabeth fully concurring—to make the vicinity of it our place of residence; and this without any expectation of ever changing our location."[11] Two of the five boys, James III, 24, and William, 22, both having attended Miami University in Ohio and Yale, were practicing law in Cincinnati. James and Elizabeth were joined by teenagers Dion and David, as well as youngsters George and Florence, in the vacant Webster House hotel in Saginaw for about six months. David distinguished himself early by driving a herd of purebred cattle about three hundred miles through the wilderness from

Ohio. Another son, Fitzhugh, was born 9 January 1842 in Saginaw. The family then settled in a renovated warehouse on the Saginaw River in what is now downtown Bay City, some twelve miles upriver from Saginaw.

The hard physical labor the frontier required was therapeutic to the failed politician, and he did not shrink from it, cutting trees, clearing land, cultivating crops, and tending horses and cattle. Over the twelve years of his residence in Lower Saginaw he purchased about 1,600 acres of land, including 358 acres at a tax sale for the incredible bargain of $4.10, just over a penny an acre.[12] This land was among large government lots platted after Gen. Lewis Cass had negotiated the Treaty of Saginaw with more than 118 Chippewa tribal chiefs in 1819. The land had been placed on sale for $5 an acre, discounted by half, and sold to speculators, who clear-cut the timber, took enormous profits, and abandoned it by failing to pay property tax: the "cut and get out" philosophy that was a widespread practice in Michigan. Birney thought he could recoup his losses in Michigan: he had been forced to sacrifice a parcel of 2,009 acres in Indiana for $4,300 to settle debts. He immediately began promoting investment in his new home territory by writing to Lewis Tappan in New York, "The place on which I live is a town site, and it must ultimately be a place of a good deal of business. I know of no place now where a small capital—say $2000 or $3000 in plain goods—could be better employed by a business man. In Saganaw City there are not regular merchants or shopkeepers—all Indian traders. Mr. William McDonald, a Scotchman in the employ of the American Fur Co. does the largest business."[13] He also offered himself as a land agent by advertising in newspapers.

When the Birneys arrived, Michigan was a Democratic stronghold; in 1836 Martin Van Buren had won 64.5 percent of the small territorial vote, 7,332 votes out of 11,377 cast. Michigan became a state in 1837. In 1840 William Henry Harrison, a Whig, prevailed by a margin of 1,516 votes over Van Buren, the Democrat, the total vote of 44,350 showing nearly a 75 percent increase in just four years, reflecting rapid population growth of the state because jobs were available in lumbering and associated enterprises.

Birney's eldest son, James III, in a letter in August 1841 questioned his fifty-year-old father's move to a wilderness area. Obviously concerned about neglecting his abolitionist crusade, Birney wrote to Lewis Tappan on 4 October 1841 about his move to Saginaw: "It seems almost out of the peopled world,—but I can't help it. I must go where I can live cheap and where I can put my boys to doing something to support themselves. I have so long neglected my private affairs, that they will no longer endure it. Wherever I may be placed in the providence of God, the A. S. cause will remain very dear to me.—To make up my mind to separate myself so far from my old friends and co-adjutors in it, has occasioned me no small struggle."[14] Joshua Leavitt commented in a letter on 18 January 1841, "It seems hard to submit to the idea that you are settled so far away, but I suppose good may come out of it, to your and to our cause."[15] Reverend Weld also was troubled about Birney's move to Saginaw, writing from Belleville, New Jersey, "I can't make it seem right for you to be on the very confines of civilization in the depths of the Michigan woods. But I suppose you have maturely considered this. When do you emerge? Or do you get no light ahead?"[16] Earlier, Weld had weighed in with, "Your description of your new home is quite a romance. In my case the woods were always a rest. Would that I could spend a week with you! Not in hunting deer by the way."[17]

However much his son and friends protested, Birney was determined. On 8 June 1842 he bought four lots in Lower Saginaw along the Saginaw River for $1,500 from James Fraser. Birney explained his reasons for the Michigan venture in a letter dated 17 August 1843 to Charles H. Stewart and Leavitt:

> My circumstances are much reduced, and to maintain my honesty, I am compelled to live in relative obscurity. On my return from England, I found myself greatly embarrassed by the failure of one for whom I have become responsible, and who could not pay, and by the refusal of another to whom I had loaned a large sum of money, and who cannot be compelled to pay. I am now here, at one of the ends of the earth, endeavoring by working all that I am capable of, by saving all that a close economy can save, to pay off what remains of my liabilities, after having, as I suppose, discharged no small part of them by the sacrifice of a large landed property that, I thought five years ago, would place me in easy circumstances for the remainder of my life.[18]

Abolitionists in Michigan anticipated Birney's arrival in the state and began to exploit his antislavery celebrity. On his initial trip to Michigan, in September 1841, he responded to requests and gave lectures on abolition to the faithful in Detroit, Ann Arbor, and Flint. Arthur L. Porter wrote from Detroit to Birney's new home in Saginaw on 25 February 1842: "The project has been started almost simultaneously and apparently without concert by leading Abolitionists in all parts of the state to run you for Governor at our next state election, subject of course to your consent. We seriously think there w'd be a good degree of probability of carrying the election." Porter displayed unwarranted enthusiasm when he wrote, "A wonderful revolution is taking place in Michigan as elsewhere. The change is particularly noticeable since the recent discussion in Congress in relation to Mr. Adams."[19] Antislavery forces had defeated a plan by Southerners to censure John Quincy Adams, who was opposing the gag rule barring discussion of petitions against slavery.

Birney's state of mind regarding the political situation in the nation was revealed when a committee in Saginaw County asked him to speak at a Fourth of July celebration in 1842. Birney responded with deep-seated emotion:

> I regret that circumstances constrain me to decline it. Two millions and a half of Native Americans—my poor despised brethren—are enslaved in this land; groaning in worse than Algerian bondage;—bought and sold, men, women and little children; as beasts in the market. The slave trade in its most revolting form is maintained in the District of Columbia, under the very eaves of the Capitol. This too whilst we have in our mouths, "All men are created equal and entitled to life, liberty and the pursuit of happiness." With such proof before me of our National Hypocrisy, I have for years declined having any part in celebrating the 4.July as the Anniversary of American Liberty. When that shall really arrive, and liberty be enjoyed by all the inhabitants of the land, no one will more cheerfully unite with the Committee in celebrating it than their Very ob't and h'ble S't, J. G. B.[20]

How wrong Mr. Porter was in his prediction was reflected in the state election results for governor in 1843, showing Birney with just 2,776 votes, while the victorious candidate, Democrat John S. Barry got 21,392 votes.

Attempting to fend off requests to become a candidate for president a second time, Birney wrote to Stewart and Leavitt. "Now, abolitionists, after all have a good deal of human nature in them," he said. "How then would they like to have their candidate for the highest office of Gov't a laboring man—one engaged daily in farming drudgery, and in the discharge of menial offices? Can they well stand it to have as their candidate one seen hoeing potatoes, rolling logs or chopping his own firewood or cleaning his own shoes? Such a candidate they would have in me."[21] But the Liberty Party faithful were not to be deterred. Elizur Wright Jr. wrote from Boston, urging Birney: "Therefore leave the City of Saginaw to grow as it may for a season. We are on the road to victory and our leader must not be browsing on the solitary and humid plains of Saginaw, among the reeds and alders and weeping willows. We want him to water the cedars which are sticking their roots down among the granite foundations of this continent."[22]

By the following year Birney was beginning to take faith in Wright's ideas, writing him on 4 March 1844:

> Even here, where you might suppose I might have privacy to my heart's content, I have not found it; nor much peace. We have a miserable population here. They would be pirates if they had courage. Their vices are lying, drinking, gambling, backbiting, etc. We have no Religious ordinances—nothing in fact of moral restraint on the population of some 130 souls that make up our settlement. If I could get away, I would. But who can control his fate? I owe debts—not very large to be sure,—and I have cattle and land—but there is no money here to buy them—and I can't get out of debt. I am tied to a stake and I must stand it—but at times it is so grievous to me, that I think I cannot stand it long.[23]

After the election of 1844, Leavitt wrote to Birney from Washington, D.C., informing him that he had read Birney's private letter "that I dare say will show his naked heart" to a Liberty convention. "I assure you it produced the deepest sensation, even to tears in many cases," Leavitt said. "The effect was deep and highly gratifying. It showed not only that you retain the full and perfect confidence of our friends, but that your services and the unmerited persecutions you have been subjected to have given you a strong hold on the best affections of their hearts. I hold you to your promise not to do anything hastily in regard to withdrawing from the field as a candidate."[24] Soon after the 1844 election, friends and relatives resumed their efforts to get Birney to move out of the Saginaw area and return to the mainstream of American political life. Leavitt offered him a salary of $1,000 a year to write for the *Boston Morning Chronicle,* which he published, and Birney considered the possibility of moving to Boston and working on the newspaper or resuming the practice of law.

William Birney wrote to his father on 28 December 1844: "I do wish a plan could be devised to enable you to leave Saginaw without pecuniary loss. You spend in looking after horses, feeding cattle and burning loses those energies which should redeem the enslaved. The age seems to demand of you the vindication of human rights—yet your free and effective action is embarrassed by petty cares. May not those cares eat into your life itself? I have ever lamented the seeming necessity which drove you to a forest life. The resumption of your profession in some commercial area would no doubt enable you to rear your shattered fortunes from its ruins."[25]

In a long letter addressed to the Liberty Party, printed in the *Signal of Liberty* on 20 January 1845, Birney vented his frustration about his low vote totals in the election, claiming that the abolitionist vote had been lowered by a scheme by Clay's friends to connect his name with opposition to the annexation of Texas. (Birney, in his fervor to assign blame for his loss, had quickly forgotten his public statements against the annexation of Texas.) "But had it never been started—had no issue whatever been joined as to annexation between the Democratic and Whig parties, our Ticket would have received not less than twenty thousand votes more than it did, and these votes would, in the main, have been drawn about equally from both the other parties." He denied being unjust to Clay or misrepresenting his private positions, "but with his public life, I did deal as one in earnest to save his country." Birney then went on to excoriate Clay as a "DUELLIST AND A SLAVEHOLDER, one of a small, self-elected and aristocratic corps, technically describing themselves as 'gentlemen of honor'—gentlemen whose fidelity to the laws of their peculiar code is shown just in proportion as they trample on the laws of every other code, human and divine." Calling it "a foreign, a bloody, an atheistic code," Birney charged that Clay had become a slaveholder "not by the accident of having slaves entailed on him—which slaveholders affect to consider as a sufficient excuse for their oppression—but deliberately—by purchase;—and this, too after he had publicly for a time, yielded up his mind to the generous impulse of the spirit of Emancipation" and instead "in effect declared himself in favor of perpetual slavery in this country." Birney was especially critical of Clay's "procuring the admission of slaveholding Missouri into the Union."[26]

The vestiges of Birney's former life as a slaveholder followed him to Michigan. He learned that Edwin, the son of his former slave and friend, Michael, was in trouble. Edwin had completed his apprenticeship in Louisville, but after his father died he mysteriously landed in, as Birney put it, "the Calaboose" in New Orleans. From Lower Saginaw in July 1845, Birney wrote the president of the Bank of Commerce, Jacob Barker, to intervene and obtain Edwin's release. Birney offered to pay, saying, "If the sum be not more than fifty dollars, I will tax my poverty to that amount, as his security for its repayment."[27] A month later Barker wrote that he had sent a Joseph Maybin, who found the boy in the Second Municipality prison, which required an authenticated copy of the deed of emancipation for his release. Barker went on to say, "There is much feeling here against Cap't I. Smith of the Steamer 'Sea Bird' for bringing him into the State in contravention of our laws—passing him off as the slave of Mr. Leach of Louisville, and this feeling is extended to the boy from a supposition that he was a party to the fraud."[28] Birney sent the deed, and Barker notified him that the boy had been released and left the city with Captain Smith, who it is supposed was employing him aboard the ship. The final correspondence from Barker came in October when Birney was informed that the captain had supplied the funds for the boy's release, incurring no expenses on Birney's account. Barker enclosed a copy of a long printed tract and noted, "I felt called upon to put forth some years since to repel unfounded and ungenerous accusations circulated against me on the race question." In the tract Barker warned that "free men of colour" should keep away from Louisiana, since "this community is justly afraid of their contaminating influence on the slaves" and had established a policy of imprisoning them for life or sentencing them to a chain gang if they persisted on remaining.[29]

Henry B. Stanton also had discussed the possibility of his moving to Boston so he could be better positioned for Liberty Party politics. "I suppose there are hardly two opinions in our ranks as to your being our next candidate for the Presidency," wrote Stanton on 11 August 1845. "The only objection is your locality—and that, not so much that you reside in Michigan, as that you are so far from the centre of the state. This objection would be in a measure obviated by your appearing at our great Conventions, such as that at Cincinnati, and the one to be held here [Boston]."[30]

Soon any decision on moving to Boston or running again for president, or even a future political life, would be taken out of Birney's hands by fate. In August 1845 in Lower Saginaw he fell heavily from a horse and was severely injured. William Birney described the accident:

> A favorite amusement of his was riding on horseback. He owned a pair of jet-black Canadian ponies. They were swift and moved well under the saddle. Mounted on these we galloped over the prairies, enjoying the bracing air of early morning or the breezes of the evening. On our last ride we were moving rapidly, side by side. My father, with extended hand, was pointing out to me a vessel in the distant horizon making her way under full sail when a prairie chicken rose with a whirr from under the feet of his pony. The animal shied, springing to one side, and my father was thrown heavily to the ground. To my inquiries he answered, "It was a bad jolt, my son, but no bones are broken."

He rode home about two miles, making no complaint, but two hours later "he had a stroke of nervous paralysis. This was the beginning of the end. For the rest of his life, twelve years and three months, he was an invalid."[31] In September, after being thrown from a horse again, he wrote to Theodore Foster about his desire to resign as Liberty Party candidate for governor of Michigan because of ill health.[32] He was partially paralyzed and had difficulty writing and speaking. He continued to write, however, on antislavery topics by dictating to his wife.

The Liberty Party candidate for governor in 1847 received fewer votes than Birney had in 1843, tallying just 2,585, but only two years later public opinion was suddenly beginning to favor abolitionist candidates. Part of the reason may have been publicity resulting from the invasions of Michigan about that time by slaveholding groups from Kentucky attempting to capture black men and women who had escaped. Although the Liberty Party faded, the Whig and Free Soil candidate for governor in 1849 closed to 23,450 votes to 27,837 for the Democrat. By 1854, with abolitionist sentiment coalescing in the new Republican Party that sprang up in Jackson, Michigan, and soon afterward in Wisconsin, Kinsley S. Bingham gained a majority of 43,652 votes to 38,675 for the Democratic candidate, John S. Barry. The "wonderful revolution" predicted prematurely twelve years before by Arthur Porter had finally come about.

The war of words, political wrangling, and armed clashes over the slavery issue were escalating even as Birney languished on his farm in Lower Saginaw, periodically trekking to Detroit to consult quacks for "water cures," electrical shock treatments, and other outlandish attempts to cure his paralysis. The Fugitive Slave Act of 1850 was a major source of Birney's continuing distress over the slavery issue as he contemplated a move from Michigan, prompted by several more strokes that made speech and writing more difficult. He had lost his place of leadership in the antislavery movement, which seemed to be lagging, personal financial struggles persisted, and "it seemed to Birney that his sons brought him trouble and worry more often than help and comfort," according to Fladeland. Doctors in Saginaw were bleeding him, as was the custom in the misguided medical circles of the day, and he resorted to electrical shock treatments in Detroit and daily cold water showers as advised by Beriah Green. Like Lincoln, he consulted a medium, a noted woman clairvoyant in New York, who seems to have relieved him only of a lock of hair and ten dollars.[33] He summed up his physical and mental status in his diary:

> Contrary to my expectations a year or eighteen months ago, I have arrived at another birth-day. I am today fifty-nine years old. I do not discover much if any material change in my malady for the last year. I do not like to go out into company. The effort to talk so as to be understood is rather difficult with me & I suppose it must be some effort on the part of those I converse with to hear. I do not wish to impose this on them. Besides, after spending some time in conversation I find that I feel somewhat exhausted & overdone. I think I shall decline it entirely hereafter. My powers of locomotion are slow & cautious. I don't think I have slept soundly for the last six months or thereabouts as I formerly did since my first attack.

Perplexed about the nature of his health problems, which a Detroit doctor had told him were "singular," Birney morbidly wished that "if we had here any good surgeon or anatomist, I would like him to examine my body when I die to see what was the nature of it."[34]

Weld had interested Birney in a communal living project near Perth Amboy, New Jersey. Fitzhugh could attend a progressive school, which Weld was to run, and many old friends were moving there. Birney paid off his last mortgage in 1851, sold his thoroughbred cattle and most of his land in the Lower Saginaw area, and achieved what he intended in his move to Michigan—profit—although some key parcels, including 116 acres fronting on the Saginaw River, were held in trust for Elizabeth by her brother, Dr. Fitzhugh. The Saginaw River land became the village of Wenona, named after the mother of Hiawatha in Henry Wadsworth Longfellow's epic poem "Song of Hiawatha." After Birney's death in New Jersey in 1857, Elizabeth returned to what was now called Bay City and sold the riverfront property to New York lumber baron Henry Sage for $10,000 in 1865, and it became the site of the largest lumber mill in the world at that time. Elizabeth developed other property into subdivisions in Bay City that bear her name. She died in 1869 and is buried in Livingston County, New York, with her husband.

Other tracts were sold to James III, who gave up his Cincinnati law practice to become a Republican politician in Michigan. His success came quickly in the Northern outpost, perhaps a result of his father's modest fame. Moral reformers seldom have been popular, and Birney's abolitionist activities at the time pinned the tag "radical" on him. However, within two years of moving to Michigan in 1856, James III was elected on the Republican ticket as state senator and in 1860 won the post of lieutenant governor, although he resigned after several months to accept appointment as a circuit judge of six mid-Michigan counties. In 1876 President U. S. Grant appointed James III as minister to The Hague in the Netherlands, where he served six years. His youngest brother, George, died of tuberculosis in Bay City at age twenty-six, and in 1858 James III established Pine Ridge Cemetery in his memory. The five-acre Victorian burial ground is on land he purchased from Dr. Fitzhugh near where his father had been injured in the fall from his horse in 1845. George is buried there in a circular family plot along with James III; his wife, Amanda; and their daughter, Sophie, Mrs. William Blackwell. There is no official memorial in Pine Ridge to James Gillespie Birney, but James III planted some cedar of Lebanon trees, the symbolic tree of the Liberty Party, in his honor.

Meanwhile, the Birneys and young Fitzhugh, in 1853, after twelve years in Saginaw and Lower Saginaw, now called Bay City, were on to Perth

Amboy, where Weld and other free thinkers had established Eagleswood commune across from New York City on Raritan Bay. Florence stayed in Bay City and married Charles Jennison, who established a large hardware business; George would stay in Bay City and die in 1856 of tuberculosis at age twenty-four. Dion stayed in Saginaw, married, and became a druggist; David was practicing law in Philadelphia where William was editing a newspaper; a daughter born to Elizabeth had died at age three in 1846. The Michigan adventure was over. Eagleswood would be Birney's last home.

CHAPTER 14

Flight to Eagleswood

*Despite the service of slaves in patriot military forces
and their work on the home front, the 1776 Constitution
of the State of New Jersey did not abolish slavery.*

—NEW JERSEY WOMEN'S HISTORY, RUTGERS UNIVERSITY

IT WAS AN IRONIC TWIST OF HISTORY THAT PLACED ONE OF THE
nation's leading abolitionists, James G. Birney, at Perth Amboy, New Jersey, which had been the state's leading port for the slave trade. And that irony was compounded after his death when two of radical abolitionist John Brown's accomplices in the raid on Harper's Ferry, Virginia, were buried there. One of Brown's most vocal supporters, transcendentalist author and poet Henry David Thoreau, also came to Perth Amboy to do surveys of the property for the landowners who were developing the Eagleswood community, the Birneys' new home.

Despite his failing health, Birney continued to keep up on the national wrangling over slavery. He clearly viewed the U.S. Constitution as an antislavery document. His most powerful statement on the subject of the Constitution and slavery had come in a late and painfully produced response to the Supreme Court's *Prigg v. Pennsylvania* ruling of 1842. The Court held that Congress had exclusive power over fugitive slaves, a perfidious ruling that led to the Fugitive Slave Act of 1850, which was embodied in the Henry Clay–crafted Compromise of 1850. Birney contended that the founders of the nation considered slavery only temporary, noting that the word "slave" was never used in the Constitution and that James Madison had rejected South Carolinian Charles Pinckney's idea to guarantee property in slaves in the historical document. Birney's treatise on the Prigg case was not completed until 1850 and thus was never published, because it was so long after the decision, but, as it turned out, his views would have been pertinent, since *Prigg* provided grounding for the Fugitive Slave Act, which was adopted that same year.[1]

Birney expanded on his *Prigg* conclusions in his "Examination of the Decision of the Supreme Court of the United States, in the Case of Strader, Gorman and Armstrong vs. Christopher Graham, Delivered at Its December Term, 1850: Concluding with an Address to the Free Colored People, Advising Them to Remove to Liberia." The title aptly stated his feeling that free black people would never be granted equal rights. The court had declined to hear the case on the basis that only the provisions of the Northwest Ordinance of 1787 that had been incorporated into new state constitutions remained valid. Birney disagreed, maintaining that the ordinance should be honored because it was a compact between the original thirteen states and the people of the territories. He hoped the Fugitive Slave Law would be ruled unconstitutional because it violated the right of habeas corpus.[2] On 21 January 1851 Birney wrote in his diary, "The Law of 1793 and its interpretation by the Supreme Court in the Prigg case I consider altogether unconstitutional . . . the amendment to it at the last session of Congress is so unconstitutional in every sense, whether we judge of it by the higher law or even by the Constitution, that I would suppose no person at all impartial could mistake it."[3] He further observed, "It must appear to many an odd turn of things that people should escape from this country to Canada, a province of the British, to secure their liberty, when we went to war with that empire because we had not liberty enough. But the times are changed and slavery produces strange anomalies."[4] He included another predictive insight: "Injustice exercised toward the colored people will naturally make us less careful of justice to one another. Both species of injustice will advance together & in proportion as we depart from justice we loosen the bonds which hold us together and degrade us."[5]

Perth Amboy traditionally had been a busy landing point for slave traders, since between 1721 and 1769 New Jersey placed no import duty upon incoming coffles. The port also was convenient to moving chained groups of black slaves into both Philadelphia and New York, where they would be placed on the auction block. The practice was no secret, since barracks had been erected there to temporarily house the incoming cargo. An attempted insurrection in 1734 was reminiscent of similar outbreaks in the South, as was the reaction of whites. Reports had circulated that a slave convicted of a crime was burned alive at Perth Amboy in full view of a large crowd of his comrades who were forced to witness the agony. About fifteen years before

Birney and his family moved in 1853 to the Eagleswood commune, at Raritan Bay, slave trading was still going on there. A New Jersey history project quotes historian Clement A. Price, who says "support for the institution was stronger in New Jersey than in any other northern colony."[6]

New England Transcendentalists led by philanthropists Marcus and Rebecca B. Spring established a utopian community in 1852 at Eagleswood, so named because it was a gathering place of the raptors who built their aeries in the tall trees along the Atlantic Coast. Eagleswood, officially the Raritan Bay Union, was the second incarnation of a commune broadly based on the principles of Charles Fourier, an eighteenth-century French philosopher and utopian socialist. Eagleswood was different than the first Fourierist venture, the North American Phalanx, formed in 1842, in that no member had to surrender private property and labor sharing was not emphasized. Fourier advocated a return to a rural tribe or extended-family living arrangement much like the ideas of Mother Ann Lee and Rev. George Ripley of the Brook Farm Association. The Transcendentalist idea of improving humankind through reform fit neatly with that of Birney and the abolitionists. However, Fourier's experiments at New Harmony, Indiana, a community formed by Robert Owen, with their orgies of eating, drinking, and free sex directed by a "philosopher of the passions," were vastly at odds with the strictly intellectual sharing by Birney and his compatriots at Eagleswood but did not go so far as the Shakers' total sexual abstinence in a similar communal living arrangement.

Author and poet Henry David Thoreau, writing to his sister, reported seeing at a "sort of Quaker meeting . . . James G. Birney, formerly candidate for the presidency, with another particularly white head and beard." Birney asked Thoreau to survey a small piece of land for him, according to the Walden Pond author, who had turned to surveying to supplement his income.[7] Theodore Weld, his aging but still intent visage by then garnished with a flowing white beard, directed the progressive, coeducational, integrated school established by the Springs under sponsorship of the Raritan Bay Union. Reformed South Carolina slaveholders Angelina (Grimke) Weld and her sister, Sarah Grimke, were teachers in the school. The school adopted progressive educational initiatives, especially regarding female students, who were encouraged to participate in sports, perform in theatrical productions, and become proficient in public speaking—activities that were not allowed by other, more traditional schools.

One reason for Birney's move from Michigan to New Jersey was so that young Fitzhugh, then eleven years old, could attend Weld's progressive school. Weld's children also attended, being taught by their mother and aunt. The school prepared Fitzhugh for Harvard, where he was a classmate of Robert Lincoln, son of the president, in Harvard's class of 1864. Although young Lincoln failed the entrance examination to the Ivy League school, after prepping at Phillips Exeter Academy he became a good student, graduating with his class in July 1864. Academically, Robert stood thirty-second in a class of ninety-nine. Although young Birney was reported by Harvard president C. C. Felton to have high academic potential, his rowdy activities put him in constant trouble with college authorities, and during a one-year suspension in 1861, when he was a sophomore, he joined the Union Army. Robert Lincoln came late to the war as a captain on Grant's staff in 1865, his duties being mainly to escort important visitors.[8]

Visiting lecturers at Eagleswood, including Thoreau, William Cullen Bryant, Ralph Waldo Emerson, Horace Greeley, Bronson Alcott, and others, enhanced the Union's "stimulating intellectual atmosphere" described by a writer, who noted that Nathaniel Peabody, New Hampshire physician and one of the nation's founders, became a member of the Union, and one of his famous daughters, Elizabeth, taught for a time in Weld's school.[9] Even *New York Tribune* editor and publisher Horace Greeley, Birney's old political antagonist, with whom he had resumed correspondence, showed up to make peace and to lecture.[10]

Eagleswood was a unique, peaceful community in a natural wooded amphitheater between the Raritan Bay and the Neversink Hills. "It was no wonder everyone was so content to stay there," Fladeland observed, "not venturing even into New York City, only twenty-five miles away, except on compulsion, and then, as Weld laughingly described, 'They rush through the streets with their fingers in their ears crying 'Life! Life! Eternal Life!'"[11]

As the nation careened toward war, Birney soon was dead after a series of strokes and physically debilitating attacks left him wishing for relief. The end came on 25 November 1857 at Eagleswood with his family gathered around. The Dred Scott decision, holding that Negroes were not citizens, seven months before his death had perhaps driven the last stake into his heart. To a man in his death throes like Birney, the decision must have seemed the final blow to the abolitionist striving that had begun more than a quarter century earlier.

As abolitionists became ever more desperate to attack slavery, and the South retaliated with increased strictures on slaves, the movement inevitably turned violent. Terrorist/abolitionist John Brown reportedly had in his pocket a canceled $100 bank draft from Birney's brother-in-law Gerrit Smith when he was captured by Col. Robert E. Lee and Lt. J. E. B. Stuart, later Confederate military leaders, during his raid on the United States

Arsenal at Harpers Ferry, Virginia, in 1859. With a force of just twenty-one men, Brown had high hopes for success. "Their plan was to gain control of the arsenal, distribute the cache of weapons to the large population of slave and free blacks in the area, whom Brown expected to be waiting for him, and incite an insurrection that would spread throughout the south and result in black freedom. It was a breathtakingly ambitious plan and it was doomed to fail."[12]

After hearing about Brown's raid and the arrests, Rebecca Spring traveled to Charles, West Virginia, to visit Brown, Absalom Haslett, and Aaron Dwight Stevens, two of the sixteen white abolitionist raiders who had been sentenced to hang along with their leader. Mrs. Spring was the daughter of Birney's early abolitionist collaborator Quaker Arnold Buffum, who was a founder of the New England Anti-Slavery Society and an early conductor on the Underground Railroad. Comforting Haslett and Stevens before their execution, she promised to bury their bodies in "free" Northern soil. True to her word, Mrs. Spring had the bodies transported to Perth Amboy and buried in a small cemetery at Eagleswood.[13]

Birney and Brown had gone to their graves, but their spirits would arise, and the movement they helped initiate would mightily demonstrate its wrath.

CHAPTER 15

The Republican Phenomenon

But for the pioneer work of the abolitionists
there would have been no Republican Party.

—LEVI COFFIN

JUST HOW DID AN UNKNOWN POLITICIAN LIKE ABRAHAM LINCOLN, who had won only brief terms in the Illinois legislature and the U.S. House of Representatives, attain the presidency of the United States in 1860? Lincoln was able to catch the rising tide of antislavery sentiment initiated in 1840 by Birney and the Liberty Party, which was carried on by the Free Soil and Republican parties for two decades, and in 1860 he won a plurality in an election split among four candidates. Fortunately for the Republicans, the pro-slavery reaction to the antislavery movement resulted in two new parties, the Southern Democrats and the Constitutional Union Party, splitting the vote and creating conditions that made possible Lincoln's election.

Although they had garnered only just over 62,000 votes in the 1844 election, the Liberty Party showing proved that political abolitionism was increasing the nation's awareness of the need for reform. The efforts of the abolitionists and their new political base had spurred the slave power to increase their hydra-headed thrusts to spread the evil practice everywhere, and the reaction from the North, while not immediately overwhelming, would grow gradually over the next three presidential election cycles. The steady acceptance of the antislavery philosophy of Birney and the pioneer antislavery Liberty Party by American voters is illustrated by the growth of the vote from Birney's minuscule 7,453 in 1840 and 62,103 in 1844 to Lincoln's 1,866,352 in 1860. In between were Martin Van Buren, with 291,263 votes on the Free Soil ticket in 1848; another Free Soiler, John

P. Hale, with 155,900 votes in 1852 (the Compromise of 1850 having mollified some voters); and the first Republican candidate, John C. Fremont, with 1,391,555 votes in 1856.

A case can be made that Lincoln was influenced by Birney's antislavery positions and his courageous stand through their common associate, Salmon P. Chase. According to Lincoln historian John Niven, "Chase had provided much of the intellectual and constitutional underpinnings of the free soil movement that eventually provided the ideology of the new Republican party."[1] Chase and Birney had collaborated in legal battles against slavery in Cincinnati, and Lincoln doubtless knew of Birney's abolitionist political activities, because Abe campaigned for Henry Clay in 1844 when Birney was the Liberty Party standard-bearer. Birney's influence clearly seems to have been carried through Chase generally to the Republican Party and specifically to Lincoln.

Birney had articulated the "higher law" theory of the constitutional protection of liberty for all in a speech to the judiciary committee of the New York legislature on 5 March 1840. "In one sense there are laws by which even the makers of the Constitution as well as the legislators are bound—those rules of right existing in the public mind prior to the Constitution," Birney recorded in his diary.[2] It was a restatement of a fundamental moral principle with roots in English law that had been used by the founders in drafting the American Constitution. Chase followed with a similar statement about eighteen months later. This idea was embraced two decades later by Lincoln and repeated by Chase when they both were contenders for the Republican presidential nomination. Chase had made a similar argument in an address to the Liberty Party convention 9 December 1841 in Columbus, Ohio.[3] "In particular, Chase made the argument that Lincoln and others adopted, linking the anti-slavery natural rights philosophy as expressed in the Declaration of Independence to the Constitution," notes Niven, observing, "Lincoln had been attracted to Chase's courageous battle for human rights in the Ohio of the 1830s through the 1850s. Lincoln shared with Chase a deep-rooted opposition to slavery."[4] Also, John Quincy Adams had cited a somewhat similar "natural law" of the Declaration of Independence in the appeal of the *Amistad* slave ship mutiny case in November 1840.[5]

It must have provided Birney great satisfaction to preside over the Southern and Western Liberty Convention in Cincinnati in June 1845. Here he stood boldly in front of two thousand sweating, cheering delegates, a chairman who had been threatened with death and run out of the same town nearly a decade previously. Although earlier he had been a pariah in Cincinnati, now an enthusiastic throng was espousing the same principles for which he had been scorned. Fladeland noted, "Many of the men who had fought Birney and *The Philanthropist* in 1836 were now advocating antislavery principles; by 1845 Ohio was one of the most completely abolitionized states."[6] Birney repeatedly asserted that the Constitution was an antislavery document and that slavery anywhere in the United States was "illegal, unconstitutional and anti-republican." This was his final public appearance as Liberty Party chieftain. Delegates "resolved to use all constitutional means to effect the extinction of slavery," wrote Richard Sewell, commenting, "The convention showed the growing strength of the coalitionists under the Liberty banner."[7]

After his riding accident later that summer, and fearing he would never recover, Birney painfully completed dictating to his wife and sons a long essay titled "Sinfulness of Slaveholding in All Circumstances; Tested by Reason and Scripture." The essay ran in the *Signal of Liberty* on 6 October 1845 and was published as a pamphlet by Charles Willcox in Detroit in 1846. In "Sinfulness," addressed to "Preachers of the gospel in the United States," Birney displayed his grasp of biblical lore and concepts, focusing on analysis of the life of the apostle Paul, for sixty pages, much of it seemingly far beyond the intellect of the average preacher. Stating more practical arguments in the preface and postscript, Birney asserted, "the writer does not believe that slavery can be established by any law. It is out of the power of man, as adultery, murder, profanity would be." To the preachers, he preached, "I will not withhold my surprise, that any of you should still use the Book of God's *love* to countenance the practice of Man's *hate*. . . . That we are prosperous, fifty or a hundred years hence, in spite of a violation of His law, by keeping our fellow creatures in bondage, proves two things,—the long-suffering mercy of God,—and the infidelity of the sentiment."[8] The pertinent statements in the document perhaps used as foundation stone by the framers of the Fourteenth Amendment were these: "The people are considered as connected with the government. Whilst the government is made for the *protection of property*, it must not forget its still higher duty, and the last necessarily flows from it— the *protection of persons*."[9] From such thoughts flowed the "due process" and "equal protection" clauses of the amendment. He thundered in the conclusion: "I am an advocate of Christianity, without which, I am surprised, that reflecting persons can live; of a firm and steady execution of the laws, *on all,* be they rich or poor, black or white; of an economical and just government to all, over whom we assume jurisdiction; of a government whose operations may be easily comprehended, by those who give their minds to understand them; and of a free and equal one, (with exceptions, of course,) such as ours was intended to be, when it came from the hands of those who made it."[10]

Birney's position that slavery was illegal and unconstitutional also was part of the platform of the Liberty Party as interpreted by New York editor, author, and religious reformer Rev. William Goodell and adopted at the Macedon Lock, New York, convention in early June 1847. Birney could not attend that convention, but he allowed his name to be affixed to the party's "Declaration and Reasons for Action." He wrote four articles published in the *National Era* outlining his views and sent an article to William Cullen Bryant for publication in the *New York Post*. Fladeland summarized his stand: "Birney's argument was based on his contention that the Union was formed with the intention that the 'establishment' of slavery was only temporary and with the expectation that those states still having slavery would keep faith by getting rid of it. By not doing so, they had broken the compact; therefore, the North no longer need consider binding those parts of the Constitution which were proslavery. He cited a Congressional duty of maintaining equal protection of the laws, consistent with the preamble of the Constitution."[11]

As the 1848 election loomed, with Birney disabled in Michigan and unavailable for what might have been his third nomination for president, the Liberty Party selected Senator John P. Hale as its candidate for president. Hale was a New Hampshire man, a former Democrat who had opposed annexation of Texas. Hale withdrew his candidacy after party leaders, including Chase, urged Liberty members to switch their allegiance to the newly forming Free Soil Party. Chase presided over the first Free Soil convention on 9 August 1848, and the Liberty Party became history; it was absorbed into the Free Soil Party, the transitional stage before the Republican Party. Van Buren ran as the Free Soil candidate in 1848, gaining 291,263 votes, more than four times Birney's 1844 total. Hale then became the Free Soil candidate for president in 1852 and fared even worse, many voters apparently convinced that the Compromise of 1850 had resolved the slavery issue.

Hale played an ironic and tragic role in history. A cantankerous critic of the Navy Department, he was defeated for reelection as senator by a Republican caucus in 1864. Lincoln had appointed him minister to Spain and met with him in the White House on the morning of 14 April 1865, the date of Lincoln's assassination. Hale's daughter was a close friend of assassin John Wilkes Booth, who apparently obtained a pass through Hale to attend President Lincoln's second inaugural. According to Benn Pitman of the U.S. Army Military Commission: "Sometime in late 1864 or early 1865, Booth entered into a serious romance with Lucy Lambert Hale, daughter of John Parker Hale, New Hampshire's abolitionist former senator. In January of 1865 the Hales moved into the National Hotel where Booth was staying.

By March Booth was secretly engaged to Lucy Hale. On March 4th Booth attended Lincoln's second inauguration as the invited guest of Lucy. Booth is known to have confided to his actor friend Samuel Knapp Chester, 'What an excellent chance I had to kill the President, if I had wished, on inauguration day!' Booth was seen with Lucy at the National Hotel on the morning of the assassination."[12] The assassin also reportedly had a photo of Lucy Hale and four other women in his pocket when he was killed by U.S. soldiers in Maryland after the shooting of Lincoln. A cold-case detective might logically theorize that Booth had targeted friendship with Lucy Hale as a way to gain access to Lincoln in order to have an assassination opportunity. Shortly before courting Lucy, Booth apparently had been in love with, sent love letters to, and gave a friendship ring to a much prettier girl, Isabel Sumner, the seventeen-year-old daughter of a Boston merchant, a relationship that seems to have ended late in 1864. John Rhodehamel and Louise Taper, chroniclers of Booth's writings, observed, "When the identity of Lincoln's assassin was revealed, there was a wild Republican scramble to obscure all traces of the love affair [with Lucy Hale]. A story denying the report of the romance appeared in *The New York Times* on 26 April."[13]

The Fugitive Slave Law of 1850 was the equivalent of Jefferson's "fire bell in the night" that he had heard during the Missouri Compromise discussions, alarming the whites of the North as well as adding motivation to Harriet Beecher Stowe to write *Uncle Tom's Cabin*. Negroes were now as anxious to get out of the North as they had been to escape the South. The Underground Railroad had to extend its tracks even farther. Birney reported in his diary in October 1851 that former slaves were streaming through Detroit heading for Canada: "Much excitement exists in this city in reference to the Fugitive Slave Bill. Every steamer, propeller & vessel from the ports in Ohio to this place has a large number of fugitive slaves that have resided for some time in various parts of Ohio on their way to Canada. Fear of the slaveholder & a return to bondage at the South nearly distracts them, consequently they are flocking to free Canada for protection. The cars from the west also bring a great number to the city & they ferry to Canada in double quick time." He estimated that two thousand blacks were crowding the Canadian villages of Sandwich, Malden, and Windsor, just across the Detroit River from Michigan. The Canadians were "very hospitable" to the fugitives, Birney related, the British army giving up its barracks at Sandwich and Malden and also housing the blacks in barns and vacant houses all up and down the St. Clair River. "Some are suffering for food," he wrote, overwhelming Canadian charitable efforts along the St. Clair River dividing Michigan and Ontario and in the lower portion of Lake Ontario near

Rochester, New York, and Niagara Falls. After visiting Montreal, he estimated that another thousand fugitives had reached that city and Toronto. Birney agonized in his diary: "Can the law of man be made to annul the law of nature? Is law made, or ought it not to be made, to do justice? Can it be made to do injustice? To continue a human being in bondage, or to the voluntary cause in any way of returning one to slavery must make us worse."[14]

The new law severely disrupted former slaves' attempts to build lives in the North. In the ten years after passage of the law, an estimated twenty thousand black men and women fled to Canada, an exodus Birney had observed. A slave girl caught in this web documented her experiences, which later were published under the pseudonym Linda Brent: "Harriet Jacobs, a fugitive living in New York, called it 'the beginning of a reign of terror to the colored population.' Free blacks, too, were captured and sent to the South. With no legal right to plead their cases, they were completely defenseless."[15]

Fugitive slave laws were becoming a key motivation in the willingness of many Northerners to join the anti-slavery movement and later the Republican Party. This was a field of philanthropic action that Birney had plowed many years before, with help from a lawyer who was destined to become an important member of the Lincoln cabinet, Salmon P. Chase.

Chase, Birney's old friend from Cincinnati, had taken so many slavery cases he became known as "Attorney General of Fugitive Slaves." One of his first cases in that arena was in defending Birney when he was charged with violating the Fugitive Slave Act in the case of the biracial girl Matilda Lawrence in March 1837. Her father, Larkin Lawrence, was a wealthy planter in southern Missouri. She was a beautiful brunette octoroon, and her skin carried so faint a tint of color as to pass for white. Her father forbade her to associate with Negroes, and her nativity was known in their county, so she also was unwelcome among whites. After a trip to New York, during which she discovered the power of her beauty through the attention of male strangers, she began to beg her father for "free papers." This he was not inclined to grant, as she was his nursemaid and companion. Stopping at a hotel near the wharf in Cincinnati, en route to St. Louis, she fled to the house of a Negro barber. After a few days in hiding, she found her way to the Birney household on Race Street and was engaged by Agatha Birney as a chambermaid and nurse. The Birneys were unaware of her history, thinking she was white, according to William Birney, who recounted details in his book about his father.

When Matilda was on an errand, she was snatched off the street by John W. Riley, a notorious slave catcher, who had a warrant signed by a justice of the peace that had been issued by William Henry Harrison, then clerk of the Common Pleas Court and later president of the United States. Birney, represented by Chase, applied to the court for a writ of habeas corpus and was spurned. The girl was quickly taken by ferryboat to Covington, Kentucky, and by steamboat to New Orleans, where she was sold. "In sending this hapless girl to a fate worse than death, the judge disregarded all laws human and divine," wrote William Birney. "He presumed that she was a colored person when the law of Ohio declared white all persons of more white blood than a mulatto."

Birney was tried on an indictment procured by his political enemies from his courthouse showdown the previous year, R. T. Lytle and N. C. Read. The accused spoke for about three hours in his own defense, maintaining that Matilda was in law a free woman. The guilty verdict in the lower court was quashed by the Ohio Supreme Court on grounds the indictment was defective. "The sympathy excited by this case throughout the North was one of the potent causes of the passage by free state legislatures of 'personal liberty' laws, designed to secure the right of trial by jury to every person claimed as a slave, and to punish as kidnappers all persons aiding or abetting in delivering as a slave any person not proved to have escaped from a slave into a free state." William Birney recalled testifying in the Matilda case himself and observed that Chase, who had spent many long hours discussing the legal aspects of slavery in Birney's library, "adopted Mr. Birney's legal and constitutional opinions on slavery in 1836."[16]

In the 1842 case of Kentucky slaveholder Wharton Jones versus John Van Zandt, an aged Ohio farmer and abolitionist charged with harboring fugitives for transporting escapees, Chase repeated Birney's principle of natural law and laid down a challenge that struck to the heart of the Fugitive Slave Law of 1793: "The law of the Creator, which invests every human being with an inalienable title to freedom, cannot be repealed by any inferior law which asserts that man is property. . . . The very moment a slave passes beyond the jurisdiction of the state, in which he is held as such, he ceases to be a slave; not because any law or regulation of the state which he enters confers freedom upon him, but because he *continues* to be a man and *leaves behind* him the law of force, which made him a slave."[17] Van Zandt had picked up a party of fugitives from Boone County, Kentucky, on the road and transported them in his wagon to his farm, where they went free. One of the slaves continued to work for Van Zandt, and both the white farmer and the Negro workman were captured by slave hunters and taken to Kentucky. Van Zandt was released but later was charged by Jones with harboring and concealing fugitives in violation of the Fugitive Slave Law. Van Zandt lost in the lower and appellate courts and appealed to the U.S.

Supreme Court. There Chase was joined by William Seward, antislavery attorney from New York, pairing for the first time future members of Abraham Lincoln's cabinet. Chief Justice Roger B. Taney and the Supreme Court found the Fugitive Slave Law to be constitutional, presaging the Dred Scott case ten years later. Two courageous lawyers—or even dozens, with righteous Van Zandt or Scott cases—couldn't reverse the tide of inequity that washed over the land. That would take the combined work of thousands of Apostles of Equality, and legions of Van Zandts, Chases, and Sewards, whose numbers were growing.

Birney and other abolitionists became even more dedicated to the campaign to end slavery. The Underground Railroad became more active, reaching its peak between 1850 and 1860, although at that point the disabled Birney was out of the mainstream of the fight, living far north in Michigan, and in New Jersey after 1853, and did not participate. Many voters who had previously been uncertain about slavery now saw its evils and began to support antislavery candidates of the Free Soil and, later, Republican parties.

Despite Free Soil nominee Martin Van Buren's opposition to a plank calling for an end to slavery in the District of Columbia, he ran under an abolitionist platform adopted from the Liberty Party. Van Buren had led a radical wing of the New York state Democratic Party called the "barnburners," which split from the party and joined the abolitionists rather than support the presidential nomination of Lewis Cass, senator from Michigan. "Radical support for Van Buren and the Free Soil party . . . hinged on the platform adopted by the Buffalo Convention," observes historian Eric Foner. "At Buffalo, of course, the radicals got what they wanted. In exchange for the nomination of Van Buren, the Barnburners gave the Liberty men carte blanche in writing the platform."[18]

Birney's home state of Kentucky was a harbinger of Southern attitudes. In 1849 another constitutional convention was held, and according to Kentucky historian Richard Carl Brown, "It was clear that Kentuckians had made their choice in favor of a more conservative attitude toward slavery. Alarmed by reformers' criticisms, defenders of slavery at the convention strengthened its legal status . . . by declaring: 'The right of property is before and higher than any constitutional sanction, and the right of the owner to a slave and to such slave and its increase is the same and as inviolable as the right to any property whatsoever.'" Kentucky voters approved the constitution of 1850 with 71,653 votes in favor and 20,302 opposed. It was Kentucky's third constitution in fifty-eight years, and it ended the hopes of those favoring gradual emancipation by state action.[19]

Sen. John Burton Thompson of Harrodsburg, Kentucky, may have personified Southern attitudes of the time in racial matters. "'Our people believe it is no harm to take away from a Spaniard or a Mexican or an Indian anything he has got, and they want,' declared Senator Thompson. When he added, 'they do not believe it is homicide or murder to kill him either,' his fellow senators laughed."[20] The extension of such a philosophy to Negroes was implicit and a historical fact. Thompson, who had earlier served in the U.S. House as a Whig, was elected as an American, or "Know Nothing," Party candidate and served in the Senate in the volatile pre–Civil War era, 1853–1859. The short-lived party was described as based mainly on "nativism and anti-Catholicism" along with opposition to the growing antislavery sentiment in the North. Strangely, many of the Know Nothings were absorbed into the Republican Party that they had opposed, according to Tyler Anbinder, a leading historian of the American Party movement.[21]

Even as the border state of Kentucky and other Southern states were stiffening against abolition, Michigan was on an opposite track. The Republican Party's fiftieth-anniversary publication states, "The Wilmot Proviso, the Fugitive Slave Law and the Kansas-Nebraska Act were the three measures which, in succession, gave occasion for the expression of the strong, but sometimes latent, anti-slavery feeling in Michigan, and eventually caused the State to take the leading part in the formation of the Republican party."[22] That latent antislavery feeling had been inspired in part by Birney in his campaigns for president in 1844 and Michigan governor in 1843 and 1845 on the Liberty Party ticket as well as in his lecturing and writing. His influence had also spread through the *Signal of Liberty* and other friendly news sheets. The Wilmot Proviso, though described as "futile" by the Republicans, "drew the line sharply between those who favored and those who opposed the extension of slavery into the territories."[23]

The Wilmot Proviso was an 1846 amendment to a bill put before the U.S. House of Representatives during the Mexican War by Pennsylvania Democrat David Wilmot that provided an appropriation of $2 million to enable President Polk to negotiate a territorial settlement with Mexico. Wilmot's amendment stipulated that none of the territory acquired in the Mexican War should be open to slavery. Debate over the bill created hostility between the sections, and the division "gave instruction to Northern men into the purposes and methods of Southern leaders." Among the Northerners so instructed was Abraham Lincoln, who in 1847 represented Springfield, Illinois, in the Thirtieth Congress. Wilmot became a Free Soiler and then a Republican and was a key figure in gaining the nomination for Abraham Lincoln. The first Republican platform, adopted at a convention in Jackson, Michigan, on 6 July 1854, dealt in large measure with slavery. The language is found in *Under the Oaks,* a 345-page history commemorating the fiftieth anniversary of the party, edited by William Stocking and published by the *Detroit Tribune* in 1904:

> The Freemen of Michigan, assembled in Convention in pursuance of a spontaneous call emanating from various parts of the state, to consider upon the measures which duty demands of us as citizens of a free State, to take in reference to the late acts of Congress on the subject of slavery and its anticipated further extension, do,
>
> RESOLVE, That the Institution of Slavery, except in punishment of crime, is a great moral, social and political evil . . .
>
> RESOLVED, That slavery is a violation of the rights of man as man; that the law of nature, which is the law of liberty, give to no man rights superior to those of another . . .
>
> RESOLVED, That the history of the formation of the Constitution, and particularly the enactment of the ordinance of July 13, 1787, prohibiting slavery north of the Ohio abundantly shows it to have been the purpose of our fathers not to promote but to prevent the spread of slavery . . .
>
> RESOLVED . . . inasmuch as the Constitution itself creates an equality in apportionment of representatives greatly to the detriment of the free and to the advantage of the Slave States . . . we hold it the duty of Congress to prevent the spread of slavery and the increase of such unequal representation . . .
>
> RESOLVED, That the repeal of the "Missouri Compromise" . . . for the creation of the territories of Nebraska and Kansas, thus admitting slavery into a region till then sealed against it by law . . . is an act unprecedented in the history of the country.
>
> . . . that one of its principal aims is to give to the Slave States such a decided and practical preponderance in all measures of government as shall reduce the North, with all her industry, wealth and enterprise, to be the mere province of a few slave holding oligarchs of the South—to a condition too shameful to be contemplated.[24]

The resolution demanded repeal of the Fugitive Slave Law and an act to abolish slavery in the District of Columbia and called for a general convention of the free and slaveholding states and appointment of a committee of five to correspond and cooperate with other states on the subject. Less than 10 percent of the resolution was comprised of matters dealing with economical administration of government, more rigid accountability of public officers, payment on national debt, reduction of taxes, preservation of school and university funds, legislation to prevent unnecessary sale of public lands, and a general railroad law encouraging investment while protecting the rights of the public. Out of approximately 2,000 words in the platform document, all but about 150 are dedicated to antislavery sentiments.

Today's official Republican line on its founding gives no credit to the Liberty or Free Soil parties and, although it admits to antislavery beginnings, does not mention the fact that it was formed mainly by abolitionists. The history traces the founding of the Republican Party to the early 1850s

> by anti-slavery activists and individuals who believed that government should grant western lands to settlers free of charge. The first informal meeting of the party took place in Ripon, Wisconsin, a small town northwest of Milwaukee. The first official Republican meeting took place on July 6th, 1854 in Jackson, Michigan. The name "Republican" was chosen because it alluded to equality and reminded individuals of Thomas Jefferson's Democratic-Republican Party. At the Jackson convention, the new party adopted a platform and nominated candidates for office in Michigan.

In 1856, the Republicans became a national party when John C. Fremont was nominated for President under the slogan: "Free soil, free labor, free speech, free men, Fremont." Even though they were considered a "third party" because the Democrats and Whigs represented the two-party system at the time, Fremont received 33% of the vote. Four years later, Abraham Lincoln became the first Republican to win the White House.

The original platform says nothing about "granting western lands to settlers free of charge" and the Liberty Party, Birney and the political abolitionists are disregarded in the contemporary Republican history.

Keys to Republican success in converting the U.S. populace to the antislavery cause, according to some historians, were shifting attention away from the effects of slavery on black men and women to the threats to the liberties and free institutions of America, and frightening the North with a conspiracy theory about Southern plots to dominate the nation."The platform gave Republicans the chance to campaign as conservatives and traditionalists who cherished the values and policies of the Founding Fathers," wrote Richard Carwardine. "Their declared intent was not innovation but restoration: they offered a 'primitivist' return to the nation's republican roots, prising the levers of power from the hands of sectional 'slaveocrats' bent on expanding slavery westward, reopening the Atlantic slave trade, and founding a new empire in the Caribbean."[25]

Greeley noted that the real impetus to the formation of the Republican

Party was provided by Congress: "The passage of the Nebraska Bill was a death-blow to Northern quietism and complacency . . . To all who had fondly dreamed or blindly hoped that the Slavery question would some-how settle itself, it cried, 'Sleep no more!' in thunder-tones that would not die unheeded."[26] George W. Julian, Free Soil candidate for vice president in 1852 and an early Republican, had a clear picture of the origins of the Republican Party. Reviewing Theodore Clarke Smith's book *The Liberty and Free Soil Parties in the Northwest* in 1898, he wrote, "The title of the book might well have been 'the genesis of the Republican party.'" That was, in fact, the subtitle of William Birney's 1890 biography of his father, *James G. Birney and His Times: The Genesis of the Republican Party.* "The repeal of the Missouri Compromise played an important part in rousing the people and speeding the march of events," he noted, "but it was merely an incident, as Mr. Smith shows, of the concerted measures which had already been set on foot for the formation of a consolidated national anti-slavery party that was to supersede all previous organizations." Julian also strikes directly to the Birney versus Garrison, politics versus moral suasion, conflict: "The attempt to overthrow slavery without political action under a government carried on by the ballot was simply preposterous, while the dissolution of the Union would leave the slave in his chains. Nor could any citizen escape complicity in slavery by declining to vote." Referencing the contributions of Birney, Salmon P. Chase, Joshua R. Giddings, and Samuel Lewis, Julian summarized, "Without the labors of these men the great cause would have made little headway, and they should be honored as brave and faithful pioneers who opened the way for the armies that were to follow."[27]

Richard Sewell explains the early Republican antislavery connection: "Not all of the new coalitions took the name Republican, and the degree of antislavery commitment varied substantially from state to state. Where radical elements were strong, as in Michigan, Wisconsin, and Vermont, the new party promptly christened itself Republican and ratified resolutions similar to the Free Soil–Free Democratic platforms of 1848 and 1852: denouncing slavery as 'a great moral, social, and political evil,' demanding its abolition in the District of Columbia and its exclusion from federal territories, urging repeal of the Fugitive Slave Law, and insisting that no other slave states be admitted to the Union."[28]

One of the most powerful influences on the formation of the Republican Party was the party's first convention in Illinois in 1856, which largely has been forgotten, as was the speech that marked the meeting as having historical significance. Whigs, Know Nothings, Free Soilers, and abolitionists came together in Bloomington, Illinois, on 29 May 1856 to hear Lincoln at a state convention designed to marshal the Republican Party to stop the spread of slavery to the west. Lincoln's speech was a lightning flash into the political brain of the country. Benjamin P. Thomas, a Lincoln biographer, recalled: "Outwardly calm, inside he was on fire. The audience sat enthralled. Men listened as though transfixed. Reporters forgot to use the pencils in their hands, so that no complete and authentic record of what may have been his greatest speech has ever been found. At the end, the hall rocked with applause. The Republican Party was reborn in Illinois, even though, because of its radical origin, Lincoln and most of the other delegates still avoided the use of that name."[29]

However, Chicago lawyer Henry C. Whitney made longhand notes of the address. Whitney, in his *Life and Works of Lincoln,* titled the speech "You Shall Not Go Out of the Union." When Lincoln said, "unless popular opinion makes itself very strongly felt, and a change is made in our present course, *blood will flow on account of Nebraska, and brother's hand will be raised against brother,*" Whitney recorded a personal comment: "The last sentence was uttered in such an earnest, impressive, if not, indeed, tragic manner, as to make a cold chill creep over me. Others gave a similar experience." Whitney noted audience reaction when Lincoln exclaimed:

- *"Kansas shall be free! [Immense applause.]"*
- *"Slavery must be kept out of Kansas! [Applause.]"*
- "Now is the time for decision—for firm, persistent, resolute action. [*Applause.*]"
- "We are in a fair way to see this land of boasted freedom converted into a land of slavery in fact. [*Sensation.*]"
- "I read once, in a blackletter law book, a slave is a human being who is legally not a *person* but a *thing.* And if the safeguards to liberty are broken down, as is now attempted, when they have made *things* of all the free negroes, how long, think you, before they will begin to make *things* of poor white men? [*Applause.*]"
- "Such are the inconsistencies of slavery, where a horse is more sacred than a man; and the essence of *squatter* or popular sovereignty—I don't care how you call it—is that if one man chooses to make a slave of another, no third man shall be allowed to object. And if you can do this in free Kansas, and it is allowed to stand, the next thing you will see is shiploads of negroes from Africa at the wharf at Charleston; for one thing is as truly lawful as the other; and there are the bastard notions we have got to stamp out, else they will stamp us out. [*Sensation and applause.*]"

The real theme, declared loudly at the apex of the peroration, addressed to Southern disunionists, was, "WE WON'T GO OUT OF THE UNION, AND YOU SHAN'T!!!"[30] That also was a clear message to Garrison and his supporters, who threatened to secede from the Union to escape Southern perpetuation of slavery under a Constitution they believed favored slavery. This speech must have gladdened the heart of Birney, who at this point was still alive in New Jersey, although he had only about a year and a half to live, and was continuing to dictate abolitionist pamphlets despite his continuing physical deterioration.

Too little attention has been paid to the reaction of voters of all stripes to Henry Clay's statement in the Senate that if the South were to be denied black slaves, it must have white ones. That bound workingmen to the party that would represent them and defused any attempt by slaveholders to make slaves of workers. The threat of white slavery was highlighted in "Republican Bulletin No. 9," issued in 1856, and used as a campaign tool. David R. Roediger observed, "Republicans continued to spill tremendous amounts of ink over the threat of white slavery, but it was seen as just that—a threat and not a reality. And the threat was increasingly seen as coming, not from capital, but from a conspiracy of slaveholders against the Republic."[31] The South had ambitions to reintroduce slavery in the North where it had existed earlier. The idea of expanding slavery to include white laborers in the North shifted the initiative from color to class. Southern politicians often noted that slavery in Greece and Rome was based not on color but on social status. They also noted that slavery sanctioned in the Bible did not specify that slaves were black. Modern observers commented: "The Fugitive Slave Law of 1850 was one way in which free whites in the Northern states were threatened with white slavery. A second way had to do with the belief that the Southern oligarchy desired to nationalize slavery and eventually enslave white laborers in the North. At face value this notion seems preposterous, but in truth, that is precisely what many believed the South ultimately intended to do."[32]

All of these discussions had the result of making Northern working people very nervous and more willing to shift allegiance to the antislavery Republican cause. That widespread motivation led to a movement that some political observers called "the Republican revolution," an unprecedented shift in public opinion, and a powerful voting trend. The threat of white working-class slavery, while perhaps not realistic, had been transmitted to very real politics.

Sewell noted that Democrats, as well as Republicans, were beginning to talk of a "Southern conspiracy" to maintain slavery and a "sellout" to the

South by Senator Stephen A. Douglas. The Dred Scott decision in 1857 prompted Democratic newspapers in DeKalb County, Illinois, and Beloit, Wisconsin, to declare that the opinion revealed "'a conspiracy between a portion of the Supreme Court Judges, Buchanan and the South . . . to retard the progress of freedom, and confirm the claims of the slave power to universal supremacy.'"[33] Michael J. McManus provides an insight: "While the emphasis changed and the moral character of original political abolitionism lessened, what stands out most is the endurance of Liberty party principles as Free Soilers and their Republican successors adapted them."[34] Major evidence of the Republican tie to the abolitionists came when James Birney III was elected Republican lieutenant governor of Michigan in 1860. The younger Birney was riding a wave of pro-abolitionist sentiment fostered not only by the raging popularity of Harriet Beecher Stowe's best-selling *Uncle Tom's Cabin,* but also by outrage in the Northern states over the 1854 Kansas-Nebraska Act allowing territories to decide whether to permit slavery and the 1857 Dred Scott decision of the U.S. Supreme Court, which said, in essence, that Negroes had no rights that a white man was bound to recognize.

The political fortunes of the abolitionists were at last in the majority after nearly three decades of work by James G. Birney and his compatriots. Birney and his fellow abolitionists had worked to soften the opposition to the antislavery movement, and politicians, notably Abraham Lincoln, picked up the cudgel. Carwardine opined, "Through several seasons of public speaking Lincoln's steady advocacy of an antislavery argument did much to shape public sentiment and to effect the displacement of the Whigs by a broader-based Republican party that aspired to national power. . . . the party was an expression of the reform-minded, optimistic Protestant evangelicalism unleashed by the religious movement known as the Second Great Awakening."[35] Lincoln's "seasons of public speaking" culminated in seven debates in a like number of Illinois towns with Senator Douglas from 21 August through 15 October 1858. The debates dealt mainly with the issue of slavery, and, ironically, the final Lincoln-Douglas verbal clash was in Alton, Illinois, the site of the 1836 murder of abolitionist editor Elijah Lovejoy, at whose funeral John Brown announced his intention to dedicate his life to ending slavery.

In the view of John Hay, Lincoln's secretary and later secretary of state under President William McKinley, "the Whig Party had gone to ruin in 1852 on account of the impossibility of combining the scattered elements of opposition to the party of pro-slavery aggression; but they themselves furnished the weapon which was to defeat them." That "weapon" was the

Kansas-Nebraska Bill, which omitted the Missouri Compromise's exclusion of slavery. Hay recalled: "This action at once precipitated the floating anti-slavery sentiment of the country; a mighty cry of resolution indignation arose from one end of the land to the other. . . . A discussion of the right and wrong of slavery became general; the light was let in, fatal to darkness. A system which degraded men, dishonored women, deprived little children of the sacred solace of home, was doomed from the hour it passed into the arena of free debate." Hay, perceiving a collective state of mind in the North at the time of the formation of the Republican Party, commented in the party's fiftieth-anniversary publication:

> It was not so easy 50 years ago to take sides against the slave power as it may seem to-day. Respect for the vested rights of the Southern people was one of our most sacred traditions. It was founded on the compromises of the Constitution, and upon a long line of legal and legislative precedents. The men of the revolution made no defense of slavery in itself; Washington, Adams, Jefferson and Franklin deplored its existence but recognized the necessity of compromise until the public mind might rest in the hope of its ultimate extinction. But after they had passed away, improvements in the culture and manufacture of cotton made this uneconomic form of labor for the time profitable, and what had been merely tolerated as a temporary necessity began to be upheld as a permanent system.[36]

William Stocking, the editor of the Republican history, gave a clear statement of the feeling among early party men by titling his first chapter "Aggressions of the Slave Power," and Hay indicated the intolerable turning point in the national situation: "Slavery entrenched itself in every department of our public life. Its advocates dominated Congress and the State Legislatures; they even invaded the pulpit and grotesquely wrested a few texts of Scripture to their purpose. They gave the tone to society; even the Southern accent was imitated in our schools and colleges." Despite the Southern dominance of national affairs, Hay said, the "conservative people of the North" were willing to tolerate slavery rather than "'cast upon our brethren in the South the burdens and perils of its abolition.'" He said: "If the slaveholders had been content with their unquestioned predominance, they might for many years have controlled our political and social world. . . . But the slaveholding party could not rest content. The ancients said madness was the fate of those judged by the gods. Continual aggression is a necessity of a false position. They felt instinctively that if their system were permanently to endure it must be extended, and to attain this object they were ready to risk everything."[37]

As we have seen, Birney's legacy to the foundation of the Republican Party has not been adequately recognized by either political activists or academic historians. However, an early Republican, A. D. P. VanBuren, observed the importance of his contribution: "James G. Birney became the leader who mustered, drilled and trained the abolition forces in Michigan for a still larger and more important field—that of national politics, and there, in two presidential contests he led them against their old foes, and although not gaining the victory, yet he handed them over to other leaders with whom, increased in numbers and discipline, they constituted the 'old guard' that turned the tide of battle in favor of the Republicans in the presidential contest in 1860."[38]

Three years before the Republican revolution that elected Lincoln, a decision of the U.S. Supreme Court threw fresh fuel on the fires of controversy. It was the Dred Scott case of 1857. The ruling defied credibility: even though black men had been voting citizens in five of the original states back to 1776, it said no slave or descendant of a slave could be a United States citizen, or ever had been a citizen. Seven of nine justices of the U.S. Supreme Court, led by former Maryland slaveholder Roger B. Taney, held that Scott had no rights that a white man was bound to respect, could not sue in a federal court, and must remain a slave. The ruling involved one man, Scott, but affected four million black men and women, slave and free. The Court took the nation back in time nearly four decades, declaring the Missouri Compromise of 1820 unconstitutional. The most inflammatory effect of the ruling was that Congress could not stop slavery in the newly emerging territories, an issue already ablaze in controversy because of the Kansas-Nebraska Act. Even the normally cautious Lincoln spoke out in disgust against the ruling in a speech delivered on 17 June 1858 at Springfield, Illinois, that was forever etched into the nation's consciousness as the "House Divided" speech. Stanley Kutler observed that Lincoln focused on the potential of the ruling to allow slavery to spread into the territories when he said, "'We shall lie down pleasantly dreaming that the people of Missouri are on the verge of making their State free, and we shall awake to the reality instead, that the Supreme Court has made Illinois a slave State.'"[39]

Sewell noted that an insightful summary of the historical progression of the pro-slavery action was provided by the *Harrisburg Telegraph*:

Seventy years ago . . . the Democrats drew a line around the States, and said to the Slave Trader, "thus far you may go, but no farther." This was the Jeffersonian Proviso. Thirty years ago they rubbed out part of the line, and said to him, "You may go into the lands South, but not into the lands North." This was the

Missouri Compromise. Five years ago they rubbed out the rest of the line, and said to him, "We leave it to the Settlers to decide whether you shall come in or not." This was the Nebraska Bill. Now they turn humbly to him, hat in hand, and say, "Go where your please; the land is all yours, the National flag shall protect you, and the National Troops shoot down whoever resists you." This is the Dred Scott decision.[40]

Thus were the combatants poised for a political revolution and sectional warfare to the extent that none could ever have imagined.

PART 3

The Civil War

CHAPTER 16

The Birneys in Battle

When the President of the United States, on the 15th day of April, 1861,
issued his proclamation calling out seventy-five thousand of the militia of
the different states, [David Bell] Birney determined to act.

—OLIVER WILSON DAVIS

THE "SOLID SOUTH," WHICH WILLIAM BIRNEY LATER OBSERVED HAD been emerging since 1824, exploded with the election of Abraham Lincoln in November 1860. Lincoln's election was the signal bell for Southern states to declare outrage over the antislavery platform of the Republican Party, secede from the Union, and form the Confederate States of America. The decision had been shaping for over several decades, but it was reinforced by "Apostles of Disunion" who fanned out across the South, according to the author of a book by that name, Charles B. Dew. Professor Dew, of Williams College, Williamstown, Massachusetts, takes pains to note he is a native of Florida who attended high school in Virginia and whose ancestors fought for the Confederacy. He describes the "apostles of disunion" as the antithesis of James G. Birney's "apostles of equality," who had campaigned for the abolition of slavery in the 1830s. The "disunionists" were Southern secession commissioners who were specifically assigned by their state governments to whip up opposition to what the rebels called "Black Republican rule." Mississippi was first to appoint commissioners to travel to every slave state in action taken by the state legislature before the end of November 1860. Other states, galvanized by fears that the Republican Party was intent on "the destruction of the institution of slavery," sent out their own commissioners. A secession convention was called in Columbia, South Carolina, a parade of rebel resignations from the U.S. Senate and

House began, and mobilization of men and arms was started. There was no retreat now from the intransigent position that slavery must be preserved. "'The tea has been thrown overboard, the revolution of 1860 has been initiated,'" the *Charleston Mercury* declared.[1] James Buchanan's vice president, John Cabell Breckenridge, son of Birney's old Princeton roommate Joseph, was the highest-ranking government official to defect to the Confederacy. Actually, Breckenridge's term was up in early 1861, and his candidacy on the newly formed Southern Democratic ticket took more than eight hundred thousand votes that might otherwise have helped elect "Little Giant" Democrat Stephen A. Douglas of Illinois instead of Lincoln.

The Civil War exploded into history when Confederate cannons directed by Gen. P. G. T. Beauregard opened on the federal Fort Sumter in the harbor of Charleston, South Carolina, on 12 April 1861. Some national spirit still prevailed, for Beauregard offered assistance to the commander, Maj. Robert Anderson, when the fort's barracks burned, and some rebels cheered the gallantry of Anderson's men even as they continued to load and fire the cannons during the intense bombardment. The author of a Confederate military history, wrote in 1899: "The spirit and language of General Beauregard in communicating with Major Anderson, and the replies of the latter, were alike honorable to those distinguished soldiers. The writer, who was on duty on Sullivan's island, as major of Pettigrew's regiment of rifles, recalls vividly the sense of admiration felt for Major Anderson and his faithful little command throughout the attack, and at the surrender of the fort."[2]

The offspring of James G. Birney were eager to join the Union cause at the outset of the war in 1861. Oldest son James III, forty-three, initially was involved in recruiting troops as lieutenant governor of Michigan, but was soon to resign and take a circuit judgeship in mid-Michigan. Two sons who would become major generals were William, forty-two, who was practicing law in Cincinnati, and David, thirty-six, a lawyer in Philadelphia and a member of a local militia unit. Two others who would soon enlist were Robert Dion, thirty-eight, a druggist in Saginaw, Michigan, and Fitzhugh, nineteen, who was studying at Harvard University. Grandson James G. IV, son of James III, was a brash youth of seventeen in Bay City, soon to enlist in the Seventh Michigan Cavalry. The enlistment of four sons and a grandson of James G. Birney represented perhaps the greatest contribution of any abolitionist family to the war effort.

William Birney and David Bell Birney were among the many "political" generals in the Union Army whose military qualifications were suspect. Others included Benjamin F. Butler, former governor of Massachusetts; explorer John C. Fremont, the first Republican presidential candidate; controversial member of Congress Daniel Sickles; John "Black Jack" Logan, another member of Congress; Lincoln crony John McClernand, who spread rumors of Grant's drinking and eventually was fired for insubordination; and Joshua Lawrence Chamberlain, a professor at Bowdoin College in Maine, who, despite his lack of military qualifications, was a highly competent commander, won the Medal of Honor at Gettysburg, and was brevetted major general. At the start of the war the regular army officers, especially West Point graduates, did not trust the skills or tactical judgment of the political appointees. David Birney and his brother William had the added burden of being the sons of a noted abolitionist at the same time that many officers were either overtly or tacitly pro-slavery. While most of the political generals had ridden only their desks and wielded few weapons besides a pen, both Birneys had spent time on the frontier in Michigan and were familiar with weapons and horsemanship, as were their brothers Robert Dion and Fitzhugh and nephew James G. Birney IV. At age seventeen, David had driven his father's herd of thoroughbred cattle three hundred miles from Ohio to Lower Saginaw, Michigan, and later had roughed it there while trading with the Indians in the employ of a Philadelphia mercantile company. William also had grown up on the Alabama and Michigan frontiers and had experienced armed conflict in Paris during the revolt of 1848. He strode in comradeship with students from the University of Bourges, France, where he taught English literature, and commanded a barricade in street fighting against royalist troops.

David Bell Birney, born in Huntsville, Alabama, in 1825, received early training at the Western Military Institute in Georgetown, Kentucky. He attended Phillips Academy in Andover, Massachusetts; studied law in Michigan; and was a successful lawyer in Philadelphia. He anticipated the onset of war in 1860 by experiencing increasing hostility from Southern businessmen he was dealing with on legal matters. Alarmed, David joined the Philadelphia City Cavalry, a militia group, and began studying military tactics. When war broke out he was named lieutenant colonel and helped recruit a regiment of the Twenty-third Pennsylvania Volunteers called "Birney's Zouaves," mainly at his own expense. Many of the colorfully clad Zouaves were members of the Philadelphia Fire Department. David Birney's first minor engagement was against Stonewall Jackson at Falling Waters, Virginia, on 2 July 1861, and he gave a creditable performance, soon winning promotion. According to his biographer, Oliver Wilson Davis, a *New York Tribune* correspondent of the time had observed, "'Just in the middle of the fight the Twenty-third Pennsylvania [Birney's regiment] came up as cool as cucumbers and pitched into the chase, flanking out a considerable distance to the left and routing the rebels from all their places of concealment. Every man was cool and deliberate and their shots told with fearful effect.'"[3]

During the three-month campaign in 1861, Lieutenant Colonel Birney was ordered to arrest a fugitive slave but examined the articles of war and, finding nothing requiring an officer to catch runaway Negroes, refused.[4] After the ninety-day enlistment, he recruited a new regiment, and by August 1861 he was on the way to Washington with seven hundred men, his fourteen-year-old son, Frank, waving the flag in front of the column. The regiment patrolled along the Potomac River. By February 1862 Birney was a brigadier general commanding a brigade in the Third Division of the Third Corps of the Army of the Potomac under Maj. Gen. Philip Kearny.

It was estimated that four-fifths of the Union generals at the start of the Civil War were Democrats, who, it was said by the radical abolitionists, "nourished a sympathy for slavery that bordered on treason," wrote T. Harry Williams. They complained that "the 'infernal hold-back pro-slavery' philosophy of the military chieftains prevented a vigorous prosecution of the war."[5] The *Congressional Globe* reported that in 1861 the poorly equipped army of sixteen thousand men had an officers corps "shot through with sympathy for the Confederacy."[6] That pro-slavery, anti-abolitionist attitude was displayed by an encounter between Maj. Gen. George B. McClellan and David Birney in trenches at Yorktown, in which a news reporter embedded with McClellan basically accused Birney of cowardice and of Maj. Gen. E. O. C. Ord's cashiering of William Birney as his black troops closed on Robert E. Lee near Appomattox on 8 April 1865.

Abolitionist families like the Welds, Beechers, Birneys, Garrisons, Tappans, and Adamses all had members in the Union Army, but none had more than the five Birneys, and none ultimately sacrificed more. The onset of war was hardly welcomed by Northerners of any political stripe while many militaristic Southerners celebrated the opportunity to perpetuate their traditional political domination on the battlefield. Crowds celebrated in Richmond and Charleston when war broke out. In the South, no doubt, the aggressive spirit of the slave patrols and the Code Duello, which justified murder by dueling in the name of honor, carried over to attitudes on the battlefield. Ironically, the constitution of the Confederacy prohibited states from seceding and barred reestablishment of the African slave trade.

The North was at an immediate disadvantage as well as being in denial about the peril the nation faced. The militia system in many states was in shambles, and Congress had not prepared for possible civil war, being preoccupied with futile schemes for sectional compromise. Even as South Carolina was preparing to secede, the Senate passed a resolution asking the war department to further reduce military expenses. There was talk of sending an army of twenty-five thousand to Richmond to squash the uprising, an action that no doubt would have been doomed to failure. Other opinions were that any conflict would be over in six months. Obviously, apathy and overconfidence were the North's greatest enemies.

A persistent question about the war is why the Union Army, given its superiority in manpower and materiel, was so unsuccessful early in the conflict. Incompetence, inexperience, and hesitancy were among the flaws of Union generals. But none of these failings seem to provide a reasonable explanation for the horrendous losses at the First Battle of Bull Run, described by Bruce Catton as "the momentous fight of the amateurs";[7] Gaines's Mill; Chancellorsville; Chickamauga; and other early Union disasters. There must have been another factor. Is it possible that the pro-slavery element in the Union Army deliberately subverted military success? However, the Union loss at Bull Run had an unintended consequence for the victorious Confederacy. Senator Charles Sumner, a Massachusetts antislavery leader who pushed for emancipation and had been severely beaten with a cane on the floor of the Senate by Rep. Preston Brooks of Georgia, told Lincoln that First Bull Run made the extinction of slavery inevitable.[8] The horrendous defeat alerted the North that its perils at the hands of the rebel armies were very real. While the South adopted a defensive strategy, the North was forced to fight on unfamiliar soil surrounded by a hostile populace. Lincoln embraced a three-cornered strategy: capture the Confederate capital of Richmond, seize control of the Mississippi River, and blockade Southern ports to prevent resupply from abroad.

The swagger of the aggressive Southerners, who considered themselves more experienced in weapons and horsemanship, sometimes backfired. On a sultry August morning near Centreville, Virginia, in the second year of the Civil War, Brig. Gen. David Bell Birney of the Twenty-third Pennsylvania Volunteers, a slim thirty-seven-year-old abolitionist with sandy hair and piercing blue eyes, was on mounted reconnaissance with companies H and K of the Second Pennsylvania Cavalry. Perhaps musing about the previous day when he found Union trains burning at Manassas Junction, Birney rode with the distracted air of a lawyer who had seen more action in a courtroom than in the field that day. The oppressive heat and hordes of flies seemed his only enemies at the moment. Birney was part of Maj. Gen. Samuel P. Heintzelman's Third Corps sent up the Potomac to join Maj. Gen. John Pope, commander of the new Army of Virginia, protecting Washington and trying to cut off Robert E. Lee's Army of Northern Virginia from the Shenandoah Valley. Suddenly a vedette reined up and informed Birney of the approach of horsemen carrying the U.S. flag. Seeing through field glasses that the horsemen were in rebel uniform, David and his men headed their mounts toward Union lines, and a chase ensued toward Manassas. One rebel, said to have been "better mounted and more daring than his comrades" and brandishing a saber, rode abreast of the skedaddling Birney, shouting, "Surrender, you're my prisoner," apparently attempting to bag the entire Union unit through capture of their leader. David Birney's biographer, Oliver Davis, recalled: "Birney, though riding at a run, replied: 'I guess not,' and raising his revolver, which he had been carrying in his hand from Centreville, fired, and unhorsed his captor, who fell to the ground, and was never again able to raise his sword against a soldier of the Union. During the afternoon it was ascertained that the enemy had fallen back on Centreville and were about thirty thousand strong."[9]

David Birney had a peripatetic record, performing heroically in some battles and bungling in others, according to reports. He assisted the one-armed iconoclast Gen. Philip Kearny, a fellow abolitionist, in the Peninsula and Pope's campaigns. Kearny was a wealthy New Yorker and law graduate of Columbia who scorned the easy life to become a professional soldier, serving in the Mexican War and on the western frontier with Jefferson Davis. Birney headed a regiment of Maine and New York men under the crusty forty-seven-year-old Kearny at Chantilly, Virginia, in August. "Those regiments engaged and drove back the enemy, though greatly inferior in numbers," recalled Davis. On 1 September Major General Kearny came up with Randolph's battery, and Birney pointed out a gap on his right created by the retiring of Gen. Isaac Ingals Stevens's units, which were in disarray. "Kearny insisted that it was impossible for such a gap to exist and said he would ride forward to see what troops were there. Birney warned him, and urged him to remain, saying he would ride into the enemy's lines, but Kearny, . . . [in Heintzelman's words,] 'pressed forward to reconnoiter in his usual gallant, not to say reckless manner,' and came upon a rebel regiment. In attempting to escape, he was killed.'" Gen. Stevens also was killed the same day in that battle. "As General Kearny did not return, General Birney supposed he had been taken prisoner, and assumed command of the division, being the ranking brigade commander on the field."[10]

Another historian, Francis Miller, wrote, "The brilliant bayonet charge by Birney, in command of the division of General Philip Kearny, who had just fallen, drove back the Confederates, and Birney held the field that night." As a violent thunderstorm raged, Birney ordered up the Thirty-eighth New York and Fifty-seventh Pennsylvania regiments to secure the victory.[11] He later was among officers who devised a medal in honor of their fallen comrade, called "the Kearny Cross," given to all officers who had fought under Kearny and also awarded by Birney to several soldiers from the Fourth Maine Volunteer Infantry Regiment, for valor at Chancellorsville. Kearny made a lasting contribution to the nation's military by devising the first corps patches from his own red blanket, the innovation coming after he had mistakenly reprimanded officers from the wrong unit. As a result, every army division today has its own unique shoulder patch.[12]

At Seven Pines, Virginia, David Birney was accused of not bringing his men up in time to participate in the battle, but a court-martial exonerated him. In a futile cause at Chancellorsville, Birney lost 1,607 men, most in the Union force, but he captured a Georgia regiment of 500 men and was highly praised for his performance by the commander, Maj. Gen. George Stoneman. According to press reports, Birney's division drove back the Confederates at midnight, recovered lost ground, and retrieved abandoned guns and caissons. Maj. Gen. Daniel Sickles's report also mentioned Birney as "making his dispositions with admirable discernment and skill." Sickles commented, "The right giving way toward the Plank road, General Birney, in person, led a portion of Hayman's brigade to the charge, driving the enemy back in confusion, capturing several hundred prisoners, and relieving Graham from a flank movement of the enemy, which exposed him to great peril, when he withdrew in good order. . . . It is difficult to do justice to the brilliant execution of this movement by Birney and his splendid command."[13]

When Maj. Gen. Hiram G. Berry was killed, creating an opening, David Birney at last won a promotion. Biographer Davis noted the highly unusual occurrence of a general officer visiting the White House and seeing the president in person, perhaps indicating the influence inherent in the Birney name. In March 1863 while David was in Washington to appear before the Committee on the Conduct of the War, he called at the White House to see the Great Emancipator. Lincoln said in jest, "Birney, why do your friends remind me of the news boys about Washington?" Birney replied, "Indeed, sir, I cannot tell." Lincoln exclaimed, "Why, they are always crying out 'Extra, Star.'"[14] Lincoln made sure Birney received the extra star in recognition of his actions at Chancellorsville. The president's unusual solicitousness toward David Bell Birney, perhaps indicating a degree of favor toward abolitionists, was evident in the fact that Lincoln wrote to Secretary of War Edwin M. Stanton on 7 March 1864 asking that Birney's nomination for promotion to major general "for meritorious service at Chancellorsville" be dated 3 May rather than 22 June 1863. "It is also represented that to make the desired change will not give Gen. Birney rank over any one who now ranks him. I shall be glad to withdraw his present nomination and make the change, if the above is a true and full statement of the facts."[15] A note was attached by the Lincoln Studies Center at Knox College in Galesburg, Illinois, saying, "General Birney's date of nomination was indeed revised, but for him to take rank from May 20, 1863, rather than from May 3 as requested."[16] Someone in the war department, for an unknown reason, had seen fit to modify Lincoln's request. Larry Tagg, the author of a history of Gettysburg's generals, observed, "Despite his lack of a military background, by the summer of 1863 Birney was a seasoned and capable combat leader."[17]

David Birney was given temporary command of Third Corps at Gettysburg, replacing Sickles, who lost his right leg on 2 July 1863 when he was struck by a cannonball. Sickles had blundered by advancing nearly a mile too far, overextending his men along the Emmitsburg Road, leaving the left flank under Birney at Devil's Den, nearly half a mile from Little Round Top, which needed to be defended. The corps thus was separated from the Union line on Cemetery Ridge, leaving soft spots at the Wheatfield and the Peach Orchard, and gaining Sickles the wrath of Maj. Gen. George Gordon Meade, overall Union commander. Birney was left with the nearly impossible task of defending the Devil's Den, the Wheatfield, and the Peach Orchard with thin lines, isolated and vulnerable to Confederate artillery fire from the south and west. Birney was unable to prevent the unit from being decimated by attacks from Confederate units and was struck twice by bullets but not seriously hurt. CSA Lt. Gen. James Longstreet himself led one assault on the Wheatfield and the Peach Orchard. Third Corps was forced to fall back, but only to its original position. Finally, units of First, Second, and Seventh Corps were joined by Maj. Gen. John Sedgwick's Sixth Corps, whose ten thousand men had marched all night, covering thirty-four miles, providing reinforcement in late afternoon and forcing Longstreet to pull back. Despite the loss of more than 40 percent of its manpower, the resoluteness of Third Corps was considered decisive in the battle by some observers, especially Gettysburg Battlefield Park historian Eric A. Campbell, who in August 2009 cited the resolve of Third Corps troops under David Birney in the aftermath of Sickles's wounding. A shell-shocked Birney was famously quoted as wishing he were already dead at the battle's end, a statement frequently interpreted as Birney's concession of loss—an untrue perception, according to later analysis by several historians. "Despite all that went wrong, in the end the III Corps contributed to a Union victory," wrote Campbell.[18]

The next night, 3 July, after Maj. Gen. George Pickett's futile charge against the Union center with 15,000 fearless Confederates failed, Lee was forced to retire to the South and the victory was Meade's. Birney's division lost 1,988 men in killed, wounded, and missing; the 141st Pennsylvania alone lost 49 men in the Peach Orchard, or about 24 percent of those engaged, one of the worst losses of any Union unit in any battle in the war.[19] The depleted Third Corps disappeared in a reorganization of the Army of the Potomac in 1864. Birney then was assigned to command the Third Division of Second Corps.

In the Battle of the Wilderness, David Birney served under the highly regarded Maj. Gen. Winfield Scott Hancock. According to historian Bruce Catton, at one point Hancock reported, "Birney has gone in and he is just cleaning them out beautifully." Soon thereafter his troops were caught in a jam. "General Birney was forced to call a halt so that he could get his troops reorganized . . . and just at this moment the van of Longstreet's hurrying columns came up and struck the disordered Federal line with a sharp counterattack." Birney's line was shattered, but he got a break when Longstreet's men became entangled with A. P. Hill's and the Confederates were forced to halt and regroup. Hancock had confidence in Birney, at Spotsylvania transferring brigades from another commander into his division.[20] "Maj. Gen. Winfield Scott Hancock's II Corps entered the Overland campaign as an excellent command, probably the best in the Army of the Potomac," wrote Catton. "Hancock had three capable and aggressive division commanders: Brigadier General Francis C. Barlow, Major General David Bell Birney, and Brigadier General John Gibbon."[21]

David Birney was arrested and court-martialed twice, apparently for specious cause, although he was quickly acquitted following support by generals Kearny and Joe Hooker, both of whom commended him. In addition, he faced vicious attacks from New York newspapers on his actions in battle, which to contemporary observers appeared to be based more on the fact that he was an abolitionist rather than on justifiable cause. He took part in a nasty exchange printed in a long column in the *New York Times* with a former reporter of the *New York Tribune,* Samuel Wilkeson, aide de camp to General Heintzelman. On 28 March 1863 Wilkeson, mistakenly addressing him as "William B. Birney," responded to David Birney's complaint of "wretched stories." Wilkeson wrote, "If you fight, sir, as stupidly as you write, I pity your brigade." Commenting on the Battle of Seven Pines, Wilkeson continued, "I said you had been ordered under arrest by Gen. Heintzelman for disobedience of orders and for cowardice." An indication that Wilkeson's vitriol may have stemmed from a connection with the proslavery McClellan was evident, for he also wrote, "Gen. McClellan was also a personal witness of the refusal one day of a 'General of the Trenches' before

Yorktown, to follow him and his Staff across an open and exposed break in the uncompleted works." David Birney had been "general of the trenches" in that battle. Regarding Williamsburg, Wilkeson wrote, "Gen. Heintzelman struck you out of that fighting society in his report of the battle; and Heintzelman is as just as he is brave." Wilkeson concluded with the charge that Heintzelman had "yielded to your importunity to let you write his report, so as to give you an opportunity to connect yourself creditably with a battle, which should have ended your military career." Birney vigorously responded on 10 April in the *Times*, noting "the utmost confidence has existed" since the Battle of Seven Pines between himself and General Heintzelman. "He has very kindly and very warmly urged my promotion, and expressed his belief in my fitness for the command of Kearny's old division." Birney then followed with a compendium of praise from General Kearny for his actions at Williamsburg, Fair Oaks, Malvern Hill, and Manassas Plains.[22]

Besides Wilkeson's connection with General McClellan, perhaps he was influenced by his former editor, Horace Greeley of the *Tribune*, still rankling over the defeat of Henry Clay, whom he had supported for the presidency, by the candidacy of David's father, James G. Birney, in 1844. David Birney's hometown *Philadelphia Inquirer*, by contrast and not surprisingly, was almost totally supportive of his military performance. Heintzelman, a full-bearded, fifty-six-year-old professional soldier who had graduated from West Point the year after David Birney was born, was relieved of command in late 1862 and assigned to command troops guarding Washington. He died in 1869.

At Fredericksburg Birney commanded the First Division of the Third Corps under Hooker. A charge of dereliction of duty leveled against David Birney at Fredericksburg was reversed, and Maj. Gen. George Stoneman praised him.[23] "During the battle Birney several times was asked to assist Meade as he broke the Confederate line and then was forced back. Birney ignored the requests, considering Meade of equal rank and waiting for orders from higher command. In testimony before the Congressional Committee on the Conduct of the War, considering Birney's actions at Fredericksburg, Meade "nowhere censures Birney for not having been up in time." Birney was not relieved from his post on the field, and the incident seems to have been a misunderstanding between Birney and Meade. Birney's biographer notes a Confederate report about the matter: "In his report of this action, the rebel General Lee says that at no part of his line were his men driven from the ground they had captured from our troops, except at the point where Birney's division drove back Early's division of Ewell's corps."[24]

Marvin Pakula, author of a picture history of the war, later charged

David Birney with blundering at the Siege of Petersburg, one outrageous error or fabrication accusing him of being responsible for sending green troops into battle and causing the loss of six thousand men.[25] This claim is perplexing, since no evidence can be found that Birney's actions were the cause of heavy loss of men at Petersburg. Apparently some erroneous newspaper reports had blamed the Negro troops under Birney's command for the disaster in the Crater, and those errors may have been the source of the mistake. However, General Hancock considered him a top commander, and he collaborated with Grant in the Overland Campaign on the drive toward Petersburg and commanded the Army of the James for several weeks just before his death. As such he was a rare breed, a non–West Point officer heading an entire army. With three of his brothers—Robert Dion, Fitzhugh, and now, David—dead, only William and nephew James G. Birney IV remained to carry the Birney name in battle and to pursue the abolitionist crusade of James G. Birney and the Apostles of Equality.

William Birney, born in Alabama and raised among slaves on his father's cotton plantation, was a Yale-educated lawyer who had been a correspondent for British and New York newspapers in 1848 when he was in France. He also was the founder of the *Philadelphia Daily Register* and had practiced law in Cincinnati. Rising quickly in the officer corps of the New Jersey volunteers, he was brevetted a major general in March 1865 shortly before the war's end.

Long after the war, William Birney was forced to defend his military record against attacks by Col. James Shaw Jr., one of his regimental commanders in the Second Division of the Twenty-fifth Corps. According to Birney, Shaw was harboring a grudge because of slights, real or imaginary, suffered while serving under him and had compiled anti-Birney charges in a pamphlet he was circulating to former military associates. Birney vigorously defended himself, publishing a twenty-eight-page booklet detailing his actions, promotions, and commendations as well as Shaw's shortcomings, which allegedly included cowardice and inept leadership. Birney wrote that he had been a captain of New Jersey volunteers at First Bull Run on 21 July 1861, claiming he had been "one of the few officers who brought their men in perfect order from the field." Joining Gen. Phil Kearny's brigade, along with his brother David, he was at Yorktown and West Point and in the Chickahominy Campaign. Captured at Gaines Mill, he was exchanged, promoted to major, and assigned by Kearny to command a Pennsylvania regiment in the Third Corps. William joined Maj. Gen. John Pope at Warrenton Junction and was in all movements preceding Second Bull Run, heading the Fifty-seventh Pennsylvania, which he reported held a rebel brigade for three hours. "Kearny declared it the most scientific fighting of the day and mentioned me with honor in his report," he noted. Birney was at Chantilly holding the picket line and was commended for a counterattack at the head of the famous New York Thirty-eighth, the Tammany Regiment, at Fredericksburg. "General [Henry Clay] Ward, my commander, published to the army, and in the press, a letter extolling it as a great feat of arms."[26]

The undistinguished third son of James G. Birney, Robert Dion Birney, had a somewhat troubled youth and struggled with his education, but became a pharmacist in Saginaw, Michigan, and a Union Army "physician," obviously with minimal qualifications. Army records show he arrived at Camp Graham near Washington, D.C., on 1 January 1862 accompanied by a servant, a not uncommon situation for wealthy enlistees. He served as a first lieutenant in Company F, Twenty-third Regiment, Pennsylvania Volunteer Infantry, headed by his brother Gen. David Bell Birney. Dion suffered from exposure in the field in the Peninsula Campaign of 1862, resigned in April, and died soon afterward.

Fitzhugh Birney enlisted after being given a one-year suspension at Harvard University in 1861 by President C. C. Felton for a variety of minor disciplinary problems.[27] Fitzhugh Birney had health problems, suffering constantly from colds and coughing up blood after a wrestling match with a friend. At Harvard the nineteen-year-old freshman, who had to wait out a year to recover his health, and his classmates, including Robert Lincoln, the president's oldest son, watched the conflict unfold after the attack on Fort Sumter. They wanted action, and the governor of Massachusetts assigned a student corps from Cambridge to guard the arsenal in Boston. It wasn't enough for young Birney. He wrote to a friend, "I must go to the war. My father sacrificed all for freedom. My brothers are already in the field. Am I not dishonoring my name and the cause with which it is identified?" After his suspension from Harvard, he was visiting his uncle Gerrit Smith, in Utica, New York, when he received a letter from his brother David offering him a first lieutenant's commission in the Twenty-third Pennsylvania Volunteers. He sought his mother's permission to accept. "Yes, if you are well," wrote Elizabeth, referring to the respiratory problems that had plagued him. He was commissioned captain and assistant adjutant general in Kearny's division under his brother David. He found duty as an aide boring and soon transferred to the Signal Corps, under Maj. Gen. George B. McClellan, and was promoted to major.[28]

Taking risks near enemy lines at Chickahominy, Fitzhugh went aloft with General Stoneman to reconnoiter defenses around Richmond. Balloons engineered by a Professor Thaddeus Lowe were used by General

Heintzelman for observation on the Virginia Peninsula. After the battle of Fredericksburg he wrote to his mother:

> "You at home must suffer more from anxiety than we do from cold, exposure, and battle. It was hard for you to know that so fierce a fight was raging, and that we three were in the hottest of it. You ask me how I felt. There is intense excitement as the tide of battle ebbs and flows. If one's own party are advancing, there is a glow of exultation; if retreating, a passion to turn the enemy back. 'Twas so the other day when Meade's Pennsylvania Reserves, to which we were support, advanced in a long, magnificent line of battle, as if on parade. All was quiet when they started, but in an instant the roar of cannon and the rattle of musketry were deafening. Twenty minutes it lasted. Then from the woods directly in front of us came out a shattered mass of troops in perfect disorder. It seems to me that I could have died a hundred deaths to turn the scale. . . . One of our colonels well describes our position that day, 'The Rebels were in the boxes and we in the pit.' It was a Roman amphitheatre, and we were the poor beasts exposed on the arena."[29]

A long account of Fitzhugh's war experiences in the *Harvard Memorial Biographies* observed, "In the third year of the war he wrote, 'I have passed over the scene of John Brown's adventurous raid. He was our leader, after all. We shall finish his work, and that "perturbed spirit" may rest in peace.'"[30]

Fitzhugh was married on Christmas Day 1863 to Laura Strattan, from an aristocratic Philadelphia family, who also had attended Reverend Weld's school in New Jersey. However, it was a short marriage with an unhappy ending. Fitzhugh took sick in the spring of 1864 with a recurrence of his lung problems. He refused to go on the sick list and stayed on duty, but finally was forced to leave the field at Cold Harbor. He was taken up the Potomac by steamer and died of pneumonia in Duddington, the old mansion of the Carroll family, cousins of his mother, at Washington on 17 June 1864. He was buried near his father in Williamsburg Cemetery at Hampton, the old homestead of the Fitzhughs and the Carrolls, in Livingston County, New York.

James G. Birney IV, son of Judge James Birney and grandson of the late abolitionist James G. Birney, enlisted from the town of Hampton in Bay County, Michigan, in the Seventh Michigan Cavalry at age eighteen and served under Gen. George A. Custer at Gettysburg. He was wounded, captured, and escaped the same day east of Gettysburg on 3 July 1863 as rebel cavalry leader J. E. B. Stuart was foiled in an attempt to flank the Union line. As Stuart brought the First Virginia up from Cress's Ridge in what later was deemed an attempt to hit the Union rear while George Pickett's charge slammed the center, Custer led the under-strength and rookie Seventh, including young Birney, in a dramatic saber charge against the Confederates at a gallop, waving his kepi on his sword and shouting, "Come on you Wolverines," a nickname that had originated among students at the University of Michigan. Struck by a hail of rebel fire and blocked by a rail fence, the unit dismounted and exchanged pistol and rifle fire with the brigade of John Chambliss. Wade Hampton's troops joined the fray and drove off the Fifth Michigan, which had come to Custer's rescue. In a counterattack the Fifth, with their seven-shot Spencers, were holding off the Confederates "when the next, and final, episode of the battle began to unfold. Shortly after 3:30 P.M.—while nearly 13,000 infantrymen were assaulting the midpoint of the Union line at Gettysburg," Hampton attacked again with obvious intentions: "to sweep his adversaries from the field." Custer then galloped beside Col. Charles Town and the First Michigan and engaged in what Col. Russell Alger called "the most gallant charge of the war."[31]

The brigade's Capt. Charles King recalled with a rhetorical flourish: "The hoarsely shouted 'Charge!' the glorious burst of cheers! The wild fury of the onset! The crash and shock of the meeting hosts—and Virginia's grand advance is done. Like Pickett's—Stuart's grand assault is turned to naught. What soldier lives who does not envy Michigan that day?" The Seventh lost 13 killed, 48 wounded, and 39 missing as the brigade's 250 casualties of 20 percent were highest of any unit in the battle.[32] A state history of the war observed, "Michigan troops were the first to be involved in the Gettysburg action and conducted the last charge that signaled the end of that bold and formidable invasion of northern soil."[33]

Young Birney was brevetted captain for bravery at Gettysburg, and General Custer presented him with a dress sword. After being on the chase of Lee and Stuart from Gettysburg through Maryland and back into Virginia, he served under Gen. Phil Sheridan. Sheridan was complimentary in a letter dated 20 May 1865 supporting young Birney's application for a commission in the regular army, noting that he was "recommended by the governor of Michigan and generals Merritt, Custer, Devins, etc. Capt. Birney is an active & intelligent young officer. He has served faithfully & with distinction during the war."[34]

The capture of Petersburg and Richmond were imminent, and Appomattox was soon to follow. On 2 April young James reported in another letter to his father, "We had a terrible fight yesterday, and gave the Johnnies a complete whipping, capturing nearly the whole of the pickets and part of Johnson's Division. It is reported that we have the South Side R.R. My division was in the fight dismounted with the 5th Army Corps. Excuse me from any more infantry fighting." He probably refers to Five Forks, where Sheridan's men, under Brig. Gen. Thomas Devin, fought dismounted and were forced to give way to Confederate infantry under generals Fitzhugh Lee and George Pickett as the armies grew more desperate, the rebels scrapping to continue against the odds and the Union men just as desperate to end the war. "The day before, March 31, we were badly whipped and I gave myself up as gone. I shall not forget that day as long as I live. I will give you the details some time. I was cut off with eight companies and at one time we were half a mile in the rear of the rebel line. We were dismounted, and when we reached our lines were completely 'played out.' I was reported wounded, captured, killed and everything else; but was merely badly demoralized. The infantry are now hard at it on the right, and I would not be surprised if we had another brush before noon." That report was undoubtedly about Dinwiddie Court House. The letter, with its blow-by-blow accounts, is the equivalent of what a war correspondent might have reported and provides documentation of fighting in the final days leading to the end. Captain Birney concluded his letter: "Peace negotiations are a humbug. They fight just as hard as they ever did. This is written on rebel paper with a rebel pencil. We have nothing now except what we capture."[35] The mention of peace negotiations must have reflected rumors among the troops about the unauthorized talks between generals Ord and Longstreet, for Grant's first message to Lee in that regard was not sent until 7 April at 5:00 P.M.

After the "grand review" in Washington on 23 May 1865, young Birney and other troops were surprised when they were not mustered out and allowed to go home but instead were combined into the First Michigan Veteran Cavalry and sent west to fight Indians. The troops traveled via the Baltimore and Ohio Railroad, thinking they were going home until the train veered west, and then were loaded aboard steamers on the Ohio and Mississippi rivers for the trip to Fort Leavenworth, Kansas. While the Fifth Michigan Cavalry and some other units were mustered out, Birney's and other units were divided into detachments for Powder River and Black Hills expeditions or service at Fort Laramie, Wyoming. One group was trapped by Indians for twelve days until reinforcements arrived. Michigan senators and congressmen protested that 1,216 men of the First, Fifth, Sixth, and Seventh Michigan Cavalry had been "unjustly held in service for six months after they had been ordered mustered out by General Pope." A special appropriation allowed each man $325 for travel home, and they were finally mustered out in Utah on 10 March 1866.[36]

Lieutenant Birney returned to Michigan, serving briefly on appointment as deputy collector of customs of the Port of Bay City, until he was replaced shortly thereafter in what some local sources considered political machinations associated with his grandfather's, father's, and uncles' notoriety as abolitionists. After being honored by other veterans and local elites at a grand banquet in Bay City, he reenlisted in the army with the rank of captain in the Ninth Cavalry. He headed a company of Negro troops, known by the Indians as "buffalo soldiers," in the Indian wars in Texas and in 1870 died mysteriously at the age of twenty-five. He was buried initially at Fort Davis, Texas, and then reinterred in a family plot in Green Wood Cemetery, Brooklyn, where his wife, Mary Deuel Birney, of New York City, and son, Newton, who died in 1868 at age seven months of a brain disorder, also are buried. Mary Birney died in 1884. James G. Birney IV apparently had met his wife while he was serving in New York City during the draft riots in 1863.

Thus closed the military careers of the five Birney offspring, who made perhaps the greatest contributions of any of the children of the abolitionists, securing their status as "Apostles of Equality." Of the five Birneys who had entered the war, only William remained alive as Reconstruction wracked the South.

CHAPTER 17

The U.S. Colored Troops
Tip the Balance

Give us a flag, all free, without a slave.

—SONG OF NEGRO SOLDIERS

DESPITE VICIOUS DEROGATION OF THEIR EFFORTS THAT BEGAN DUR-
ing the war and has persisted in Civil War historiography, the military
abolitionists played an important role in that they were willing to recruit
and lead Negro troops, thus providing the Union with an extra 10 percent of manpower that may have been the key to victory. The Birneys were
invaluable leaders because they had been raised with slaves on their father's
Alabama plantation and understood, perhaps better than most other Northern officers, how to motivate black soldiers. The flood of former slaves and
freedmen to the Union Army deprived the Confederacy of services that were
vital to the military effort. Lincoln's decision to use Negro troops was long
delayed. A history of the war explains, "But, at the time of the Civil War
the Negro was closely associated in the public mind with the political causes
of the strife. The prejudice and opposition against the use of colored troops
was so strong that the war was half finished before they were organized to
any extent."[1] Some historians theorize the Negroes "freed themselves" by
refusing to work any longer for their masters, by escaping to Union lines,
and by joining the Union Army. When the decision to enlist Negroes was
finally made, as a noted abolitionist William Birney was among the first
Union officers named to head the recruiting efforts. The 186,000 Negroes
who ultimately served in the United States Colored Troops strengthened the
Union Army immeasurably as manpower grew short.

David Birney's instincts about refusing to return fugitive slaves were upheld when on 13 March 1862 President Lincoln issued an order forbidding any Union officer from returning a fugitive slave. A history of the Negro troops summarizes how Union policies regarding slaves morphed into their enlistment: "From the beginning of the war Negroes had been a subject of debate. Even before Bull Run, on May 26, 1861, General B. F. Butler had declared that all fugitive slaves would be considered as contraband of war. Congress, however, decided in August that all slaves confiscated should be held subject to the decision of the United States courts."[2] War Department General Orders No. 1, issued on 2 January 1863, authorized enrollment of colored men in the army and navy; the order came the day after Lincoln had issued the Emancipation Proclamation. "No soldier hailed its appearance with more joy than General [David] Birney," his biographer wrote. "He had long hoped for it, and believed that its publication would strengthen the strong man and animate the weak. He had buckled on his sword, because he believed that this rebellion was begun by men whose principal object was to perpetuate the curse of slavery upon our land, while he had determined that, so far as lay in his power, as a man and as a soldier, the curse should be removed."[3]

The war department finally issued General Orders No. 143 on 22 May 1863 establishing a special bureau for organization of black enlisted troops. With the Confederacy opposed to arming slaves, the Union had a field day enlisting black troops from Southern states, including South Carolina, Alabama, Mississippi, Louisiana, Arkansas, and Tennessee. Negro units had grown from 58 to 140 regiments by 1863, providing over 100,000 blacks in uniform. More than 1,500 whites applied to the screening boards in Washington, Cincinnati, and St. Louis for appointment as officers to lead black troops in combat. Only 517 were found qualified; the other nearly 1,000 were rejected for physical or mental shortcomings. Whites were eager for appointment as officers leading black troops, because obviously by this time the willingness of Negroes to fight had been proven in such battles as Island Mounds, Missouri, on 28 October, 1862; Milliken's Bend, Louisiana, on 7 June 1863; and Fort Wagner, South Carolina, on 18 July 1863.

Ten days after the battle of Cedar Mountain, Virginia, on 9 August 1862, New York newspaper publisher Horace Greeley published his famous letter to Lincoln, "The Prayer of Twenty Millions," urging Lincoln to free the slaves as a means of weakening the Confederacy." Lincoln's response, concluding with the words "a personal wish that all men everywhere could be free," has been interpreted as preparing the nation for a momentous announcement. On 22 September 1862 the Emancipation Proclamation was issued, and on 1 January 1863 the final proclamation was made that "Negroes would be received into the military and naval service of the United States Corps."[4]

Historian John T. Hubbell wrote: "The Emancipation Proclamation, issued on January 1, 1863, called for the enrollment of blacks in the Union Army and Navy. It was contained in an almost offhand passage—fully in keeping with Lincoln's tendency to hint, approach indirectly, and finally, defend the stated policy. Yet the proclamation was fundamental. It was a war message, a political document. The government of the United States, through the Office of the President, was now unequivocally on the side of emancipation and of bringing black men into the army of the Republic."[5]

Lincoln became convinced by mid-1862 that the emancipation of slaves in the seceded states would be necessary to win the war as well as to discourage Great Britain and France from helping the Confederacy. He believed that Negroes would fight for their own freedom and meet the Union's desperate need for more volunteers. "With Maj. Charles W. Foster at the helm," writes military historian Joseph T. Glatthaar, "the Bureau of Colored Troops administered more than 186,000 black and white officers and men, and at one time had over 123,000 soldiers in uniform—a force larger than the field armies that either Lt. Gen. Ulysses S. Grant or Maj. Gen. William T. Sherman directly oversaw at the height of their campaigns in 1864 and 1865. Blacks alone did not win the war, but timely and extensive support from them contributed significantly and may have made the difference between a Union victory and stalemate or defeat. Free and slave, they tipped the delicate balance of power squarely in favor of the North."[6]

The nation's record in dealing with black soldiers has featured sporadic fits of racism overcome only by desperate need for help. U.S. armies in the Revolutionary War and the War of 1812 had reluctantly employed Negro troops in times of crisis while periodically barring them based on political, racial grounds. An almost totally ignored factor of the Civil War is that the Confederate Army was the first to enlist Negroes. Two weeks after Fort Sumter a Negro unit was reported marching through Atlanta on the way to Virginia. In June 1861 the legislature of Tennessee had authorized enlistment of Negroes, and seventy free Negroes joined the Confederate Army in Lynchburg, Virginia. On 2 January 1864, the Irishman Gen. Patrick Cleburne presented his proposal to emancipate all slaves who would fight for the Confederacy, along with their families, stating, "As between the loss of independence and the loss of slavery, we assume that every patriot will freely give up the latter—give up the negro slave rather than be a slave himself."[7]

Several historians have observed that Cleburne's motivation was based on the anticipation of Confederate defeat and the end of slavery. He reportedly felt such a move perhaps would gain recognition of the South by England and would slow Union recruitment of black soldiers. He even stated a hope that if the South abolished slavery blacks would desert the Union Army and join the Confederacy.

"He saw Confederate defeat as very likely and with it the end of slavery," reports historian Mauriel Phillips Joslyn. "So, if the South were to lose its slaves, it would be better to at least gain the political independence for which it was fighting. Voluntarily ending slavery, he believed, would cause England, which had instituted emancipation in its possessions in the 1830s, to openly side with the South. He further felt that such a move on the part of the Confederacy would sap the Union's efforts to use black soldiers against it. He even asserted that Southern-born Black Union soldiers would no longer see a need for their services and would desert, return home and take up arms for the Confederacy!"[8]

However, as the war continued, the traditional Southern view of slaves prevailed. CSA general Howell Cobb observed a widely accepted principle concerning the use of Negro troops by the Confederacy: "You can't keep black and white troops together and you can't trust Negroes by themselves. Use all the Negroes you can get for purposes for which you need them but don't arm them. The day you make soldiers of them is the beginning of the end of the revolution. If slaves make good soldiers, our whole theory of slavery is wrong."[9] Cobb's lack of trust of Negroes was confirmed by the experience of Union major general Benjamin Butler, whose troops took New Orleans. Butler saw that the black "native guards" had not left the city when it was abandoned by white Confederates. "He sent for several of the most prominent colored men of the city," wrote historian Charles Wesley, "and asked why they had accepted service under the Confederate Government which was set up for the purpose of holding their brethren and kindred in eternal slavery. They replied that they dared not to refuse, that they had hoped by serving the Confederates to advance nearer to equality with the whites and they had longed to throw the weight of their class with the Union forces and with the cause with which their own dearest hopes were identified."[10]

A political decision inherent in the system of slavery was at the basis of the rejection of Negro troops in the Confederate Army. Early in the war the Confederate Congress had made it a crime punishable by death for any white person to train any Negro or biracial person to arms. Although there were no reports of whites being executed for that offense, a number of lynchings of armed Negroes were reported through the end of the war when, ironically, what the South needed most was soldiers of any color who knew weaponry and would fight in its defense. Confederate abandonment of Negro troops after the early days of the war was described by Christian A. Fleetwood, a former soldier, who observed, "But the primary successes of the South closed its eyes to its only chance of salvation, while at the same time the eyes of the North were opened. In 1865, the South saw, and endeavored to remedy its error. On March 9, 1865, the Confederate Congress passed a bill, recommended by General Lee, authorizing the enlistment of 200,000 Negroes; but it was then too late."[11] The war ended with Lee's surrender to Lt. Gen. Ulysses S. Grant on 9 April 1865 at Appomattox, Virginia.

The North had its philosophical problems, too, with enlistment of Negroes. Historian Robert C. Kennedy observed that in the spring of 1862, when Gen. David Hunter raised a regiment of Negroes in South Carolina for Union service, he was met with the attitude of "this is a white man's war." Democratic congressman Charles A. Wickliffe, of Bardstown, Kentucky, introduced a resolution inquiring whether a regiment of fugitive slaves was being raised and whether the war department had given authority for such action. The resolution was referred to General Hunter by Secretary of War Edwin M. Stanton. Hunter's letter in reply to the query cited instructions by Gen. W. T. Sherman and former secretary of war Simon Cameron "to employ all loyal persons offering their services in defense of the Union and for the suppression of this rebellion in any manner I might see fit, or that the circumstances might call for." Hunter wryly noted, "[I]t is the masters who have, in every instance, been the 'fugitives,'—running away from loyal slaves as well as loyal soldiers, and whom we have only partially been able to see—chiefly their heads over ramparts, or, rifle in hand, dodging behind trees, in the extreme distance. In the absence of any 'fugitive master' law, the deserted slaves would be wholly without remedy, had not the crime of treason given them the right to pursue, capture, and bring back those persons of whose protection they have been thus suddenly bereft." He noted, "I have clothed, equipped and armed the only loyal regiment yet raised in South Carolina," and expressed the hope that by the end of next fall he would "be able to present to the Government from forty-eight to fifty thousand of these hardy and devoted soldiers." A reading of the letter on the floor of the House by the clerk "brought out such a storm of laughter, from both friends and foes, that further action was impossible. The beginning of 1863 saw the opening of the doors to the Negro in every direction. For two years the fierce and determined opposition had kept them out, but now the bars were down and they came pouring in."[12]

Born in Alabama six years before his brother David, William Birney entered the Union Army in 1862 as a captain in the Fourth New Jersey Infantry, being promoted to major before Chancellorsville. Commissioned a brigadier, he recruited black troops in Maryland, emptying jails and slave pens and sending soldiers into the plantation areas to secure more recruits. His activities annoyed loyal Maryland slaveholders, who complained to Lincoln. The president telegraphed Colonel Birney on 3 October 1863, saying "Please give me as near as you can the number of slaves you have recruited in Maryland. Of course, the number is not to include the free colored. A. LINCOLN." Birney responded the same day, "Yours just received. Between 1,250 and 1,300, as near as I can judge. WM. BIRNEY." Lincoln then telegraphed, "Take care of colored troops in your charge, but do nothing further about that branch of affairs until further orders. Particularly do nothing about General Vickers, of Kent County." Birney wrote the adjutant general on 13 October, informing him of Lincoln's order and commenting, "the general in question was formerly a noisy constitutional Union man, but has recently, and on the slave question, become a virulent enemy of the government and associate with known secessionists." He also mentioned a Judge Carmichael, "who is so vindictive and dangerous an enemy to the Government. They are, I am happy to say, not sustained by the mass of the population, which earnestly desires the enlistment of the negro, especially the slaves. My officers went unarmed and alone through nearly every county in the central part of the Eastern Shore, and everywhere received aid and sympathy from the people, except the rebel sympathizers among the slave-owners and except a few politicians." Lincoln appointed a three-man board to review claims by "alleged owners of slaves who may be enlisted" and to approve compensation of $300 per slave enlisted as long as the owners swore oaths of allegiance to the government. Colonel Birney was directed to provide copies of all muster rolls. The order provided "any slave so enlisting shall be forever free."[13] At Camp Birney, which Colonel Birney established near Baltimore, some of the Negro troops had no weapons and were forced to train with broomsticks. Nevertheless, they seemed to find army life attractive, noted abolitionist minister Col. Thomas Higginson, commander of the Union's First South Carolina. "As to camp life, they have little to sacrifice; they are better fed, housed and clothed than ever in their lives before."[14] Higginson observed that as a race they had never attempted a widespread insurrection against their Southern masters and attributed this to the general hopelessness of their situation. He commented: "They had no knowledge, no money, no arms, no drill, no organization—above all no mutual confidence. . . . They had no mountain passes to defend, no country or communities to protect."[15]

William Birney was relieved of recruiting duty on 12 February 1864 and was ordered to Hilton Head, South Carolina, in command of the Seventh and Ninth Regiments, U.S. Colored Troops. He planned to raise fifteen more Negro regiments in South Carolina, Georgia, and Florida, writing from Beaufort, South Carolina, asking Maj. Charles W. Foster to gain approval to give each recruit forty acres of land and furnish his family commissary stores at cost. "How legislators can imagine we can raise troops at $7 a month I cannot see. The man must have $2 for himself, and he cannot support his family on the other $5. Hence the great numbers of desertions in this department . . . because their families were starving. The field here is black for the harvest and I wish to be in with my sickle."[16] Birney never received a response to this request, and the regiments were not raised, although in June 1864 the pay for black troops was equalized to the thirteen dollars monthly received by the white soldiers.

Birney has been credited with a major role in subduing Florida, a state that was providing vast supplies of beef to Confederate forces, even though he was only assigned there during five months of 1864. Birney occupied Jacksonville and conducted mid-summer raids into steamy eastern Florida with two regiments of Negro troops, confiscating an estimated $2 million worth of cattle, horses, and mules; arms, cartridges and powder; rail cars; lighters; and a sawmill. Birney's troops also destroyed cornfields, torpedo manufactories, and tore up bridges, railroads, and telegraph lines. Birney's Raid in late April 1864 destroyed the Starke plantation, said to be the most productive plantation in the DeLeon Springs area, east of Pensacola in the Florida Panhandle. His troops destroyed a grist mill and riverboats, liberated slaves, and took some rebel prisoners. Confederates considered it an attempt by the Yankees to "redeem themselves" for their defeat in February at the Battle of Olustee, although Birney had not been present at that battle. A. G. Brown, a U.S. Treasury agent accompanying Birney and his troops, reported that the expedition up the St. John's River started on 26 April on two transport steamers loaded with Negro troops and towing six large boats. "'At Welaka, . . . ninety miles above Jacksonville, . . . [w]e seized here a quantity of cotton . . . The next night, reached Sanders, where we quartered ourselves on an old hoary-headed virulent rebel, who said, if he were young, he would fight us twenty years. The next morning we confiscated his slaves and carried off the old traitor's horses.'" Failing to capture Starke, the proprietor, described as "a notorious rebel," the Union troops nevertheless intercepted a rebel messenger with important letters relating to blockade runners. Two schooners, blockade runners from Nassau, were confiscated along with the cotton they carried. The raid, Brown concluded, "'has cleared the country east of the St. John's of rebels, and has put into the hands of the government not less than two hundred thousand dollars worth of property, in cotton and beef-cattle.'"[17]

There were conflicting opinions in his command about William Birney, one Negro soldier writing, "There is but one man that can make the 'Florida Expedition' a perfect success with the forces composed chiefly of colored troops, and that man is Genl. Birney. The men of the regiment would follow him anywhere, and our confidence in him is unbounded. He is a stern soldier but his heart is in the right place; and he feels that is a part of his mission on earth to elevate our race."[18] A vastly different view was taken by a Lieutenant Norton of the Eighth U.S. Colored Troops, no doubt a white officer, since few blacks were given command posts, "who complained that 'the District of Florida' is cursed by a commander called Brigadier General Birney. It seems to be a sort of dunce block for the government—a place where they send men good for nothing in any other place. He is utterly unable to be quiet or let anybody else be." Norton also complained again that Birney had ordered the Eighth U.S. Colored Troops to camp on a horse cemetery and made them stand in a pelting rain for two hours on a wharf.[19]

Birney recalled, "I accepted the rank of colonel of colored troops, Mr. [Edwin] Stanton [Secretary of War] saying, jestingly, that I should not have my brigadiership until I had raised a regiment." Birney explained his relationship with and conclusions about the Union Army's use of Negroes as soldiers:

> Going into the colored troops was personally a sacrifice to me. My friends generally were surprised and grieved at it. But I had gone into the army to aid in abolishing slavery; I thought the national interest demanded the use in the army of a vast neglected physical force; I had confidence that, by entire devotion to the work, a most efficient body of troops could be put into the field, and I hoped that the opposition and prejudice of officers high in rank might be so moderated as to give the colored troops a fair chance of distinction in the field. In this hope I was grievously disappointed, as impartial history will show. For a long time, we were kept on the outskirts of the war, and when at last, through the efforts of Gen. Butler and the good sense of Gen. Grant, we were united with the body of the army, our opportunities of distinction were quietly slipped away from us. The only unpleasant part of my military life was caused by my endeavors to prevent discrimination against the colored troops and their officers.[20]

Obviously, the final comment was primarily aimed at an incident at Appomattox when General E.O.C. Ord prevented Birney and the Negro troops from ending the conflict against Lee and his rebels.

Thomas Morris Chester, the black correspondent of the *Philadelphia Press,* who was present at the front in Virginia, reported "the enthusiastic admiration of the colored troops under Gen. Wm. Birney for that gallant officer. They are all from Maryland and were taken from the plantations of their former owners by the General, whom they regard as their deliverer." Chester observed, "The secret of Gen. Birney's success is, that he treats his men as any other gallant officer would regard the defenders of the Union." The writer also commented that "the colored troops have cheerfully accepted the conditions of the Confederate Government, that between them no quarter is to be shown. Those here have not the least idea of living after they fall into the hands of the enemy, and the rebels act very much as if they entertained similar sentiments with reference to the blacks. Even deserters fear to come into our lines where colored troops may be stationed."[21]

One of the few times the two Birney brothers who were general officers were known to have collaborated in battle produced a spectacular, if bloody, victory. Brig. Gen. William Birney, leading a brigade of Negro troops, was commanded by his brother Maj. Gen. David Bell Birney, heading Tenth Corps, at the Battle of New Market Heights, Virginia, in September 1864. William's brigade attacked Fort Gregg, an action marked by heroism, but one that ultimately was unsuccessful. The battle pitted Robert E. Lee's "Grenadier Guards," the First, Fourth, and Fifth Texas and Third Arkansas regiments of infantry under Lt. Col. Frederick S. Bass, against Col. Samuel Duncan's brigade of U.S. Colored Troops. A battlefield history by Michael D. Gorman reported, "During this time Generals Grant and Birney rode alongside of the troops towards the head of the column. General Grant's presence was instantly known to the soldiers, and acted like magnetism along the whole line." When regimental commander Col. John W. Ames called retreat, Gen. David Birney countermanded the order and called for a renewed attack on the rebel works. "They marched onward and soon carried the works at the intersection of the New Market and Mill roads."[22]

Despite massive losses, including all of their officers, the Negro troops under Sgt. Powhatan Beatty continued their charge and took the heights. Cpl. James Miles lost an arm but continued fighting, loading and discharging his piece with one hand. Miles and thirteen other black soldiers and two white officers won the Medal of Honor for heroism at New Market. A Negro soldier William Birney had recruited in Maryland, Sgt. Major Christian A. Fleetwood, described the act that won him the Medal of Honor citation as follows: "Saved the regimental colors after eleven of the twelve color guards had been shot down around it."[23] (The official federal citation stated that only two color guards had been shot down.) The Negro troops' assault on

Fort Harrison breached Lee's line around Richmond the first time. Union pressure north of the James River forced Lee to weaken his Petersburg lines in response. It was the closest Yankee troops had come to Richmond, with some units just two miles away and able to see church spires in the city.

Meanwhile, David Birney had become ill with what was described as "malarial fever" but may have been typhoid, in the first few days of October, but refused to leave the field. Despite his weakness from disease and medicine, he rose upon hearing of an enemy movement on 7 October and mounted his horse, Eclipse, and rallied troops until noon, when he was placed in an ambulance but remained on the battlefield until the action was over at dusk. In what was known as the Battle of Darbytown Road, Lee's counterattack was repulsed and cost about one thousand rebel dead, with Union losses at only about one hundred. John Townsend Trowbridge, a Northern journalist who visited the battlefield shortly after the war, wrote, "Butler's colored regiments formed unflinchingly under fire and made their gallant charge, wiping out with their own blood, the insults that had been heaped upon them by white troops."[24]

David Birney, physically exhausted by his exertions, and ill, finally was relieved by General Grant and sent home aboard the *Greyhound,* Butler's dispatch boat, on 10 October to Philadelphia to recuperate. He reached Philadelphia on 11 October, Election Day, and despite his weakened condition insisted on being taken to the polls. He had to overcome a Copperhead (antiwar, pro-slavery) challenge to his qualifications but finally was able to vote and cast his ballot for Lincoln and the entire Republican ticket. On 18 October 1864, just eleven days after leading his troops at New Market, David Birney was on his deathbed. About noon he tried to rise and said, "Boys, the road through the woods will soon be completed; we must move on it cautiously, and make an attack on the flank." Later in the day he called to his bodyservant, straightened up, waved his hand, and said, "John, tell the staff to get ready, I'm going now." It was just an hour before his death. His last delirious words were "Keep your eyes on that flag, boys." He was thirty-nine.[25]

At this point in the war William Birney commanded the Second Division of the Twenty-fifth Corps, the only all-Negro unit in the Union Army. While many white Union officers, personified by General Ord, were unconvinced of the fighting ability of the Negro troops, as well as wary of the idea of mixing white and black troops, a white officer leading the 102nd Michigan U.S.C.T. in Florida sent a letter home that attested:

There are strong arms and brave hearts under the black skins that the enemy may well dread to meet in a conflict for life. We have marched side by side, camped on the same ground, and worked in the trenches with white regiments, and there has never been any feeling of enmity or aversion displayed by the white soldiers—the contrary has been the case. The old notion, that the colored soldier would have a demoralizing effect upon the army is all nonsense. The white soldier is only too glad to have assistance, no matter what the color is. The fact is, colored troops are a success and have done and are doing more than was expected of them by their most earnest advocates.[26]

As troop shortages, illness, and desertions continued to plague the Southern army, Robert E. Lee's version of Gen. Patrick Cleburne's proposal to enlist and free Negroes was finally adopted by the Confederate Congress, but not until 18 February 1865, when the struggle was nearly over. At that point the hard-pressed rebel soldiers, especially, were heartily in favor of support from Negroes. According to historian John Horn, "The Confederates gave the United States Colored Troops the highest accolade available. In February 1865 the Southern soldiers in Lee's command voted overwhelmingly to admit to their ranks free blacks and slaves. Recruitment had barely begun when the Confederacy collapsed."[27]

Although some of the estimated four million black slaves in the South proved their fidelity to their homeland by refusing to oppose the Yankees, there were legions who could hardly wait to serve the Union in opposition to their white masters. By the time Lee convinced Confederate leaders to try to use the black manpower resource and grant freedom to the slaves who fought, as well as to their families, the war was nearly over. It was, of course, a futile hope "All but the most dull witted of slaves comprehended the absurdity of fighting for their own bondage," observed William Marvel, author of a history of the Appomattox Campaign, "and only the direst necessity could induce any black man, slave or free, to enlist; two condemned burglars became the first volunteers, offering their services on the day they were to have been hanged."[28] Much of the Northern population had the same prejudices against Negroes as were found in the South, but Lincoln's decision to enlist black men came in time, however, to provide useful manpower while the rebels refused to admit the need for them, or were so adamant against their use in battle, until it was far too late. And the black troops knew that if the Union won, they and their families and countrymen would gain freedom—a goal they could not bank on if they fought for the South.

Had Lee convinced Jefferson Davis to come to the decision to recruit and arm blacks earlier than in the last week of the war, the rebels might well have had the manpower to win. By the week before Appomattox, Lee had mustered only thirty-six Negro soldiers who were to be given their freedom if the South won, according to some reports. Black Union troops under Maj. Gen. William Birney, commander of the Twenty-fifth Corps, some of whom were former slaves he had recruited in Maryland, were on hand at the fateful confrontation that forced Lee to surrender at Appomattox, Virginia, on 8–9 April 1865. It was a dramatic and telling meeting that spoke directly to philosophical and sectional racial attitudes: abolitionist Yankee Birney versus Confederate cavalier Lee. The wisdom of Lee's decision still echoes. "Years after Lee's death, Jefferson Davis said Lee told him he would carry on guerrilla warfare for twenty years rather than surrender," said Professor John Y. Simon, of Southern Illinois University, editor of "The Papers of U.S. Grant." Professor Simon amplifies: "However, this is pure Davis, the politician and Confederate. Lee was the premier military man of honor and recognized defeat. He was a true American and understood that the battle, and the cause, were lost at Appomattox."[29]

Therefore, after reviewing the long and troubled history of the use of Negro troops, it could fairly be said that one man—Jefferson Davis—singlehandedly stopped the Confederacy from enlisting Negro soldiers and contributed to the defeat of his cause, and that one man—Abraham Lincoln—initiated enlistment of Negro soldiers and helped assure Union victory.

CHAPTER 18

Appomattox Sundays

If slaves make good soldiers, our whole theory of slavery is wrong.

—CSA GEN. HOWELL COBB

ROBERT E. LEE AND HIS ARMY OF NORTHERN VIRGINIA HAD FOUGHT on long after any reasonable expectation that the Confederate cause could be successful, according to historian Clifford Dowdey, who estimated 30 September 1864 at Fort Harrison near Richmond (where major generals David and William Birney had been among the commanders of black Union troops) as "close as any to the date when nothing remained to support the most desperate hope."[1] So the war went on for six more months and thousands more died in vain for the "lost cause." Apparently Lee had realized for months the situation was hopeless, although Confederate president Jefferson Davis was still blindly optimistic and in total denial of the perilous condition of his army and impending defeat. Lee's despair was so great, according to one historical report, he even pondered the ultimate escape—allowing himself to be shot in the line of duty. As he looked out over the battle lines, facing defeat, he wrote in a letter to his wife, Mary, that he had briefly contemplated the unthinkable: "'How easily I could be rid of this, and be at rest! I have only to ride along the line and all will be over! . . . But it is our duty to live. What will become of the women and children of the South if we are not here to protect them?'"[2] Lee's papers reveal that Lee, Gen. James Longstreet, and Secretary of War John Breckenridge all agreed as early as February 1865 that there was no hope the war could be won, "but no one was willing to assume the responsibility of trying to convince Davis of this."[3]

The four-year bloodbath was nearing a dramatic climax. The final act of the drama appropriately opened in a house of the Lord. It was a gloomy

Sunday morning, 2 April 1865. Jefferson Davis, president of the Confederate States of America for the past four years, sat quietly in St. Paul's Episcopal Church at the corner of Grace and Ninth streets, in Richmond, Virginia. Davis, gaunt, his face grim with stress and pockmarked by malaria from his younger days, worshiped in pew number 63 in St. Paul's, also joined by his aide, Frank Lubbock, the governor of Texas, and the army's chief of ordnance, Gen. Josiah Gorgas. Churchgoers heard explosions from the nearby James River that confirmed the looming danger. Union ships were bombarding, Confederate powder magazines were exploding, and Union troops under Grant were preparing to breach the thin defenses and storm the capital to end the bloody four-year conflict that both North and South had grown to despise. A hush enveloped the church as the Reverend Dr. Charles Minnigerode, pastor of St. Paul's, intoned with a German accent, "The Lord is in his holy temple: let all the earth keep silence before him." The silence was about to be broken. It was 11:00 A.M. when the solemnity of the service was invaded by footsteps, whispers, and signs of alarm among the worshipers. General Lee had already told government officials the city was indefensible and the army must retreat soon, statements punctuated by the explosions on the river from the direction of City Point. But Davis, true to form, did not take the news as final and had gone stolidly to church. The aged sexton of St. Paul's, William Irving, stopped the dispatch bearer, an eager young boy, in the vestibule. "I must see President Davis," said the boy, handing him a note. "General Lee telegraphs that he can hold his position no longer. Come to the office immediately. Breckenridge."[4] Irving eased into the sanctuary with the fateful missive from the Confederate secretary of war, Gen. John Breckenridge. Davis and other officials tiptoed out of the service, their grave faces revealing fear that the glorious days of the Confederacy were at last coming to an end.

Despite the turmoil in Richmond, Jeff Davis held a brief cabinet meeting and then ordered a slave named John Davis to crate up his marble bust; the servant promised to "put it where no Yankee will ever find it." David Bradford, another servant, was sent to retrieve the silver spoons and forks that he had reminded Davis had been forgotten.[5] Gun carriages were being destroyed and cannons spiked. Whisky gushed in the gutters from smashed barrels to keep it from looters and Yankees, and rebel guards whipped federal prisoners for their jeering catcalls, unleashed as they were being marched, howling, out of the capital. Most pathetic was the last coffle of slaves, under the whip of a veteran trader, one Robert Lumpkin, who operated a notorious slave jail in downtown Richmond. Charles Carleton Coffin, an author and war correspondent traveling with the advancing Union Army days before the fall of Richmond, found Lumpkin "shipping out fifty men, women and children. This sad and weeping fifty, in handcuffs and chains were [he declared] the last slave coffle that ever shall tread the soil of America."[6] Coffin later recalled his impressions of the fall of Richmond and the fires consuming the city: "General Ewell crosses the bridge, riding an iron gray horse. He wears an old faded cloak and slouch hat. He is brutal and profane, mingling oaths with his orders. Following him is John Cabell Breckenridge, the long black glossy hair of other days changed to gray, his high, broad forehead wrinkled and furrowed. The Rebel troops behold the conflagration as they wind along the roads and through the green fields towards the southwest, and memory brings back scenes of their earlier rejoicing. It is the 2nd of April, four years lacking two weeks since the drunken carousel over the passage of the ordinance of Secession."[7]

Despite the turmoil, Davis auctioned his goods and reported to his wife, Varina, by letter that he had received $28,400. The type of currency was not disclosed. He described the actions of the Negro slaves: "Called off on horseback to the Depot, I left the servants to go down with the boxes and they left. Tippy—Watson came willingly, Spencer came against my will, Robert, Alf., V. B. and Ives got drunk—David Bradford went back from the Depot to bring out the spoons and forks which I was told had been left— and to come out with Genl. Breckenridge; since then I have not heard from either of them." That evening, Davis, his personal staff, cabinet members, and hangers-on, entrained for Danville, in southern Virginia. On his arrival there he issued, on 4 April, a proclamation of extreme political correctness: "Let us not despond my countrymen; but relying on the never failing mercies and protecting care of our God, let us meet the foe with fresh defiance, with unconquered and unconquerable hearts. Relieved from the necessity of guarding particular points, our army will be free to move from point to point, to strike the enemy in detail far from his base."[8] Later he would admit that the statement, "viewed by the light of subsequent events, it may fairly be said was oversanguine."

Lee and Longstreet revealed the desperation of the Confederate situation in an exchange of letters considering arming government staff members in Richmond and impressing gold from banks to procure supplies as well as ideas of making peace through negotiations with General Grant. Longstreet wrote Lee on 7 March 1865: "The gold is in the country, and most of it is lying idle. Let us take it at once and save Richmond, and end the war. If we hold Richmond and keep our cotton, the war cannot last more than a year longer. If we give up Richmond we shall never be recognized by foreign powers until the government of the United States sees fit to recognize us. If we hold Richmond and let the enemy have our cotton, it seems to me that we shall furnish him the means to carry on the war against us." Longstreet estimated the Union force, comprised of the armies of the Potomac and James and Sheridan's cavalry, at 111,000 against Lee's 39,897.[9]

General Birney's colored troops marched in wonder into the Confederate capital on 3 April, having been evacuated only hours before by Lee's Army of Northern Virginia. Singing "John Brown's Body," they paraded through rows of flaming buildings. Notorious slave dealer Robert Lumpkin was surprised by the Confederate decision to abandon Richmond, as he had not yet managed to sell his latest shipment of slaves. As Richmond's Negroes cheered, Union troops halted without command outside Lumpkin's slave jail to pay tribute to the throng packing the windows while the slaves inside broke into a grateful song, "Slavery Chain Done Broke at Last." Lumpkin had marched his valuable coffle (estimated to be worth $50,000) to the train station the previous night, when they were observed by the author Coffin. However, Lumpkin was unable to get passage on the last train out, since it had been reserved for President Davis, so he marched the slaves back through the streets of Richmond to the jail and locked them in for the night. The next morning the Twenty-eighth Colored Infantry, the only Negro unit from Indiana, part of Maj. Gen. August Kautz's First Division of the Twenty-fifth Corps, commanded by Brig. Gen. Charles S. Russell, opened the jail and set the slaves free. Author James W. Loewen observes: "Robert Lumpkin's occupation—slave dealer—abruptly ceased to exist. We do not know how he spent that day, April 3, when his world turned upside down. But he soon realized that he loved Mary Ann, the black woman he had bought a decade earlier who had already borne him two children. Not long after the liberation of Richmond, he married her."[10]

Black soldiers from Birney's division were among the first troops into Petersburg, twenty-five miles from Richmond, the same day. As the Confederates exited the capital and the rail center, the Union force took chase with the Negro soldiers out front. Among the units under Maj. Gen. William Birney pursuing Lee's army beginning on 3 April was the Thirty-first U.S. Colored Troops from New York, organized during April 1864 on Hart Island under Col. Henry C. Ward. The unit was consolidated with the Thirtieth Connecticut Colored Volunteers and included black Canadians and other foreign-born black soldiers. The Thirty-first was one of thirty-two regiments comprising the Twenty-fifth Corps. It was present at the mine explosion during the siege of Petersburg and was one of the first units into Richmond. The Twenty-fifth Corps was composed of colored troops from the Tenth and Eighteenth Corps, consolidated 3 December 1864 under the command of Maj. Gen. Godfrey Weitzel. William Birney's Second Division accompanied the Army of the James under General Ord on a march from the James River to Hatcher's Run, a movement that began on 27 March 1865. Birney's division was present in the fighting at Petersburg and followed Lee's army to Appomattox from 3 April to 8 April 1865. General Sheridan reported capturing an incensed and indignant rebel courier riding a mule on 4 April whose dispatches, hidden in his shoe, revealed Lee's position at the town of Amelia Court House, his need for provisions, and an estimate of his numbers since the request to the commissary for three hundred thousand rations probably indicating a ten-day supply for about thirty thousand men.[11]

Approximately two thousand U.S. Colored Troops (about 3 percent of the federal force) made the one-hundred-mile march from Richmond and Petersburg to Appomattox Court House with Birney as part of Ord's Army of the James and were involved in the last days of the war. The black troops passed through the villages of Blacks & Whites, Nottoway Court House, Burkeville Junction, Rice's Station, Farmville, and Walker's Church.

In contrast to the Union's marching juggernaut of Negro soldiers hot on Lee's heels, the rebels' tentative, long-delayed attempt to organize colored troops had little success. However, a brigade of Confederate States Colored Troops had been assembled in Richmond, and a Union chaplain observed a gray-clad company with their muskets stacked constructing breastworks along a retreat route to Painesville. The unit was attacked on 5 April by Union cavalry, believed to be the only time Negro Confederate troops were ever in battle. When Lee surrendered at Appomattox, thirty-six Negroes were listed on the Confederate paroles. Most were noncombatants—either servants, free blacks, musicians, cooks, teamsters, or blacksmiths.

The Union chase was nearing its end. Near Appomattox Court House, a short, curly-haired, steely-eyed officer, Maj. Gen. E. O. C. Ord rose in his stirrups and squinted into the sun to better scan the valley. As his mount shook his head, whinnied softly, and scuffed the ground restlessly, Ord peered across the fields of bluebells, pendulous blooms swaying in the soft breeze and, far away, sparkling like blinking dots of sun on a flat green sea. To a waiting courier, General Ord blurted, "Tell General Birney to get his men back, out of sight. Behind the trees would be best." The courier, a fresh-faced lieutenant, hesitated, and said carefully, "Sir, begging your pardon, General Birney's men are moving fast to cut off the Rebs. He's in hot pursuit . . . Sir?" Ord spat angrily, "You have my orders, lieutenant, now go!"

It was the morning of 8 April 1865. Maj. Gen. William Birney had marched his men one hundred miles from Richmond, the last forty miles taking all night. Although exhausted, they were exhilarated to catch sight of Robert E. Lee's rebel troops. Somehow they had found strength to keep their legs and feet moving. They were grim-faced, determined Negro troopers of the Second Division, Twenty-fifth Corps, Army of the James. They had been patrolling swamps and pastures in Florida eight months before when word came from General Grant to head north. They were needed in Virginia to cut off the rebels, to help end the war. It was going to be over soon, they thought, the excitement of the time giving them superhuman endurance. "Keep moving, end this damn thing now," they thought. "Keep moving." The term "foot cavalry," which Stonewall Jackson's troops had coined, came to mind. They were just like horses with boots.

On a nearby hill Birney leaned forward on his mount, straining to see through the glass. He could see tiny specks, men in blue, sweeping through the valley below, flowing inexorably southwest. On far hillsides, gray dots rose to the summit, disappeared for a time, then reappeared on the next summit, fading into the horizon after mounting each succeeding crest. Suddenly a courier appeared, yellow-fringed cape flapping, lathered mount's hooves clattering on the rocky hillside. With Ord's order, Birney's face turned purple. He puffed near to exploding, exclaiming, "What? We're not to be allowed to end it!" He thought, "We're so close we can see their bare feet, ragged uniforms, many with no muskets, spavined, starving horses . . . We can wrap it up. What is Ord thinking?" Despite the courier's message, Birney kept his men going forward.

At the barricades with the students revolting against France's King Louis Philippe in 1848, seeking jobs and the right to vote, William Birney, then professor of English literature at the University of Bourges, had been filled with the spirit of freedom. The corrupt, oppressive regime of the last king of France had been defeated, and universal suffrage and the right to work were being embraced. Now, with hundreds of former black slaves at his back, he was feeling the same power that had intoxicated him in France. This time the conflict involved the goal of universal freedom, fulfillment of the promise of America. It was not to be, however. Birney and his Negro troops would not be allowed to pursue what some had romantically thought was a chance to capture Robert E. Lee.

With his troops near Farmville during a lull in the chase, Birney saw a horse far in the distance, coming fast. "What's this?" he thought. "Somebody in a big hurry. But who and for what purpose?" Soon General Ord galloped up, curtly summoned him to ride alongside, snapping unceremoniously, "General Birney, you are relieved of duty." Birney had figured for some time that his part in the grand battle for freedom was nearly over. Ord had made that clear by keeping his men away from the front whenever possible, assigning them distasteful tasks and camp areas away from water and supplies. Birney believed the general had resented the fact that Birney's men were first into Petersburg and that others had marched into Richmond with Maj. Gen. Godfrey Weitzel. "What was I to do, hold them back?" Birney thought, smiling. "Troops have begun to call something easy 'like Grant took Richmond'; hell, it was Weitzel who took Richmond." Ord directed Birney to report to City Point to await a new assignment.

The entire Twenty-fifth Corps of Negro troops was ordered to Texas to attempt control of the Apache and other Indians.[12] The Indians called the Negro soldiers "buffalo soldiers," because, in the Indians' view, they fought with the ferocity of wild buffaloes, and their black, kinky hair resembled the shaggy, curly manes between the horns of the hulking animals. The buffalo soldiers, some in Texas led for several years by Capt. James G. Birney IV, would make history as fierce, relentless fighters taming the frontier. Blasting a letter to Maj. Gen. Benjamin F. Butler, Birney charged Ord with "discrimination against the Negro troops on the final campaign." Birney complained that his mistreatment by Ord occurred because he was "damned as a Butler man." He accused Ord of discrimination against Negro troops, including keeping them away from the front whenever possible. "He was much chagrined at my getting into Petersburg first and censured me for it," Birney wrote to Butler.[13] In a letter to Butler, General Weitzel confirmed that the Twenty-fifth Corps of Negro troops had entered both Petersburg and Richmond first and observed that Birney felt he was being put down by Ord because his troops had been alert, discovered the evacuation, and therefore were first to enter Petersburg.

Historian Bernarr Cresap observed: "Ord's management of the black troops was in keeping with his previous attitudes on matters racial and political. His conservatism meant that Ord was willing to forgive rebellious Southerners and forget their sin of secession if they would but return to the Union. Further, it meant that the black people should be free, but, as they were unprepared to assume responsibilities, they would have to be looked after. Those views stand in contrast with those of Birney, a self-styled Radical, with those of Butler, and with those of many others that the Southerners must be punished and their ex-slaves elevated." Cresap drew the conclusion that Ord "probably thought of the war as an unfortunate encounter between gentlemen brought on by unscrupulous politicians." Although Birney's black troops had acquitted themselves well under fire, Ord still looked on them as auxiliary to white troops, and Cresap concluded, "If he had his way there would have been no Negro soldiers enlisted in the Union Army."[14]

Maj. Gen. Joshua Lawrence Chamberlain, Maine's famed hero of Little Round Top at Gettysburg, in his recollection of the last action at Appomattox, stated, "One striking feature I can never forget—Birney's black men abreast of us, pressing forward to save the white men's country."[15] Chamberlain recalled Birney's Negro soldiers on the march, perhaps on the eighth of April, but by the ninth they were no longer under Birney's command, for he had been relieved of duty and sent to the rear by General Ord. The Second Division was split, Doubleday's brigade being assigned to the First Division Twenty-Fourth Corps under Robert S. Foster, and the Third Brigade of William W. Woodward posted to John W. Turner's Independent Division.

No explanation of William Birney's dismissal was given by Ord, according to Cresap, although the commanding general hinted in his official reports that Birney's work was unsatisfactory. What Chamberlain's statement confirms is that Birney's troops were in the vanguard of the attack, no doubt on 8 April, just before the abolitionist general clashed with Ord over the order to hold back his troops. If, as Cresap contended, Ord had been in position to "annihilate" Lee, it seems likely that it was Birney and his black troops who had put him in that position on 8 April. It is frightening to speculate what the aftermath of the war might have been like if Birney's black troops had killed or captured Lee; obviously, a whole new tone would have been set between the combatant "nations" from that point on, and the reaction to the end of the war may have been even more troubled than it turned out to be. Perhaps even more horrible to contemplate is the thought that if Lee had broken out on 9 April and joined Joe Johnston, guerilla warfare might have plagued the nation, caused more death and destruction, and done even more damage to the cause of national unity. Also, would a bloody or humiliating end for Lee and the Confederates have changed the murderous attitudes of John Wilkes Booth and his coconspirators? Had Grant been on the scene 8 April, would he have allowed Birney's black troops to advance on Lee and end the war by capture or annihilation? Of course, we will never know. But Ord's decision, based more on philosophical, sympathetic affinity with the South than on military tactics, came dangerously close to prolonging the conflict. As it was, with Birney exiled to City Point and his Negro units operating under other commanders, Lee's last hope was still alive for one more day after his close call.

Early on the morning of 9 April, Lee, with about seven thousand weary men, followed by stragglers, set out for Appomattox Station in hungry desperation, hoping to find their lost rations. Once fed, Lee planned to head his men for Lynchburg across the James River, and from there they would have a chance to escape to the South. The last battle opened at 5:00 A.M.

with a futile charge by John B. Gordon's troops. A historical site notes the dialogue: "Gordon sent word to Lee around 8:30 A.M. . . . 'my command has been fought to a frazzle, and unless Longstreet can unite in the movement, or prevent these forces from coming upon my rear, I cannot go forward.' Receiving the message, Lee replied, 'There is nothing left for me to do but to go and see General Grant, and I would rather die a thousand deaths.'"[16] Lee, of course, was unaware that he had perhaps been spared one of those proverbial thousand deaths at the hands of Birney's Negro troops the previous day.

The war was rapidly nearing a climax. Lee had sent a tentative note to Grant on 7 April inquiring as to terms of a possible surrender, and Grant responded just as tentatively, then was called away from the front for a day, leaving Ord in charge. Lee's officers were keenly aware of their predicament, and a grave-faced delegation of Confederate officers called on Lee in his tent the night of 8 April. They were artillerists William N. Pendleton and Edward Porter Alexander, both brigadiers, and Maj. Gen. John Gordon. The trio had concluded the situation was hopeless and decided to advise Lee to capitulate. They had tried the idea on Longstreet before seeing Lee but found no support for surrender. In fact Longstreet had cautioned that urging a superior officer to surrender during wartime was an offense punishable by execution. As a major general, Gordon was the highest ranking of the trio, having won a second star at Spotsylvania. He was a slightly built thirty-three-year old Georgian commanding Johnson's division of the Army of Northern Virginia. Wounded in the head at Antietam, he liked to show fellow officers the hole in his hat that released blood as he continued the fight. "Parson" Pendleton, full-whiskered Episcopal priest and Lee's close friend as well as chief of artillery, was the eldest at age fifty-five. He was a West Point graduate who had resigned from the military, becoming a teacher and then a priest before joining the Confederate cause. He was a brigadier with mainly administrative duties in charge of reserve ordnance. Brigadier General Alexander, thirty, was Longstreet's artillery chief who had been seriously wounded in the Battle of the Crater. Graduating third in his class at West Point, he had helped devise the U.S. Army's "wigwag" system of communicating by waving flags by day and using torches by night. He resigned from the army and joined the Confederates in 1861. At First Bull Run he used wigwag against his former collaborator, Union signal corps chief Maj. Albert J. Myer, to warn rebels of the Union advance.

Even this imposing group of officers could not convince the indomitable Confederate commander it was time to surrender. Lee declined the group's recommendation, offered by his friend and coreligionist Parson Pendleton, with most considerate courtesy. An officer of lesser character may not have been so kind to subordinates. Gordon, who had been promoted to lieutenant general late in the war, led the last charge. So the Civil War actually lasted one day longer, and more blood was spilled unnecessarily. To Pendleton fell the task of informing an exhausted Lee, reclining by a tree, of the failure of the last charge and the loss of more men, reducing the First Virginia to less than a hundred hungry, wounded, and disconsolate rebels. Abandoned muskets and swords littered the ground, and off in the distance Sheridan's cavalry was seen headed for Appomattox Station to capture rebel rations. Lee responded to the bad news in typical indomitable, if delusional, fashion: "I trust it has not come to that; we certainly have too many brave men to think of laying down our arms. They still fight with great spirit, whereas the enemy does not. And besides, if I were to intimate to General Grant that I would listen to terms, he would at once regard it as such evidence of weakness that he would demand unconditional surrender, and sooner than that I am resolved to die. Indeed, we Must all be determined to die at our posts." Historian Morris Schaff issued a pithy comment in an article titled "The Sunset of the Confederacy" in the *Atlantic Monthly* many years later: "Is it not inconceivable that Lee should have said that our men lacked spirit? Go ask any living veteran of the Army of Northern Virginia whether our troops quailed from the day the campaign began till their general, Cox, fired the last volley at Appomattox. No, no, General Pendleton, you certainly misunderstood General Lee, or General Lee was amazingly misinformed: never, never did the old Army of the Potomac show more spirit."[17]

Lee instructed his corps commanders to send out flags of truce to suspend the hostilities and wrote a note to Union lieutenant general Ulysses S. Grant requesting an interview "to arrange the surrender of the Confederate Army of Northern Virginia." Even when convinced there was only the slimmest shred of hope, the overweening pride of the Confederates nearly kept them from surrender, the historical source claims: "Word soon came from Grant that he was pushing to the front to meet with Lee. Gen. James Longstreet came up as Lee was preparing to leave for Appomattox Court House. Still game, Longstreet said to Lee, 'General, unless he offers us honorable terms, come back and let us fight it out.'"[18] But the terms were honorable—even, some say, generous—and Grant was gracious in the negotiations, providing rations and allowing the rebels to keep their horses that would be necessary for the coming growing season. Jay Winik analyzed: "These terms were probably more than Grant was authorized to offer, but he knew President Lincoln would agree. He had told Grant: 'Let them all go, officers and all. I want submission and no more bloodshed . . . treat them liberally all around.

We want those people to return to their allegiance to the Union and submit to the laws.'"[19]

Lee's son, Capt. Robert E. Lee, Jr., summed up the status of the Confederate Army after falling back one hundred miles "before its overpowering antagonist" at the end: "The Army of Northern Virginia ceased to be recruited; it ceased to be adequately fed. It lived for months on less than one-third rations. It was demoralized, not by the enemy in its front, but by the enemy in Georgia and the Carolinas. Finally, from mere exhaustion, less than eight thousand men with arms in their hands, of the noblest army that ever fought 'in the tide of time,' were surrendered at Appomattox to an army of 150,000 men; the sword of Robert E. Lee, without a blemish on it, was sheathed forever."[20] At the peace talks in the McLean house at Appomattox, Grant recalled that Lee had repeated the position taken earlier by Jefferson Davis. After exchanging pleasantries and reminiscing about the Mexican War, Grant reported, "General Lee remarked to me again that their army was organized a little differently from the army of the United States (still maintaining by implication that we were two countries)."[21]

Gordon, who directed the final desperate attack, later observed: "General Longstreet's forces and mine at Appomattox, numbered, together, less than 8,000 men; but every man able to bear arms was still resolute and ready for battle. There were present three times that many enrolled Confederates; but two thirds of them were so enfeebled by hunger, so wasted by sickness, and so foot-sore from constant marching that it was difficult for them to keep up with the army. They were wholly unfit for duty. It is important to note this fact as explaining the great difference in the number of those who fought and those who were to be fed. At the final meeting between General Lee and General Grant rations were ordered by General Grant for 25,000 Confederates."[22] Historian Henry Steele Commager observed that some twenty-eight thousand soldiers of the Army of Northern Virginia were paroled at Appomattox; the others had "melted away."[23]

Grant ordered the Union troops not to celebrate as their former enemies stacked their weapons, a spirit reminiscent of rebels cheering the bravery of Union troops under attack at Fort Sumter in 1861. Grant wrote in his memoirs: "When news of the surrender first reached our lines our men commenced firing a salute of a hundred guns in honor of the victory. I at once sent word, however, to have it stopped. The Confederates were now our prisoners, and we did not want to exult over their downfall."[24]

The Confederate retreat from Richmond and Petersburg to Appomattox spanned successive Sundays. Services at the beginning and the end of the one-hundred-mile journey were in great contrast. The first Sunday was one of religion still steeped in Confederate hope while the second, Palm Sunday, saw a purely civil ending to a four-year military apocalypse without benefit of clergy.

After the surrender most of the Army of the Potomac joined other Union troops in the Grand Review in Washington. But no black troops marched down Constitution Avenue before the cheering throng. General Ord had sent them all to Texas. The only Negroes in the parade were comically dressed "contrabands" playing buffoons, dancing, singing, and clowning to entertain the crowds. Yes, freedom was fairly won on the battlefields with the help of courageous black troops. But there would be nothing fair about the future for the Negroes.

Epilogue

ABRAHAM LINCOLN, JAMES G. BIRNEY AND THREE OF HIS SONS AND a grandson, and many of their collaborators were long dead as the signs of the apocalyptic four-year Civil War still were evident on ten thousand battlefields in the devastated South at the end of Reconstruction. The final Union and Confederate death toll combined was about 630,000—2 percent of the nation's population. Many forlorn graves are marked "unknown" to this day. More than three million veterans headed for home, some hobbling on one leg or with flapping sleeves, all hoping to rebuild lost lives and rekindle neglected loves. The long crusade of the Apostles of Equality appeared to be a victory, but its effects would not be realized to any great extent for another century. In actuality, the denial of rights to black men and women that occurred during the time of slavery didn't end in the United States until civil rights laws were passed in the mid-1960s, more than a century after the Emancipation Proclamation. No social scientist, historian, or author is capable of explaining satisfactorily the train of racist-motivated events that have violated the spirit of the nation since Appomattox. All we can do here is try to illuminate, in "our poor power to add or detract, "as Lincoln said at Gettysburg, some of the aspects of the human drama that in many ways is an interminable struggle.

The "sinful" loophole in the Constitution created by Thomas Jefferson and Benjamin Franklin had been closed in 1868 with the ratification of the Fourteenth Amendment, inspired in part by James G. Birney's philosophies, which says: "No state shall make or enforce any law which shall abridge the privileges or immunities of citizens of the United States; nor shall any state deprive any person of life, liberty or property, without due process of law; nor deny to any person within its jurisdiction the equal protection of the laws." But perhaps no constitutional amendment had less effect, at least for the century following the Civil War.

The fact that the Fourteenth Amendment, which makes us unique among nations, exists today is a marvel. President Andrew Johnson vetoed the Civil Rights Act of 1866, which conferred citizenship and guaranteed equal rights to Negroes, but Congress overrode the veto on 9 April. South-ern states unanimously rejected the Fourteenth Amendment to the U.S. Constitution, adopted by Congress on 13 June 1866, "guaranteeing" due process and equal protection under the law to all citizens and granting citi-zenship to Negroes. The Fourteenth Amendment was proposed to the state legislatures by the Thirty-ninth Congress on 13 June 1866. On 28 July 1868 the secretary of state declared it to have been ratified by the legislatures of twenty-eight of the thirty-seven states. Due process and equal protec-tion were concepts that had been espoused by James G. Birney based on the Declaration of Independence and the general concepts of the preamble to the Constitution, which he asserted covered both states and territories. Birney, who died in 1857, four years before the Civil War began, also had contended that Congress had been delegated the duty of maintaining equal protection of the laws and abolishing slavery, since it was a natural right that was the province of God. This was a concept he had adopted from Rev. David Rice, the Presbyterian "Apostle of Kentucky" of the late eigh-teenth and early nineteenth centuries. Biographer Fladeland summarized Birney's natural right philosophy: "God alone being the source of right with which government is invested, no people, no nation, could take from an individual his natural rights. There is no obligation to obey a government which attempts to destroy such rights. Slavery, he concluded, had no legal existence. It continued simply because slaveholders had usurped the govern-ment and misinterpreted the Constitution. It was not only the power but the duty of Congress to abolish it."[1]

It has been nearly a century and a half since its adoption, but writers and legal scholars have only recently begun to give James G. Birney credit for help-ing develop the concepts that undergird the Fourteenth Amendment. In the light of history, the main contribution of Birney and the Apostles of Equality was their part in laying the groundwork for the transformation of the United States from a pro-slavery nation to one that opposed it. The realization of full equality is a work in progress that has been going on interminably, prolonged by deep-seated attitudes passed from generation to generation.

One of the most difficult tasks has been the granting of full voting rights to black citizens. Before the Reconstruction Acts there were 627,000 white voters and no black voters in the South, but Reconstruction added 703,000 black voters. Although the numbers would seem to indicate Negro par-ity, they were never to achieve the full potential of their apparent voting power. In fact they were made virtually powerless by Democratic efforts to suppress their votes and their rights after Reconstruction was ended by a corrupt bargain.

Another postwar program with much promise was the Freedmen's Bureau, officially the Bureau of Refugees, Freedmen, and Abandoned Lands. However, the bureau was a flawed agency, which failed to achieve its advance billing and potential mainly because it immediately came under attack after it launched operations to benefit former slaves and free Negroes. "The creation of the Freedmen's Bureau in March 1865 symbolized the widespread belief among Republicans that the federal government must shoulder broad responsibility for the emancipated slaves, including offering them some kind of access to land," observes Reconstruction historian Eric Foner.[2] Established by Congress as a division of the war department just before Lincoln's assassination, the bureau supervised relief and education of refugees and freedmen, including providing rations, clothing, and medicine. The bureau also assumed custody of confiscated lands or property in the former Confederate states, border states, the District of Columbia, and Indian Territory. Records were created and maintained by headquarters, assistant commissioners, and state superintendents of education.

Despite its patronage mission, the bureau was powerless to stop violence; although the war and slavery officially were over, they were not really over in the minds of some Confederate diehards. The toxic environment was described by Georgia state representative Abram Colby, a Negro leader in Greene County, in testimony before Congress in 1871: "No man can make a free speech in my county. I know I cannot do it in my county and I do not believe any Republican can. I do not believe it can be done anywhere in Georgia. If you go there you will be killed, or shot at, or whipped, or run off."[3] Representative Colby had been attacked in 1869; his back had been badly injured and he lost the use of his left hand, but in his role as a legislator he continued to oppose violence.

What happened in the South is that many former Confederates had no intention of being "reconstructed." And, of course, it was their land and their people, so no peaceful force on earth could change them if they were determined to resist. The social scheme in the South, where blacks were subservient to whites, was institutionalized in the compromises that had allowed the founding of the nation. According to slavery historian James Z. George, "These compromises were founded on the concession on all sides that slavery was a State institution, subject to the will of each State to establish or abolish as it should deem best in its own judgment."[4]

So it was no surprise that an indomitable people who had defeated the world's greatest military power, the British, mainly on their own ground, would not yield easily to Yankee domination even after their land had been ravaged and people decimated by Civil War. "A movement calling itself the 'Readjusters' sprang up in many parts of the South, addressing itself to hamstringing or repealing much of the direly needed social legislation that had been enacted during Reconstruction," notes Southern historian Stetson Kennedy. "The fledgling public schools systems were a prime target, and appropriations or bond issues intended for them were either voided or diverted."[5] The Readjusters, who soon became known as the Ku Klux Klan under a more formal organization, followed a spirit of vigilantism similar to that of an Irish movement called the Whiteboys, who also used white cloth disguises in their night attacks. The rural, mainly Catholic, Irish group sought "readjustment" for tenant farmers who were suffering abuses at the hands of British landlords. Much as the Klan rampaged through the Southern countryside supposedly defending the rights of white farmers against black former slaves, the Whiteboys (without the racial motivation on which the Klan activity was based) did the same in Ireland.

A British history observed, "Assembling by night with their shirts, employed as upper garments to prevent discovery, they assailed the property and dwelling of the Tythe Farmers, and various outrages were committed by those who, from their disguised dress, were denominated *Whiteboys.*" The secret agrarian association, operating in the mid to late eighteenth century, used violence targeting landlords and tax collectors on behalf of tenant farmers. Their grievances included excessive rack rents, tithe collection, priests' dues, and evictions.[6] French author Gustave de Beaumont, in his history of Ireland, wrote about the Whiteboys:"One of their usual punishments (and by no means the most severe) was taking people out of their beds, carrying them naked in winter on horseback for some distance, and burying them up to their chin in a hole filled with briers, not forgetting to cut off one of their ears."[7] So, again, as in the case of dueling, rural vigilantism in the United States came from Irish roots. And Irish and Scotch Irish immigrants were numerous on the frontiers of the American South.

James Birney III, the grave-visaged eldest son of James G. Birney, at the time a forty-eight-year-old lawyer and former Congregational minister, had sought the post as head of the Freedmen's Bureau as the war was coming to an end. Known familiarly as Judge Birney because of his six years on the circuit bench in Michigan during and just after the war, he had written Abraham Lincoln in February 1865 seeking appointment to the post as "commissioner of Freedmen." The opening sentence of his letter, in the light of history, was not only eerily prophetic but also an indication that the pair had met and apparently had talked of Birney's interest in working for freed slaves after the war. "As I may not have another interview with you, I submit in writing the following statement," Birney's letter began. He cited support from the Michigan delegation in Congress and state officials and noted, "For thirty years I have been conversant with the discussions pertaining to the elevation of the black man. My early life was spent in Alabama and Kentucky." In his letter, Birney also noted the death of three of his brothers in service and that "one [William] is in command of four thousand colored troops, and having raised seven regiments of colored troops in Maryland is said to have broken the back of slavery in that state," adding, "My eldest son is also in the army." A letter from Secretary of the Treasury Salmon P. Chase endorsing Judge Birney's earlier effort to win appointment as a U.S. senator was enclosed in the communication to Lincoln, and Judge Birney appended a note urging the president to read Chase's earlier letter of support.[8]

With the war coming to a conclusion in February and March 1865, the president was no doubt preoccupied with military matters and did not reply to Birney's application. In fact the Freedmen's Bureau was not established by Congress until 3 March 1865, and the war ended on 9 April with Lee's surrender to Grant at Appomattox. Then, after Lincoln's assassination on 14 April 1865, the political climate grew colder for abolitionists as Republicans sought to reunite the country. It could be assumed that because of Birney's father's fame as an abolitionist leader and his familiarity with the family, Lincoln might have appointed the younger Birney.

As it was, however, Maj. Gen. Oliver Otis Howard, a troop commander who had lost his right arm in combat, was named by Lincoln's successor, President Andrew Johnson, in May as the first head of the Freedmen's Bureau. General Howard (1830–1909) was born in Maine and attended Bowdoin College and West Point, where he taught mathematics in the mid-1850s. The Civil War had cut short his aim to become a minister, but he transferred his moral influence to troops, urging them to attend prayer and temperance meetings, thus becoming known as "the Christian general." Howard's arm had to be amputated after severe wounding at Fair Oaks. He commanded troops in several important battles, and despite disasters at Chancellorsville and Gettysburg, he was awarded the Medal of Honor in 1893 for heroism at Fair Oaks. He led the Army of the Tennessee on Sherman's March to the Sea. Besides advocating black suffrage, he worked to provide lands to blacks, helped integrate his church, and founded a Negro college in the District of Columbia, now Howard University. He also was superintendent of the U.S. Military Academy in 1881–1882 and founded Lincoln Memorial University in Harrogate, Tennessee, for "mountain whites."

During its first year the Freedmen's Bureau built about four thousand schools and one hundred hospitals and homes, plus providing food, for former slaves at a cost of $17 million. The following year, as white backlash grew,

President Johnson vetoed extension of the bureau's power and also quashed the Civil Rights Bill aimed at neutralizing Black Codes, which restricted former slaves from voting, sitting on juries, testifying against whites, carrying weapons, and working in certain jobs. General Howard headed the Freedmen's Bureau for eleven years, from May 1865 to July 1874. After the suppression of the first year by President Johnson, his leadership seems to have amounted mainly to record-keeping rather than law enforcement or providing protection to black men and women under assault by the Klan and other white supremacists. The records of the Freedmen's Bureau contain a compendium of violence and murder that erupted against black people in the South immediately after the Civil War.

The Ku Klux Klan, established in Pulaski, Tennessee, in May 1866, obviously in response to the Civil Rights Act, launched a regional campaign of terror under former Confederate cavalry leader Gen. Nathan Bedford Forrest in 1867. Besides blacks, Klan targets included whites favoring black rights, immigrants, and Republicans, both black and white. Masked night riders in white sheets also inflicted "summary vengeance" on successful black businessmen and black workers who attempted to form trade unions. "Reconstruction and Republican political domination caused unprecedented bitterness and passionate resistance among white southerners, accounting for the rise of the Ku Klux Klan and other night-riding orders," writes William Warren Rogers Jr. "The perception of the Republicans' nefarious behavior, and the resulting political violence, emblematically played out in Alabama."[9]

David W. Blight, in his book *Race and Reunion,* says that "selective political assassinations destroyed the Republican Party and rendered independent black political and economic life untenable." He cites the deaths of about four hundred people, mostly Negroes, between 1868 and 1871, across the South. In the old Birney homestead of Madison County, Alabama, including the town of Huntsville, "Klan beatings and hangings became weekly and even daily events during the election months" in 1868 and 1869. In rural central Kentucky (the Birney birthplace region) in the first ten years after the war, Blight cites estimates that at least three hundred people, mostly Negroes, perished at the hands of lynch mobs.[10]

Ku Klux Klan Grand Wizard Forrest, a former slave trader and dashing Confederate cavalry commander, had infamously entered the history books as the commander at Fort Pillow, Tennessee, where black soldiers were massacred by Confederates in April 1864. The Klan was to enforce the Black Codes aimed at controlling Negroes. In 1868 the Ku Klux Klan drew up a series of questions for people who wanted to join its organization:

- Are you now, or have you ever been, a member of the Radical Republican Party?
- Did you belong to the Federal Army during the late war, and fight against the South during the existence of the same?
- Are you opposed to Negro equality, both social and political?
- Are you in favor of a white man's government in this country?

Assaults by the Klan and Southern states and communities on voter rights prompted Congress in 1869 to pass the Fifteenth Amendment, which supposedly guaranteed suffrage of black Americans. Segregation was widespread both in the North and South, but reverse Reconstruction began to institute racist laws to offset constitutional protections and civil rights legislation.

The Freedmen's Bureau's "Reports of Murders and Outrages" listed hundreds of similar violent events and deaths in Alabama, Georgia, Louisiana, North Carolina, South Carolina, Tennessee, Texas, Virginia, and Washington, D.C. Some "white on white" offenses were against Union loyalists. The bureau explained the contents of the reports as follows:

> Records relating to murders and outrages and reports of murders, outrages, and riots were submitted by subordinate and field officers in either tabular or narrative form. Although the term "outrage" meant any criminal offense, it usually referred to violent crimes by or against freedmen. The reports usually included the date of the incident and the county in which it took place; the names and race of the injured and accused parties; a brief description of the incident and the action taken, if any, by civil authorities and by the bureau; and the outcome. Most of the reports pertain to crimes committed by whites against freedmen, but crimes of whites against whites, freedmen against freedmen, and freedmen against whites were also reported. In addition to the reports, for some states there are registers of murders and outrages that contain the same type of information as the reports, and may have been compiled from them. There are also lists of murders of freedmen and lists and reports of arrests.[11]

One report, dated 3 November 1868, to Bt. Col. J. R. Lewis, USS, assistant commissioner, state of Georgia, from "Agent in Charge" A. Sawyer, was addressed with unfortunately formal wording to the sub-district headquarters in Savannah: "Colonel: I have the honor to submit herewith report of murders, outrages &c committed on colored people from Jany. 1st to Oct. 31st 68."[12] The use of the word "honor," it must be assumed, was inadvertent as a matter of common usage in correspondence, but the average reader would no doubt wonder if it was in fact commentary.

Strangely, the Freedmen's Bureau issued no report of government action or of local civil prosecution against the perpetrators of crimes against black citizens or white Unionists. Apparently officials of the bureau were content to list the "murders and outrages" and feel they had done their job. An explanation for the bureau's powerlessness was posed by slavery historian Ira Berlin: "Although the bureau often lacked resources to do more than make written note of the abuses of freed people brought to its attention, bureau agents scattered across the South conducted censuses, undertook investigations, recorded depositions, filed reports, and accumulated letters authored by ex-slaves and interested whites."[13]

An Alabama historian, Edward Chambers Betts, commented, "At first these bureaus were conducted by the federal military authorities, but after the war their management was entrusted to 'loyal Union men,' 'Carpetbaggers.' These institutions," he said, "if properly conducted, might have been of inestimable worth to the nation as a whole, serving in a large measure to readjust the shattered economic conditions at the South. But such was not their purpose, and as a consequence their presence threatened the very existence of civilization at the South, and for a time substituted Ethiopian for Caucasian supremacy." Betts no doubt spoke for many Southerners when he wrote: "The South was not the original importer of the slave, but became a slave section naturally and logically. It was not to be expected that a factor which had become so deeply embedded in its economic life could be eliminated in the twinkling of an eye. . . . No savage race the world has ever known, had conferred upon it so speedily, the blessings of civilization and Christianity, as that portion of this African people which thus came into immediate and continuous contact with the splendid civilization of the Old South."[14]

Only one of the Birneys, William, ultimately played a role in Reconstruction, and that was a brief one. William had displayed courage during the war but perhaps more so after the war. His decision to return to rebel Florida after being removed from command at Appomattox by General Ord would put him face-to-face, on their ground, with the rebels he had fought there. There was to be no sunshine and palm trees for the son of one of the nation's most noted abolitionists, himself a prominent member of that antislavery clan. William's experience in postwar civil government in Florida would prove almost as harrowing as the war. The toxic tone had been set by the suicide a week before Appomattox of the governor, John Milton, descendant and namesake of the famed English poet. Governor Milton had declared in his final message to the legislature that "death would be preferable to reunion" with the Yankees and shot himself. Young Men's Democratic

Clubs and the Ku Klux Klan were rampaging against black men and women and Republicans like Birney sent to administer Reconstruction, reported Ralph L. Peek in *Florida Historical Quarterly*.[15]

Birney had been appointed district attorney for Florida's Fifth Judicial Circuit, headquartered in Alachua County at Gainesville. This section of the state was one of two that "furnished the setting of the most sustained and vicious outbreaks during 1868–1871," according to Peek. "The organized campaign of violence and lawlessness "was the result of four years of total and devastating war, which had demoralized society in all Southern states," the historian wrote. Citing a July 1866 issue of the *New York Times*, Peek wrote: "Mounting disorders had resulted in suspension of civil government in Alachua and four nearby counties—Madison, Levy, Santa Rosa and Escambia."[16]

"Young Men's Democratic Clubs incorporated local white men who perpetrated threats, physical assaults, floggings and murders, all for the purpose of making the Democratic Party paramount and defeating the Republicans," according to later testimony before the Congressional Joint Select Committee on Condition of Affairs in the Late Insurrectionary States.[17] Negro and white Republicans were prime targets, and dozens were killed or intimidated to subdue Negro voters. In Alachua County there were nineteen such murders during those times. "The audacity of members of the resistance groups is revealed by an attack on William Birney . . . designed to kill Birney and eliminate him from the political scene, launched in open daylight in the streets of Gainesville," wrote Peek. "Birney managed to outdistance his pursuers in a protracted footrace and escaped harm."[18] The sight of a federal prosecutor fleeing for his life on foot on a main street in a Florida town must have seemed quite hilarious for the pursuing former Confederates as well as an unforgettable terror for the former Union major general. One can only imagine what would have happened to the dignified Birney had he been caught by pursuers.

The campaign to cow black voters also was active in Alabama, notes Foner: "Localities added poll taxes of their own. Mobile levied a special tax of five dollars on every adult male 'and if the tax is not paid,' reported the city's black newspaper, 'the chain gang is the punishment.'"[19] Peek summarized, "The cases cited above reveal a deep, fundamental antipathy between the races and the determination of the Southern white people to establish white supremacy at all costs. The physical violence inflicted on Negroes as a means of economic and political control was intensified by the racial hatred which became stronger with the progress of Reconstruction." He concluded, "The survey of records of the lawless era leads to the obvious conclusion that the former Confederates were determined to regain their former status at any cost."[20]

The situation in Alabama was similar to that in Florida, according to Betts, noting that the turmoil created by the Freedmen's Bureau "created a necessity for some sort of social regulator. And out of these conditions logically resulted the 'Invisible Empire,' whose mandates were executed by the Ku Klux Klan." The rise of the Klan was prompted, in part, by Negro arrogance and unruliness, according to Betts. "Upon emancipation from slavery every negro man acquired a dog and a gun," he wrote, noting this had been prohibited under slavery. "Negroes would march through the streets, armed, in military formation, and execute drills about the court house . . . loiter about the streets, acting boisterously; using abusive and obscene language, discharging firearms and making threats of violence against the whites; taking particular care to make themselves most offensive to those they especially disliked. In short, the 'carpet-baggers' contrived every conceivable means of intimidating the Southern whites into submission to Negro domination and social equality." However, neither additional Union troops nor martial law was effective in suppressing the Klan's "social regulation." Just before the presidential election of 1868, Betts reported, a riot took place when about fifteen hundred of the Ku Klux Klan rode into the city and paraded the streets, both horses and men cloaked in white sheets. Presumably, the horse was recognizable as the property of a man whose identity would then be known. Shots allegedly fired by Negroes sparked the riot, several of whom were injured, and a "scalawag" judge from a neighboring county was killed. "This is only one of many similar 'Negro riots' enacted in the South, and accredited to the Ku-Klux-Klan, as 'outrages,'" Betts stated.[21]

Radical Republican congressman Benjamin Butler, the abolitionist and former Union Army general under whom David and William Birney had served, called the Klan the "Invisible Empire of the South" in complaining to President Ulysses S. Grant and calling for an investigation in 1870. Grant ordered a federal grand jury investigation into the Klan, and a report was issued in 1871. The grand jury reported:

> There has existed since 1868, in many counties of the state, an organization known as the Ku Klux Klan, or Invisible Empire of the South, which embraces in its membership a large proportion of the white population of every profession and class. The Klan has a constitution and bylaws, which provides, among other things, that each member shall furnish himself with a pistol, a Ku Klux gown and a signal instrument. The operations of the Klan are executed in the night and are invariably directed against members of the Republican Party. The

Klan is inflicting summary vengeance on the colored citizens by breaking into their houses at the dead of night, dragging them from their beds, torturing them in the most inhuman manner, and in many instances murdering.[22]

Congress passed the Ku Klux Act in 1871, giving the president the power to suspend habeas corpus in counties where racial incidents occurred. Butler commented on the law that resulted from Grant's action: "By the bill this murdering of negroes by Ku Klux riders at night was to be deemed conspiracy, and punished by fine and imprisonment. But the prisoner would first have to be convicted by a Southern jury, and upon these juries other members of the Ku Klux could serve if their own cases were not on trial. That bill was passed, and the government made great show of enforcing it."[23] However, some observers concluded the Klan already had practically disappeared because its objective of white supremacy in the South had been achieved.

"By the latter part of 1871, the application of the Ku Klux Enforcement Act had brought a cessation of violence and a restoration of peace. By this time the Democrats had consolidated their power in most of the counties of Florida and the battle was over," the House report summarized.[24] A committee of Congress met in Huntsville in October 1871 to investigate the Klan, reported the historian, saying, "Many of Huntsville's most prominent citizens were called before this inquisitorial body for examination." The committee reported the following table of crimes: killed, 6; outrages, 19; shootings, 5; whippings, 19. "So far as is known no one in Madison County was ever punished for participation in the activities of the Ku-Klux-Klan," summarized Betts.[25]

Texas was perhaps a worse example of legalized murder, but at least the authorities made an effort to enforce the laws. "Texas courts indicted some 500 white men for the murder of blacks in 1865 and 1866, but not one was convicted. 'No white man in that state has been punished for murder since it revolted from Mexico,' commented a Northern visitor. 'Murder is considered one of their inalienable state rights.'" Bureau records listed some of the "reasons" for an estimated one thousand murders of blacks by whites in Texas from 1865 to 1868. According to Foner, one victim was killed for failing to remove his hat, another wouldn't give up his whiskey flask, and a white man 'wanted to thin out the blacks a little.'" Former slave Henry Adams testified that "over two thousand colored people" were murdered in 1865 near Shreveport, Louisiana.[26]

The term "waving the bloody shirt" entered the nation's lexicon during this wave of violence after the beating of school superintendent Allen

P. Huggins in Aberdeen, Monroe County, Mississippi, on the night of 9 March 1871. Huggins received seventy-five lashes with a leather stirrup as punishment for the "crime" of educating Negro children. The story was broadcast in the South that former Union general Ben Butler, an abolitionist, had waved Huggins's bloody shirt on the floor of Congress in his jeremiad calling for a Ku Klux Klan control bill. "Waving the bloody shirt" would become "the standard expression of dismissive Southern contempt whenever a Northern politician mentioned any of the thousands upon thousands of murders, whippings, mutilations, and rapes that were perpetrated against freedmen and freedwomen and white Republicans in the South in those years." There was no bloody shirt except in the minds of Southern extremists incensed by any criticism of their violent deeds. Historian Stephen Budiansky comments, "*The bloody shirt* perfectly captured the inversion of truth that would characterize the distorted memories of Reconstruction the nation would hold for generations after. . . . [It] turned the very act of Southern white violence into wounded Southern innocence, turned the very blood of their African American victims into an affront against Southern white decency."[27]

Radical Republicans in Congress led by Butler assured passage of the Ku Klux Klan Act in April 1871 giving the president power to suspend habeas corpus in troubled areas. With the new power President Grant declared martial law against the white vigilantes in the South, especially targeting South Carolina. Suspected Klan leaders were rounded up and tried in federal courts, destroying the Klan in South Carolina. Grant's campaign against the Klan was popular with Northern voters, and he won a second term, declaring "states lately at war with the General Government are now rehabilitated." He invited black men and women to the inaugural ball for the first time in history.

The Klan supposedly died out because the objectives of white supremacy had been achieved, but racism lingered deep in some hearts and minds in both South and North. Five years later the hatred that had been simmering burst out in an explosion of violence that was to change history. It was really a reigniting of the Civil War that was to cascade across the South and end Reconstruction after eleven turbulent years. From letters, diaries, and news reports, Budiansky has chronicled the July 1876 massacre of Negroes in Hamburg, Edgefield County, South Carolina, at the hands of the Sweetwater Sabre Club, so-called rifle clubs, and other avengers under leadership of former Confederate generals Wade Hampton, Matthew C. Butler, Benjamin "Pitchfork" Tillman, and Martin Witherspoon Gary. "The Democratic campaign that fall became indistinguishable from a series of military triumphs. On streets where, eleven years before, the freedmen had paraded in humble celebration of freedom, Wade Hampton's men came now as conquerors."[28]

Judge Albion W. Tourgee, although a "carpet-bagger" from Ohio, wrote a pithy comment on the Klan in his book *A Fool's Errand: By One of the Fools*: "One can not but regard with pride and sympathy the indomitable men who, being conquered in war, yet resisted every effort of the conqueror to change their laws, their customs, or even the personnel of their ruling class."[29] In smoothing over an oppressive Reconstruction, the Republicans ceded black votes to the Democrats, too, for years after the era ended with perhaps the most corrupt, and damaging, bargain of them all. The end of lawless Reconstruction came with an even more lawless crescendo: the election of 1876 followed by nearly a century of resistance to change as defined so accurately by Judge Tourgee.

A biographer of Rutherford B. Hayes, Ari Hoogenboom, documents the corrupt bargain of 1876 in which the Democrats in the South agreed to give up the presidency won fairly by Samuel Tilden in exchange for the Republicans pulling troops out of the South. The key actor in the drama was the infamous Dan Sickles, the former congressman who had been acquitted of killing his wife's lover in 1858 and who, as commanding general of Third Corps, had lost his leg to a cannonball and been replaced at Gettysburg by David Bell Birney. Night owl Sickles, returning from an election night at the theater, stopped by Republican headquarters to find it deserted, disconsolate campaign chair Zachariah Chandler, a senator from Michigan, having retired with a bottle of whiskey. Perusing the returns, which appeared to show a Democratic victory, Sickles saw a glimmer: if the close vote in several Southern states could be reversed, the Republicans could win by a single electoral college tally. Firing telegrams to GOP operatives in South Carolina, Louisiana, and Florida directing them with the code for manipulation of results "hold your state," Sickles staved off a 283,000-vote victory by Tilden and launched a four-month wrangle.[30]

Election boards in Florida, South Carolina, and Louisiana invalidated enough returns from violence-torn counties to make Hayes victorious, observes historian Foner. An electoral commission dominated by Republicans voted 8–7 to give Florida, as well as disputed votes in the other two states, to Hayes. A threatened Democratic filibuster was called off when a settlement was reached: Hayes would withdraw all federal troops from the South, appoint a former Whig from the South to the cabinet, and look favorably on internal improvements such as railroads in the South.[31] Attempts to organize a Republican party in the South failed, and Democrats, many of them former Whigs, remained loyal to their party, although they cooperated often with their Northern rivals.

The deal that put Hayes in the White House ended Reconstruction. Negroes who had held government positions under Reconstruction were out and black people were barred from voting by grandfather clauses and poll taxes. Mississippi governor Adelbert Ames, a Republican from Maine sent South, declared, "A revolution has taken place—by force of arms— and a race are disenfranchised—they are to be returned to a condition of serfdom—an era of second slavery." Thomas Hall, an eighty-one-year-old former slave, mourned, "The Yankees helped free us, so they say, but they let us be put back in slavery again."[32] Thus, the corrupt deal in 1876 that put Hayes in the White House in exchange for the withdrawal of federal troops from the South marked the end of federal efforts to protect the civil rights of Negroes. The Readjusters had won. Reconstruction was over!

Increased oppression of black men and women in the South, not unlike the days of slavery before the Civil War, was resumed after an interval of eleven years after the Civil War. The aftermath of Reconstruction is a litany of oppression and violence against black people rivaled only by the era of slavery. Thus began a century-long rollercoaster of federal civil rights legislation offset by nullifying efforts by states, in many cases supported by court rulings. "After the Civil War many Southern states were determined to try and limit the rights of former slaves," says contemporary observer Boz Hod. "One of the biggest fears in society was the mixing of the races; this was something the white people vowed to stop."[33]

In 1883 the Supreme Court invalidated the Civil Rights Act of 1875. The court held the act unconstitutional and ruled that the Fourteenth Amendment did not forbid citizens from discriminating, holding that the amendment applied only to states. Fourteen Southern states officially segregated railroad passenger cars from 1881 to 1907. These actions led to the landmark 1896 Supreme Court case of *Plessy v. Ferguson*. Radical Republican judge Tourgee served without fee as lead counsel in the test case brought by a New Orleans Citizens Committee to Test the Separate Car Act. Homer Adolph Plessy, a free, light-colored black man (actually seven-eighths white), had been fined twenty-five dollars by New Orleans parish judge John Ferguson for taking a seat in a "whites only" rail car in Louisiana in 1892. For his act of planned disobedience, Plessy was removed from the rail car and arrested. The Supreme Court ruling enshrined the "separate but equal" doctrine by holding that the Thirteenth and Fourteenth Amendments protected political, but not social, equality. The ruling established the doctrine that federal law protected segregation, a concept that survived until the *Brown v. Board of Education* case in 1954.

In 1890 the Mississippi Plan was adopted, which provided for literacy tests to bar blacks from voting. Seven other Southern states—South Carolina, Louisiana, North Carolina, Alabama, Virginia, Georgia, and Oklahoma—over the following twenty years embraced the same type of disenfranchisement laws. In 1910 Baltimore adopted a city ordinance setting boundaries of white and black neighborhoods. Similar municipal laws were passed in Dallas, Texas; Greensboro, North Carolina; Louisville, Kentucky; Norfolk, Virginia; Oklahoma City, Oklahoma; Richmond, Virginia; Roanoke, Virginia; and St. Louis, Missouri. The Supreme Court in 1917 held the Louisville ordinance unconstitutional, thus setting a precedent nullifying such laws.

After more than fifty years, federal segregation roared back with the administration of Woodrow Wilson, a Democrat, in 1913. Workplaces, restrooms, and lunchrooms were segregated by federal mandates. President Wilson viewed the 1915 motion picture *Birth of a Nation,* a propaganda piece for the Klan by David W. Griffith, in the White House, declaring it to be "like writing history with lightning. And my only regret is that it is all terribly true."[34] Although apparently decrying the tale, Wilson did nothing to stop the racism and in fact institutionalized it in the federal government. That movie, depicting Klansmen as heroic vigilantes restoring order in a Southern town before, during, and after the Civil War, set the tone for revival of the Klan and a decade and a half of the organization's influence in American civic and political life. Promoters like erstwhile preacher William J. Simmons made large sums selling memberships, robes, and other Klan regalia. The Klan published newspapers, operated radio stations, supported political candidates, and tried to position itself like a local civic organization. Although secrecy was still attempted, most people in local communities were aware of the identities of prominent Klansmen. At its height, 1926 through 1928, thousands of Klansmen marched down Constitution Avenue in Washington, D.C., in annual parades.

Violations of constitutional rights of black men and women in the South were not addressed until the civil rights legislation of the 1960s, and racially motivated violent incidents have continued to occur occasionally, perhaps as much or more in the North as in the South. Large sections of Detroit were burned in race riots in 1967, New York City had racial violence in 1986 and 1991, and Cincinnati erupted in 2000, the latest outbreak being one of a series going back to the early days of the Ohio River city that borders Kentucky.

Persistent attitudes among the populace in the South about the Civil War, Negroes, and Republicans were explained in part by the Federal Writers' Project, a Works Project Administration research effort during the Great Depression: "In Virginia, strangers often are amazed to find how near seems the War between the States. The reason is that the conflict reached every family, brought them all together in defense, left most of them impoverished, and then produced during Reconstruction a type of government that made political unity a racial necessity. Prior to 1860, Virginia was divided not unevenly between Whigs and Democrats. After the war, disfranchisement and the carpetbaggers' venal misguidance of the freedmen made men Democrats because they were white and had been Confederates."[35] Alabama historian Virginia Van der Veer Hamilton's views are instructive: "Scholars of the American South have consistently noted the region's characteristic resistance to change and have pondered the reasons for such marked reluctance. W. J. Cash, in his interpretation of southerners, attributed the tendency to a closed state of mind (he called this the 'Savage Ideal') which suppressed dissent and enforced conformity. Cash believed that the 'Savage Ideal' was rooted in the South's defensive posture on slavery and that it spread later to equate every criticism with disloyalty, 'making criticism so dangerous that only a madman would risk it.'"[36] In recent decades Republicans have become ascendant in the South, in a sense switching places philosophically with regard to racial attitudes with the Democrats of the post–Civil War years and into the 1960s.

William Birney, who had found Florida a little too hot after his harrowing escape from the Klan on the streets of Gainesville in 1867, moved to Washington, D.C., where he was appointed district attorney. He would serve in other governmental posts, develop a subdivision, and write a biography of his father published in 1890. Birney and his wife, Catherine Hoffman Birney, had four daughters and four sons. His eldest child, Catherine Hoffman Birney, born in Ohio, was a musician and wrote a biography of the Grimke sisters, Southerners who, like Birney, were important figures in the struggle over slavery. William Birney died at his daughter's home in Forest Glen, Maryland, a Washington suburb, in 1907, at the age of eighty-eight, after cutting down a tree and suffering a stroke. According to his great-grandson Herman Hoffman "Topper" Birney, of Huntsville, Alabama, the aged former general found that his view from his room to the landscape outside was blocked by the tree, and, being the man of action that he was, grabbed an ax and felled the offending tree. He was stricken the next day. William is buried in Oak Hill Cemetery, in Georgetown, D.C. In his 1890 book, titled *James Gillespie Birney and His Times: The Genesis of the Republican Party,* William Birney reflects on his father's life, the struggle for constitutional rights for whites and blacks, and the formation of the Republican Party as a result of the effort begun by his father and his Liberty Party compatriots.

The Liberty Party's role in forming the basis for the Republican Party, as documented in William Birney's biography of his father, was totally ignored in some early Republican histories. For example, William Livingstone's party history, published in 1900, inexplicably jumps from the growth of antislavery sentiment after the Missouri Compromise to the 1848 start of the Free Soil Party, failing to even give passing mention to the Liberty movement. Was Livingstone taking his cues from Birney and Liberty detractor Theodore Roosevelt? Roosevelt had gone a step further in his 1886 biography of Thomas Hart Benton, stating, "The Liberty Party, in running Birney, simply committed a political crime, evil in almost all its consequences," adding that "they in no sense paved the way for the Republican Party, or helped forward the anti-slavery cause, or hurt the existing organizations." Roosevelt was clear regarding his animosity, declaring that Birney was of "the classes that were chiefly instrumental in the election of Polk" and therefore responsible for the war with Mexico. He expanded: "Owing to a variety of causes, the Abolitionists have received an immense amount of hysterical praise, which they do not deserve, and have been credited with deeds done by other men, whom they in reality hampered and opposed rather than aided." His revisionist ideas tortuously continued: "Lincoln in 1860 occupied more nearly the ground held by Clay than that held by Birney." Roosevelt outrageously went on to claim that the Republicans "would never have meddled with slavery" except for the South's rebellion and the "unscrupulous, treacherous ambition of such men as [Jefferson] Davis, [president of the Confederacy], [John B.] Floyd [secretary of war in the Buchanan administration] and the rest."[37] Obviously, Roosevelt had never read the original Republican platform declaring all-out war against slavery, or chose to ignore it for political purposes. Such machinations have caused Birney's legacy to be falsely tarnished and his accomplishments ignored for a century and a quarter since Roosevelt's treacherous claims hit print.

Maj. Gen. David Bell Birney is buried in Philadelphia, where a plaque in his honor has been erected on the façade of the famous Bookbinders restaurant. After the general's death in 1864, his widow, Antoinette Jennison Birney, became a Carry Nation–like figure in Bay City, Michigan, urging temperance and an end to rowdy activities by lumberjacks along Water Street, known as "Hell's Half Mile," where Birney's home had been located. Her family's hardware building on the Birney site has been converted to luxury condominiums. The valiant David Birney would have no rest for eternity. Grave robbers in 1996 invaded his casket and stole his ornate sword, which subsequently became an Internet auction item.

In many ways the nation still struggles to understand the effects of the sudden emancipation of a long downtrodden race of slaves and the destructive impact of forced Reconstruction that was an attempt to transform the political agenda and social mores of a region of proud, independent people. The South is not alone in the sins of the soul. Civil War–era historian Louis S. Gerteis has commented on the aftermath of war, "Northern and southern whites shared attitudes about race that bound them together in a culture that survived the Civil War to deny African Americans full equality."[38]

Slowly, inexorably—but painfully—America continues the struggle to purge the sins of the founders who created a nation only by making a devil's compromise over human rights. The U.S. Senate and House and most of the Southern states have "expressed regret" for slavery but have parsed the wording of their resolutions in fear of demands for monetary reparations. The murderous days of the Civil Rights campaigns of the 1960s are recalled in museums like one for Rosa Parks, who became the "mother" of the movement by refusing to give up her seat on a bus in Montgomery, Alabama, in 1955. Today black men and women are voting; using lunch counters, bathrooms, and drinking fountains; and attending schools and universities as equals for the most part. Martyrs like Rev. Martin Luther King Jr. have been elevated to near-sainthood, but still the arguments over inferiority and the cause of the Civil War persist, and periodic violence perpetuates the stain of inhumanity on this nation despite its claim to be the freest in world history. We must continue to remind ourselves and our neighbors that progress in human rights can be maintained only by perpetual vigilance. The evolution of our political, constitutional, and legal structure and the part played in shaping them by James G. Birney, his descendants, and the Apostles of Equality are readily discernible. A greater appreciation of their contributions will add to the civility of the national discourse that continues interminably on issues of race and age-old intersectional conflicts.

Birney's Writings

Address to the Cliosophic Society, in *Southern Advocate,* Huntsville, Alabama, 1829

To Justin Martyr, in *Democrat,* Huntsville, Alabama, 1830

"African Colonization," in *The Democrat,* 1832

"Washington Centennial Address," in *Southern Advocate,* 1832

"The Colonization Society," in *Democrat,* 29 November 1832

"Colonization of the Free Colored People, No. 1," in *Democrat,* 16 May 1833

"Colonization of the Free Colored People, No. 2," in *Democrat,* 23 May 1833

"Colonization of the Free Colored People, No. 3," in *Democrat,* 30 May 1833

"Colonization of the Free Colored People, No. 4," in *Democrat,* 6 June 1833

"Colonization of the Free Colored People, No. 5," in *Democrat,* 13 June 1833

"Colonization of the Free Colored People, No. 6," in *Democrat,* 20 June 1833

"Colonization of the Free Colored People, No. 7," in *Democrat,* 27 June 1833

"Colonization of the Free Colored People, No. 8," in *Democrat,* 4 July 1833, and in *Southern Mercury,* Huntsville, Alabama, 10 July 1833

"Colonization of the Free Colored People, No. 9," in *Democrat,* 11 July 1833, and in *Southern Mercury,* 10 July 1833

"Colonization of the Free Colored People, No. 10," in *Democrat,* 18 July 1833, and in *Southern Advocate,* 6 July 1833

"Colonization of the Free Colored People, No. 11," in *Democrat,* 25 July 1833, and in *Southern Advocate,* 23 July 1833

"Colonization of the Free Colored People, No. 12," in *Democrat,* 1 August 1833, and in *Southern Advocate,* 30 July 1833

"Colonization of the Free Colored People, No. 13," in *Democrat,* 8 August 1833, and in *Southern Advocate,* 6 August 1833

"Colonization of the Free Colored People, No. 14," in *Democrat,* 15 August 1833, and in *Southern Mercury,* 10 August 1833

"Colonization of the Free Colored People, No. 15," in *Democrat,* 15 August 1833

"Constitution and Address of the Kentucky Society for the Gradual Relief of the State from Slavery," 11 December 1833

"Prospective Gradual Emancipation," *African Repository and Colonial Journal,* 10 (April 1834)

Mr. Birney's Letter to the Churches: To the Ministers and Elders of the Presbyterian Church in Kentucky, 1834

Letter on Colonization Addressed to the Rev. Thornton J. Mills, Corresponding Secretary of the Kentucky Colonization Society, 1834

Address to the Ladies of Ohio, 1835

"Vindication of the Abolitionists: Reply to Resolution of a Body of Alabama Citizens," 1835

Correspondence between James G. Birney, of Kentucky, and Several Individuals of the Society of Friends, 1835

To the Patrons of the *Philanthropist,* 1835

To the Editor of the *Olive Branch,* 1835

To Colonel William L. Stone, 1836

"American Slavery vs. Human Liberty," 1836

Letters to the Presbyterian Church, 1836

Philanthropist (weekly), January 1836 to September 1837

Correspondence between the Hon. F. H. Elmore, one of the South Carolina Delegation in Congress, and James G. Birney, one of the Secretaries of the American Anti-Slavery Society, 1838

"To the Governors of Southern States and Their Replies," in *Emancipator,* 1838

A Letter on the Political Obligations of Abolitionists, with a Reply by William Lloyd Garrison, 1839

Stanton and Birney to the Executive Committee of the Massachusetts Abolition Society, 27 November 1839

Speeches in England, 1840

To the *Signal of Liberty,* 1841

To the Editor of the *Free Press,* 1842

"The American Churches the Bulwarks of American Slavery," 1842

"Speech at Pontiac, Michigan," in *Signal of Liberty,* 5 September 1842

"Memorial to the Legislature of the State of Michigan," in *Signal of Liberty,* 30 January 1843

"Headlands in the Life of Henry Clay," 1844

To the Editor of the *Albany Patriot,* 1845

To the President of the Michigan State Anti-Slavery Society, 1846

To the Editor of the *Signal of Liberty,* 1846

"The Sinfulness of Slaveholding in All Circumstances; Tested by Reason and Scripture," 1846

"Can Congress, under the Constitution, Abolish Slavery in the States?" in *Albany Patriot,* 12 May 1847, 19 May 1847, 26 May 1847, and 2 April 1847

"Senatorial Opinions on the Right of Petition," *Massachusetts Quarterly Review* 3 (1849–1850): 431–459

"Senatorial Speeches on Slavery," *Massachusetts Quarterly Re*view 3 (1849–1850): 1–40

To the Christian Anti-Slavery Convention, 1850

"Examination of the Decision of the Supreme Court of the United States in the Case of Strader, Gorman and Armstrong vs. Christopher Graham, Delivered at Its December Term, 1850: Concluding with an Address to the Free Colored People, Advising Them to Remove to Liberia," 1852

"Concise Examination of Certain Passages and Events in the Bible, Divested of the Miraculous Character" (Christianus, pseud.), 1856

"Concise Examination of Certain Supernaturalisms of the Bible, as Commonly Understood" (Christianus, pseud.), 1856

"Multum in Parvo; or Short Treatises on Future Life, Immortality, Conscience, Prayer, the Sentence of the Serpent, the Esoteric and Exoteric Doctrines, Truth and Falsehood" (Christianus, pseud.), 1856

Brief Statements and Arguments on I. "Our First and Last Presidents;" II. "Forgiveness;" III. "How Dreams Were Thought of in Old Times, and How Now Among Rude Tribes and Nations;" IV. "Rationale of Slaveholding;" V. "Father, Son and Visitant;" VI. "Historical Morceaux about Play Actors;" VII. "Women's Rights;" VIII. "England and America;" IX. "How Shall We Judge of Others?" X. "A Standard" (Christianus, pseud.), 1857

First Republican Platform

Adopted "Under the Oaks," on Morgan's Forty, Jackson, Michigan, 6 July 1854. Published in Under the Oaks, *50th Anniversary History of the Republican Party, William Stocking, ed., Detroit, MI: Detroit Tribune, 1904.*

The Freemen of Michigan, assembled in Convention in pursuance of a spontaneous call, emanating from various parts of the State, to consider upon the measures which duty demands of us as citizens of a free State, to take in reference to the late acts of Congress on the subject of slavery and its anticipated further extension, do

RESOLVE, That the Institution of Slavery, except in punishment of crime, is a great moral, social and political evil; that it was so regarded by the Fathers of the Republic, the founders and best friends of the Union, by the heroes and sages of the Revolution who contemplated and intended its gradual and peaceful extinction as an element hostile to the liberties for which they toiled; that its history in the United States, the experience of men best acquainted with its workings, the dispassionate confession of those who are interested in it; its tendency to relax the vigor of industry and enterprise inherited in the white man; the very surface of the earth where it subsists; the vices and immoralities which are its natural growth; the stringent police, often wanting in humanity and speaking to the sentiments of every generous heart, which it demands; the danger it has already wrought and the future danger which it portends to the security of the Union and our Constitutional liberties—all incontestably prove it to be such evil. Surely that institution is not to be strengthened against which Washington, the calmest and wisest of our Nation, bore unequivocal testimony; as to which Jefferson, filled with a love of liberty, exclaimed: "Can the liberties of a Nation be ever thought secure when we have removed their only firm basis, a conviction in the minds of the people that their liberties are the GIFT OF GOD? that they are not to be violated but with his wrath? Indeed I tremble for my country when I reflect that God is just; that His justice cannot sleep forever; that, considering numbers, nature and National means only, a revolution of the wheel of fortune, and exchange of situation is among possible events; that it may become probably by supernatural interference. The Almighty has no attribute which can take sides with us in such a contest." And as to which another eminent patriot in Virginia, on the close of the revolution, also exclaimed: "Had we turned our eyes inwardly when we supplicated the Father of Mercies to aid the injured and oppressed, when we invoked the Author of righteousness to attest the purity of our motives and the justice of our cause, and implored the God of battles to aid our exertions in its defense, would we not have stood more self-convicted than the contrite publican?" We believe these sentiments to be as true now as they were then.

RESOLVED, That slavery is a violation of the rights of man as man; that the law of nature, which is the law of liberty, gives to no man rights superior to those of another. That God and nature have secured to each individual the inalienable right of equality, and violation of which must be the result of superior force; and that Slavery, therefore, is a perpetual war upon its victims; that whether we regard the institution as first originating in captures made in war, or the subjection of the debtor as the slave of his creditor, or the forcible seizure and sale of children by their parents or subjects by their king, and whether it be viewed in this Country as a "necessary evil" or otherwise, we find it to be, like imprisonment for debt, but a relic of barbarism as well as an element of weakness in the midst of the State, inviting the attack of external enemies, and a ceaseless cause of internal apprehension and alarm. Such are the lessons taught us, not only by the histories of other commonwealths, but by that of our own beloved country.

RESOLVED, That the history of the formation of the Constitution, and particularly the enactment of the ordinance of July 13, 1787, prohibiting slavery north of the Ohio abundantly shows it to have been the purpose of our fathers not to promote but to prevent the spread of slavery. And, we, reverencing their memories, and cherishing free Republican faith as our richest inheritance, which we vow, at whatever expense, to defend, thus publicly proclaim our determination to oppose by all the powerful and honorable means in our power, now and henceforth, all attempts, direct or indirect, to extend slavery in this Country, or to permit it to extend into any region or locality in which it does not now exist by positive law, or to admit new Slave States into the Union.

RESOLVED, That the Constitution of the United States gives to Congress full and complete power for the municipal government of the territories thereof, a power which from its nature cannot be, either alienated or abdicated without yielding up to the territory an absolute political independence, which involves an absurdity; that the exercise of this power necessarily looks to the formation of States to be admitted into the Union; and on the question whether they shall be admitted as Free or Slave States Congress has a right to adopt such prudential and preventative measures as the principles of liberty and the interests of the whole country require; that this question is one of the gravest importance to the free States, inasmuch as the Constitution itself creates an equality in the apportionment of Representatives, greatly to the detriment of the free and to the advantage of the Slave States. This question, so vital to the interests of the Free States (but which we are told by certain political doctors of modern times is to be treated with utter indifference), is one which we hold it to be our right to discuss; which we hold it the duty of Congress in every instance to determine an unequivocal language, and in a manner to prevent the spread of slavery and the increase of such unequal representation. In short, we claim that the North is a party to the new bargain, and is entitled to have a voice and influence in settling its terms. And in view of the ambitious designs of the Slave Power, we regard the man or the party who would forego this right, as untrue to the honor and interest of the North and unworthy of its support.

RESOLVED, That the repeal of the "Missouri Compromise," contained in the recent act of Congress for the creation of the territories Nebraska and Kansas, thus admitting slavery into a region till then sealed against it by law, equal in extent to the 13 old states, is an act unprecedented in the history of the country, and one which must engage the earnest and serious attention of every Northern man. And as Northern freemen, independent of all former party ties, we here hold this measure up to the public execration for the following reasons:

That it is a plain departure from the policy of the fathers of the Republic in regard to slavery, and a wanton and dangerous frustration of their purposes and their hopes.

That it actually admits and was intended to admit slavery into said Territories, and thus (to use the words applied by Judge Tucker, of Virginia, to the fathers of that commonwealth) "sows the seeds of an evil which like leprosy hath descended upon their posterity with accumulated rancor, visiting the sins of the fathers upon succeeding generations." That it was sprung upon the country stealthily and by surprise, without necessity, without petition and without previous discussion, thus violating the cardinal principle of Republican government, which requires all legislation to accord with the opinions and sentiments of the people.

That on the part of the South it is an open and undisguised breach of faith, as contracted between the North and South in the settlement of the Missouri question in 1820, by which the tranquility of the two sections was restored, a Compromise binding upon all honorable men.

That it is also an open violation of the Compromise of 1850, by which, for the sake of peace and to calm the distempered impulse of certain enemies of the Union and at the South, the North accepted and acquiesced in the odious "Fugitive Slave Law" of that year.

That it is also an undisguised and unmanly contempt of the pledge given to the country by the present dominant party at their National Convention in 1852, not to "agitate the subject of slavery in or out of Congress," being the same Convention which nominated Franklin Pierce to the Presidency.

That it is greatly injurious to the free states, and to the territories themselves, tending to retard the settlement and to prevent the improvement of the country by means of free labor, and to discourage foreign immigrants resorting thither for their homes.

That one of its principal aims is to give to the Slave States such a decided and practical preponderance in all the measures of government as shall reduce the North, with all her industry, wealth and enterprise, to be the mere province of a few slave holding oligarchs of the South—to a condition too shameful to be contemplated.

Because, as openly avowed by its Southern friends, it is intended as an entering wedge to still further augmentation of the slave power by the acquisition of the other territories, cursed with the same "leprosy."

RESOLVED, That the obnoxious measure to which we have alluded ought to be repealed, and a provision substituted for it, prohibiting slavery in said territories, and each of them.

RESOLVED, That after this gross breach of faith and wanton affront to us as Northern men, we hold ourselves absolved from all "compromises," except those expressed in the Constitution, for the protection of slavery and slave-owners; that we now demand measures of protection and immunity for ourselves, and among them we demand the REPEAL OF THE FUGITIVE SLAVE LAW, and an act to abolish slavery in the District of Columbia.

RESOLVED, That we notice without dismay certain popular indications by slaveholders on the frontier of said territories of a purpose on their part to prevent, by violence, the settlement of the country by non-slaveholding men. To the latter, we say: Be of good cheer, persevere in the right, remember the Republican motto, "THE NORTH WILL DEFEND YOU."

RESOLVED, That postponing and suspending all differences with regard to political economy or administrative policy, in view of the imminent danger that Kansas and Nebraska will be grasped by slavery, and a thousand miles of slave soil be thus interposed between the free states of the Atlantic and those of the Pacific, we will act cordially and faithfully in unison to avert and repeal this gigantic wrong and shame.

RESOLVED, That in view of the necessity of battling for the first principles of republican government, and against the schemes of the aristocracy the most revolting and oppressive with which the earth was ever cursed, or man debased, we will co-operate and be known as REPUBLICANS until the contest be terminated.

RESOLVED, That we earnestly recommend the calling of a general convention of the Free States, and such of the Slaveholding States, or portions thereof, as may desire to be there represented, with a view to the adoption of other more extended and effectual measures in resistance to the encroachments of slavery; and that as committee of five persons be appointed to correspond and co-operate with our friends in other states on the subject.

RESOLVED, that in relation to the domestic affairs of the State we urge a more economical administration of the government and a more rigid accountability of the public officers, a speedy payment of the balance of the public debt, and the lessening of the amount of taxation, a careful preservation of the Primary School and University Funds, and their diligent application of the great objects for which they were created, and also further legislation to prevent the unnecessary or imprudent sale of the lands belonging to the State.

Although this was the first statement of Republican Party principles, agreed upon at a state convention, the party held a national convention in Philadelphia and on 18 June 1856 and adopted similar wording of a much shorter platform statement also declaring opposition to polygamy as well as slavery and adding goals of a railroad to the Pacific and improvement of rivers and harbors. There was no mention in the latter platform of economical government, payment of public debt or reduction of taxes as in the first document.

Notes

INTRODUCTION

1. Elizabeth Fladeland, *James Gillespie Birney: Slaveholder to Abolitionist* (Ithaca, NY: Cornell University Press, 1955), 72–73.
2. William Birney, *James Gillespie Birney and His Times* (New York: D. Appelton and Company, 1890), 102–103.

CHAPTER 1. RISING IMMIGRANT TIDES

1. Scholars in recent years have documented 23,844 transatlantic slaving voyages fostered by "political entities in Africa organized as states with structures of power and administration," according to Professor Bernard Bailyn of Harvard University, who calls Atlantic study "a still-forming historic sub-discipline." Remarks at Atlantic History Conference, Harvard University, Cambridge, Massachusetts, 21 June 2007.
2. Floyd Windom Hayes, *A Turbulent Voyage* (Lanham, MD: Rowman and Littlefield, 2000), 64. Hayes asserts that 237,025 slaves were shipped here from 1715 to 1775, and of those 35,727 died, a mortality rate of 15.1 percent.
3. Aaron Fogelman, "The Atlantic World, 1492–1860s: Definition, Theory and Boundaries," paper presented at Atlantic History Conference, Harvard University, Cambridge, Massachusetts, 21 June 2007.
4. James Oliver Horton and Lois E. Horton, *Slavery and the Making of America* (New York: Oxford University Press, 2005), 22–24.
5. Hugh Thomas, *The Slave Trade* (New York: Simon and Schuster, 1997), 519.
6. Douglas Harper, "Northern Profits from Slavery, " Slavery in the North, http://www.slavenorth.com/profits.htm, 9 July 2007.
7. Douglas Harper, introduction page, Slavery in the North, http://www.slavenorth.com/index.htm, 9 July 2007.
8. Thomas, *Slave Trade,* 519.

9. J. C. Furnas, "Patrolling the Middle Passage," *American Heritage* 9 (October 1958): 7, 19.

10. Gary B. Nash, "Franklin and Slavery," *Proceedings of the American Philosophical Society* 150, no. 4 (December 2006): 618–635.

11. Rebecca Yamin, *Digging in the City of Brotherly Love: Stories from Philadelphia Archaeology* (New Haven, CT: Yale University Press, 2008), 51.

12. Bernard Bailyn and Aaron Fogelman, remarks at Atlantic History Conference, Harvard University, Cambridge, Massachusetts, 21 June 2007.

13. Marcus Rediker, *The Slave Ship: A Human History* (New York: Penguin, 2008), 10.

14. "Brown University Committee Examines Historical Ties to Slavery," *Boston Globe,* 5 March 2004.

15. Rodney Stark, *For the Glory of God: How Monotheism Led to Reformations, Science, Witch Hunts, and the End of Slavery* (Princeton, NJ: Princeton University Press, 2003), 349.

16. William Birney, *James G. Birney and His Times: The Genesis of the Republican Party* (New York: D. Appleton and Company, 1890), 2. The name John for the father of James Birney is used here for convenience; genealogical searches have not revealed his true given name. The National Archives of Ireland reports that all records involving Protestants prior to 1922 were destroyed in a fire.

17. Personal correspondence with Ken Birney of Toronto, Ontario, Canada, regarding the genealogy of the Birney name.

18. Joseph B. Meehan, *The Birthplace of General Philip Sheridan of the American Civil War* (New York: P. J. Kennedy and Sons, 1926); P. H. Sheridan, *Personal Memoirs of P. H. Sheridan* (New York: Charles L. Webster and Co., 1888).

19. Richard C. Brown, "The Richest Man in Danville," [*Danville*] *Kentucky Advocate* (Bicentennial Edition), 21 July 1976, 12.

20. Memoranda of Marshall, Birney, Green and Fry Families, Made Up by the Late Mrs. McAfee, of Ky., for Wm. Birney, manuscript copy in William Clements Library, University of Michigan, Ann Arbor, Michigan.

21. W. Birney, *James G. Birney and His Times,* 5.

CHAPTER 2. BIRTHING KENTUCKY AND A BIRNEY

1. As is the case with the father of Birney Senior, the first name of his sister is unknown. "Margaret" is used for convenience, but she was called "Aunt Doyle," and even William Birney in his writings never mentions her given name.

2. Edward Steers, *Lincoln Legends: Myths, Hoaxes and Confabulations Associated with Our Greatest President* (Lexington: University Press of Kentucky, 2007), 65.

3. Asa C. Barrow, "David Barrow and His Lulbegrud School, 1801," *Filson Club History Quarterly* 7 (April 1933): 88–93.

4. Betty Fladeland, *James Gillespie Birney: Slaveholder to Abolitionist* (Ithaca, NY: Cornell University Press, 1955), 7.

5. Beriah Green, *Sketches of the Life and Writings of James Gillespie Birney* (Utica, NY: Jackson and Chaplin, 1844), 2. Green also was president of Oneida Institute, a manual labor school that enrolled blacks as well as whites.

6. W. Birney, *James G. Birney and His Times,* 27.

7. William Kauffman Scarborough, *Masters of the Big House: Elite Slaveholders of the Mid-Nineteenth Century South* (Baton Rouge: Louisiana State University Press, 2003), 67.

8. Lucien Beckner, Transcription of Rev. John Dabney Shane's Interview with Mrs. Sarah Graham of Bath County, *Filson Club History Quarterly* 9, no. 4 (1935): 222–241.

9. Carl Sandburg, *Abraham Lincoln: The Prairie Years and the War Years* (New York: Galahad Books, 1993), 7–8.

10. Maria T. Daviess, *History of Mercer and Boyle Counties* (Harrodsburg, KY: *Harrodsburg Herald,* 1924), 7.

11. *Memoranda of Marshall, Birney, Green and Fry Families.*

12. James Hopkins, *A History of the Hemp Industry in Kentucky* (Lexington: University Press of Kentucky, 1951), 24–30.

13. W. Birney, James G. *Birney and His Times,* 4. Detail about the success of the elder Birney's enterprises is also cited in Calvin M. Fackler, *Early Days in Danville* (Louisville: Standard Printing Co., 1941), 236.

14. Matthew Mason, *Slavery and Politics in the Early American Republic* (Chapel Hill: University of North Carolina Press, 2006), 14.

15. Dwight Lowell Dumond, *Antislavery: The Crusade for Freedom in America* (New York: W. W. Norton, 1966), 29.

16. Vernon P. Martin, "Father Rice, the Preacher Who Followed the Frontier," *Filson Club History Quarterly* 27, no. 4 (1953): 324–330.

17. Lowell H. Harrison, *Kentucky's Road to Statehood* (Lexington: University Press of Kentucky, 1992), 19–30.

18. Even though in 1784 his friend, Rev. David Rice had organized Presbyterians in and around Danville into what was known as Concord Church, the elder Birney had gravitated toward the more socially prominent, at least in Danville during that period, Episcopalians. Later he was a founding member of the Trinity Episcopal Church. Personal conversation with the late Right

Reverend David Bell Birney IV, Danville, Kentucky, 1999. Bishop Birney, a great-great-grandson of James G. Birney, died in 2004.

19. Samuel's son, Dr. Ephraim McDowell, studied medicine at the University of Edinburgh in Scotland and became known as "the father of surgery in America." In 1809 he performed the world's first ovarian tumor removal on forty-seven-year-old Jane Todd Crawford of Greensburg, Kentucky, and in 1812 he removed kidney stones from seventeen-year-old James K. Polk of Mecklenberg County, North Carolina. Lamar A. Gray, "Ephraim McDowell: Father of Abdominal Surgery," *Filson Club History Quarterly* 43 (July 1969): 216–229. (Dr. McDowell was the uncle of James G. Birney's wife, Agatha McDowell.) Polk went on to become the eleventh president of the United States in the 1844 election, with a little help from Dr. McDowell's relative by marriage, James G. Birney, who ran on the Liberty Party ticket and took enough votes from Henry Clay to give Polk the victory.

20. *Tracy/McDowell Family History,* chapter 61, www.thetracyfamilyhistory.net, 26 April 2010.

21. Alexander Leitch, *A Princeton Companion* (Princeton, NJ: Princeton University Press, 1978).

CHAPTER 3. ROOTS OF THE CONFLICT OVER SLAVERY

1. Ira Berlin, *Many Thousands Gone: The First Two Centuries of Slavery in North America* (Cambridge, MA: Harvard University Press, 1998), 12.

2. J. Winston Coleman Jr., "The Code Duello in Ante-Bellum Kentucky," *Filson Club History Quarterly* 30 (April 1956): 125–140. After Dickinson called Jackson "a worthless scoundrel, a poltroon and a coward," the general challenged him. With pistols at eight paces, after Jackson had been wounded on the first shot he coldly shot his antagonist dead. The wound near his heart was not fatal, because the bullet hit a rib, but it was believed to be a contributing cause of Jackson's death nearly forty years later.

3. Elbert Smith, *The Death of Slavery: The United States, 1837–1865* (Chicago: University of Chicago Press, 1967), 44.

4. Coleman, "Code Duello," 129–130.

5. Jim Gannam, "May the Best Man Win," *Coastal Antiques and Art* (March 2002): 1.

6. Bertram Wyatt Brown, *Honor and Violence in the Old South* (New York: Oxford University Press, 1986), 5.

7. E. Smith, *Death of Slavery,* 45.

8. Fladeland, *James G. Birney,* 17.

9. American Convention for Promoting the Abolition of Slavery and Improving the Condition of the African Race, "First Convention at Philadelphia, 1–7 January 1794," *Minutes, Constitution, Addresses, Memorials, Resolutions, Reports, Committees and Anti-Slavery Tracts, 1794–1829*, vol. 1 (New York: Bergman Publishers, 1969).

10. Ibid., 1108–1109.

11. Otto A. Rothert, "The Tragedy of the Lewis Brothers," *Filson Club Quarterly* 10 (October 1936): 235.

12. Horace Greeley, *Recollections of a Busy Life: Including Reminiscences of American Politics and Politicians, From the Opening of the Missouri Contest to the Downfall of Slavery* (New York: J. B. Ford and Co., 1868), 284.

13. Wendy McElroy, "The Abolitionist Adventure," paper published by the Independent Institute, Oakland, CA (2003). Available online at http://www.independent.org/newsroom/article.asp?id=1439.

14. Winthrop S. Hudson, *Religion in America: An Historical Account of the Development of American Religious Life* (New York: Macmillan, 1981), 182–183.

15. Emerson Klees, *The Crucible of Ferment: New York's Psychic Highway* (Rochester, NY: Friends of the Finger Lakes Publishing, 2001).

16. Carl N. Degler, *Out of Our Past: The Forces That Shaped Modern America* (New York: Harper and Row, 1984), 194–195.

17. Julian P. Bretz, "The Economic Background of the Liberty Party," *American Historical Review* 34, no. 2 (1929): 250–264.

18. Theodore Clarke Smith, *The Liberty and Free Soil Parties of the Northwest* (New York: Longmans, Green and Company, 1897), 100–101.

19. James G. Blaine, *Twenty Years in Congress: From Lincoln to Garfield* (Norwich, CT: Henry Bill Publishing Co., 1884), 23.

20. Carl Schurz, *Life of Henry Clay* (New York: Houghton Mifflin, 1887), 43.

21. William Lee Miller, *Arguing about Slavery: The Great Battle in the United States Congress* (New York: Alfred A. Knopf, 1996).

22. Bryan-Paul Frost and Jeffrey Sikkenga, eds., *History of American Political Thought* (Lanham, MD: Lexington Books, 2003), 272.

23. Greeley, *Recollections of a Busy Life*, 285, 215.

24. David Brion Davis, *The Slave Power Conspiracy and the Paranoid Style* (Baton Rouge: Louisiana State University Press, 1969), 11–12.

25. Dumond, *Antislavery*, 60.

26. Protest made to Illinois House of Representatives, 3 March 1837, "Lincoln on Slavery," Lincoln Home National Historic Site, National Park Service, http://www.nps.gov/liho/historyculture/slavery.htm, 31 March 2008.

27. "Correspondence, between the Hon. F. H. Elmore, one of the South Carolina delegation in Congress, and James G. Birney, one of the secretaries of the American Anti-Slavery Society," *From Slavery to Freedom: The*

African-American Pamphlet Collection, 1824–1909, Rare Book and Special Collections Division, Library of Congress.

28. Fladeland, *James Gillespie Birney,* 163.
29. J. C. Furnas, *The Road to Harper's Ferry* (New York: William Sloane Associates, 1959), 319.
30. Dumond, *Antislavery,* 249–250.
31. Monique Prince, University of North Carolina Library, "Documenting the American South," http://docsouth.unc.edu/neh/weld/summary.html, 26 May 2010.
32. Bruce Catton and William Catton, *Two Roads to Sumter: Abraham Lincoln, Jefferson Davis, and the Road to the Civil War* (New York: McGraw Hill, 1963), 17.
33. Furnas, *Road to Harper's Ferry,* 319.
34. James G. Birney, "Cases of Conscience—Political Abolitionism," *The American Whig Review: A Whig Journal of Politics, Literature, Art and Science,* vol. 2 (New York: George H. Colton, 1845), 6.
35. Ibid., 4.

CHAPTER 4. TRAPPED IN THE GOLDEN CIRCLE

1. Virginia Van der Veer Hamilton, *Alabama: A History* (New York: W. W. Norton, 1984), 3.
2. Ibid.
3. James Birney Sr. to James G. Birney, 24 November 1818, Birney Papers, William L. Clements Library, University of Michigan, Ann Arbor, MI.
4. Ibid.
5. James F. Hopkins, "The Production of Hemp in Kentucky for Naval Use," *Filson Club Historical Quarterly* 23 (January 1949): 34–51.
6. Willis Brewer, *Alabama: Her History, Resources, War Record and Public Men: From 1540 to 1872* (Montgomery, AL: Barrett and Brown, 1872), 361.
7. Benjamin F. Shearer, ed., *The Uniting States: The Story of Statehood for the Fifty United States,* vol. 1: *Alabama to Kentucky* (Westport, CT: Greenwood, 2004), 44.
8. Fladeland, *James Gillespie Birney,* 19.
9. Thomas Jones Taylor, "Early History of Madison County," *Alabama Historical Quarterly* (Fall 1930): 316.
10. Thomas McAdory Owen, *Transactions of the Alabama Historical Society,* 4 vols. (Montgomery, AL: Brown Printing Co., 1899), 3:154–157.

11. Louis S. Gerteis, review of John W. Quist, *Restless Visionaries: The Social Roots of Antebellum Reform in Alabama and Michigan* (Baton Rouge: Louisiana State University Press, 1998), in *American Historical Review* 105, no. 5 (2000): 1741.

12. Plantation record book, Birney Papers.

13. W. Birney, *Birney and His Times*, 41–42, 23.

14. James Birney to James G. Birney, 10 April 1821, Birney Papers.

15. William McDowell to James G. Birney, 7 April 1821, Birney Papers.

16. W. Birney, *Birney and His Times*, 37–39.

17. William Warren Rogers, Robert David Ward, Leah Rawls Atkins, Wayne Flynn, *Alabama: The History of a Deep South State* (Montgomery: University of Alabama Press, 1994), 110–113.

18. Plantation record book, Birney Papers.

19. Burton J. Hendrick, *Statesmen of the Lost Cause: Jefferson Davis and His Cabinet* (New York: Literary Guild of America, 1939), 77.

20. W. Birney, *Birney and His Times*, 45.

21. Beriah Green, *Sketches of the Life and Writings of James Gillespie Birney* (Utica, NY: Jackson and Chaplin, 1844), 7–8.

22. Theodore Dwight Weld, *American Slavery As It Is: Testimony of a Thousand Witnesses* (New York: American Anti-Slavery Society, 1839), 46.

23. W. Birney, *Birney and His Times*, 63.

24. Edward Chambers Betts, *Early History of Huntsville, Alabama: 1804–1870* (Montgomery, AL: Brown Printing Co., 1916), 33–40.

25. Albert James Pickett, *History of Alabama: And Incidentally of Georgia and Mississippi from the Earliest Period* (Charleston, SC: Walker and James, 1851).

26. Thomas McAdory Owen, *History of Alabama and Dictionary of Alabama Biography* (Chicago: 1921), 3:152–55; Constitution of the State of Alabama (6 December 1819), Art. VI, Sec. 1, cited in Fladeland, *James Gillespie Birney*, 20.

27. *Journal of the Proceedings of the Board of Trustees of the University of Alabama at Their First Session, 1822* (Montgomery: Alabama Collections, University of Alabama Library), 260–261, cited in Fladeland, *James Gillespie Birney*, 33.

28. W. Birney, *Birney and His Times*, 61–62.

29. Oliver W. Davis, *Life of David Bell Birney, Major General United States Volunteers* (Philadelphia: King and Baird, 1867), 2.

30. *Nation* 50 (Jan. 1, 1890–June 30, 1890), 206–207. "Fathers and Sons," unsigned review of *James G. Birney and His Times*, by William Birney (New York: D. Appleton and Company, 1890). Here the *Nation* errs; Edward Everett served as Harvard president from 1846 to 1859. When Birney visited Boston in 1830, Josiah Quincy was president, serving from 1829 to 1845.

The article was mainly a scathing review of William Birney's biography of his father, calling it a defamation of William Lloyd Garrison.

31. The university eventually became a military school, training troops for the Confederacy during the Civil War, and all but seven buildings were subsequently burned by Union troops. A new era began in 1871, and in 1880 Congress granted forty thousand acres of coal lands, worth an estimated $250,000, as partial compensation for damages during the war.

32. Samuel J. May, *Some Recollections of Our Antislavery Conflict* (Boston: Fields, Osgood and Co., 1869), 207–208.

33. Owen, *Transactions,* 5:95.

34. McElroy, "Abolitionist Adventure."

35. W. Birney, *Birney and His Times,* 68.

36. Ibid., 88.

CHAPTER 5. DEFENDING THE CHEROKEE, LAUNCHING ABOLITION

1. Albert James Pickett, *Pickett's History of Alabama* (Montgomery, AL: River City Publishing, 2003), 139–147.

2. Sumter was later a general in the Continental Army during the Revolutionary War and later went on to become a U.S. senator and a champion of state's rights. The historic Civil War fort in the harbor of Charleston, South Carolina, bears his name.

3. Henry Timberlake, *The Memoirs of Lt. Henry Timberlake: The Story of a Soldier, Adventurer, and Emissary to the Cherokees, 1756–1765,* edited by Duane H. King (Cherokee, NC: Museum of the Cherokee Indian Press, 2007).

4. Hamilton, *Alabama,* 150.

5. H. W. Brands, *Andrew Jackson: His Life and Times* (New York: Random House, 2005), 435.

6. Ricky L. Hendricks, "Henry Clay and Jacksonian Indian Policy: A Political Anachronism," *Filson Club History Quarterly* 60, no. 2 (1986): 218–238.

7. Fladeland, *James Gillespie Birney,* 35–36.

8. W. Birney, *Birney and His Times,* 56.

9. Mary Hershberger, "Mobilizing Women, Anticipating Abolition: The Struggle against Indian Removal in the 1830s," *Journal of American History* 86, no. 1 (1999).

10. James G. Birney to C. C. Clay, 26 April 1832, Dwight Lowell Dumond, ed., *Letters of James Gillespie Birney* (Gloucester, MA: Peter Smith, 1966) [hereafter cited as Birney Letters], 1:2–5.

11. Brands, *Jackson*, 488–489.
12. Theda Perdue and Michael D. Green, *The Cherokee Nation and the Trail of Tears* (New York: Penguin Group, 2007), 134.
13. Brands, *Andrew Jackson*, 489. Birney and Clement C. Clay were inducted into the Alabama Lawyers Hall of Fame on 7 May 2010.
14. Fladeland, *James Gillespie Birney*, 36–37.
15. Gerard N. Magliocca, "The Cherokee Removal and the Fourteenth Amendment," *Duke Law Journal* 53, no. 3(2003).
16. Garrett Epps, "The Antebellum Political Background of the Fourteenth Amendment," *Law and Contemporary Problems* 67 (2004).

CHAPTER 6. THE COLONIZATION DEBACLE

1. Carroll was one of the wealthiest men in the country and was only titular head of the ACS, being, in historian Dwight Dumond's opinion, "a feeble old man without pronounced convictions either for colonization or emancipation." Carroll, who had been a member of the Continental Congress from Maryland and later a U.S. senator, was the last surviving signer of the Declaration of Independence. He died on 14 November 1832.
2. Birney to Ralph R. Gurley, 23 August 1832, Birney Letters, 1:22.
3. Daniel S. Dupre, *Transforming the Cotton Frontier: Madison County, Alabama, 1800–1840* (Baton Rouge: Louisiana State University Press, 1997), 168, 205. Dupre reveals that Birney's pastor, the Reverend John Allan, Presbyterian minister and father of William Allan, who later collaborated with Birney during the Lane Seminary Debates, was a prominent slaveholder in Huntsville.
4. James Birney Sr. to Birney, 10 January 1832, Birney papers.
5. Birney to Gurley, 24 January 1833, Birney Letters, 1:50–53.
6. Birney Letters, 1:v–vi.
7. Ibid.
8. "Africans in America," PBS Online, http://www.pbs.org/wgbh/aia/part3/3narr4.html, 12 January 2008. As a youthful sailor, Forten had been captured by the British and held prisoner in England, where he was exposed to abolitionist influences. Back in America he was apprenticed to a sailmaker, eventually owning the business and building a fortune of more than $100,000.
9. B. L. Rayner, *Life of Thomas Jefferson*, edited by Eyler Robert Coates Sr., ch. 12, "Establishing Religious Freedom," University of Virginia Alderman Library online resources, http://etext.virginia.edu/jefferson/biog/lj12.htm, 13 July 2010.

10. Philip Shaw Paludan, "Lincoln and Colonization: Policy or Propaganda?" *Journal of the Abraham Lincoln Association* 25, no. 1 (2004).

11. Dupre, *Transforming the Cotton Frontier,* 219–221.

12. Letter from Henry Clay to John Switzer, 19 May 1831, New York: *Gilder Lehrman Institute of American History.*

13. Dupre, *Transforming the Cotton Frontier,* 223.

14. Lowell H. Harrison, *The Antislavery Movement in Kentucky* (Lexington: University Press of Kentucky, 1978), 39.

15. James M. Gifford, "Some New Light on Henry Clay and the American Colonization Society," *Filson Club Historical Quarterly* 50 (October 1976): 372–374.

16. "Table of Emigrants," *African Repository and Colonial Journal* 30, no. 1 (1854): 121.

CHAPTER 7. BIRNEY'S EPIPHANY

1. Daniel Mallory, ed., *The Life and Speeches of Henry Clay* (New York: Robert P. Bixby and Co., 1844), 1:363–364.

2. Ibid.

3. John Breckenridge had introduced the resolutions in the Kentucky legislature but died eight years later.

4. *The Papers of Thomas Jefferson: The Kentucky Resolutions of 1798,* vol. 30: *1 January 1798 to 31 January 1799* (Princeton, NJ: Princeton University Press, 2003).

5. William Birney, *Birney and His Times,* 72.

6. Chris Morris, University of Texas, Arlington, review of Daniel S. Dupre, *Transforming the Cotton Frontier: Madison County, Alabama, 1800–1840* (Baton Rouge: Louisiana State University Press, 1997), for H-SHEAR, H-NET List of the Society for the History of the Early American Republic (March 1999).

7. Birney to Ralph R. Gurley, 11 December 1833, Birney Letters, 1:97.

8. John D. Christian to Birney, 30 Aug. 1831, Birney Letters, 1:1.

9. George M. Frederickson and Christopher Lasch, "Resistance to Slavery," edited by John H. Bracey Jr., *American Slavery: The Question of Resistance* (Belmont, CA: Wadsworth, 1971).

10. Fladeland, *James Gillespie Birney,* 48.

11. Henry C. Whitney, *Life and Works of Abraham Lincoln: Lincoln the Citizen* (New York: Lincoln Centenary Association, 1892), 1:73.

12. Sandburg, *Lincoln,* 19.

13. Abraham Lincoln to Joshua Speed, August 24, 1855," in *The Collected Works of Abraham Lincoln,* edited by Roy P. Basler (New Brunswick, NJ: Rutgers University Press, 1953–1955). Available at Abraham Lincoln Online,: Speeches and Writings, http://showcase.netins.net/web/creative/lincoln/speeches/speed.htm, 3 February 2008.

14. Marli Frances Weiner, *Mistresses and Slaves: Plantation Women in South Carolina,* 1830–80 (Champaign: University of Illinois Press, 1997), 97; Mary Chestnut, http://multiracial.com/site/content/view/460/37, 9 January 2007.

15. Lawrence R. Tenzer, *The Forgotten Cause of the Civil War: A New Look at the Slavery Issue* (Manahawkin, NJ: Scholars Publishing House, 1997), 37.

16. A.D. Powell, *"Passing" For Who You Really Are: Essays in Support of Multiracial Whiteness,* (Palm Coast, FL: Backintyme Publishing, 2005).

17. *The Abolitionist: Or Record of the New England Anti-Slavery Society,* edited by a committee (Boston: Garrison and Knapp, 1833), 178–189.

18. Birney to Gurley, 3 December 1833, Birney Letters, 1:97.

19. Fladeland, *Slaveholder James Gillespie Birney,* 41.

20. Conrad J. Engelder, *The Churches and Slavery: A Study of the Attitudes toward Slavery of the Major Protestant Denominations,.* Ph.D. dissertation, the University of Michigan, 1964. (Note: Engelder was a student of anti-antislavery scholar Prof. Dwight L. Dumond.)

21. "Mr. Birney's Letter to the Churches," 2 September 1834, Labadie Special Collections, Bentley Historical Collections, The University of Michigan. Emphasis in the original.

22. Hershberger, *Mobilizing Women,* 38.

23. Fladeland described him as follows: "Birney, in middle age, was still a handsome man. His brown hair was beginning to gray, and he had added weight, but the years had given him even more self-assurance coupled with a more serious dignity. He was not above enjoying the limelight."

24. Fladeland, *Slaveholder James Gillespie Birney,* 110–112.

25. Birney to Gurley, 24 September 1833, American Colonization Society Papers, cited in Fladeland, *Slaveholder James Gillespie Birney,* 71.

26. Birney to Gerrit Smith, 21 March 1835, Birney Letters, 1:189.

27. Birney to William Jay (a noted London Congregationalist minister), 5 October 1840, Birney Letters, 2:605.

28. C. C. Goen, "Broken Churches, Broken Nation: Regional Religion and North-South Alienation in Antebellum America," *Church History: Studies in Christianity and Culture* 52, no. 1 (1983): 22.

29. Whitney, *Life and Works,* 162–163. Emphasis in original.

30. Telephone conversation with Herman Hoffman "Topper" Birney, of Huntsville, Alabama, a great-great-grandson of James G. Birney, 19 October 2006.

CHAPTER 8. SAVING THE SOUTH FROM DESTRUCTION

1. Nathan Green to Birney, 26 August 1833, Birney Letters, 1:86.
2. Birney to Gurley, 24 September 1833, Birney Letters, 1:89.
3. Fladeland, *James Gillespie Birney,* 73.
4. Birney to Gurley, 11 December 1833, Birney Letters, 1:98–99.
5. Ibid., 110.
6. Harrison, *Antislavery Kentucky,* 42.
7. Fladeland, *James Gillespie Birney,* 85–86.
8. Ibid., 85–89.
9. James G. Birney Emancipation Document, Mercer County Deed Book 19, p. 32, recorded October 1934 in Mercer County Court Microfilm 191820 (KDLA); manumission ceremony cited in W. Birney, *Birney and His Times,* 139, and Fladeland, *James Gillespie Birney*, 82–83.
10. Lewis Bond to Birney, 31 August 1835, Birney Letters, 1:240–241.
11. John Jones to Birney, 19 September 1835, Birney Letters, 1:245.
12. W. Birney, *Birney and His Times,* 181–182.
13. Birney to Gerrit Smith, 13 September 1835, Birney Letters, 1:243–244.
14. Fladeland, *James Gillespie Birney,* 94.
15. Endorsement by Birney to letter from Henry Clay to Birney, 16 September 1834, also citing diary entry of 16 September 1834, Birney Letters, 1:135.
16. Ibid., 94–95.
17. Ibid.
18. Levi Coffin, *Reminiscences of Levi Coffin, the Reputed President of the Underground Railroad* (Cincinnati: Robert Clark and Co., 1880), 719–726.
19. Fladeland, *James Gillespie Birney,* 90–91.

CHAPTER 9. THE TAR AND FEATHERS AGENDA

1. Charles F. Goss, *Cincinnati: The Queen City, 1788–1912* (Cincinnati: S. J. Clarke Publishing Co., 1912), 1:83.
2. Ibid. 1:168.
3. W. Birney, *Birney and His Times,* 217.
4. Fladeland, *James Gillespie Birney,* 128.
5. Replica copy of the *Philanthropist,* 1 January 1836, published by New Richmond, Ohio, Historical Society, 1976, in author's personal possession.
6. "The Philanthropist," in *New Richmond, Ohio: Historical Collections 1997,* edited by Aileen M. Whitt (New Richmond, OH: Historical New Richmond, Inc., 1997), 92.

7. *Philanthropist,* 29 January 1836, 1.

8. W. Birney, *Birney and His Times,* 217.

9. Fladeland, *James Gillespie Birney,* 132.

10. W. Birney, *Birney and His Times,* 219.

11. Henry Howe, "Achilles Pugh," *Historical Collections of Ohio: An Encyclopedia of the State* (Norwalk, OH: Laning Printing Co., 1896), 2:769.

12. Charles T. Greve, *Centennial History of Cincinnati and Representative Citizens* (Chicago: Biographical Publishing Co., 1904), 585.

13. W. Birney, *Birney and His Times,* 219.

14. Graphic in Birney Letters, 1:342.

15. Alpha (unknown) to Birney, July 1836, in Birney Letters, 1:342.

16. Beriah Green, *Sketches of the Life and Writings of James Gillespie Birney* (Utica, NY: Jackson and Chaplin, 1844), 50.

17. Clara Longworth de Chambrun, *Cincinnati: Story of the Queen City* (New York: Charles Scribners' Sons, 1939), 168.

18. *Philanthropist,* 23 September 1836; American Anti-Slavery Society, Fourth Annual Report, New York (1837), 82–87.

19. Joan Hedrick, *Harriet Beecher Stowe: A Life* (New York: Oxford University Press, 1994), 104–109.

20. Greve, *Centennial Cincinnati,* 127.

21. *Philanthropist,* 7 August 1838, 3.

22. Albert B. Hart, *Salmon P. Chase* (New York: Chelsea House, 1980), 48–52.

23. Jacob W. Schuckers, *The Life and Public Services of Salmon Portland Chase* (1874; New York: Da Capo Press, 1970), 77.

24. Diary of James G. Birney, entries for 29 February–6 March 1840.

25. Schuckers, *Life and Public Services,* 48–49.

26. John Niven, "Lincoln and Chase: A Reappraisal," *Journal of the Abraham Lincoln Association* 12, no. 1 (1991): 5.

27. A. D. P. Van Buren, "Michigan in Her Pioneer Moments," in *Michigan Pioneer and Historical Collections,* vol. 17 (Lansing, MI, 1892).

28. Ibid.

29. Wendell Phillips Garrison and Francis Jackson Garrison, *William Lloyd Garrison, 1805–1879: The Story of His Life Told by His Children,* 4 vols. (New York: Century Co., 1885), 1:276.

CHAPTER 10. LINCOLN'S PROPHET

1. Joseph H. Borome, "Henry Clay and James G. Birney: An Exchange of Views," *Filson Club Historical Quarterly* 35 (April 1961): 122–124.

2. Bertram Wyatt-Brown, *Lewis Tappan and the Evangelical War against Slavery* (Baton Rouge: Louisiana State University Press, 1997), 273.

3. Theodore Clarke Smith, *The Liberty and Free Soil Parties in the Northwest* (New York: Longmans, Green and Co., 1897), 36.

4. Wyatt-Brown, *Lewis Tappan,* 273.

5. Stephen P. Budney, *William Jay: Abolitionist and Anticolonialist* (Westport, CT: Praeger, 2005), 72.

6. Birney to Myron Holley, Joshua Leavitt, and Elizur Wright Jr., 11 May 1840, Birney Letters, 1:562–574.

7. Ibid.

8. Ibid.

9. Dwight Lowell Dumond, *Antislavery Origins of the Civil War in the United States* (Ann Arbor: The University of Michigan Press, 1959), 51.

10. Ballot in Birney Papers, William L. Clements Library, The University of Michigan, Ann Arbor, Michigan.

11. Furnas, *Road to Harper's Ferry,* 364.

12. Gabor S. Boritt, *Lincoln and the Economics of the American Dream* (Memphis, TN: Memphis State University Press, 1978), 78, cited in Carwardine, 328.

13. Birney Papers, William L. Clements Library, the University of Michigan, Ann Arbor, Michigan.

14. Mrs. Stanton's memory must have failed her about the ship, since she was writing nearly sixty years after the trip to England. She recalled being aboard the *Montreal* when the vessel was in fact the *Great Western,* the first steamer to establish transatlantic service. The *Montreal* was not built until 1848, and she plied the Liverpool-to-Montreal route. Elizabeth Cady Stanton, *Eighty Years and More: Reminiscences (1815–1897), of Elizabeth Cady Stanton* (New York: European Publishing Co., 1898), 74–83.

15. Ibid.

16. Ibid.

17. Henry Mayer, *All on Fire: William Lloyd Garrison and the Abolition of Slavery* (New York: St. Martin's Griffin, 1998), 266–267.

18. Henry B. Stanton, *Random Reflections* (Johnstown, NY: Blunck and Leaning, 1885), 48, cited in Fladeland, *Slaveholder James Gillespie Birney,* 198.

19. Elizabeth Cady Stanton, *Reminiscences,* 89.

20. Mayer, *All on Fire,* 290–291.

21. Elizur Wright to Daniel O'Connell, 20 October 1838, Correspondence of Daniel O'Connell, 6:2566.

22. Elizabeth Stanton, *Reminiscences,* 91.

23. Neil A. Hamilton, *Rebels and Renegades: A Chronology of Social and Political Dissent in the United States* (New York: Routledge, 2002), 91.

24. R. L. Morrow, "The Liberty Party in Vermont," *The New England Quarterly* 2, no. 2 (1929): 238.

25. "Address from the People of Ireland," *Signal of Liberty*, 6 April 1842, 1.

26. John F. Quinn, *Father Mathew's Crusade: Temperance in Nineteenth-Century Ireland and Irish America* (Amherst: University of Massachusetts Press, 2002), 86–97.

27. *Liberator*, 4 February 1842.

28. *Signal of Liberty*, 6 April 1842, 1.

29. Brian Dooley, *Black and Green: Fight for Civil Rights in Northern Ireland and Black America* (Chicago: Pluto Press, 1998), 11–12.

30. Fladeland, *Slaveholder James Gillespie Birney*, 205.

31. Vincent Peter Lannie, "Profile of an Immigrant Bishop: The Early Career of John Hughes," *Pennsylvania History: A Journal of Mid-Atlantic Studies* 32, no. 4 (October 1965): 366–379. Hughes was the first Catholic archbishop in the United States, having been appointed by Pope Pius IX. In 1841, he established St. John's College in the Bronx, later to become Fordham University.

32. Theodore W. Allen, *The Invention of the White Race,* vol. 1: *Racial Oppression and Social Control* (London: Verso, 1994), 168–169.

33. Thomas F. Moriarity, "The Irish American Response to Catholic Emancipation," *Catholic Historical Review* 64 (1980): 366–372.

34. Dooley, *Black and Green,* 13.

CHAPTER 11. HENRY CLAY'S NEMESIS

1. Michigan Pioneer and Historical Society, *Historical Collections: Collections and Researches Made by the Michigan Pioneer and Historical Society* (Lansing: Robert Smith Printing Co., 1900), 28:237.

2. W. Birney, *Birney and His Times,* 88.

3. Joel H. Silbey, *Storm Over Texas: The Annexation Controversy and the Road to Civil War* (New York: Oxford University Press, 2005), 76–77.

4. Albert B. Hart, *American History Told by Contemporaries: National Expansion, 1783–1845* (New York: Macmillan Publishing Co., 1901), 646–649.

5. Elizur Wright, *Emancipator and Free American,* 26 October 1843, 16 November 1843.

6. "Birney Is the Man," *Signal of Liberty,* 22 July 1844.

7. John J. Marshall, "Birney: By a Slaveholder Who Knows Him," *Signal of Liberty,* 14 October 1844.

8. Dumond, *Antislavery,* 93.

9. Beriah Green, *Sketches of the Life and Writings of James Gillespie Birney* (Utica, N.Y.: Jackson and Chaplin, 1844).

10. William Birney, *Birney and His Times,* 354–355.

11. Michael F. Holt, *The Rise and Fall of the American Whig Party: Jacksonian Politics and the Onset of the Civil War* (New York: Oxford University Press, 1999), 206.

12. Dumond, *Antislavery,* 303.

13. William Ellery Channing, *The Works of William E. Channing, D.D* (Boston: American Unitarian Association, 1890), 752.

14. Eugene Barker, "Public Opinion in Texas Preceding the Revolution," American Historical Association, *Annual Report of the American Historical Association for the Year 1911.* 2 vols. (Washington, D.C., 1913), 1:219n1.

15. Clay's instincts about the dangers of a Mexican War were realized when his son, Lt. Col. Henry Clay Jr., thirty-five, died leading his regiment, the 2nd Kentucky Volunteers, in the Battle of Buena Vista in 1847.

16. Horace Greeley, *Recollections of a Busy Life* (New York: J. B. Ford and Co., 1868), 165–166.

17. Horace Greeley, response to *Rochester (NY) Daily Union,* in *New York Tribune,* 7 January 1864.

18. Anonymous, "A Tribute to James Birney," 22.

19. Ibid.

20. "James G. Birney," *New York Times,* 3 February 1852.

21. Michigan Pioneer and Historical Society, *Historical Collections,* 28:237.

22. William Livingstone, *Livingstone's History of the Republican Party* (Detroit: William Livingstone, 1900), 1:6.

CHAPTER 12. UNCLE TOM COMES ALIVE

1. Joan Hedrick, *Harriet Beecher Stowe: A Life* (New York: Oxford University Press, 1994), 104–109.

2. Henry Louis Gates Jr. and Hollis Robbins, *The Annotated Uncle Tom's Cabin* (New York: W. W. Norton, 2007), xxxiii.

3. Huntington Lyman, "Address Delivered at Oberlin College Jubilee Celebration," in *Lane Seminary Rebels,* edited by W. G. Ballentine (Oberlin, OH: Oberlin Jubilee, 1883), 63.

4. Fladeland, *James Gillespie Birney,* 81.

5. Charles Beecher, ed., *Autobiography, Correspondence, Etc., of Lyman Beecher,* (New York: Harper, 1864), 2:323. Emphasis in original.

6. Lyman, *Lane Rebels,* 63.

7. Ibid.

8. James A. Thome, *First Annual Report of the American Anti-Slavery Society* (New York: Dorr and Butterfield, 1834), 12.

9. Harriet Beecher Stowe, *Uncle Tom's Cabin: Or Life Among the Lowly* (Boston: Houghton, Osgood and Company, 1879), 9.

10. *Debate at the Lane Seminary, Cincinnati: Speech of James A. Thome, of Kentucky, Delivered at the Annual Meeting of the American Anti-Slavery Society, May 6, 1834; Letter of the Rev. Dr. Samuel Cox, against the American Colonization Society* (Boston: Garrison and Knapp, 1834). Emphasis in original.

11. Lyman, *Lane Rebels,* 62–64.

12. Dumond, *Antislavery,* 262–263.

13. R. J. M. Blackett, "The Press and Abolition," *Atlanta History: A Journal of Georgia and the South* 42, no. 1–2 (1998).

14. Birney Diary, 27 November 1851, 335.

15. "Harriet Beecher Stowe's Life and Time," Harriet Beecher Stowe Center, Harriet Beecher Stowe House and Library, 2005. Available online at http://www.upa.pdx.edu/IMS/currentprojects/TAHv3/Content/Not_Posted/Harriet_Beecher_Stowe.pdf.

16. Betty L. Fladeland, "James G. Birney's Anti-Slavery Activities in Cincinnati, 1835–1837," *Bulletin of the Historical and Philosophical Society of Ohio* 9, no. 4 (1951): 160.

17. Unsigned review [Gamaliel Bailey] of *Uncle Tom's Cabin, National Era,* 15 April 1852.

18. Edwin DeLeon, "[From] *Valedictory,*" *Charleston Mercury,* 13 August 1852.

19. Thomas F. Gossett, *Uncle Tom's Cabin and American Culture* (Dallas: Southern Methodist University Press, 1985).

20. Michigan Pioneer and Historical Society, "The Anti-Slavery Bible," *Historical Collections,* 28:238.

21. Correspondence between Leonard Bacon, on behalf of Mrs. Stowe, and Birney in late 1852 and early 1853, cited in Birney Letters, 2:1159–1163. Harriet Beecher Stowe, *A Key to Uncle Tom's Cabin: Presenting the Original Facts and Documents Upon Which the Story Is Founded, Together With Corroborative Statements Verifying the Truth of the Work* (Boston: John P. Jewett and Co., 1853).

22. Ibid., 1161.

CHAPTER 13. MICHIGAN'S "WONDERFUL REVOLUTION"

1. Richard Reeves, *American Journey: Traveling with Tocqueville in Search of Democracy in America* (New York: Simon and Schuster, 1982), 210.

2. Gerard Fergerson, introduction to *Marie; or, Slavery in the United States,* by Gustave de Beaumont (Baltimore: Johns Hopkins University Press, 1999), x.

3. Reeves, *American Journey.* During his research in 1980, I guided Reeves on a tour of Saginaw and Bay City.

4. Floyd B. Streeter, *Political Parties in Michigan* (Lansing: Michigan Historical Commission, 1918).

5. David G. Chardavoyne, "Michigan and the Fugitive Slave Acts," *Court Legacy* 12, no. 3, (2004): 1–2.

6. Ralph Naveaux, *Invaded on All Sides: Engagements at Frenchtown and the River Raisin in the War of 1812* (Monroe, MI: Ralph Naveaux, 2008), 11.

7. Coffin, *Reminiscences.*

8. Chardavoyne, "Michigan and the Fugitive Slave Acts," 4–6.

9. Ibid., 9.

10. John W. Quist, "The Great Majority of Our Subscribers Are Farmers: The Michigan Abolitionist Constituency of the 1840s," *Journal of the Early Republic* 14 (Fall 1994).

11. Birney to Dr. Daniel Fitzhugh, 19 November 1841, Birney Collection, Bay County Historical Society, Bay City, MI.

12. Saginaw County, 1843 tax sale records, Birney Papers, Clements Library.

13. Birney to Lewis Tappan, 27 May 1842, Birney Letters, 2:694–696.

14. Birney to Lewis Tappan, 4 October 1841, Birney Letters, 2:636.

15. Joshua Leavitt to Birney, 18 January 1841, Birney Collection, Bay County Historical Society, Bay City, MI.

16. Weld to Birney, 23 May 1842, Birney Letters, 2:692–694.

17. Weld to Birney, 22 January 1842, Birney Letters, 2:662–664

18. Birney to Charles H. Stewart and Joshua Leavitt, 17 August 1843, Birney Letters, 2:754–758.

19. Arthur L. Porter to Birney, 25 February 1843, Birney Letters, 2:674.

20. Birney to Saginaw City Committee of Arrangements, 25 June 1842, Birney Letters, 2:700.

21. Birney to Stewart and Leavitt, 17 August 1843, Birney Letters, 2:757.

22. The Lebanon cedar was the campaign symbol adopted by the Liberty Party. Elizur Wright to Birney, 16 September 1843, Birney Letters, 2:759–761.

23. Birney to Elizur Wright, 4 March 1844, Birney Letters, 2:797–798.

24. Joshua Leavitt to Birney, 18 December 1844, Birney Letters, 2:888–891.

25. William Birney to Birney, 28 December 1844, Birney Letters, 2:892–894.

26. Birney to the Liberty Party (printed in the *Signal of Liberty*, 20 January 1845), Birney Letters, 2:894–910.
27. Birney to Jacob Barker or Joseph Maybin, 12 July 1845, Birney Letters, 2:953.
28. Barker to Birney, 5 August 1845, Birney Letters, 2:957.
29. Barker to Birney, 2 October 1845, Birney Letters, 2:975.
30. Henry Stanton to Birney, 11 August 1845, Birney Letters, 2:957–961.
31. W. Birney, *Birney and His Times*, 374–375.
32. Theodore Foster to Birney, 12 September 1845 Birney Letters, 2:967, citing earlier letter from Birney, undocumented.
33. Fladeland, *James Gillespie Birney*, 267–268.
34. Birney Diary, 4 February 1851, Birney Letters, 31.

CHAPTER 14. FLIGHT TO EAGLESWOOD

1. Fladeland, *James Gillespie Birney*, 277.
2. Ibid., 279.
3. Birney Diary, 21 January 1851, Birney Collection, Clements Library, 21–22.
4. Ibid., 2.
5. Ibid., 50.
6. Clement A. Price, *Freedom Not Far Distant: A Documentary History of Afro-Americans in New Jersey* (Newark: New Jersey Historical Society, 1980).
7. Letter dated 1 November 1856, in F. B. Sanborn, "The Emerson-Thoreau Correspondence: Emerson in Europe," *Atlantic Monthly* (June 1892).
8. Student files and administrative records pertaining to Robert Lincoln and Fitzhugh Birney, Harvard Archives, Harvard University.
9. Benjamin Thomas, *Theodore Weld, Crusader for Freedom* (New Brunswick, NJ: Rutgers University Press, 1950), 227.
10. Fladeland, *James Gillespie Birney*, 286.
11. Ibid.
12. John Stauffer, *The Black Hearts of Men: Radical Abolitionists and the Transformation of Race* (Cambridge, MA: Harvard University Press, 2001), 237.
13. Maud Honeyman Greene, "Raritan Bay Union, Eagleswood, New Jersey," *Proceedings of the New Jersey Historical Society* 68, no. 1 (1950). In 1899 the bodies were disinterred and the remains transported to North Elba, New York, high in the Adirondack Mountains near Lake Placid. There they were reburied on Brown's farm with the bodies of Brown and other Harpers Ferry conspirators.

CHAPTER 15. THE REPUBLICAN PHENOMENON

1. John Niven, "Lincoln and Chase, a Reappraisal," *Journal of the Abraham Lincoln Association* 12, no. 1 (1991): 3.
2. Diary of James G. Birney, entries for 29 February through 6 March 1840, Birney Collection, William Clements Library.
3. Schuckers, *Chase,* 48–49.
4. Niven, "Lincoln and Chase," 10.
5. John Quincy Adams to Roger S. Baldwin, 11 November 1840, Gilder Lehrman Collection, Gilder Lehrman Institute of American History, New York, 582.
6. Fladeland, *James Gillespie Birney,* 254.
7. Richard H. Sewell, *Ballots for Freedom* (New York: W.W. Norton, 1980), 126.
8. James G. Birney, *Sinfulness of Slaveholding in All Circumstances, Tested by Reason and Scripture* (Detroit: Printed by Charles Willcox, 1846), 5.
9. Ibid., 58.
10. Ibid., 60.
11. Fladeland, *James Gillespie* Birney, 264.
12. Benn Pitman, U.S. Army Military Commission, *The Assassination of President Lincoln and the Trial of the Conspirators* (New York: Moore, Wilstach and Baldwin, 1865), 45.
13. John Rhodehamel and Louise Taper, eds., *Right or Wrong, God Judge Me: The Writings of John Wilkes Booth* (Champaign: University of Illinois Press, 2001), 136.
14. Birney Diary, William L. Clements Library, University of Michigan.
15. Linda Brent [Harriet Jacobs], *Incidents in the Life of a Slave Girl,* edited by Lydia Maria Francis Childs (1861; New York: Harcourt Brace, 1973), 195.
16. W. Birney, *Birney and His Times,* 261–265.
17. Salmon Portland Chase, *Reclamation of Fugitives from Service: An Argument for the Defendant Submitted to the Supreme Court of the United States at the December Term, 1846, in the Case of Wharton Jones vs. John Van Zandt* (Cincinnati: Printed by R. P. Donough and Co., 1847), 84. Emphasis in original.
18. Eric Foner, *Free Soil, Free Labor, Free Men: The Ideology of the Republican Party before the Civil War* (New York: Oxford University Press, 1995), 124–125.
19. Richard Carl Brown, *History of Danville and Boyle County Kentucky, 1774–1992* (Danville, KY: Bicentennial Books, 1992), 4.
20. William L. Barney, *The Road to Secession: A New Perspective on the Old South* (New York: Praeger, 1972), 51.
21. Tyler Anbinder, *Nativism and Slavery: The Northern Know-Nothings and the Politics of the 1850s* (New York: Oxford University Press, 1994).

22. William Stocking, ed., *Under the Oaks: Commemorating the Fiftieth Anniversary of the Founding of the Republican Party at Jackson, Michigan, July 6, 1854* (Detroit: *Detroit Tribune*, 1904), 11.

23. Ibid., 16–19.

24. Ibid.

25. Carwardine, *Lincoln: A Life*, 119.

26. Greeley, *Recollections of a Busy Life*, 294.

27. George W. Julian, review of *The Liberty and Free Soil Parties in the Northwest*, by Theodore Clarke Smith, *American Historical Review* 4, no. 1 (1898): 180–183.

28. Sewell, *Ballots for Freedom*, 265.

29. Benjamin P. Thomas, *Lincoln: A Biography* (Carbondale: Southern Illinois University Press, 1952), 166.

30. Marion Mills Miller, ed., *Life and Works of Abraham Lincoln*, by Henry C. Whitney, 9 vols. (New York: Lincoln Centenary Association, 1907), 3:276–279, 282, 299, 302.

31. David R. Roediger, *The Wages of Whiteness: Race and the Making of the American Working Class* (London: Verso, 1991), 81.

32. Lawrence R. Tenzer and A. D. Powell, "White Slavery, Maternal Descent, and the Politics of Slavery in the Antebellum United States," paper originally presented at University of Nottingham Institute for the Study of Slavery, July/August 2004.

33. Sewell, *Ballots for Freedom*, 301.

34. Michael J. McManus, *Political Abolitionism in Wisconsin, 1840-1861*, (Kent, OH: Kent State University Press, 1998).

35. Carwardine, *Lincoln: A Life*, xi–xii.

36. John Milton Hay, cited in Stocking, *Under the Oaks*, 166.

37. Ibid.

38. A. D. P. Van Buren, *Michigan Historical Society Reports*, 17:249.

39. Stanley I. Cutler, *The Dred Scott Decision: Law or Politics?* (Boston: Houghton Mifflin, 1967), 4–5.

40. Sewell, *Ballots for Freedom*, 301.

CHAPTER 16. THE BIRNEYS IN BATTLE

1. Charles B. Dew, *Apostles of Disunion: Southern Secession Commissioners and the Causes of the Civil War* (Charlottesville: University of Virginia Press, 2001), 22–25.

2. Ellison Capers, "The War Begins! Fort Sumter," in *Confederate Military History,* edited by Clement A. Evans (1899), 5:17–18.

3. Oliver Wilson Davis, *Life of David Bell Birney: Major General United States Volunteers* (Philadelphia: King and Baird, 1867), 22.

4. Ibid., 106.

5. T. Harry Williams, *Lincoln and the Radicals* (Madison: University of Wisconsin Press, 1941), 16.

6. Don E. Fehrenbacher, "Lincoln's Wartime Leadership: The First Hundred Days," in *Essays from the Journal of the Abraham Lincoln Association,* edited by Thomas F. Schwartz (New York: Fordham University Press, 1999), 63.

7. Bruce Catton, *The Civil War* (New York: Houghton Mifflin, 2004), 42.

8. Charles Sumner to Wendell Phillips, 3 August 1861, in Sumner, *Selected Letters,* 2:74, cited in James M. McPherson and William J. Cooper Jr., *Writing the Civil War: The Quest to Understand* (Columbia: University of South Carolina Press, 1998), 263.

9. Davis, *Life of David Bell Birney,* 62.

10. Ibid., 70.

11. Francis Trevelyan Miller, ed., *The Photographic History of the Civil War* (New York: The Review of Reviews Co., 1911), 2:51.

12. Davis, *Life of David Bell Birney,* 73–73, History of 57th Regiment Pennsylvania Volunteers, http://www.pa.roots.com/pacw/infantry/57thorg.html, 15 May 2010.

13. Report of Maj. Gen. Daniel E. Sickles, USA, Commanding the Third Army Corps, "The Chancellorsville Campaign," 20 May 1863, Washington, D.C., Official Records of the War of the Rebellion, ser. 1, vol. 25, pt. 1, 385, 390; "Battle of Chancellorsville," from *Harper Brothers American History,* vol. 2, http://www.sonofthesouth.net/leefoundation/battle-chancellorsville.htm, 9 June 2008.

14. Davis, *Life of David Bell Birney,* 110–111.

15. Abraham Lincoln to Edwin M. Stanton, 7 March 1864 (Gen. David B. Birney), The Abraham Lincoln Papers at the Library of Congress, ser. 3, General Correspondence, 1837–1897.

16. Abraham Lincoln Correspondence, Lincoln Studies Center, Knox College, Galesburg, Illinois.

17. Larry Tagg, *Generals of Gettysburg: The Leaders of America's Greatest Battle* (Cambridge, MA: DaCapo Press, 2003), 66.

18. Eric A. Campbell, "Death of the III Corps: What Was Daniel Sickles Thinking When He Practically Destroyed His Own Corps at Gettysburg?" *Civil War Times* 48, no. 4 (August 2009): 34–38. (The bones of Sickles's right leg, and the cannonball that injured him, are still on display at the Walter Reed Medical Center in Washington, D.C.)

19. Col. William F. Fox, "The Colored Troops, History of Their Organization, Their Losses in Battle and by Disease," in *Fox's Regimental Losses* (Albany, NY: Albany Publishing Company, 1889).

20. Bruce Catton, *Grant Takes Command* (Boston: Little, Brown and Company, 1968), 195–197.

21. Bruce Catton, *The American Heritage New History of the Civil War* (New York: Metro Books, 1996), 422.

22. Samuel Wilkeson, "Samuel Wilkeson to Brig. Gen. Birney," *New York Times*, 28 March 1863, 2; and Brig. Gen. David Bell Birney, "A Statement From Gen. Birney," *New York Times*, 10 April 1863, 2.

23. Davis, *Life of David Bell Birney*, 110–111.

24. Ibid., 87–102.

25. Marvin H. Pakula, *Centennial Album of the Civil War* (New York: Castle Books, 1960), 86.

26. William Birney, *General William Birney's Answer to Libels Clandestinely Circulated by James Shaw, Jr., Collector of the Port of Providence, Rhode Island, with a Review of the Military Record of the Said James Shaw, Jr., Late Colonel of the Seventh U.S. Colored Troops* (Washington, D.C.: Stanley Snodgrass Printer, 1878), 4.

27. Fitzhugh Birney file, student records, Harvard Archives, Pusey Library, Harvard University.

28. Elbridge J. Cutler, "Fitzhugh Birney," *Harvard Memorial Biographies,* edited by Thomas Wentworth Higginson (Cambridge, MA.: Sever and Francis, 1866), 2:440.

29. Ibid., 2:442.

30. Ibid, 2:440.

31. Edward Longacre, *Custer and His Wolverines: The Michigan Cavalry Brigade* (Conshohocken, PA: Combined Publishing, 1997), 143–165.

32. Asa B. Isham, *Seventh Michigan Cavalry of Custer's Wolverine Brigade* (New York: Town Topics Publishing, 2000), 29.

33. Jno. Robertson, comp., *Michigan in the War, State of Michigan*, 3 vols. (Lansing: W. S. George and Co., 1882), 1:410–411.

34. Philip Sheridan to Army Headquarters, endorsement on application for regular army appointment of James G. Birney IV, 20 May 1865, U.S. Archives.

35. Letter from Lt. James G. Birney IV to Judge James Birney, dated 2 April 1865, published in *Bay City [Michigan] Journal,* 13 April 1865.

36. Robertson, *Michigan in the War,* 1:453.

CHAPTER 17. THE U.S. COLORED TROOPS TIP THE BALANCE

1. William F. Fox, "The Colored Troops," *Regimental Losses in the American Civil War, 1861–1865* (Albany, NY: Albany Publishing Company, 1889). Available online at http://www.civilwarhome.com/chapt6.htm, 10 July 2008.
2. Ibid.
3. Davis, *David Bell Birney,* 105–106.
4. Miller, *Photographic History of the Civil War*, 32.
5. John T. Hubbell, "Abraham Lincoln and the Recruitment of Black Soldiers," *Journal of the Abraham Lincoln Association* 2 (1980): 17.
6. Joseph T. Glatthaar, *Black Glory: The African American Role in Union Victory* (New York: Oxford University Press, 1992), 138.
7. Robert F. Durden, *The Gray and the Black: The Confederate Debate on Emancipation* (Baton Rouge: Louisiana State University Press, 1972), 29–32.
8. Mauriel Phillips Joslyn, ed., *A Meteor Shining Brightly: Essays on Maj. Gen. Patrick Cleburne* (Milledgeville, GA: Terrell House, 1997).
9. Maj. Gen. Howell Cobb to Hon. James A. Seddon, Secretary of War, Jan. 8, 1865, *Official Records of the War of Rebellion,* ser. 4, vol. 3, Washington, Government Printing Office, 1900, 1009.
10. Charles H. Wesley, "The Employment of Negroes as Soldiers in the Confederate Army," *The Journal of Negro History* 4, no. 3 (1919): 244.
11. Christian A. Fleetwood, "The Negro as a Soldier," in *Masterpieces of Negro Eloquence,* by Alice Moore Dunbar-Nelson (New York: The Bookery Publishing Company, 1914), 194.
12. Edward Everett and Frank Moore, eds., *The Rebellion Record, a Diary of American Events with Documents, Narratives, Illustrative Incidents, Poetry, Etc.* (New York: G.P. Putnam, 1863), 538–539.
13. Abraham Lincoln and William Birney, (telegraph correspondence), *Official Records of the War of Rebellion,* vol. 3, (S#124,) Adjutant General's Office, Bureau for Organization of Colored Troops, October 1863.
14. Thomas Wentworth Higginson, *Army Life in a Black Regiment* (Boston: Fields, Osgood and Company, 1870), 10.
15. Ibid., 248.
16. Col. William Birney to Maj. Charles Foster, *Official Records of the War of Rebellion,* ser. 3, vol. 4 (S#125), 12 April 1864.
17. Lewis G. Schmidt, *The Civil War in Florida: A Military History,* vol. 1: *Florida's East Coast* (Allentown, PA: Schmidt Publishing, 1989), 1172.
18. Edwin S. Redkey, ed., *A Grand Army of Black Men: Letters from African-American Soldiers in the Union Army, 1861–1865* (Cambridge: Cambridge University Press, 1992), 55.
19. Schmidt, *Civil War in Florida,* 1166, 1177.

20. W. Birney, *General William Birney's Answer,* 4, 5.

21. Thomas Morris Chester, *Thomas Morris Chester, Black Civil War Correspondent: His Dispatches from the Virginia Front,* edited by R. J. M. Blackett (Baton Rouge: Louisiana State University Press, 1989), 109–110.

22. Michael D. Gorman, "The Union Perspective at the Battle of New Market Heights,." Washington, D.C.: National Park Service website, http://nps.gov/archive/rich/union.htm, 3 March 2008.

23. Ibid.

24. John Townsend Trowbridge, *The South: A Tour of Its Battlefields and Ruined Cities, a Journey through the Desolated States, and Talks with the People* (Hartford, CT: L. Stebbins, 1866), 200.

25. Davis, *Life of David Bell Birney,* 278.

26. 1st Lt. H. H. Alvord, Co. C, 102nd U.S.C.T., "Letter From Lieut. Alvord," printed in *The Weekly Press and Times,* Bay City, Michigan, 1 October 1864.

27. John Horn, *The Petersburg Campaign: June 1864–April 1865* (Great Campaigns) (Coshokocken, PA: Combined Publishing, 2000), 8.

28. William Marvel, *Lee's Last Retreat: The Flight to Appomattox* (Chapel Hill, NC: The University of North Carolina Press, 2002), 5.

29. John Y. Simon, *On the Road to Appomattox: Grant and Lee from War to Peace,.* Washington, D.C., online audio program recorded at the Smithsonian Institution, Nov. 9 November, 1998, http://civilwarstudies.org/OnlinePrograms/simon/start.htm, 14 June 2007.

CHAPTER 18. APPOMATTOX SUNDAYS

1. Clifford Dowdey, *Lee's Last Campaign: The Story of Lee and His Men against Grant* (Boston: Little Brown, 1960), 369.

2. Thomas L. Connelly, *The Marble Man: Robert E. Lee and His Image in American Society* (Baton Rouge: Louisiana State University Press, 1978), 192.

3. Clifford Dowdey and Louis H. Manarin, eds., *The Wartime Papers of Robert E. Lee* (New York: Virginia Civil War Commission, 1961), 898.

4. James C. Clark, *Last Train South: The Flight of the Confederate Government from Richmond* (Jefferson, NC: McFarland and Company, 1984), 13.

5. Burke Davis, *To Appomattox: Nine April Days, 1865* (New York: Rinehart and Company, 1959), 113–115.

6. Charles Carleton Coffin, *Four Years of Fighting: A Volume of Personal Observation with the Army and Navy from the First Battle of Bull Run to the Fall of Richmond* (Boston: Ticknor and Fields, 1866), 501.

7. Ibid., 542.

8. Jefferson Davis, *The Papers of Jefferson Davis,* vol. 11: *September 1864–May 1865,* edited by Lynda Lasswell Crist (Baton Rouge: Louisiana State University Press, 2004), 503–504.

9. James Longstreet, *From Manassas to Appomattox: Memoirs of the Civil War in America* (Bloomington: Indiana University Press, 1960), 593–594, 650.

10. James W. Loewen, *Lies across America: What Our Historic Sites Get Wrong* (New York: Simon and Schuster, 2007), 283. After Lumpkin's death in 1867, Mary Ann Lumpkin leased his former slave jail to a Negro minister, Rev. Nathan Colver, who established a school for freed slaves. Founded by the American Baptist Home Missionary Society and the National Theological Institute, the school grew into what is now Virginia Union University. The jail site, now a parking lot, was excavated by archaeologists in 2008.

11. Philip H. Sheridan, "The Last Days of the Rebellion," in *Battles and Leaders of the Civil War,* vol. 6, edited by Peter Cozzens (Chicago: University of Illinois Press, 2004) 526. A ration was considered food for one soldier for one day; the rebel ration, though somewhat reduced, generally followed the Union allowance of 12 oz. of pork or bacon or 20 oz. of fresh or salt beef, 22 oz. of soft bread or flour, 16 oz. of hard bread, or 20 oz. of cornmeal.

12. Bernarr Cresap, *Appomattox Commander: The Story of General E.O.C. Ord* (New York: A. S. Barnes and Company, 1981), 222. The late author was a distant relative of General Ord, whose full name was Edward Ortho Cresap Ord.

13. William Birney to Benjamin F. Butler, 23 April 1865, B. F. Butler Papers, Manuscript Division, Library of Congress, Washington D.C.

14. Cresap, *Appomattox Commander,* 221.

15. Joshua Lawrence Chamberlain, *The Blue and the Gray: The Story of the Civil War as Told by the Participants,* edited by Henry Steele Commager (New York: Bobbs-Merrill Co., 1950), 1133.

16. "The Appomattox Campaign," National Park Service website, http://www .nps.gov/apco/appomattox-campaign.htm, 24 May 2010.

17. Morris Schaff, "The Sunset of the Confederacy," *Atlantic Monthly* 110 (1912): 98. Ohioan Schaff, an 1862 West Point graduate, was a Union general who wrote several books about the Civil War.

18. Thomas Nelson Page, *Robert E. Lee: Man and Soldier* (New York: Charles Scribner's Sons, 1911), 573.

19. Jay Winik, *April 1865: The Month That Saved America* (New York: Harper-Collins Publishers, 2001), 68.

20. Capt. Robert E. Lee, Jr., *The Recollections and Letters of Robert E. Lee* (New York: Barnes and Noble Books, 2003), 147.

21. Ulysses S. Grant, *Personal Memoirs of U. S. Grant* (New York: Charles L. Webster and Company, 1886), 2:496.

22. John B. Gordon, *Reminiscences of the Civil War* (New York: Charles Scribner's Sons, 1903), 443.
23. Henry Steele Commager, *The Blue and the Gray: The Story of the Civil War as Told by Participants* (New York: The Fairfax Press, 1982), 2:1145.
24. Grant, *Memoirs*, 2:496.

EPILOGUE

1. Fladeland, *James Gillespie Birney,* 264.
2. Eric Foner, *A Short History of Reconstruction* (New York: Harper and Row, 1990), 31.
3. Abram Colby, quoted in *Testimony Taken by the Joint Select Committee on the Condition of Affairs in the Late Insurrectionary States,* vol. 7 (Washington, D.C.: Government Printing Office, 1872), 699.
4. James Z. George, *The Political History of Slavery in the United States* (New York: Neale Publishing Company, 1915), Book 1, 17.
5. Stetson Kennedy, *After Appomattox: How the South Won the War* (Gainesville: University Press of Florida, 1995), 283.
6. *The History of Origins, . . . by A Literary Antiquity* (London: Sampson Low, 1824), 128–130. Emphasis in original.
7. Gustave de Beaumont, *Ireland: Social, Political, and Religious* (1839; Cambridge: Belknap Press, 2006), 73.
8. Judge James Birney to President Abraham Lincoln, February 1865, Abraham Lincoln Papers, Library of Congress.
9. William Warren Rogers Jr. "For the Destruction of Radicalism: A Reconstruction Case Study," *Alabama Review: A Quarterly Journal of Alabama History* (July 2009): 191.
10. David W. Blight, *Race and Reunion: The Civil War in American Memory* (Cambridge: Harvard University Press, 2001), 114.
11. "Freedmen's Bureau Records Relating to Murders and Outrages against Freedmen," Freedmen's Bureau Online, http://freedmensbureau.com/outrages.htm.
12. "Records of the Assistant Commissioner for the State of Georgia," Freedmen's Bureau Online, http://freedmensbureau.com/georgia/outrages10.htm.
13. Ira Berlin, ed., *Freedom: A Documentary History of Emancipation, 1861–1867,* series 1, vol. 1: *The Destruction of Slavery* (Cambridge, MA: Cambridge University Press, 1982), xviii.
14. Betts, *Early History of Huntsville,* 104, 122.
15. Ralph L. Peek, "Lawlessness in Florida, 1868–1871," *Florida Historical Quarterly* 40 (July 1961): 165.

16. Ibid., 164.
17. Ibid.,165.
18. Ibid., 168.
19. Foner, *Short History of Reconstruction,* 96.
20. Peek, "Lawlessness in Florida," 172, 184.
21. Betts, *Early History of Huntsville,* 118, 114–115, 119.
22. Benjamin Franklin Butler, *Autobiography and Personal Reminiscences of Major-General Benj. F. Butler* (Boston: A. M. Thayer and Co., 1892), 962.
23. Ibid.
24. Ibid.
25. Betts, *Early History of Huntsville,* 119, 120.
26. Foner, *Short History of Reconstruction,* 95, 53.
27. Stephen Budiansky, *The Bloody Shirt: Terror after Appom*attox (New York: Penguin, 2008), 1–5. Emphasis in original.
28. Ibid., 247.
29. Albion W. Tourgee, *A Fool's Errand: By One of the Fools, The Famous Romance of American History* (New York: Fords, Howard, and Hulburt, 1879), 2: 247.
30. Ari Hoogenboom, *Rutherford B. Hayes: Warrior and President* (Lawrence: University Press of Kansas, 1995), 274.
31. Foner, *Short History of Reconstruction*, 243–244.
32. Ibid., 236, 259.
33. Boz Hod, *Terrorism in America: The Ritualistic Murder of Blacks* (Decatur, IL: AOM Publishing Unit, Inc., 2005), 132.
34. Thomas J. Knock, "'History with Lightning': The Forgotten Film Wilson," Baltimore, MD: The Johns Hopkins University Press, *American Quarterly* 28, no. 5 (1976): 523–543.
35. *Virginia: A Guide to the Old Dominion.* Federal Writers' Project (London: Oxford University Press, 1940), 5.
36. Hamilton, *Alabama,* 173.
37. Theodore Roosevelt, *Thomas Hart Benton* (Boston: Houghton Mifflin Company, 1886), 292–295.
38. Louis S. Gerteis, review of *The Meaning of Slavery in the North,* edited by David Roediger and Martin H. Blatt (New York: Garland, 1998), *Civil War History* 45, no. 1 (1999): 70.

Bibliographic Essay

T<small>HE DEARTH OF ACADEMIC WRITING ABOUT THE CAREER OF</small> J<small>AMES</small> Gillespie Birney leaves one wondering about the independence of thought among historians throughout the past century and a half since Birney's death. We have seen how Theodore Roosevelt's vicious condemnation of Birney's political initiatives in his biography *Thomas Hart Benton* (Houghton Mifflin, 1886) caused negative effects on the Birney historiography. Apparently taking cues from a powerful political source such as Roosevelt, historians began ignoring both Birney and the Liberty Party in histories of the Republican Party. A prime example is William Livingstone's *History of the Republican Party* (William Livingstone, 1900), which fails to even mention Birney or the Liberty Party contributions to its establishment. The list of supposedly comprehensive histories of the Republican Party as well as the antislavery movement that ignore Birney is as puzzling as it is long, and I would not attempt a compilation here. The Birney situation brings to mind an error in original reporting that is carried forward interminably until someone takes note and makes corrections. It is on that cusp of history that, hopefully, I stand.

PRIMARY SOURCES

Without the *Letters of James Gillespie Birney* in two volumes, compiled and edited by Dwight Lowell Dumond at the University of Michigan (Peter Smith, 1966), the task of evaluating Birney's contributions would have been vastly more difficult, if not impossible. While Birney's weekly newspaper, the *Philanthropist* (Achilles Pugh, 1836–1837), has much ideological posturing about the antislavery movement, it reveals little about Birney's life during those tumultuous years in Cincinnati.

Among the outstanding works that do credit Birney and the Liberty Party and put them in historical perspective are Richard Sewell's *Ballots for*

Freedom (W.W. Norton and Company, 1980) and Eric Foner's *Free Soil, Free Labor, Free Men: The Ideology of the Republican Party before the Civil War* (Oxford University Press, 1995). Also important are Dwight Lowell Dumond's *Antislavery: The Crusade for Freedom in America* (W.W. Norton and Company, 1966) and *Antislavery Origins of the Civil War in the United States* (University of Michigan Press, 1959). The primary source for much early Republican history is *Under the Oaks,* edited by William Stocking (Detroit Tribune, 1904).

Major sources of information about Birney's life are William Birney's *James G. Birney and His Times: The Genesis of the Republican Party* (D. Appleton and Company, 1890); Betty Fladeland's *James Gillespie Birney: Slaveholder to Abolitionist* (Cornell University Press, 1955), adapted from a 1952 doctoral dissertation at the University of Michigan; and Beriah Green's 1844 campaign piece, *Sketches of the Life and Writings of James Gillespie Birney* (Jackson and Chaplin, 1844). The Harriet Beecher Stowe connection with Birney, together with some details on his activities in Cincinnati, is carried in Joan Hedrick's *Harriet Beecher Stowe: A Life* (Oxford University Press, 1994).

Some of Birney's political collaborations are tracked in Albert B. Hart's *Salmon P. Chase* (Houghton Mifflin, 1899) and Jacob W. Schuckers's *The Life and Public Services of Salmon Portland Chase* (D. Appleton and Company, 1874). Henry Mayer's biography of William Lloyd Garrison, *All On Fire* (St. Martin's Griffin 1998), gives detail on the conflict between Birney and Garrison, as does the four-volume biography *William Lloyd Garrison: The Story of His Life,* by Garrison's sons, Wendell Phillips Garrison and Francis Jackson Garrison (The Century Co., 1885). Some perspective on the 1844 presidential campaign is furnished by Horace Greeley's *Recollections of a Busy Life* (J.B. Ford and Co., 1868) and Joel H. Silbey's *Storm Over Texas* (Oxford University Press, 2005), although detail on Birney's role is noticeably lacking in both books.

LOCAL HISTORIES

Local histories that incorporate details about Birney's early days in Kentucky and Alabama include, from Kentucky: Calvin Fackler's *Early Days in Danville* (The Standard Printing Co., 1941) and Richard Carl Brown's *History of Danville and Boyle County Kentucky* (Bicentennial Books, 1992); from Alabama: Thomas McAdory Owen's *Transactions of the Alabama Historical Society* (The Alabama Historical Society, 1899), Edward Chambers Betts's

Early History of Alabama, 1804–1870 (The Brown Printing Co., 1916), and Daniel Dupre's *Transforming the Cotton Frontier: Madison County, Alabama, 1800–1840* (Louisiana State University Press, 1997). A perusal of the files of the *Filson Club Historical Quarterly,* published at Louisville by the Filson Historical Society, allows a reader and researcher an unparalleled source of background on social and political activities in Kentucky during the Birney era and some insights into the conflict between Henry Clay and James G. Birney, the McDowell family, dueling, the Lincoln family, Rev. David Rice, and the Lewis brothers' (nephews of Thomas Jefferson) mayhem and tragedy. A newspaper article by Richard Carl Brown, "The Richest Man in Danville," in the *Kentucky Advocate* (Kentucky Advocate, 1976), is a good source for the limited information available on James Birney Sr., the Irish immigrant and father of James G. Birney. Lowell H. Harrison's *Kentucky's Road to Statehood* (The University Press of Kentucky, 1992) is an outstanding source for understanding the early ferment over human rights in that state, a pivotal region in the intersectional conflict that followed.

SLAVERY IN GENERAL

Although scant information is available on Birney, key works on slavery in general include Ira Berlin's *Many Thousands Gone: The First Two Centuries of Slavery in North America* (Harvard University Press, 1998), James Oliver Horton and Lois E. Horton's *Slavery and the Making of America* (Oxford University Press, 2005), and Hugh Thomas's *The Slave Trade* (Simon and Schuster, 1997). Douglas Harper has done valuable online documentation in *Slavery in the North, Northern Profits from Slavery* (www.slavenorth.com/profits.htm). Floyd Windom Hayes III writes authoritatively in *A Turbulent Voyage* (Rowman and Littlefield, 2000) of Atlantic traffic in slaves as does Marcus Rediker with his masterful *The Slave Ship: A Human History* (Penguin Group, 2008). Our understanding of the slave trade was enhanced by attendance in 2007 at the Atlantic History Conference at Harvard University, where noted historians Bernard Bailyn and Aaron Fogelman were key speakers.

BACKGROUND ON THE CAUSES OF THE WAR

Charles B. Dew's *Apostles of Disunion: Southern Secession Commissioners and the Causes of the Civil War* (University of Virginia Press, 2001) is an exposé of immense proportions, revealing a calculated campaign by Southerners to incite the war, an aspect of the conflict mystifyingly ignored for the long decades since the war. William L. Barney's *The Road to Secession* (Praeger Publishers, 1972) also concisely addresses the issues smoldering during the run up to the war. David Chardavoyne's "Michigan and the Fugitive Slave Acts," an article in the *Court Legacy,* the U.S. District Court Eastern District of Michigan newsletter, http.mied.uscourts.gov/HistoricalSociety/pages/newsletters.php provides invaluable insight into the long-term conflict between slaveholders in Kentucky and abolitionist-minded Michigan residents that contributed to the escalation of enforcement of fugitive slave laws and the mushrooming sectional dispute.

MILITARY BACKGROUND ON BIRNEY'S SONS AND GRANDSON

The main military history treating the career of David Bell Birney is an old but relatively comprehensive biography attributed to a fellow Union Army officer, Oliver W. Davis (King and Baird, 1867). The book mysteriously did not list the name of the author. The *New York Times* (March-April 1863) published the unusual and volatile charges and counter-charges between reporter Samuel Wilkeson and David Birney. Besides his response to a postwar attack by a fellow officer, *William Birney's Response to Libels . . .* (Stanley Snodgress, 1878), there is little historiography on the career of William Birney. What documentation there is of William Birney's campaign in Florida is found in Lewis G. Schmidt's *The Civil War in Florida* (L. G. Schmidt, 1989), a multivolume effort of merit. *Appomattox Commander,* by Bernarr Cresap (A.S. Barnes and Company, Inc., 1981), and Edward Longacre's *A Regiment of Slaves* (Stackpole Books, 2003) provide much of the information readily available on the activities of William Birney and his black troops during the dramatic last days of the war. Michael D. Gorman has written persuasively online "The Union Perspective at the Battle of New Market Heights" for the National Park Service, www.nps.gov/archive/rich/union.htm. The Official *Records of the Civil War* are confusing and filled with gaps about the contribution of the U.S. Colored Troops, the firing of

William Birney by General Ord, as well as the assignment of black troops to Texas immediately after Appomattox. The *B. F. Butler Papers* in the Library of Congress shed some light on those activities. General information on the contribution of the black troops has emerged relatively recently, especially Joseph T. Glatthaar's *Black Glory* (Simon and Schuster, 1992), letters edited by Edwin Redkey in *A Grand Army of Black Men* (Cambridge University Press, 1992), and R. J. M. Blackett's *Thomas Morris Chester: Black Civil War Correspondent* (Da Capo Press, 1989).

The *Harvard Memorial Biographies* (Sever and Francis, 1866) provide what little information there is on Fitzhugh Birney's brief career in the Civil War. We are left to consult scattered newspaper accounts in the *Weekly Press and Times* and the *Bay City Journal* (1864–1865), mainly gathered from letters between young Birney and his father, Judge James Birney, about James G. Birney IV's exploits serving under Gen. Phil Sheridan late in the war. There are two books, Longacre's *Custer and His Wolverines* (Combined Publishing,1997) and Asa B. Isham's *Seventh Michigan Cavalry* (Blue Acorn Press, 2000), referencing the grandson's early exploits under George Armstrong Custer, including his heroic role at Gettysburg. Clifford Dowdey, in *Lee's Last Campaign: The Story of Lee and His Men against Grant* (Little, Brown and Company, 1960) portrays the hopelessness of the "Lost Cause" interspersed with indomitable enthusiasm for Confederate victory in the latter days of the war. Burke Davis's *To Appomattox: Nine April Days, 1865* (Rinehart Company, 1959) takes a reader into Richmond in those fateful times, and James C. Clark's *Last Train South: The Flight of the Confederate Government from Richmond* (McFarland and Company, Inc., 1984) takes the reader out of Richmond as the war is concluding. Nothing can compare with Charles Carleton Coffin's *Four Years of Fighting . . .* (Ticknor and Fields, 1866) for firsthand observations throughout the war.

RECONSTRUCTION SOURCES

Eric Foner's *A Short History of Reconstruction* (Harper and Row, Publishers, 1990) is valuable for perspective on that era while Ralph L. Peek documents some of William Birney's harrowing days as a Reconstruction prosecutor in Florida in *Florida Historical Quarterly* (Florida Historical Society, 1961). Stephen Budiansky's *The Bloody Shirt: Terror after Appomattox* (Viking Penguin, 2008) documents the worst of that lamentable time in history. Ari Hoogenboom's *Rutherford B. Hayes: Warrior and President* (University Press of Kansas, 1995) provides invaluable insight about the "corrupt bargain" that ended Reconstruction, put Republican Hayes in the White House instead of the actual winner of the 1876 presidential race, Democrat Samuel Tilden, and consigned blacks to virtual continuation of slavery for nearly a century. Stetson Kennedy's *After Appomattox: How the South Won the War* (University Press of Florida, 1999), is illuminating about how white voting supremacy was maintained with violence, as is the Public Broadcasting Service's website, Reconstruction: The Second Civil War, http://www.pbs.org/wgbh/amex/reconstruction/. There is no finer source of the "big picture" in the century and a half since the war than that provided by David W. Blight with his *Race and Reunion: the Civil War in American Memory* (Harvard University Press, 2001).

It is not my intention here to list every secondary source on James G. Birney and his sons, especially since solid information relating directly to Birney is so sparse. The importance of Birney's role must be extrapolated and synthesized from myriad sources, as was the intent of my effort in this book. The National Park Service lists online documentation, some of it written by eminent authorities but not available in print, on various campaigns and aspects of the war, including Abraham Lincoln, slavery in general, the gag rule and other Congressional issues, dueling, black soldiers, and Reconstruction.

A review of the literature indicates that much research and documentation needs to be done to more thoroughly enlighten the reading public on the Birneys and the Liberty Party as well as the transitional phases to the Republicans and how this is all connected to the Civil War. Obviously, the body of work to date leaves a rich field for academic study and historiography. Unfortunately, we must leave that to future generations and hope that this book serves as a catalyst to meet an unfulfilled need.

Index

AASS. *See* American Anti-Slavery Society
abolition, 4, 31, 44, 69, 89, 92, 182, 205;
David Bell Birney, 201, 203, 211; James
Birney III, 239; and James G. Birney,
xi, xiii, 47, 57, and James G. Birney
IV, 210; and William Birney, 211, 222,
230, 242; James G. Birney's transition from colonization to immediate
emancipation, 28, 59, 61, 91; British, 8,
36, 139, 271 n 8; and Salmon P. Chase,
115; Cincinnati, 107–9, 110, 112, 146,
147, 148; City Abolition Society, 110;
and Clement C. Clay, 81–83, 99; Henry
Clay, 121, 137, 141, 188; colonization,
73–80, 84, 95; conservative, 129; and
William Lloyd Garrison, 62; gradual,
37, 61, 79; *Liberator*, 85; and Abraham Lincoln, 176, 189, 201; military,
211; movement, 7–8, 58, 72, 80, 88,
90, 155; New Jersey, 36, 169; newspapers, 87, 100, 102; New York, 36,
40; non-Garrisonian, 41; and Daniel
O'Connell, 130, 132–34; Philadelphia,
4, 8; *Philanthropist*, 110, 114, 116, 140;
political, 11, 14, 17, 41, 123, 126, 128,
189; propaganda, 39; pro-slavery opposition, 105, 113; Quakers, 26, 35, 47;
radical, 10, 53, 198; Republicans, 32,
135, 185–86, 191, 251; *Signal of Liberty*, 138, 159; societies, 36; Southern
concerns, 18, 23, 43, 96, 190; Union
generals, 200, 244, 246; U.S. Congress,
37, 40, 42, 45–46; vote for president
131, 140–41, 143, 159, 160–63, 166,
167, 175
Abolition of Slavery Act (Britain), 127

ACS. *See* American Colonization Society
Adams, Henry, 245
Adams, John, 14, 21, 43; Massachusetts
constitution, 31
Adams, John Quincy, 58, 62, 100, 102,
116, 162, 176; gag rule, 42–45
Africa, 20, 80, 95, 148; captives, 4;
deportation of Negroes, 25, 28, 36, 73,
76–77, 84, 88; slavery, 5, 8, 112, 121,
198, 242; slave ships, 3–4, 6–7, 78,
187, 263 n 1
African Americans, 246, 252
African Repository and Colonial Journal, 71,
79, 96
Alabama, 35, 65, 75, 252; "Alabama Fever,"
49; Alabama Historical Society, 67;
James G. Birney in, xi, 11, 49–63, 66,
74, 78–79, 81, 93, 96; blacks' voting
rights, 249; black troops, 212; Cherokees, 67–68, 70; Henry Clay, 141;
Colonization Society, 53, 83–84; Congress, 61; constitutional conventions,
56; Creeks, 68, 71; Andrew Jackson
in, 58–59; Ku Klux Klan, 240–41;
legislature, 63, 102; presidential vote
for Birney, 131; Reconstruction, 242–
44; removal of American Indians, 66,
71; slavery, 56, 58, 63, 81, 102, 139;
Supreme Court, 53, 62; Territorial Legislature, 70. *See also* Madison County,
AL; Mobile, AL; Montgomery, AL
Alachua County, FL, 243
Albany, NY, 40, 124, 137, 154, 156
Alcott, Bronson, 172
Alexander VI, 5
Alger, Russell, 208

Alien and Sedition Acts, 82
Allan, John, 98, 271 n 3
Alsberry, H. A., 141
Ambrister, Robert, 59
American Anti-Slavery Society (AASS), 37,
  102, 123, 148, 159; annual meeting,
  147; and Birney, 23, 43, 45–47, 87, 115,
  121, 267 n 27; book publishing, 38, 46–
  47, 88, 121; Cleveland meeting, 122;
  "Correspondence Between the Hon.
  F. H. Elmore and James G. Birney,"
  121; founding, 87; and William Lloyd
  Garrison, 41, 134; second anniversary
  meeting, 90; and James A. Thome,
  147–48; and "Elizur" Wright, 98
American Baptist Home Missionary Soci-
  ety, 288 n 10
American Bible Society, 123
American Board of Commissioners for
  Foreign Missions, 70
American Colonization Society (ACS),
  80, 88, 146; and James G. Birney, 71,
  74, 83, 90, 95, 96–97, 105, 156; and
  Charles Carroll, 74, 271 n 1; and Henry
  Clay, 71, 79; constitution, 76; and
  Samuel H. Cox, 148; formation, 76;
  and Ralph R. Gurley, 74, 79
American Convention for Promoting the
  Abolition of Slavery and Improving the
  Condition of the African Race, 36–37
American Fur Co., 160
*American Journey: Traveling with Tocqueville
  in Search of Democracy in America*
  (Reeves), 155
American Revolution, 7, 67
American Whig Review, 48
American Whig Society, 28
Ames, Adelbert, 248
Ames, John W., 219
Anderson, Robert, 196
Andover, MA, 197
Annotated Uncle Tom's Cabin, The (Gates),
  145–46
Anti-Slavery Reporter, 98
Apostles of Equality, 32, 182, 195, 205,
  210, 235–36, 252
Appomattox, VA: Appomattox Court
  House, 227, 232; Appomattox Station,

230, 232; Civil War, 198, 218, 221–22,
  230, 233, 235, 242; surrender, 116,
  208, 215, 227, 239
Arbuthnot, Alexander, 59
Atlantic slave trade, 5
Augusta, KY, 147
Autauga County, AL, 59
Avery, George, 107

back-to-Africa movement, xiii
Bacon, Leonard Woolsey, 152
Bailey, Gamaliel, 41–42, 114, 122–23
Bailey, John, 24
Bailyn, Bernard, 7, 263 n 1
Balkins, Foster, 83–84, 87
Baltimore, MD, 80, 209, 216, 249
Banshee, 80
Baptists, 15, 16, 24, 49, 61, 92; rural, 74.
  See also American Baptist Home Mis-
  sionary Society; Emancipation Baptists;
  Little Mount Separate Baptist Church;
  Little Pigeon Creek Baptist Church;
  Salem Association of Baptists
Bardstown, KY, 215
Barker, Eugene, 140–41
Barker, Jacob, 164–65
Barrow, Asa, 16
Barrow, David, 15–16
Barry, John S., 162, 166
Basking Ridge, NJ, 76
Bay City, MI, 251
Bay County, MI, 207
Beaufort, SC, 217
Beauregard, P. G. T., 196
Beaumont, Gustave de, 153, 156, 238;
  Democracy in America, 154, 155; *Marie;
  or, Slavery in the United States*, 155
Beaver Wars, 153
Beckham, William, 155
Beckley, Guy, 41, 158
Beecher, Catharine, 69
Beecher, Edward, xi, 74
Beecher, Henry Ward, 74, 146
Beecher, Isabella, 145
Beecher, Lyman, 69, 145, 146
Bell, Joshua Fry, 99
Belleville, NJ, 161
Berlin, Ira, 32, 242

Berry, Hiram G., 201
Bethel AME Church, 75
Betts, Edward Chambers, 58, 242, 244, 245
Bibb, William Wyatt, 57
Bible, 59, 74, 83, 158; as slavery defense, 31, 52, 89, 188
Bill of Rights, 24, 27, 31, 88
Bingham, Kinsley S., 166
Birney, Agatha McDowell, 26–27, 50, 65, 93, 112, 121, 180, 266 n 19
Birney, Amanda, 167
Birney, Anna Maria, 15, 33
Birney, Antoinette Jennison, 251
Birney, Arthur Hopkins, 78, 93
Birney, Catherine Hoffman, 250
Birney, David Bell, 61, 93, 159–60, 195, 196, 197, 205; buried, 251–52; Civil War, 74, 199, 201, 203, 206, 219, 247
Birney, David Bell, IV, 197, 211, 265 n 18
Birney, Fitzhugh, 160, 167, 171, 172, 196, 197, 205, 206, 207
Birney, Florence, 159
Birney, Frank, 198
Birney, George, 93, 159; death, 167, 168
Birney, Herman Hoffman "Topper," 250
Birney, James, III, 93, 159, 196; burial, 167; establishes Pine Ridge Cemetery, 167; judge, 238–39; lieutenant governor of Michigan, 189, 196; minister to The Hague, 167; seeks post as head of the Freedmen's Bureau, 238–39
Birney, James G.: abolition, 95–105; Alabama, xi, xiii, 49–63, 66, 72; American Anti-Slavery Society (AASS), 23, 43, 45–47, 87, 115, 121, 267 n 27; *American Churches: The Bulwarks of American Slavery*, 152; American Colonization Society (ACS), 71, 74, 83, 90, 95, 96–97, 105, 156; antislavery, 79, 81–93, 95–105; bar examination, 26; birth, 13–14; in Cincinnati, 92, 100, 107–17, 145, 150, 180; Civil War, 195–210; and Clement C. Clay, 70, 71, 78; and Henry Clay, 25, 26, 77, 102–5, 116, 121, 135–44; colonization, 75, 78, 96; considering move from Michigan, 166; considering move to Illinois,

74–75; "Constitution and Address of the Kentucky Society for the Gradual Relief of the State from Slavery," 97; Danville, KY, 14, 16, 21, 26, 37, 91, 95; death, 167; disabling accident, 165, 178; drinking, 25, 59, 101; early years, 3–11, 14, 16; emancipation society in Kentucky, 60–61; "Examination of the Decision of the Supreme Court of the United States, in the Case of Strader, Gorman and Armstrong vs. Christopher Graham," 170; first abolition leader, 11; Fourteenth Amendment, 236; frees his slaves, 98; gradual emancipation, 97; and Horace Greeley, 44; Huntsville, AL, 57, 60, 74, 84, 98, 131, 240; Kentucky legislature, 35; Liberty Party, 131, 163, 177; and Abraham Lincoln, 175–76, 201, 238, 239; "Lincoln's Prophet," 121–34; marries Agatha McDowell, 26–27; Mississippi, 74, 78; moves from Kentucky to Ohio, 105; moves from Michigan to New Jersey, 171; moves to Kentucky from Alabama, 93, 96; and Native Americans, 72; and Negroes, 53, 60, 83, 89, 115, 124, 148, 180–81; New Jersey, 171, 182, 188, 205, 207; opposition to Andrew Jackson, 58; in Philadelphia, 25–26, 27, 37, 77, 114, 136; and James K. Polk, 266 n 19; prediction of Civil War, 34, 46, 125; presidential vote for, 75, 116, 126, 131, 137, 139, 154; Princeton University, 18, 25, 32; resigns as Liberty Party candidate for governor of Michigan, 165; resigns from American Colonization Society, 79, 83, 90, 97, 105; "Sinfulness of Slaveholding in All Circumstances; Tested by Reason and Scripture," 177; slaveholder, 56–57; splits with William Lloyd Garrison, 116; student of Alexander J. Dallas, 25; writings, 253–55
Birney, James G., IV, 9, 197, 205, 207–10, 229
Birney, James, Sr., 4, 9, 11, 15, 35, 99, 264 n 1; business partner of David Gillespie, 14; Danville, KY, 10, 15, 50, 91, 108, 265 n 18; emancipation, 35; Kentucky,

20–22; marries Martha Reed, 10; religious beliefs, 26
Birney, John, 9
Birney, Margaret, 93
Birney, Martha, 78, 93
Birney, Martha (Reed), 10, 14
Birney, Mary Deuel, 210
Birney, Newton, 210
Birney, Robert Dion, 93, 159, 196, 197, 205
Birney, William, 60, 93, 159, 196, 205, 211; attack on, 243, 250; buried, 250; Civil War, 59, 74, 239; district attorney, Florida Fifth Judicial Circuit, 243; *James Gillespie Birney and His Times: The Genesis of the Republican Party*, 250–51, 269 n 30; Reconstruction, 210, 242–43
Birney, Gillespie, & Company, 14
Birth of a Nation, 249
Bishop, Robert Hamilton, 16
Black Codes, 76, 240
Blackett, R. J. M., 149
Black Hawk War, 71
blacks, proposal for transportation to Liberia after the Civil War, 80
Blackwell, Sophie (Birney), 167
Blaine, James G., 41
Bloomfield, Joseph, 36
Bond, Lewis, 100
Bookbinder's restaurant, 251
Booth, John Wilkes, 178–79, 230
Borome, Joseph H., 122
Boston, MA, 150, 162, 179, 206; and James G. Birney, 61, 145, 165, 269 n 30; and Aaron Burr, 116; and William Lloyd Garrison, 39, 85, 132
Boston Morning Chronicle, 138, 163
Bowdoin College, 150, 197, 239
Bowie, Jim, 136, 141
Bowling Green, KY, 55
Bradley, James, 146
Brands, H. W., 67
Brazil, 6
Breckenridge, John, 82
Breckenridge, John Cabell, 196, 223, 224, 225, 272 n 3
Breckenridge, Joseph Cabell, 18, 82, 225

Brent, Linda, 180
Bretz, Julian P., 40
Brewer, Willis, 51
British Navy blockade of Africa, 6
British Parliament, 42, 88
British Penal Laws, 130
Brook Farm Association, 171
Brooks, Preston, 199
Brown, A. G., 217
Brown, John, 158, 169, 172, 173, 189, 207, 281 n 13
Brown, Moses, 8
Brown, Richard Carl, 10, 182
Brown University, 8
Brown v. Board of Education, 249
Brunswick, ME, 150
Brush, Elijah, 156
Bryant, William Cullen, 172, 178
Buchanan, James M., 90, 189, 196, 251
Budiansky, Stephen, 246
Buffum, Arnold, 37, 90, 173
Bullock, Joseph J., 101
Bull Run, 199, 212; First Bull Run, 199, 205, 231; Second Bull Run, 205
Bureau of Refugees, Freedmen, and Abandoned Lands, 237, 238, 239, 240, 241, 244
Burke, Rosabella, 80, 227
Burkeville Junction, VA, 227
Burr, Aaron, 25, 28, 34, 116
Butler, Benjamin F., 196, 212, 214, 218, 220, 229, 244, 245
Butler, Eliza, 70, 71
Butler, Matthew C., 246
Butler, Pierce, 6

Calhoun, John C., 10–11, 32, 55; compact theory of government, 45; gag order, 134; politics, 58; senator, 42–43; slavery, 47, 79, 100; vice presidential candidate, 63; War of 1812, 157
Campbell, Alexander, 112
Campbell, Eric A., 202
Camp Graham, 206
Caribbean, 5, 86, 185
Carroll, Charles, 74, 155, 156, 207, 271 n 1

Carter, Robert, 141
Carwardine, Richard, 185, 189
Cash, W. J., 250
Cass, Lewis, 70, 157, 160, 182
Cass County, MI, 156, 157, 158
Cassopolis, MI, 157, 158
Catholics, 130, 132, 183, 277 n 31; anti-Catholic sentiment, 112, 133, 183; Ireland, 129; Irish, 9, 134, 238; Irish immigrants, 4
Catton, Bruce, 47, 199, 203
Catton, William, 47
Centre College, 35, 90, 98, 105
Chamberlain, Joshua Lawrence, 197, 230
Chambrun, Clara Longworth de, 113
Chancellorsville, VA, 199, 201, 216, 239
Chandler, Zachariah, 247
Channing, William Ellery, 42, 140
Chapman, Reuben, 53
Chapman, S., 54
Chardavoyne, David, 156, 158
Charleston, SC, 66, 187, 196, 198, 270 n 2
Charleston Mercury, 151, 196
Charlestown, MA, 51
Chase, Salmon P., 41, 114–15, 123, 176, 178, 180–82, 186, 239
Cherokees, xii, 49, 52, 65–72, 102
Chester, Samuel Knapp, 179
Chester, Thomas Morris, 219
Chestnut, James, Jr., 87
Chestnut, Mary Boykin, 87
Chickasaw, 68, 72
Child, Lydia Maria, 126
Choctaw, 68, 72
Christian, John D., 83
Christiancy, Isaac P., 143
Christianity, 100, 147, 177, 239, 242; fundamentalist, 65; among Negroes in Africa, 76; and slavery, 5, 95, 97
Christian Journal, 108
Chronicles of a Kentucky Settlement (Watts), 38
Cincinnati, OH, 42, 88, 105, 212, 249; abolition, 107–9, 110, 147, 148; anti-slavery publications, 107–12, 123, 140, 142, 145; Birney in, 92, 107–17, 145, 150, 176, 180

Cincinnati Gazette, 107
Cincinnati Journal, 145, 146
Cincinnati Republican, 110
Cincinnati Whig, 108
City Abolition Society, 110
civil rights, 235, 241, 248, 249, 252
Civil Rights Act of 1866, 235–36, 240
Civil Rights Act of 1875, 248
Civil Rights Act of 1964, 11
Civil War, 9, 11, 195–234, 235, 270 n 31; Appomattox, 223–34; Birneys in battle, 195–210; James G. Birney's prediction of, 34, 46, 91, 125; and Henry Clay, 141–42; colored troops, 211–22; Emancipation Proclamation, 16, 212–13; and John Hughes, 133–34; and the poor and humble, 91; postwar, 240, 250, 252; *Uncle Tom's Cabin*, 147, 150, 151
Clark, George Rogers, 13
Clarkson, Thomas, 130
Clay, Cassius, 137
Clay, Clement C., 51, 53, 56, 79–80; abolition, 81–82, 83, 99; and James G. Birney, 70, 71, 78; Congress, 71
Clay, Henry, 29, 32, 52, 67, 176, 188, 251; John Quincy Adams's defeat of, 62; and James G. Birney, 77, 102–5, 116, 121–22, 125, 135–44, 148; William Ellery Channing's letter to, 42; coloniza-tion, 75, 76; Compromise of 1850, 169; Congress, 68; delegate to peace conference, 26; duel with Humphrey Marshall, 33; Fugitive Slave Law, 25, 149, 158; hemp grower, 51; Mexican War, 278 n 15; opposition to Andrew Jackson, 68; political collaboration with James G. Birney, 25, 56, 77, 102; presidential defeats, 100, 204, 266 n 19; senator, 158; slaveholder, 44, 164; Speaker of the House, 24–25; War of 1812, 157; Whigs abandon, 130; white slavery, 188
Clements Library, 127
Clinton, MS, 100
Cliosophic Society, 28
Cleburne, Patrick, 213, 221
Cobb, Howell, 57, 214, 223

Code Duello, 32, 33, 34, 198
Coffin, Charles Carleton, 224–25, 226
Coffin, Joshua, 90
Coffin, Levi, 104, 157, 175
coffin ships, 4
Colby, Abram, 237
Coleman, J. Winston, Jr., 33
College of New Jersey, 17. *See also* Princeton University
colonization, 69, 73, 123, 271 n 1. *See also* Alabama: Colonization Society; American Colonization Society; Kentucky: Colonization Society
colored troops, 211–21
Columbus, Christopher, 5
Columbus, OH, 115, 176
Colver, Nathan, 288 n 10
Comet, 84
Commentaries on the Laws of England (Blackstone), 25
Concord Church, 265 n 18
Confederacy, 18, 91, 134, 195, 196, 223–26, 270 n 31; and colored troops, 211, 212–15, 221–22, 227; Union Army sympathy for, 198–99
Confederate Congress, 214, 215, 221
Congo Square, 8
Congressional Committee on the Conduct of the War, 204
Congressional Globe, 198
Congressional Joint Select Committee on Condition of Affairs in the Late Insurrectionary States, 243
Connecticut, 7, 18, 36; black laws, 116; Thirtieth Colored Volunteers, 226; vote for president for James G. Birney, 131, 139. *See also* Litchfield, CT; New Haven, CT
constitutional conventions, 6, 13, 23. *See also* Kentucky: constitutional convention; United States: constitutional convention
Constitutional Union Party, 175
Continental Army, 36, 270 n 2
Continental Congress, 27, 36, 271 n 1
Convention of Color, 77
Cootehill, Ireland, 3, 9

Cornwallis, Charles, 9
Cortland, NY, 146
County Cavan, Ireland, 3, 9, 14, 20
Courier and Enquirer, 132
Covington, KY, 113
Cox, Samuel H., 148, 232
Crawford, James, 24
Crawford, Jane Todd, 266 n 19
Creeks, 52, 59, 66, 67, 68, 71, 72, 86
Crittenden, John J., 56
Cromwell, Oliver, 9, 130
Crosswhite, Adam, 157
Cuba, 6
Cuffe, Paul, 76
Custer, George A., 207

Dallas, Alexander J., 25, 27, 114
Dallas, George M., 136
Dallas, TX, 249
Danville, KY, 10, 25, 26, 29, 101; aristocracy, 15, 27; James Birney Sr., 10, 15, 21, 37, 50, 91, 108, 265 n 18; James G. Birney, 14, 26–27, 50, 91, 95–98, 105; Centre College, 35; constitutional conventions, 11, 15; Kentucky Academy, 14; Kentucky Anti-Slavery Society, 90; New Madrid earthquake, 38; politics, 24; Woodlawn, 21–22
Danville Academy, 35
Danville, VA, 225
Davies, Samuel, 23, 107
Daviess, Maria T., 20
Davis, David Brion, 44
Davis, Jefferson, 29, 32, 57, 71, 200, 251
Davis, John, 224
Davis, Joseph Emory, 57
Davis, Oliver W., 61, 195, 197, 200, 201
Davis Hotel, 76
Declaration of Independence, xii, 4, 13, 124, 126, 156, 176, 236, 271 n 1; and slavery, 22, 31, 52, 88, 98, 115
Degler, Carl N., 40
Delaware, 36; vote for president for James G. Birney, 131, 139
Democracy in America (Tocqueville), 154, 155
Detroit, MI, 157

Detroit Tribune, 184
Devil's Den, 202
Dew, Charles B., 195
Dickey, William, 38
Dickinson, Charles, 32, 266 n 2
District of Columbia, 28, 237, 239; abolishment of slavery, 42, 43, 46, 133, 162, 182; Georgetown, 45, 250; Republican platform, 184, 186, 260
Dooley, Brian, 133, 134
Douglas, Stephen A., 189, 196
Dowdey, Clifford, 223
Doyle, Margaret, 14–15, 264 n 1
Dublin, Ireland, 3, 14, 132
Dumond, Dwight Lowell, 23, 44, 46, 76, 124, 138, 140
Dupre, Daniel S., 74, 79, 271 n 3

Eagleswood, 168, 169–73
Earle, Thomas, 37, 124, 126, 131
Eastern Michigan University, 159
Edwards, Ninian W., 126
Edwards, Ninian W., Jr., 127
Elizabeth I, 5
Elmore, Franklin H., 45, 121
emancipation: Alabama, 52–53, 63; and James G. Birney, 75, 79, 111, 124; in Britain, 127–28, 130, 149, 214; and Catholics in Ireland, 133–34; and Henry Clay, 78, 104, 164; deeds of, 99, 164; general, 117; gradual, 8, 35, 60, 91, 97, 103, 122, 182; Gradual Emancipation Act of 1780, 8; immediate, 74, 91, 96, 97; in Kentucky, 24–25, 61; and Robert E. Lee, 80; and Abraham Lincoln, 213; New York, 116; North Carolina, 62–63; obstacles, 23; of slaves, 76, 244, 252, 271 n 1; and Charles Sumner, 199; voluntary, 79; in West Indies, 42, 121
Emancipation Baptists, 15, 16
Emancipation Proclamation, 16, 212–13, 235
Emerson, Ralph Waldo, 172
Engelder, Conrad J., 89, 273 n 20
Epps, Garrett, 72
Equiano, Olaudah, 5

Erie Canal, 40, 154, 156
Everett, Edward, 61, 269 n 30

Fackler, Calvin M., 14, 265 n 13
Fairbank, Calvin, 104
Fearn, Thomas, 95
Federalists, 10, 14, 44
Federalist Papers, The, 27
Federal Writers' Projects, 250
Felton, C. C., 172, 206
Fergerson, Gerard, 155
Ferguson, John, 248
Fifteenth Amendment, 241
Finley, Robert, 76
Finney, Charles Grandison, 39, 40, 59, 89
First Republican Platform, 257–62
Fitzhugh, Daniel, 154, 159, 167
Fitzhugh, Elizabeth, 128
Fladeland, Elizabeth L., viii; on abolitionist publishing, 105; on James G. Birney in Michigan, 166; on James G. Birney's death at Eagleswood, 172; on James G. Birney's dialogue with Henry Clay, 102, 103, 104; on James G. Birney's early attitude toward slavery, 16, 45, 51; on James G. Birney's influence on Harriet Beecher Stowe, 145, 150; on James G. Birney's Native American contacts in Alabama, 60, 68; on James G. Birney's transition from slaveholder to abolitionist, 96; on James G. Birney's views on unconstitutionality of slavery, 177–78, 236; on influence of students at Lane Seminary on James G. Birney, 146; on mob opposition in Cincinnati, 109, 111; physical description of James G. Birney, 273 n 23
Fleetwood, Christian A., 215, 219
Florida, 59, 195; and William Birney, 250; Fifth Judicial Circuit, 243; and Freedmen's Bureau, 244; Rutherford B. Hayes's election, 247; and Ku Klux Enforcement Act, 245; and Negro regiments, 217; removal of American Indians, 71; Seminole War, 68; and slavery, 133; suicide of John Milton, 242; war, 124, 218, 220, 228, 242. *See also* Alachua County, FL; Gainesville, FL

Florida Historical Quarterly, 243

Florida War, 58, 124

Floyd, John B., 251

Fogelman, Aaron, 5, 7

Foner, Eric, 182, 237, 243, 245, 247

Forest Glen, MD, 250

Forrest, Nathan Bedford, 240

Fort Davis, TX, 210

Fort Detroit, MI, 153

Forten, James, 37, 73, 75, 76, 77, 148, 271 n 8

Fort Harrison, VA, 220, 223

Fort Leavenworth, KS, 209

Fort Pillow, TN, 240

Fort Sumter, SC, 19, 206, 213, 233

Fort Wagner, SC, 212

Foster, Charles W., 213, 217

Foster, Robert S., 230

Foster, Theodore, 41, 158, 165

Fourier, Charles, 171

Fourteenth Amendment, 72, 177, 235, 236, 248

Franklin, Benjamin, 3, 7, 13, 32, 36, 190, 235

Franklin, Deborah, 7

Fraser, James, 161

Frederick County, MD, 78

Fredericksburg, MD, 204, 206, 207

Frederickson, George M., 84

Free African Society, 8

Freemason's Hall (London), 129

Freedmen's Bureau, 237, 238–42; "Reports of Murders and Outrages," 241

Free Soil Party, xiii, 92, 131, 148, 166, 185, 251; merger with Republican Party, 143, 175, 189; presidential candidates, 178, 182

Fremont, John C., 176, 185, 196

Freneau, Philip, 28

Friends. *See* Quakers

Friends of Humanity, 16

fugitive slave laws, 6, 50, 115, 170, 180, 183, 184; of 1850, 25, 149, 158, 179, 188, 260; repeal, 186, 260; of 1793, 22, 181

Furnas, J. C., 7, 46, 47, 126

Gainesville, FL, 243, 250

Garrard, James, 24

Garrison, William Lloyd, 198; and the American Anti-Slavery Society, 87, 123, 147, 148; and the Cherokee Removal movement, 72; clash with Birney over antislavery strategy, 40, 41, 89, 139, 186, 188; *Liberator*, 39, 45, 62, 79, 85, 116; and opposition to colonization, 95; promotes Daniel O'Connell letter, 132–34; and the "woman question," 128–29

Gary, Martin Witherspoon, 246

Gates, Seth M., 116, 134

Gentry, Allen, 86

Gentry, James, 86

George, James Z., 237

George III, 66

Georgetown, D.C., 45, 250

Georgetown, KY, 102, 197

Georgia, 199, 237; and blacks' voting rights, 249; and Cherokees, 49, 66, 67, 68, 69, 70, 71; and the Confederacy, 201, 233; and Creeks, 66, 68; and Ku Klux Klan, 241; and Negro regiments, 217; and removal of American Indians, 71; and slavery, 56, 57

Gerteis, Louis S., 252

Giddings, Joshua, 41, 116, 186

Gifford, James M., 79

Gillespie, David, 14

Glasgow, KY, 101

Goen, C. C., 92

Gold Rush, California, 49

Goodell, William, 178

Goss, Charles F., 107, 108

Gossett, Thomas F., 151

Gradual Emancipation Act of 1780, 8

Graham, Sarah, 19, 201

Grant, Ulysses S., 167, 209, 213, 218, 220, 228; at Appomattox, 215, 233, 239; collaboration with David Bell Birney, 205, 219; drinking, 197; final campaign, 224, 225, 229–32; and Ku Klux Klan, 244–45, 246

Great Britain, 127, 136, 140, 157, 213; American Revolution, 13; and Ireland,

3, 5, 9; and slavery, 7, 8, 40, 127; Treaty of 1814, 102

Great Depression, 250

Great Western, 127, 276 n 14

Great Western Steam Ship Company, 127

Greeley, Horace, 38–39, 43–44, 141–42, 172, 185, 204, 212; Congress, 143

Green, Beriah, 17, 113, 135, 166, 265 n 5

Green, John, 97

Green, Michael D., 71

Green, Nathan, 95

Green Bottom Inn, 51, 58

Greene Academy Cliosophic Society, 88

Greene County, GA, 237

Greensboro, NC, 249

Greensburg, KY, 266 n 19

Green Wood Cemetery (Brooklyn), 210

Greve, Charles, 114

Grimke, Angelina, 38, 46, 47, 72, 171, 250

Grimke, Sarah, 171, 250

Gurley, Ralph R., 74, 79, 88, 96, 97

Hale, Charles, 109, 110, 111, 112, 147

Hale, John P., 116, 175, 178

Hale, Lucy Lambert, 178, 179

Hamilton, Alexander, 14, 27, 116; death, 26; duel, 34

Hamilton, Neil A., 131

Hamilton, Virginia Van der Veer, 49, 50, 67, 250

Hamilton County (OH) Courthouse, 109

Hammond, Charles, 107, 112

Hampton, Wade, 208, 246, 247

Hancock, Winfield Scott, 203, 205

Hanks, Dennis, 20

Hanks, John, 85, 86

Hanks, Nancy, 20, 37

Hanover County, VA, 23, 102

Harper, Douglas, 6

Harper's Ferry, VA, 158, 169, 173, 281 n 13

Harrisburg, PA, 125

Harrisburg Telegraph, 191

Harrison, Lowell, 24, 79

Harrison, William Henry, 124, 125, 126, 130, 160, 180

Harrodsburg, KY, 183

Harrogate, TN, 239

Harvard Memorial Biographies, 207

Harvard University, 7, 18, 61, 172, 196, 206, 239, 263 n 1, 269 n 30

Haslett, Absalom, 173

Haughton, James, 132

Hawkins, John, 5

Hay, John, 189–90

Hayes, Rutherford B., 247–48, 263 n 2

Hedrick, Joan, 145

Heintzelman, Samuel P., 199, 200, 203, 204, 207

Hendricks, Ricky L., 68

Henry, Prince "The Navigator," 5

Hershberger, Mary, 69

Hibben, Paxton, 121

Hilton Head, SC, 217

Holley, Myron, 122, 123

Holt, Michael F., 140

Hoogenboom, Ari, 247

Hopkins, Arthur F., 53, 60, 95

Hopkins, James F., 21, 22, 50, 60, 78, 95

Horton, James Oliver, 5

Horton, Lois E., 5

Howard, Oliver Otis, 239, 240

Hubbell, John T., 213

Huggins, Allen P., 246

Hughes, John, 132, 133–34, 277 n 31

Hughes, Morgan, 19

Hughes Station, 19

Huntsville, AL, 50, 51, 53, 55, 89; James G. Birney in, 57, 59–60, 74, 84, 131; cemetery, 93; colonization, 78; Congress, 56, 245; constitutional convention, 56; female seminary, 61, 69; Andrew Jackson visit, 58; Klan, 240, 245; Masonic Lodge, 58, 63; James Monroe visit, 51; Presbyterian Church, 74; slavery, 85, 271 n 3

Huntsville Democrat, 74, 95

Huntsville Southern Advocate, 90

Illinois, 154, 175, 189, 191; James G. Birney considers move to, xi, 74–75; Black Hawk War, 71; constitutional conventions, 127; economic growth, 40;

legislature, 44; Abraham Lincoln in Congress, 183; Abraham Lincoln's election to state legislature, 92; presidential vote for James G. Birney, 131, 139; removal of American Indians, 71; Republican convention, 186–88; Sauk Indians removed, 70; Springfield, 126

Indiana, xi, 85, 140, 154, 158, 160, 226; presidential vote for James G. Birney, 131, 139; Shippingport, 33. *See also* New Harmony, IN; Pigeon Creek, IN; South Bend, IN

Indian Removal Act, 68, 70, 72, 83, 155

Indian Territory, 65, 72, 237

Ireland, 14, 15, 20, 27, 238; James G. Birney visit, 127, 129, 130; Code Duello, 32–33, 34; O'Connell letter, 131–34; slavery, 11

Irish, 4, 8, 9, 10, 11, 16; immigrants, 3, 4, 8, 9, 10; Scotch Irish, 8

Jackson, Andrew, xii, 51, 66, 67, 70, 76; James G. Birney's opposition to, 58; Congress, 43, 69; kills Charles Dickinson, 32; president, 43; removal of American Indians, 69, 72, 83, 155; victory at New Orleans, 35

Jackson, MI, 166, 184, 185, 257

Jackson County, MI, 58

Jay, John, 27, 122, 123

Jay Treaty, 153, 157

Jefferson, Lucy, 37

Jefferson, Thomas, 25, 116, 179, 257; colonization, 75, 77; Constitution, 235; death, 38; Declaration of Independence, 13, 22, 31; Democratic-Republican Party, 185; "Kentuckey resolves," 82; murder of slave by nephews, 37–38, 104; *Notes on the State of Virginia*, 23; slavery, 27, 52, 79, 122, 190

Jefferson County, KY, 19

Jennison, Charles, 168

Jewett, J. P., 150

"John Brown's Body," 226

Johnson, Andrew, 235, 239–40

Johnson, Richard M., 130–31

Johnson's Division, 208, 231

Jones, Bill, 157

Jones, John, 101

Jones, Wharton, 181

Joslyn, Mauriel Phillips, 214

Julian, George W., 186

Kansas, 184, 187, 259, 261; Fort Leavenworth, 209

Kansas-Nebraska Act, 158, 183, 189, 190, 191

Kautz, August, 226

Kavenaugh, Charles, 24

Kearny, Philip, 198, 200–1, 203, 204, 205–6

Kennedy, Robert C., 215

Kennedy, Stetson, 238

Kentucky, xi, 108, 109, 122, 123, 131; attitude toward blacks, 20, 50; James Birney Sr. in, 9–11; James G. Birney in, xii, 49, 97, 105, 152; churches and slavery, 89; Henry Clay in, 81, 122; Code Duello, 32–35; colonization, 90, 96–97, 98; constitution, 13, 24, 31; hemp business, 50–51; influence in Cincinnati, 107, 112–13, 140, 146; "Kentuckey resolves," 82; last meeting of James G. Birney and Henry Clay, 102–4; legislature, 50, 65, 158; Abraham Lincoln's roots, 19–20; manumission of slaves, 99; Michigan raids, 157–58, 166; opposition to James G. Birney, 105; presidential vote for James G. Birney, 131; pro-slavery activities, 79; Reconstruction, 240; slave population, 32; slavery, 19, 74–75, 86, 103–5, 182; statehood initiative, 13, 15. *See also* Augusta, KY; Harrodsburg, KY; Knob Creek, KY; Mercer County, KY; Washington County, KY

Kentucky Academy, 14

Kentucky Gazette, 38

Kentucky Society for the Gradual Relief of the State from Slavery, 61, 83, 97

Key, Francis Scott, 76

Kimball, J. H., 149; "Emancipation in the West Indies," 121

King, Charles, 208

King, Martin Luther, Jr., 252
Klees, Emerson, 40
Knights of the Golden Circle, 63
Knob Creek, KY, 37
Know Nothing Party, 183, 186
Ku Klux Klan, 238, 240, 243, 244–46
Kutler, Stanley, 191

Lane Seminary, 88, 98, 121, 148, 271 n 3
Lasch, Christopher, 84
Lawrence, Larkin, 115, 180
Lawrence, Matilda, 115, 180
Lebanon cedar, 167, 280 n 22
Lee, Ann, 171
Lee, Henry, 28
Lee, Robert E., 80, 172, 223–24, 225;
    Appomattox, 230–33, 239; and David
    Bell Birney, 199, 204, 219–20; and
    James G. Birney IV, 208; and William
    Birney, 198, 218, 226–28; enlistment of
    blacks, 215, 221–22
Lee, Robert E., Jr., 233
Lee, Fitzhugh, 209
Leitch, Alexander, 28
Leon, Edwin De, 151
Leroy, NY, 134
Lewis, Charles, 37, 293
Lewis, Isham, 37–38, 293
Lewis, J. R., 241
Lewis, Lilburne, 37–38, 293
Lewis, Samuel, 186
Lewisburg, VA, 82, 125
Lexington, KY, 14, 24, 25, 33, 51, 61, 102,
    103
Lexington Intelligencer, 98
Liberator, 39, 45, 62, 79, 85, 116
Liberty Almanac, 137
*Liberty and Free Soil Parties in the North-
    west, The* (Smith), 186
Liberty Party, xiii, 14, 25, 132; antislavery
    issues, 182–83; James G. Birney as
    leader, 165, 177; James G. Birney presi-
    dential candidate of, 25, 44, 266 n 19;
    campaign of 1840, 121–27, 130–31,
    134, 154; campaign of 1844, 121–22,
    137–39, 163–64; college students join,
    148; convention, 176–77; formation,

123–25, 116; influence on Republican
    Party, 143, 175–76, 185, 189; and
    Michigan, 159, 162; and Ohio, 41,
    115; and Philadelphia, 126; Theodore
    Roosevelt denies abolitionist influences
    on Republican Party, 251; and slavery,
    124, 178; votes in Michigan, 166
Library of Congress, 80
Lincoln, Abraham, I, 19
Lincoln, Abraham, vii, viii, ix, 29, 32, 126,
    166; abolition, 189; antislavery views,
    84, 85, 86–87, 92, 176, 191, 199, 216;
    assassination, 178–79, 237, 239; James
    G. Birney influence, 58, 74, 115, 201,
    251; and James Birney III, 238–39;
    birth, 20; and Salmon P. Chase, 114–
    15, 176, 180; Civil War, 150, 195–97,
    199, 211, 212, 221, 222, 235; coloniza-
    tion, 77; Congress, 144; debates, 189;
    Emancipation Proclamation, 212–13;
    and Ulysses S. Grant, 232; and John P.
    Hale, 178–79; "Higher Law" doctrine,
    115; "House Divided" speech, 125; and
    John Hughes, 134; Illinois legisla-
    ture, 44–45, 92, 127, 144, 183, 187;
    Michigan, 154; and James K. Polk, 143;
    president, 145, 175, 185, 191, 195,
    220; as soldier, 71; as a youth, 37
Lincoln, Josiah, 19
Lincoln, Mordecai, 19
Lincoln, Nancy Hanks, 37
Lincoln, Robert, 172, 206
Lincoln, Sarah Bush Johnston, 15
Lincoln, Thomas, 15, 16, 19, 20, 37, 85
Lincoln Memorial University, 239
Lincoln Studies Center, 202
Litchfield, CT, 147
literacy tests for blacks to vote, 249
Little Mount Separate Baptist Church, 15
Little Pigeon Creek Baptist Church, 15
Livingston, William, 28, 251
Livingston County, NY, 159, 167, 207;
    Court, 38
Logan, John "Black Jack," 197
London Coffee House, 8
London Sun, 129
Longfellow, Henry Wadsworth, 167

"Long Nine," 127
Loughead, James, 34
Louisiana, 74, 78, 141, 165, 212, 241, 247, 248, 249; removal of Indians, 71; Shreveport, 245
Love, William, 65
Lovejoy, Elijah, 114, 189
Lowe, Thaddeus, 206
Lumpkin, Mary Ann, 288 n 10
Lumpkin, Robert, 224–25, 226, 288 n 10
Lundy, Benjamin, 37, 79
lynch club, 57, 58
Lytle, R. T., 110, 181

Macedon Lock, NY, 178
Madison, George, 27
Madison, James, 25, 115; and the American Whig Society, 28–29; colonization, 75, 77; influence on James G. Birney, 52, 73; and slavery, 27, 122, 169; and Virginia resolutions, 82
Madison, Margaretta, 27
Madison County, AL, 52, 56, 58, 74, 79, 83, 240, 243, 245
Magliocca, Gerard N., 72
Maine, 51, 116, 139, 197, 200, 230, 239, 248; Brunswick, 150; Fourth Volunteer Infantry Regiment, 201; vote for president for James G. Birney, 131, 139
Mali, 5
Manassas Junction, VA, 199, 200
Manassas Plains, VA, 204
Mansfield, Lord, 70
manumission, 18, 54, 56, 98
Manumission Society of North Carolina, 62
Marshall, Humphrey, 33–34
Marshall, John J., 21, 33–34, 49, 50, 55, 67, 70, 122, 138
Marshall, MI, 157
Marshall's Reports, 138
Martineau, Harriet, 130
Maryland, 179, 271 n 1; William Birney, 216, 219, 222, 239; Civil War, 208; Forest Glen, 250; Frederick County, 78; slavery, 36, 156, 191, 216
Mason, George, 103

Mason, Matthew, 23
Mason-Dixon Line, 8, 34, 40, 61, 79
Masonic Lodge, 26, 125, 139; Huntsville, AL, 58
Massachusetts, 89, 116, 196, 199, 206; Anti-Slavery Society, 139; constitution, 31; presidential vote for James G. Birney, 126, 131, 137, 139; and slavery, 6; and Whigs, 43; and women, 151. *See also* Andover, MA; Charlestown, MA; Medford, MA; Williamstown, MA
Massachusetts Abolitionist, 123
Mathew, Theobald, 132
Matthews, Michael, xi, 16, 54, 83, 99, 105, 152
May, Samuel J., 61
Maybin, Joseph, 164
Mayer, Henry, 129
McChord, John, 54
McClellan, George B., 198, 203, 204, 206
McDowell, Agatha, 26, 27, 266 n 19
McDowell, Ephraim, 266 n 19
McDowell, Samuel, 27
McDowell, William, 27, 53, 55
McElroy, Wendy, 39
McManus, Michael J., 189
Meade, George Gordon, 202, 203, 204; Pennsylvania Reserves, 207
Medford, MA, 126
Mercer County, KY, 14, 19, 26; Mercer County Courthouse, 54, 99
Methodists, 24, 49, 74, 92; Mother Bethel African Methodist Episcopal Church, 8
Mexican War, 34, 137, 143, 183, 200, 233, 278 n 15
Mexico, 140, 141, 183, 245, 251; government, 136, 144; Knights of the Golden Circle, 63; slavery, 84
Miami (OH) University, 159
Michigan, 70, 75, 143, 151, 153–68, 179, 182, 183; antislavery, 122, 156–57, 158; James G. Birney's abolition lectures, 161; Birneys in, 160, 161, 164, 165, 178, 182, 189, 191, 197; and Democrats, 160; and economic growth, 40; and Fifth Cavalry, 208, 209; and First Cavalry, 208; and first Republican

platform, 257–61; and First Veteran Cavalry, 209; and Liberty Party, 159; Lower Saginaw (Bay City), 159, 160, 161; and 102nd U.S.C.T. in Florida, 220; and radicals, 186; and removal of Indians, 71; Saginaw, 159; and Seventh Cavalry, 196, 207; and Sixth Cavalry, 209; Treaty of Saginaw, 160; vote for president for James G. Birney, 75, 116, 131, 139; and Whigs, 160. *See also* Bay City, MI; Cass County, MI; Detroit, MI; Jackson, MI; Marshall, MI

Michigan Freeman, 158

Michigan State Anti-Slavery Society, 159

Middle Passage, 5

Miller, Francis, 200

Miller, William Lee, 42, 99

Mills, Thornton J., 98

Milton, John, 242

Mississippi, 10, 96, 100; James G. Birney in, 74, 78; black troops, 212; black voting rights, 249; Clinton, 100; Monroe County, 246; and Reconstruction, 248–49; River, 13, 51, 67, 68; slavery, 36, 38, 179, 184, 186, 190, 195, 259

Missouri, removal of Indians, 71

Missouri Compromise, 116, 191, 251; and Henry Clay, 102; and slavery, 36, 38, 179, 184, 186, 190, 259

Mobile, AL, 50, 243

Monroe, James, 25, 51, 76, 122

Monroe County, MS, 246

Montgomery, AL, 252

Montreal, 127, 276 n 14

Moore, Gabriel, 62

Morris, Chris, 83

Morris, Thomas, 123, 139–40

Mother Bethel African Methodist Episcopal Church, 8

Mount Morris, NY, 159

National Era, 150, 178

National Hotel, 178, 179

National Intelligencer, 137

Native Americans, 155; attack on Lincoln ancestors, 19; James G. Birney defends, 57, 58, 59, 72; land grabs by whites, 52,

68; prejudice against, 65, 67; rights of, 60; and slaves, 5; and smallpox, 66

Naveaux, Ralph, 157

Negroes, 76, 179, 183, 187, 250; anti-slavery, 57, 75; James G. Birney's relationship with, 53, 60, 83, 89, 115, 124, 148, 180–81; Christians, 76; in Cincinnati, 113, 115; and Dred Scott decision, 172; education, 239, 246, 288 n 10; emigration to Africa, 35, 36, 59, 77; free Negroes, 8, 24, 73; Hamitic myth, 20; Abraham Lincoln's relationship with, 86; Michigan, 156; population, 8, 63, 96, 111; prejudice against, 65; rights of, 60, 189, 236, 248; runaways, 198; slavery, 7, 22, 38, 81, 103, 225, 237; students, 146; troops, 205, 210, 211–12, 226, 227, 228–31, 234; value of, 21; violence against, 108, 240–45, 246; voting rights, 248; in West Indies, 149

Nelson County, VA, 19

New England, 5–6, 22, 32, 70, 156, 159, 171, 173; slavery, 8, 16

New Hampshire, 114, 116, 172, 178; vote for president for James G. Birney, 131, 139

New Harmony, IN, 171

New Haven, CT, 137

New Jersey, 28; abolition, 36; Birneys in, 171, 182, 188, 205, 207; constitution, 169; and Fourth Infantry, 216; and slavery, 170–71; vote for president for James G. Birney, 131, 139. *See also* Basking Ridge, NJ; Belleville, NJ; Perth Amboy, NJ

New Kent, VA, 83

New Orleans, LA, 78, 115, 164, 181; Battle of, 35, 38, 59, 66; Citizens Committee to Test the Separate Car Act, 248; and Civil War, 214; and Abraham Lincoln, 84–87

New West, 19

New World, 4, 6, 7, 73

New York, 5, 132, 168; and abolition, 36, 40; and the American Anti-Slavery Society, 45, 46, 90, 98, 115, 122, 123,

147; and antislavery, 39, 140; James G. Birney in, 61, 75, 90, 114, 115, 130, 137; James G. Birney voyage from, 127; Henry Clay defeat, 141, 143; and Democratic Party, 182; and emancipation, 116; Erie Canal, 154; legislature, 176; and Liberty Party convention, 178; newspapers, 203, 205, 212; and slave trade, 170; and Thirty-eighth Regiment, 200, 206; and Thirty-first U.S. Colored Troops, 226; Van Buren defeat in, 126; vote for president for James G. Birney, 24–25, 122, 126, 131, 137, 139. *See also* Albany, NY; Cortland, NY; Leroy, NY; Macedon, NY; North Elba, NY; Peterboro, NY; Rochester, NY; Utica, NY; Warsaw, NY; Westchester County, NY

New York, NY, racial violence, 249

New York Independent, 141

New York Post, 178

New York Times, 142, 155, 179, 203, 243

New York Tribune, 141, 172, 197, 203

Nicholas, George, 24

Niven, John, 115, 176

North Carolina, 39, 54, 62, 63, 66, 241, 249

North District (Baptist) Association, 15

North Elba, NY, 281 n 13

Northern Illinois University, 5

Northwest Ordinance, 35, 105, 157, 170

Oates, Stephen, 77

Oberlin (College) Anti-Slavery Society, 148

O'Connell, Daniel, 26, 129–30, 131, 132, 133, 134

Offutt, Denton, 85

Ohio, 247, 249, 250; abolition, 177; antislavery convention, 42; antislavery meetings, 122; David Bell Birney in, 159–60, 197; James G. Birney, xi, 75, 145–46, 154, 254; Cincinnati, 112–16, 123, 145, 149, 159; and economic growth, 40; and fugitive slaves, 179; Lane Seminary, 146–48; and Liberty Party, 41, 176; New Richmond, 109, 112, 123; River, 33, 86, 105, 107, 146, 184, 209, 249–58; Springboro, 114;

Supreme Court, 115, 181; and Underground Railroad, 107; vote for president for James G. Birney, 126, 131, 139

Old Hickory. *See* Jackson, Andrew

Oneida Institute, 88, 265 n 5

Ord, E. O. C., 198, 209, 218, 220, 227–31, 234, 288 n 12

Owen, Robert, 171

Owen, Thomas McAdory, 60

Paludan, Philip Shaw, 77

Peek, Ralph L., 243

Pendleton, William N., 231–32

Pennock, Abraham L., 37

Pennsylvania, 6, 10, 13, 36, 116, 122, 207; Anti-Slavery Society, 130; constitutional convention, 124; and Fifty-seventh regiment, 200, 205; general emancipation, 35; legislature, 37; Meade's Reserves, 207; 141st regiment, 203; and Second Cavalry, 199; and Third Corps, 205; Twenty-third Pennsylvania Volunteers (Birney's Zouaves), 197, 199, 206; vote for president for James G. Birney, 131, 139. *See also* Harrisburg, PA; Philadelphia, PA; Washington County, PA

Perdue, Theda, 71

Perth Amboy, NJ, 5, 167, 169, 170, 173

Peterboro, NY, 101, 137

Philadelphia, PA, xii, 3, 4, 5, 6, 7, 14; abolition societies, 36–37; American Anti-Slavery Society, 87; antislavery, 61; David Bell Birney in, 168, 197, 220, 251; and Fitzhugh Birney, 207; James Birney Sr. in, 9, 35, 99; James G. Birney law studies, 25–26, 27, 51, 114, 136; City Cavalry, 197; colonization, 73, 75–77, 148; and Liberty Party, 126; Negro population, 8; Philadelphia Fire Department, 197; and Quakers, 8; and slave trade, 170

Philadelphia Daily Register, 205

Philadelphia Inquirer, 204

Philadelphia Press, 219

Philanthropist, 42, 101, 116, 123, 140, 177; defense by Salmon P. Chase, 114–15; mob action, 109, 112–14

Phillips, Wendell, 129, 134
Phillips Exeter Academy, 172, 197
Pickett, Albert James, 59, 66
Pickett, George, 202, 208, 209
Pigeon Creek, IN, 86
Pinckney, Charles, 6, 169
Pitman, Benn, 178
Pius IX, 277 n 31
Plessy, Homer Adolph, 248
Plessy v. Ferguson, 248
Poinsett, Joel R., 136
Polk, James K., 143, 251, 266 n 19; presidential candidate, 44, 135–36, 140–41; Texas issue, 142, 183
Polk, Josiah, 77–78
Pope, John, 199, 200, 205, 209
Pope, Thomas, 54
Porter, Arthur L., 161–62, 166
Porter, Edward, 231
Powell, A. D., 87
Powell, David, 158
Presbyterians, xi, 24, 26, 69, 92, 101, 102, 271 n 3; and abolition, 159; and James Birney Sr., 265 n 18; and James G. Birney, 89; and Robert Finley, 76; in Kentucky, 89; reform-minded, 59, 74; and David Rice, 11, 13, 18, 23, 236; and Scots-Irish, 9
Price, Clement A., 171
Priestly, James, 16, 17
Prigg v. Pennsylvania, 169–70
Prince, Monique, 46
Princeton University, 18; and abolitionists, xii; James G. Birney at, 18, 25, 26, 32, 35, 51, 114; Joseph Cabell Breckenridge at, 18, 82, 196; George M. Dallas, 136; Daniel Fitzhugh at, 154; David Rice at, 17, 18, 23; Samuel Stanhope Smith at, 17, 52
Pugh, Achilles, 112, 114
Pulaski, TN, 240

Quakers, xii, 8, 47, 85, 112, 116, 171, 173; Massachusetts, 76; Michigan, 156; Philadelphia, 8, 26, 35, 37
Quinn, John F., 132
Quist, John W., 159

Race and Reunion (Blight), 240
rations, 227, 230, 232, 233, 237, 288 n 11
Readjusters, 238, 248. *See also* Ku Klux Klan
Reconstruction, 11, 210, 235–48, 250, 252; Acts, 236; and James Birney III, 238–39; and William Birney, 59, 242–43; and Freedmen's Bureau, 237–39, 242; and Ku Klux Klan, 238–41; 244–47; and Negro voting rights, 236
Rediker, Marcus, 7–8
Red Sticks, 66, 67
Reed, John, 10, 11, 15, 16, 19, 32, 54
Reed, Lettice Wilcox, 10
Reed, Martha, 10, 14
Reed's Station, 19
Republican (Cincinnati), 110
Republicans, xiii, 175–92, 237; antislavery, 18, 42, 98, 135, 142, 148, 166, 239, 244; James G. Birney influence, 14, 41, 92, 159, 167; and William Birney, 250–51; and colonization, 77; first platform, 257–61; John C. Fremont, 196; Rutherford B. Hayes election, 247–48; as Klan targets, 240–41, 243; Liberty Party influence, 123, 131, 166, 251; and Abraham Lincoln, 29, 127, 220; Michigan, 153–68; organization, 143; platform, 195; presidential nomination, 115; principles, 45, 125; radical, 246; and Theodore Roosevelt, 251
resolutions of 1798 and 1799, 82
Revolution: American, 5, 7, 28, 67, 257; French, 44; Texas, 136
Revolutionary War, 13, 15, 27, 107, 116, 153, 213, 270 n 2
Rhodehamel, John, 179
Rhode Island, 5, 6, 8, 36, 61, 139, 158; vote for president for James G. Birney, 131, 139
Rhys, Thomas, 23
Rice, David, Jr., 11, 13, 15, 18, 22–24, 265 n 18
Rice, David, Sr., 23
Riley, John W., 180
Ripley, Ann Lee, 171
Ripley, George, 171

Robards, Rachel, 33
Rochester, NY, 137, 180
Rogers, William Warren, Jr., 240
Roosevelt, Theodore, 251
Rose, Howell, 59
Rush, Benjamin, 36, 58
Russell, Charles S., 226

Saffin, James, 107, 108
Saginaw, MI, 137, 139, 154, 196, 197, 206
Salem Association of Baptists, 16
Sandburg, Carl, 20, 86
Sangamon County, IL, 44
Sauk Indians, 70
Sawyer, A., 241
Scarborough, William Kauffman, 18
Schaff, Morris, 232
Schurz, Carl, 42
Scotland, 3
Scott, Dred, 158, 172, 182, 189, 191, 192
Second Great Awakening, 39, 40, 159, 189
Second Seminole War, 124
Sedgwick, John, 202
segregated neighborhoods, 249
Seminoles, 59, 68, 72; Second Seminole War, 124
Seven Pines, VA, 201, 203, 204
Seward, William H., 115, 182; "Irrepressible Conflict" speech, 125; as Secretary of State, 134
Sewell, Richard, 177, 186, 188, 191
Shane, John Dabney, 19, 20
Sharp, Granville, 36
Shaw, James K., Jr., 205
Shawnees, 66
Sheridan, Philip H., 9, 208, 209, 226, 227, 232
Sherman, Roger, 7
Sherman, William T., 213, 215; March to the Sea, 239
Shreveport, LA, 245
Sickles, Daniel, 197, 201, 202, 247, 284 n 18
Sierra Leone, 5
Signal of Liberty, 34, 41, 163, 183; James G. Birney's "Bible argument," 158; James G. Birney's "Sinfulness" essay,

177; John Marshall letter, 138; Daniel O'Connell letter, 131–33; subscribers, 159
Sigourney, Lydia, 69
Silbey, Joel H., 136
Simmons, William J., 249
slaveholders, 23–24, 34, 37, 260; abolitionist opposition, 42, 44, 46, 88, 101, 129; antislavery movement, 116, 190; James Birney Sr., 10–11, 15; James G. Birney, 26, 57, 61, 81, 91, 98; Charles Carroll, 156; Henry Clay, 164, 188; and colonization, 73, 79, 95, 97; Dred Scott ruling, 191; Fugitive Slave Law, 181; Grimke sisters, 171; Lane Seminary, 146; legal arguments, 236; Liberty Party, 133; Maryland, 216; Michigan raids, 157; in Philadelphia, 7; Republican platform, 260; slavery defenders, 105, 151; Samuel Stanhope Smith, 18; in *Uncle Tom's Cabin*, 149–52; and voter opinions, 138, 140, 143, 149
slavery, conflict over, 31–48
slave ships, xii, 3, 7–8, 66, 176, 263 n 1
slave traders, 5
Smith, Elbert, 33, 34
Smith, George, 24
Smith, Gerrit, 91, 101, 137; allegedly finances John Brown's raid, 172; backs abolitionist political action, 122–23; becomes Birney's brother-in-law, 154; Fitzhugh Birney visits, 206; embraces religious reform, 40
Smith, I., 164
Smith, Samuel Stanhope, 17–18, 35, 36, 52
South Bend, IN, 158
South Carolina: black troops in, 212, 215, 216; Constitution, 6; elections in, 247; and Ku Klux Klan, 246; nullification crisis, 102; secession, 195, 198; and slavery, 39, 46, 81, 87, 171; and voter rights, 241, 249. *See also* Beaufort, SC; Charleston, SC; Hilton Head, SC
Southern Advocate, 90, 95
Southern Honor: Ethics and Behavior in the Old South (Brown), 34
Speed, Joshua, 86

Spring, Marcus, 171
Spring, Rebecca B., 171, 173
Springboro, OH, 114
Springfield, IL, 126
Stanton, Edwin M., 201, 215; and William
    Birney, recruitment of black troops, 218
Stanton, Elizabeth Cady, 40, 128, 129,
    130, 276 n 14; *Reminiscences*, 127
Stanton, Henry, 123, 127, 148, 165
Stark, Rodney, 8
Starke plantation, 217
Stearns, George L., 126
Stevens, Aaron Dwight, 173
Stevens, Isaac Ingals, 200
Stewart, Alvan, 122
Stewart, Charles H., 161, 162
Stocking, William, 190; *Under the Oaks*,
    184
Stone, Dan, 44
Stoneman, George, 201, 204, 206
Stowe, Harriett Beecher,
    145–46,149–50,152
Strattan, Laura, 207
Sumter, Thomas, 66, 270 n 2
Switzer, John, 78
Swope, Benedict, 24

Tagg, Larry, 202
Taney, Roger B., 182, 191
Taper, Louise, 179
Tappan, Arthur, 40, 123, 146,198
Tappan, Lewis, 40, 90, 122, 123, 129, 160,
    198
Taylor, Thomas Jones, 52
Tecumseh, 66
Tennessee, 52, 54, 57; antislavery society,
    36; James G. Birney slave rescue, xi, xii,
    xiii, 87; and black troops, Confederate,
    213; and black troops, Union, 212; and
    colonization, 74, 78; Klan assaults in,
    241; murderer's extradition blocked, 58;
    slavery opinion, 63. *See also* Fort Pillow,
    TN; Harrogate, TN; Pulaski, TN
Tennessee Valley, 49
Tenzer, Lawrence R., 87
Texas, 224; James G. Birney position
    on, 139, 164; John Calhoun favors

acquisition, 63; Henry Clay's chang-
    ing position on, 137, 143; dispute over
    annexation of, 42; 1844 election issue,
    142; John P. Hale opposes annexation,
    178; James K. Polk's political message
    on, 136, 140
Third Party movement, 43
Thirteenth Amendment, 248
Thomas, Benjamin P., 187
Thomas, Hugh, 5, 6
Thome, James A., 147, 148–49; "Emanci-
    pation in the West Indies," 121
Thompson, John Burton, 183
Thoreau, Henry David, 169, 171, 172
Thornton, Russell, 65, 98
Ticknor, George, 61
Tillman, Benjamin "Pitchfork," 246
Timberlake, Henry, 65, 67; *Timberlake's
    Memoirs*, 66
Todd, John, 23
Tourgee, Albion W., 248; *A Fool's Errand:
    By One of the Fools*, 247
Tracy, Jim, 27
Trail of Tears, 65, 67, 71
Transcendentalists, 171
Transylvania University, 16, 61
Travis, William Barret, 136, 141
Treaty of Paris, 13
Triana, AL, 55
Trinity Episcopal Church, 265 n 18
Troutman, Francis, 158
Turner, John W., 230
Turner, Nat, xii, 39, 42, 56, 62, 82, 84
Tutwiler, Henry, 61

Uncle Tom's Cabin (Stowe), 74, 114,
    149–50, 151–52, 179, 189
Underground Railroad, 77, 107, 123, 156,
    157, 173, 179, 182
Union, 24, 58; James G. Birney, 178;
    cavalry, 9; and Civil War, 133; and
    Henry Clay, 78, 164; dissolution, 110;
    formation, 31; and Fugitive Slave Law,
    158; and William Lloyd Garrison, 41;
    and John Hughes, 133–34; and Andrew
    Jackson, 71–72; and Abraham Lincoln,
    188; and William Livingston, 28; and

James Madison, 27; Northwest Ordinance, 35; religion, 92; David Rice, 22; right of petition, 43; right to bear arms, 33; secession, 82, 86, 87, 195; slavery, 42, 45, 46, 52, 63, 91; slave states, 186; statehood, 15, 24, 25, 51; and Texas, 136–37, 139, 140
Union Army, 32, 74, 91, 172, 195–234, 244
United States Colored Troops, 211–22
United States Constitution, 57, 58, 102; James G. Birney's opinions, 47–48, 110–11, 169; Henry Clay's opinions, 82; compromise, 190; constitutional convention, 6; and the Fourteenth Amendment, 72, 177, 235–36; higher law, 115, 176; laws of Georgia "repugnant to," 70; and the Liberty Party, 133; loophole, 235; preamble, 178; and the Republican platform, 258–60; Southern view, 188; statehood, 51
University of Alabama, 60, 61, 131
University of Edinburgh, 266 n 19
University of Georgia, 76
University of Michigan, 148, 208
University of North Carolina, 46
U.S. Army, 32, 71, 72, 154, 231; emancipation, 78; Military Commission, 178
U.S. Congress, 35, 100, 138, 157, 162, 239; and abolition, 37, 40, 42, 45, 46; and antislavery, 116, 131, 184, 190, 191, 236, 237, 257; bans fur trade by foreigners, 154; and colonization, 79; Fifteenth Amendment, 241; Fourteenth Amendment, 236; Fugitive Slave Act, 133, 150, 169, 170; Fugitive Slave Law, 22, 158; Joint Select Committee on Condition of Affairs in the Late Insurrectionary States, 243; Ku Klux Act, 245; lack of preparation for civil war, 198; Nebraska Bill, 186; and Radical Republicans, 246; and slave trade, 7, 212; Thirtieth Congress, 183; Thirty-ninth Congress, 236
U.S. House of Representatives, 24, 35, 36, 43, 56, 62, 102, 175, 183
U.S. Military Academy, 80, 239

U.S. Navy, 6, 51
U.S. Supreme Court, 248, 249; and Salmon P. Chase, 114; and Cherokee, 70–71; Civil Rights Act of 1875, 248; Dred Scott decision, 189, 191; John Marshall, 21, 33, 49, 67; *Prigg v. Pennsylvania*, 169–70; Bushrod Washington, 76; *Worcester v. Georgia*, 72. *See also* individual court cases
Utica, NY, 206

Van Buren, A. D. P., 116
Van Buren, Martin, 124, 125, 126, 130, 131, 160, 175, 178, 182
Van der Veer Hamilton, Virginia, 49, 67, 250
Van Zandt, John, 181–82
Vermont, 24, 39, 70, 116, 131, 139, 186; presidential vote for Birney, 131
Vesey, Denmark, 39
Virginia, xii, 57; abolition society, 36; Appomattox, 215, 222, 233; Army of Northern Virginia, 223, 231–32, 233; attitudes, postwar, 250; Bill of Rights, 31; and David Bell Birney, 199; cavalry, 208; Cedar Mountain, 212; Chantilly, 200; and Henry Clay, 102, 125; constitutional conventions, 24; Danville, 225; and Charles B. Dew, 195; Farmville, 228; Harper's Ferry, 169, 173; House of Burgesses, 24, 27; Thomas Jefferson, 23, 60; Kentucky County, 19–20; larceny law and slaves, 84; legislature, 76; Lynchburg, 213; militia, 66; New Kent, 83; New Market Heights, 219; Peninsula Campaign, 207; Petersburg, 226–27; Presbytery of Hanover, 23; John Reed, 10; resolutions, 82; Thomas Rhys immigrates to, 23; Richmond, 224–27, 249; Seven Pines, 201; and slavery, 6, 86; and slavery laws, 17; slavery poll, 63; and Judge Tucker, 259; Turner revolt, 39, 56, 62; white slavery, 87. *See also* Chancellorsville, VA; Manassas Junction, VA; Manassas Plains, VA; Seven Pines, VA; Yorktown, VA

Walker, Caleb S., 109

Walker, John William, 57, 62, 109, 113

Walker's Appeal, 39, 62

Walker's Church, 227

Walter Reed Medical Center, 284 n 18

Ward, Henry Clay, 206, 226

War of 1812, xii, 22, 38, 49, 51, 52, 66, 157, 213

Warsaw, NY, 123

Washington, Bushrod, 76

Washington, D.C., 28, 150; American Colonization Society, 74, 76; antislavery convention, 37; David Bell Birney in, 201; Robert Dion Birney in, 206; Civil War, 198, 199; Grand Review, 209; Klan parades, 249; violence, 241

Washington, George, 7, 27, 32, 52, 122, 137, 138, 190; president, 13; Yorktown, VA, 9

Washington, Martha, 7

Washington County, KY, 37

Washington County, PA, 123

Webb, R. D., 132

Webster, Daniel, 55, 61, 76, 159

Weld, Theodore, 198; *American Slavery As It Is: Testimony of a Thousand Witnesses*, 38, 46, 47, 58, 150, 152; James G. Birney collaboration, 63, 88, 98, 102, 104; Cherokee Removal opposition, 72; colonization, 75; Eagleswood commune, 168; Lane Seminary debates, 146–48; progressive school, 167, 171; Seventy Apostles, 89, 149

Westchester County, NY, 123

Western Luminary, 98

West Indies, 42, 88, 121, 142, 149

West Point, 34, 80, 197, 204, 205, 231, 239

Whig, 110

Whig Party, 138; dies out, 135

Whigs, 123; abolitionists, 124; James G. Birney, 58, 102, 131, 159, 164; Henry

Clay, 130, 140; 143, 189; William Henry Harrison campaign, 125; Abraham Lincoln, 92; Michigan votes, 166; Martin Van Buren, 126

Whig Society, 28, 29, 43

Whiteboys, 238

white slavery, 87

Whitney, Eli, 32

Whitney, Henry C., 85, 92–93; *Life and Works of Lincoln*, 187

Whittier, John Greenleaf, 116

Wilberforce, William, 9, 26, 89, 127, 148

Willcox, Charles, 177

Williams, T. Harry, 198

Williamsburg, VA, 204

Williams College, 195

Williamson, R. M., 141

Williamstown, MA, 195

Wilmot, David, 183

Wilmot Proviso, 183

Wilson, Woodrow, 249

Winik, Jay, 232

Wirt, William, 67, 70, 114

Woodford County, IL, 16

Woodlawn, 17, 21, 22

Woods, Alva, 61

Woodward, Augustus B., 157

Woodward, William W., 230

Worcester, Samuel, 70, 71, 72

Worcester v. Georgia, 70, 72

Works Project Administration, 250

World Anti-Slavery Convention, 127, 128, 134

Wright, Elizur, 98, 130, 137

Wright, Elizur, Jr., 162–63

Yale University, 18, 159, 205

Yamin, Rebecca, 7

Yancey, William Lowndes, 32

Yorktown, VA, 9, 198, 204, 205

Young, John C., 98

Young Men's Democratic Clubs, 243